INDIVISIBLE

INDIVISIBLE

Indigenous Human Rights

Edited by Joyce Green

FERNWOOD PUBLISHING · HALIFAX & WINNIPEG

Editing: Jessica Antony
Cover artwork: Christi Belcourt, *Bird Song*, 30" x 40", acrylic on canvas,
private collection, www.christibelcourt.com
Cover design: John van der Woude
Printed and bound in Canada by Hignell Book Printing

Published by Fernwood Publishing
32 Oceanvista Lane, Black Point, Nova Scotia, B0J 1B0
and 748 Broadway Avenue, Winnipeg, Manitoba, R3G 0X3
www.fernwoodpublishing.ca

Fernwood Publishing Company Limited gratefully acknowledges the financial support
of the Government of Canada through the Canada Book Fund and the Canada Council
for the Arts, the Nova Scotia Department of Communities, Culture and Heritage,
the Manitoba Department of Culture, Heritage and Tourism under the
Manitoba Publishers Marketing Assistance Program and the Province of Manitoba,
through the Book Publishing Tax Credit, for our publishing program.

Library and Archives Canada Cataloguing in Publication

Indivisible: indigenous human rights / edited by Joyce Green.

Includes bibliographical references and index.
ISBN 978-1-55266-683-8 (pbk.)

1. Indigenous peoples—Civil rights. 2. Native peoples—Civil
rights—Canada. 3. Indigenous peoples—Legal status, laws, etc.
4. Native peoples—Canada—Legal status, laws, etc. 5. Native
peoples—Canada—Government relations. 6. Human rights.
I. Green, Joyce A. (Joyce Audry), 1956–, editor

K3247.I63 2014   342.08'72   C2014-905195-6

Contents

Acknowledgements

Many political and other professionals, activists and scholars contribute to the project of confronting Indigenous human rights abuses in the settler states. Additionally, community activists, human rights advocates and social movements are part of this project. The Idle No More movement is one such contributor and has served as a catalyst and inspiration to many troubled by the continual denial of or justification of Indigenous human rights abuses. This collection is dedicated to all those who, in their many roles and locations, defend Indigenous human rights. It is especially dedicated to those who imagined and animated Idle No More.

My teaching career has been enriched by many brilliant, thoughtful, committed students, for whom scholarship is a vocation and to whom colonialism, racism, sexism, capitalism and other forms of oppressive power relations have been serious subjects for scholarly consideration. Many have gone on to be engaged citizens and agents of change. This book is also dedicated to all my former students, who are too numerous to name. I do want to single out those who have been particularly steadfast in the scholarship and politics of justice: Nick Bonokoski, Mike Burton, Diedre Desmarais, Simon Enoch, Veldon Coburn, Nicole Leach, Alyssa Melnyk, Michael Boldt Radmacher, Jennifer Ruddy and Gina Starblanket. The academy and the country are better for your work.

Books rely on a cadre of dedicated professionals for their presentation and publication. I am indebted to the excellent, supportive and knowledgeable crew at Fernwood Publishing. This crew includes the publisher, Wayne Antony; the copyeditor Jessica Antony; the production coordinator Beverley Rach; the inputter Debbie Mathers; the proofreader Brenda Conroy; the promotions coordinator Nancy Malek; and all those who work with them.

This book rests between covers graced with the work of Métis artist Christi Belcourt. The title of the piece is *Bird Song*, 30" x 40", acrylic on canvas, private collection. Readers wanting to see more of Belcourt's work may visit <christibelcourt.com>.

Author Biographies

Christi Belcourt is a Michif visual artist and author whose ancestry originates from the historic Métis community of Lac Ste. Anne, Alberta. Like generations of Aboriginal artists before her, she celebrates the beauty of natural world while exploring nature's symbolic properties. Her work can be found within the public collections of the National Gallery of Canada, the Gabriel Dumont Institute, the Indian and Inuit Art Collection, the Art Gallery of Ontario, the Canadian Museum of Civilization and the Thunder Bay Art Gallery. Belcourt was recently named the 2014 Ontario Aboriginal Arts Laureate by the Ontario Arts Council. Follow Christi on Twitter, @christibelcourt, or visit her website, <christibelcourt.com>.

Craig Benjamin works for Amnesty International Canada as a coordinator of the human rights organizations' campaigns in solidarity with Indigenous peoples in Canada. He also represented Amnesty International at the United Nations during the finalization and adoption of the *U.N. Declaration on the Rights of Indigenous Peoples* in Canada. Before joining Amnesty International in 1998, Benjamin worked with a wide range of Indigenous peoples' organizations in North America, Latin America, Southeast Asia and the Pacific to support their advocacy on the international stage.

Gwen Brodsky practises law in Vancouver, teaches law at UBC and has taught in the Akitsiraq Law Program in Iqaluit. She is Director of the Poverty and Human Rights Centre in Vancouver. She is a leading expert on equality rights and the *Canadian Charter of Rights and Freedoms*. Recently, she was counsel to Sharon McIvor in a constitutional challenge to sex discrimination in the status provisions of the *Indian Act*, and she represented the Native Women's Association of Canada on the murders and disappearances of Aboriginal women and girls at the Inter-American Commission on Human Rights. Currently, she is a Distinguished Visiting Scholar at the University of British Columbia Faculty of Law.

Elizabeth Comack is Professor of Sociology at the University of Manitoba, where she teaches sociology of law and feminist criminology. She is also a member of the Manitoba Research Alliance, a broad coalition of academics and community partners engaged in research on Aboriginal and inner-city racialized poverty and inequality. Her recent publications include *"Indians Wear Red": Colonialism, Resistance, and Aboriginal Street Gangs* (co-authored with Lawrence Deane, Larry Morrissette and Jim Silver, 2013), *Racialized Policing: Aboriginal People's Encounters with the Police* (2012) and *Out There/In Here: Masculinity, Violence, and Prisoning* (2008).

Mary Eberts helped develop the equality provisions enshrined in the *Canadian Charter of Rights and Freedoms* and has argued some of Canada's touchstone equality cases before the Supreme Court. She is a co-founder of the Women's Legal Education and Action Fund, an organization devoted to litigation and education on women's equality rights, and was litigation counsel to the Native Women's Association of Canada. Eberts is author of numerous books, articles and book chapters. Recognition for her work includes the Governor General's Award in Honour of the Persons' Case, the Law Society of Upper Canada Medal, the YWCA Woman of Distinction Award, the Distinguished Service Award of the Canadian Bar Association-Ontario, the Women's Law Association of Ontario President's Award and several honorary doctorates.

Joyce Green is Professor of Political Science at the University of Regina, currently on long-term disability leave. Her research includes issues of decolonization and of democracy in Canada. Her published work to date has primarily dealt with Indigenous-state relations, Indigenous feminism, citizenship, identity and racism in Canada's political culture. She is the editor of *Making Space for Indigenous Feminism* (2007). She is English, Ktunaxa and Cree-Scottish Métis, and her family's experiences have provoked much of her scholarly and political work.

Brenda L. Gunn is Assistant Professor in the Faculty of Law, University of Manitoba, where she teaches constitutional law and the rights of Indigenous peoples in international law. She has worked on the U.N. Expert Seminar on Implementation of National Legislation and Jurisprudence Concerning Indigenous Peoples' Rights, and the U.N. Expert Mechanism on the Rights of Indigenous Peoples. Her research focuses on international and domestic protection of Indigenous peoples' rights. She produced a handbook entitled *Understanding and Implementing the U.N. Declaration on the Rights of Indigenous Peoples.* She remains actively involved in the international Indigenous peoples' movement. Brenda Gunn is a member of the Métis Nation.

Paul Joffe is a member of the Québec and Ontario bars. He specializes in human rights and other issues concerning Indigenous peoples at the international and domestic levels. For over two decades, he has been actively involved in international standard-setting processes including those relating to the *United Nations Declaration on the Rights of Indigenous Peoples;* the draft *American Declaration on the Rights of Indigenous Peoples* at the Organization of American States; and the *Indigenous and Tribal Peoples Convention, 1989.* He is co-editor and contributor to *Realizing the U.N. Declaration on the Rights of Indigenous Peoples: Triumph, Hope, and Action* (2010).

Rauna Kuokkanen is Sámi from Ohcejohka (Utsjoki), Northern Finland. She is Associate Professor of Political Science and Aboriginal Studies at the University of Toronto, where she teaches Indigenous politics and rights. Her current research examines indigenous self-determination and the gendered processes of self-government in Canada, Greenland and the Nordic countries among the Sámi. She is the author of *Reshaping the University: Responsibility, Indigenous Epistemes and the*

Logic of the Gift (2007) and *Boaris dego eana: Eamiálbmogiid diehtu, filosofiijat ja dutkan* (As Old as the Earth: Indigenous Knowledge, Philosophies and Research; ČálliidLágádus Sámi Academica Series, 2009). She has translated a Sámi children's book into English (*The White Stone*, 2011, Davvi Girji), edited the anthology on contemporary Sámi literature *Juoga mii geasuha* (2001) and published numerous articles on Indigenous research paradigms, education and critical theory, Indigenous literatures, comparative Indigenous politics, globalization and Indigenous women. She was the founding chair of the Sámi Youth Organization in Finland and has served as the Vice-President of the Sámi Council.

Andrea Smith is co-founder of the Boarding School Healing Coalition. She is currently Associate Professor of Media and Cultural Studies at University of California, Riverside. She is author of *Native Americans and the Christian Right* (2008) and *Conquest: Sexual Violence and American Indian Genocide* (2005), which received the Gustavus Myers Outstanding Book Award, and co-editor of *Theorizing Native Studies* (2014). She is of Cherokee descent.

Maggie Walter is Professor of Sociology in the School of Social Sciences at the University of Tasmania. She has served as the Policy and Law member on the Australian Institute of Aboriginal and Torres Strait Islander Studies Research Advisory Council, on the steering committee of the national Longitudinal Study of Indigenous Children and as Secretary of the Native American and Indigenous Studies Association. She has published articles and book chapters about citizenship, globalization and Indigenous resistance. She is co-author with Chris Andersen of *Indigenous Statistics: A Quantitative Methodology* (2013). Maggie Walter is a descendant of the trawlwoolway people from northeastern Tasmania.

Honoured in Their Absence
Indigenous Human Rights
Joyce Green

Human rights have become a hallmark of international law and are often claimed as an attribute of democratic political orders. Indeed, Canada's current federal government links human rights with democracy in its critique of other states, such as Russia in connection with its annexation of Crimea, and as a justification for Canada's military role in Afghanistan and for its support of Israel. Since 1948 human rights have been formally acknowledged within the international political and legal order, most significantly with the *Universal Declaration of Human Rights* and its covenants on both civil and political, and social, economic and cultural rights. Richard Falk (2000: 133) suggests that these instruments are the "normative foundation" for Indigenous rights claims and particularly for the claim of self-determination of peoples, which the Conventions endorse in their identical Article 1. In 2010 the *United Nations Declaration on the Rights of Indigenous Peoples* (referred to as the Declaration or the UNDRIP subsequently and throughout this book) replicated that recognition of the right of self-determination and enumerated other Indigenous rights. Indigenous self-determination "has become a major international human rights movement" (Russell 2005: 335; see also Anaya 1996: 129–33).

In international law, fundamental human rights have been enumerated and protected since the adoption of the *Universal Declaration of Human Rights* in 1948 and are now considered a customary part of international law. Human rights are understood to be universal. Indigenous rights inure only to Indigenous peoples. And yet the authors in this book frame Indigenous rights as human rights. Somewhere between the universality of our humanity and the particularity of our social, political, cultural, gendered and historical experiences, the lives of human beings are lived in specific, often inequitable and unjust contexts that benefit from human rights protection. Indigenous peoples need the full panoply of human rights and, additionally, Indigenous rights "to be." The most fundamental human right is the right to exist, both as an individual and in one's community. That right is followed by the rights to the conditions that make life meaningful and equitable in social and political contexts.

Indigenous rights, which are a response to the profound violence of colonialism, are anti-genocidal. Genocide is defined by Article 2 of the *Convention on the Crime and Punishment of Genocide* (U.N. 1948) as:

> any of the following acts committed with the intent to destroy, in whole

or in part, a national, racial, religious or ethnic group, such as: (a) Killing members of the group; (b) Causing serious bodily or mental harm to members of the group; (c) Deliberately inflicting on members of the group conditions of life calculated to bring about its physical destruction in whole or in part; (d) Imposing measures intended to prevent births within the group; and (e) Forcibly transferring children of the group to another group.

The historical record of settler states shows that all of these acts have been committed by the states or their agents against Indigenous peoples (see, for example, Russell 2005; Smith 2005; Comack 2012: 66–88; Savage 2012; Daschuk 2013). Justice Murray Sinclair, Chair of Canada's Truth and Reconciliation Commission, has called Canada's residential school policy genocidal (Comack 2013: 8; see also Woo 2011: 21–22). Canada and, generally speaking, all of the Anglo settler states with similar histories of colonialism are continuing these practices, now sanctified by law, framing historical state actions that can only be seen as genocidal for Indigenous peoples.

Colonialism is generally understood to be a phase of imperialism. The latter involves the expansion of political, territorial and economic hegemony by states that, in the process, subsume or obliterate the populations heretofore occupying a territory and exercising political, territorial and economic jurisdiction upon it, often differently than the imperial invaders. The former involved the creation of institutional and administrative apparatuses to serve imperial needs, import the legal and cultural orders of the imperium and create permanent populations of settlers from the imperium on the "new" territories so occupied (Woo 2011: 88). These processes include imperialism as ideology, a key component of which was the uncivilized and uncivilizeable nature of the "savages" being displaced, which persists still in the colonial imagination (Brantlinger 1995: 44, 55; Brownlie 2012; Savage 2012) and is encoded in systemic racism sustaining settler privilege and Indigenous subordination (Green 2005; Gordon 2011: 66-133). Western imperialism, the form that affected Indigenous peoples in today's settler states, is unique, according to Jan Nederveen Pieterse and Bhikhu Parekh (1995:1), because "it involved a different mode of production (capitalism) and technology (industrialism) and took on a virtually global scope."

Indigenous peoples share experiences of colonization, racism, loss of territory and resources and political and legal subordination. In this sense, Indigeniety is relational, as its political relevance emerges only in conditions of colonization. "It is in the unequal imposed relationship of colonialism that Aboriginality [or Indigeniety] emerges as a political distinction from others. [Aboriginal rights] are rights claimed against the colonial state, by virtue of political and cultural precedence to the colonial state, without which there would be no need for the concept [of Aboriginality]" (Green 2005: 231). Russell writes that, in Australia,

"The sense of aboriginal identity ... had evolved largely through the condition of being colonized" (2005: 135).[1] All Indigenous peoples struggle for a range of fundamental rights, in particular rights to land and self-determination. Thus, Indigenous human rights are framed by the reality of Indigenous lives, which are in turn framed by the realities of colonialism, its citizen and institutional beneficiaries, and its ideological justifications.

Colonialism and Decolonization

These realities of colonialism have been shaped by state-specific policies, practices and political and economic structures. Now there is an international effort through the United Nations "to establish worldwide standards on the rights of Aboriginal peoples which are acceptable to those peoples" (Russell 2005: 33) and offer a measure of self-determination for those who have been racialized and oppressed through state colonialism. Indigenous human rights are claims against that oppression and for liberation.

Indigenous human rights are now explicitly recognized in the *U.N. Declaration on the Rights of Indigenous Peoples* and, arguably, in the Canadian *Constitution Act 1982*, section 35, which "recognize[s] and affirm[s]" the "existing aboriginal and treaty rights" of Indigenous peoples in Canada. These include "Indians, Inuit and Métis" peoples. Moreover, Indigenous peoples in settler states are also (not uncontroversially, given our colonial experiences) within the citizen community of the settler state and are entitled to all of the human rights protections afforded by state laws, such as Canada's *Charter of Rights and Freedoms* and the *Canadian Human Rights Act*, and, of course, to all rights protections in international law.

Subsequent to the passage of the *Universal Declaration of Human Rights* and attached covenants, international law has recognized the need for rights specificity, tailored to categories of life experiences, which have been recognized by the *Convention on the Elimination of Discrimination Against Women* (CEDAW) (U.N. 1979); the *Convention on the Rights of the Child* (U.N. 1989); the *Convention on the Rights of Persons with Disabilities* (U.N. 2006); and the *Declaration on the Rights of Indigenous Peoples* (U.N. 2010). James Anaya has argued that international human rights law imposes a duty on states, which is effectively a responsibility for the political executive to guarantee enjoyment of human rights and to provide remedies for their violation. This includes securing Indigenous peoples' rights requiring "contemporary treaty and customary norms grounded in the principle of self-determination" (Anaya 1996: 130; see also 129–33). For both Indigenous peoples and settler states, animation of the right of self-determination has the potential to create durable and just relationships with some degree of mutuality. As Russell writes, "It is, after all, the principle of self determination of peoples that finally provides the normative basis for Indigenous decolonization" (2005: 136–37). Thus Indigenous human rights, which include the right to self-determination, will be foundational in obtaining decolonization.

Both the theoretical consideration and the legal protection of human rights have become more nuanced: while we are all human, we are contextualized by our social, cultural, historical and other situations, and our rights must be similarly contextualized. Despite this recognition, however, there is still an impulse evident in political discussions, and in some theoretical work, to set Indigenous rights apart from the human rights framework. Peter Kulchyski (2013) has argued that Indigenous rights are not human rights, but rather are collective rights that protect culturally specific practices and are not compatible with human rights theory. Other scholars have made efforts to distinguish Indigenous liberatory struggles from other decolonizing struggles: the "salt water" thesis proposed that real colonialism occurred elsewhere, over there, on lands not contiguous to the occupying state; and "internal colonialism" was of a different order, requiring different analyses and political solutions than classical colonialism. All of this has served to minimize the reality of the violent imposition of colonialism in settler states and to deny its logical political and legal implications. Another strand of critique has suggested that the "Western" origins of the notion of human rights makes the "imposition" of those rights on non-Western communities another act of imperialism. However, John-Andrew McNeish and Robyn Eversole's work suggests that different cultural and national communities make the concept of human rights authentically their own in the process of analyzing their conditions and making their claims (Eversole, McNeish and Cimadamore 2005: 99). In this view, then, human rights theory is Indigenized as Indigenous scholars, activists and communities claim Indigenous rights against states, corporate actions and institutional behaviours.

Indigenous rights have been opposed as a concept and as a claim by settler states. Indeed, it took decades of work and much political diplomacy on the part of Indigenous scholars, politicians and activists and their allies to bring the international community to a virtual consensus on the necessity of adopting the *Declaration on the Rights of Indigenous Peoples.*

In Canada it took decades of struggle by Indigenous activists, including international lobbying, to obtain a consensus among non-Indigenous political elites that Indigenous rights should be recognized in the Canadian Constitution. Despite this, there is a cadre of political and corporate actors and academics hostile to Indigenous rights who argue for assimilative goals and for an ahistorical "equality" that ensures erasure or minimization of the historical record of state oppression of Indigenous peoples (see for example Flanagan 2002; M. Smith 1996). Consequently, Indigenous peoples are perpetually in political and legal struggles with settler state and corporate entities, seeking recognition, implementation and protection of Indigenous human rights. The relationship is adversarial and every right won is through struggle on the hostile terrain of settler state courts and legislatures. And, in the process, many cases are lost, also setting legal precedent that constrains future challenges.

In Australia, decades of legal and political struggle led to the precedential decision of that country's High Court in Mabo (for Eddie Koiki Mabo, who initiated the case) that included the observation that Australia was not and never had been *terra nullius* ("empty land" — thus belonging to no one) and therefore Aboriginal people must be recognized in and potentially compensated for historical acts of dispossession. However, the Court diminished the positive effect of its decision by upholding "the extinguishment of native title by valid acts of imperial, Colonial state, Territory or Commonwealth Governments [and] affirmed terra nullius by introducing a new form of extinguishment into the common law" (Moreton-Robinson 2014; see also Moreton-Robinson 2001: 164–65).

In Aotearoa New Zealand, Maori political struggle has produced a partial accommodation by the state of Maori rights under the Treaty of Waitangi, including (fairly minimal) accommodations within the country's Parliament and recognition of Maori land rights that has *de facto* failed to protect Maori lands.

The U.S. experience is shaped by a history of military force by the state, and the minimalist formula of the "domestic dependent nations" doctrine introduced by the Marshall legal trilogy (after then-Chief Justice John Marshall). Invoked ever since, this doctrine has effectively subordinated Indigenous nations in the U.S. to its political regime.

Sami have gained a measure of political recognition in their territories outside of Russia and in Scandinavia, including the Sami Parliament, but still struggle for political autonomy and land rights. Norway, Sweden and Finland have limited their recognition of Indigenous rights to cultural aspects only, with little to no acknowledgement of Indigenous land rights. In spite of the establishment of the Sami Parliaments in each of these countries, they exercise very limited formal authority or decision-making power (Kuokkanen 2009). In 2005, the draft Nordic Sami Convention was submitted to the Nordic ministers in charge of Sami affairs and the presidents of the three Sami Parliaments for their approval, with the objective of strengthening the Sami rights to language, culture and livelihoods. The negotiations on ratifying the Convention, however, have been delayed.

All Indigenous peoples still struggle against the legal, political and economic impositions of the settler states that have appropriated their territories and sovereignties, and that have, in the process, violated Indigenous human rights. All Indigenous peoples seek to secure a measure of their traditional territories and economic and political autonomy within those territories. And all Indigenous peoples find that the settler states, the colonizers and their political, economic and legal apparatuses set the possibilities and parameters for Indigenous liberation so as to minimize the effect on the states (Gordon 2010: 101).

Recognizing Indigenous rights requires recognizing the oppressive history and contemporary practices of settler states. Recognition requires some critical engagement with assumptions about and practices of the economic order of capitalism. It requires an appreciation of the racialization of Indigenous peoples as a state stratagem that legitimates their exploitation and blames contemporary

Indigenous peoples for their suffering consequent to that exploitation. It is a critical scholarly position and, like other critical scholarly work, positions itself against the dominant canon in order to read a different analysis into the historical, legal and political record. In this book, the foundational claim is that Indigenous rights are a species of human rights, not a separate set of rights, which must be recognized and implemented as part of the liberatory struggle against oppression and erasure. The general analytical thread that binds all the authors in this book together is that Indigenous human rights are indivisible, not segregated from each other.

Indigenous peoples have, globally, lived with the depredations of imperialism, colonialism and capitalism, most cataclysmically launched in the Americas in 1492 with the adventures of Cristobal Colon, better known as "Columbus." The subsequent appropriation of Indigenous lands and the oppression of Indigenous peoples have been legitimated by nationalism, by economic ideology, by social science theories (of stages of development and cultural evolution), by Christian theological interpretations (justifying Indigenous cultural annihilation), by racism and by settler state law in the service of colonial and settler sovereignty and interests. Thus, the rights of Indigenous peoples have been sacrificed on altars of non-Indigenous interests in favour of those who profit at Indigenous expense. Settler state oppression of Indigenous peoples has been justified, sanitized and mythologized so thoroughly that discussing it has, in the words of Donald Worme, become a "preposterous taboo" (Comack 2012: 9). And yet, "colonialism is not simply a historical artefact" (Comack 2012: 66). Its consequences shape the lives of contemporary Indigenous and non-Indigenous people, and taint the relationship between them.[2]

Despite their involuntary and forced incorporation into settler states, Indigenous peoples have been denied not only self-determination but also the general rights and benefits of citizenship in the state (Green 2005; Thobani 2007: 67–102). The federal and provincial governments of Canada have often treated Indigenous peoples as outside of the citizenship community for the purposes of rights protection — especially where recognition would have economic consequences for governments, such as in education, health care, community safety such as fire protection, child welfare services and so on. Other settler states have been similarly unwilling to treat Indigenous rights within the human rights paradigm and thus as a reasonable obligation on governments, preferring to conceive of these rights as historical and extinguishable. The reality that Indigenous human rights include a claim to land and against the sovereignty of settler states has framed a political problematic for state recognition: none are willing to confront and remedy Indigenous rights violations as a consequence of state occupation and oppression.

The conceptual fuzziness some attribute to Indigenous human rights has made it easier for settler states to ignore them while claiming to protect human rights. This is especially true where rights claims involve territory, sovereignty, recognition of and reparations or restitution for the injuries suffered under colonialism. For example, in Canada Indigenous peoples have had to carry land claims to the hostile terrain of settler state courts over many decades to obtain small and circumscribed measures of justice (Gordon 2011: 101); education in First Nation communities continues to be dramatically underfunded by the federal government relative to the funding per student in provincial schools; Indigenous health has a profile characteristic of the extreme impoverishment of the "third world," including higher infant mortality rates; and the settler state persists in a bizarre recognition/denial approach to colonialism (see Comack, Green, this volume). Thus, colonialism is treated as only historical rather than as a continuing process; its perpetrators are seen as temporally and legally separate from contemporary democratic governments and settler populations.

All of the settler states deny Indigenous claims to land and sovereignty and have fought those claims in courts and in their political arenas, as in Canada with the Calder (SCC 1973) and Delgamuukw (SCC 1997) cases and in Australia with the Mabo (HC 1998; HC 1992) and Wik (HC 1996) cases. Where states have acknowledged the violence and consequences of historical policies of colonialism by past governments, the acknowledgement has been in such a compartmentalized fashion that it permits contemporary governments to conceive of colonial events as merely historical and to insulate their present practices that violate Indigenous rights from the analysis of past events. In this way, for example, Canadian recognition of the violence of residential schools has not extended to state remediation of the consequences, neither for education, nor for community and family suffering and disintegration, nor for health care, child welfare and so on. At the time of writing, the Canadian government refuses to strike a royal commission inquiry into over six hundred missing and murdered Indigenous women, despite being urged to do so by U.N. Special Rapporteur on Indigenous Peoples James Anaya (*Star* 2013). It persists in a "law and order" agenda that disproportionately incarcerates Indigenous offenders, for longer and with less chance of parole. Andrea Smith (2005:139) indicates that the U.S. shares this approach: "Native people are per capita the most arrested, most incarcerated, and most victimized by police brutality of any ethnic group in the country."

The failure to recognize Indigenous rights as human rights has also contributed to the popular mythologies in settler states that naturalize the political and economic order that has privileged settlers at the expense of Indigenous peoples. These are the bases of structural racism. The artificial and erroneous theoretical divide between Indigenous and other human rights has been useful for propaganda purposes, but is not intellectually defensible. Indigenous rights claims are too often recast by states as interests requiring consultation rather than rights requiring recognition and animation. Consultation is not treated as the UNDRIP's "free, prior and informed consent" but as a conversation with no clear framework for either engagement or resolution (see Benjamin, Joffe, this volume). Indigenous rights are generally not seen to be sufficient to trump economic and political initiatives by state or corporate actors. For example, in Canada, approval of certain oil and gas pipeline and related export facilities proposals will be granted if the "net benefit" to the state "outweighs" Indigenous rights (and environmental concerns), which will necessarily be trodden on.

Indigenous resistance to rights violations is not infrequently misrepresented by mainstream media and politicians as radical, illogical, anti-progressive and romantic rather than practical (see, for example, Cronlund Anderson and Robertson 2011). The worst of anti-Indigenous rhetoric labels Indigenous resistance as terrorism — the ultimate political epithet in the post-9/11 world. Thus settler state publics are presented with official and media versions of "the natives are restless," rather than getting detailed contextual coverage of the issues animating Indigenous peoples. The lack of comprehension within dominant societies contributes to their impatience with and intolerance for Indigenous rights activism, and to a lack of political pressure on government to resolve these matters honourably.

In sum, the argument in this book is that Indigenous/Aboriginal rights are a species of human rights essential for the realization of human rights of Indigenous people and peoples in the context of settler states. Moreover, settler states are obliged to respect and animate these rights, despite the evident tensions in political and economic interests between elite capitalists, settler citizens and Indigenous peoples.

The contributors to this book are all scholars of and advocates for Indigenous peoples' fundamental human rights. Legal scholars take up law as an instrument of (in)justice. Social scientists take up the theoretical and policy framework that constructs privilege and oppression. Their material has the potential to, via education, create measures of empathy, justice and enlightenment. Activist scholars show how engagement in advocacy for Indigenous human rights generally or specifically can produce transformation.

Theorizing and Contextualizing Indigenous Human Rights

Joyce Green begins with the context that Canada, a settler state created on the territories of and at the expense of Aboriginal peoples, opposed the 2007 United Nations adoption of the *Declaration on the Rights of Indigenous Peoples* and, despite ratifying it in November 2010, has qualified its significance to the point of meaninglessness. She locates the struggle for Indigenous rights in the Canadian constitutional framework and juxtaposes the Harper Government's resistance to the Declaration against the Canadian context for Aboriginal human rights and the implications of the Declaration for Canadian compliance with international law and for domestic policies.

Elizabeth Comack begins her chapter by quoting Canadian Prime Minister Stephen Harper: "We [Canada] also have no history of colonialism," volunteered at a press conference at the G20 (an international forum of the world's twenty largest economies) "Pittsburgh Summit" in September 2009. The difficulties of confronting colonialism in Canada are evident when the prime minister is comfortable making such an astounding assertion. Comack proceeds to document the justice system basis for colonialism in Canada, particularly its manifestation through racialized policing, which disproportionately and negatively affects Indigenous people. Police forces are tasked with creating and re-creating order in society. In the case of settler societies like Canada, that order is imbued with racial oppression. Comack observes: "So long as Canadians are content (and privileged) in their denial of colonialism — and the damage created by that ongoing legacy — the potential for the Canadian state to meet its obligations to the Indigenous peoples and to comply with its international obligations as spelled out in the *U.N. Declaration on the Rights of Indigenous Peoples* will be seriously restricted."

Maggie Walter writes that national suffrage was extended to Australian Aborigines in the 1960s, the last of the so-called Aboriginal protection laws was scrapped in the 1980s and land rights became at least a legal reality in the 1990s. Why then, she asks, are Aborigines still struggling for rights of recognition now? The answer can be found in the "race bind" deployed to justify racially differentiated policies and the everyday normalcy of racialized disrespect. The "race bind," she writes, is "the place where the dominant discourses of individualism, free market capitalism and the embedded stratification of race privilege/disprivilege meet. The result is a toxic discursive paradox that denies the concept of race itself" while blaming Indigenous misery on the individual choices of Indigenous people. This paradox obliterates Indigenous human rights.

Andrea Smith uses the struggle for reparation for American Indian boarding school abuses in the United States to examine the complexity of using human rights frameworks within settler states. Smith notes that while human rights movements can potentially co-opt anti-colonial struggles, human rights campaigns can also be useful organizing strategies leading to more radical emancipatory strategies later. Smith explores how activists can most fruitfully advance the human rights of Indigenous peoples.

Several authors, particularly Gwen Brodsky, Mary Eberts and Rauna Kuokkanen, take up the gendered nature of colonial oppression and of Indigenous human rights. A gendered analysis shows that while colonialism affects all Indigenous peoples, it does not affect women and men identically. Their work supports Andrea Smith's assertion that "Colonial relationships are themselves gendered and sexualized" (Smith 2005: 1) and her observation that "sexual violence has served as a tool of colonialism and white supremacy" (2005:137). Each of these authors reveals a different facet of Indigenous women's human rights, experienced as violations rather than implementations of rights.

Gwen Brodsky writes about Sharon McIvor's petition to the United Nations Human Rights Committee. The petition proposes that, despite several legislative amendments, the *Indian Act* criteria for Indian status still discriminate against Indian women and their descendants. Furthermore, Canada's legal and governmental institutions have failed repeatedly and deliberately over an excessively long period of time to remedy *Indian Act* sex discrimination. Brodsky argues that the U.N. Human Rights Committee should require Canada to end *Indian Act* sex discrimination once and for all.

Rauna Kuokkanen proposes a human rights framework that connects Indigenous self-determination to the human rights of Indigenous women. Kuokkanen examines these interconnections with a particular focus on the question of violence against women. She contends that for Indigenous self-determination to be successful, it must also address the question of violence against Indigenous women. That is, Indigenous women are entitled to human rights as *Indigenous women* — and Indigenous political orders are obliged to recognize gendered rights and rights violations if these political orders are to be legitimate within the framework of international human rights law.

Mary Eberts argues that the deployment of colonial "Victorian" patriarchy in Canadian culture and particularly through the *Indian Act* creates a cultural and legal architecture characterized by the fusion of racism, misogyny and colonialism. This has constructed Indigenous women as a "population of prey," the proof of which is evident in both standard quality-of-life indices and in the awful and disproportionate phenomenon of missing and murdered Aboriginal women. In Eberts's view Canada is responsible for the *Indian Act* and for refusing to expunge the racist and sexist elements from its Indian status provisions.

Brenda Gunn argues that the rights recognized and affirmed in the U.N. Declaration can be used as a framework for interpreting the scope of protected rights under s. 35(1) of Canada's *Constitution Act, 1982*. Gunn examines the principle, much ignored in Canada, that domestic and international law should be congruent. She concludes that crucial Supreme Court of Canada decisions, and some important strands of dissent in other decisions, point toward a need for a more robust incorporation and application of international rights instruments to Canada.

Craig Benjamin reviews the concept of "free, prior and informed consent" (FPIC) in the evolution of international human rights standards, and argues that meaningful consultation requires the possibility of consent being either granted or withheld. That is, FPIC must be more than mere consultation: it must include the ability to make decisions about land, resources, culture and so on. Benjamin argues that the principle of FPIC is necessary to the reconciliation of Indigenous and non-Indigenous peoples and that adoption of this principle in the regulation of resource development would ultimately benefit both.

Paul Joffe shows that, despite its endorsement of the U.N. Declaration, the Canadian government continues to counter Indigenous peoples' human rights, and to devalue and minimize the Declaration. In Joffe's view, Canada's actions, which include "government actions relating to Indigenous peoples' rights to land and resources; food security, environment and climate change; free trade; essential services; and children's rights" (Joffe, this volume), violate the rule of law and core

Canadian constitutional principles of justice, democracy and non-discrimination. He warns that the consequences of such conduct are likely to perpetuate Indigenous impoverishment and rights abuses.

Lawyers Gwen Brodsky, Paul Joffe, Mary Eberts, Brenda Gunn and Andrea Smith bring legal analyses to bear on the framework of settler state law and of international law as they affect Indigenous human rights. Brodsky, Eberts and Rauna Kuokkanen foreground Indigenous women in their powerful analyses. Elizabeth Comack and Joyce Green take up the historical and contemporary force of colonialism in Canada. Craig Benjamin, Green and Joffe examine the politics and law of the Canadian government's obstruction of the progress of international law and state protection of Indigenous human rights. Maggie Walter shows how race and racism have played, historically and now, to the extreme disadvantage of Aborigines in Australia.

The synthesis of these arguments leads to the inescapable conclusion that Indigenous human rights are indeed indivisible: the human rights of Indigenous peoples must include recognition of their Indigeniety and the specific rights that flow from that profoundly political identity, together with the rights that all human beings are supposed to enjoy. The human rights of Indigenous people are injured when their rights as Indigenous people are violated. To be fully and authentically human, Indigenous peoples must be able to be Indigenous — in cultural, economic, political, ecological and other ways. To be fully human, Indigenous peoples must be as able as any other community to adapt their practices and cultures — the exercise of these rights — to the conditions in which they live: these are not archaic rights frozen at some historical pre-colonial point, but the rights of living, adapting contemporary communities.

Indigenous human rights are remarkably vulnerable to abrogation at the behest of or through the indifference of what are profoundly racist and misogynist settler states. Settler states privilege primarily white settler populations, capitalist economic relations and policy and legal regimes predicated on the erasure of Indigenous sovereignty, humanity, autonomy and equality. Herein lie the main barriers to achieving Indigenous human rights.

Indigenous Human Rights and Decolonization

While Indigenous human rights have been overwhelmingly honoured in their absence by settler states, it is not politically or legally impossible for these states to now commit to the constitutional, economic and political protection and implementation of these rights. States have come some distance since imperialism and colonialism were seen as unproblematic by their historical practitioners. Most settler states now have a sense of shame about their oppression of Indigenous peoples, evident in the propaganda that is used to minimize this history and also in the efforts made to distance contemporary political and social orders from the events of recent and historical oppression. It would be cathartic, as well as just, to move to a robust defence of the rights that have been so violated. Moreover, such state action would serve to move Indigenous and settler peoples past our shared oppositional past and create the conditions for more amicable future relationships. Finally, such state action would bring settler states into compliance with the international (and in at least Canada's case, domestic constitutional) obligations to protect Indigenous human rights. While remedies will not be universal or quickly achieved, political will is an essential first ingredient in a path to reconciliation and decolonization. Importantly, no reconciliation or decolonization can occur unless the state recognizes and ceases current acts of colonialism: this is not solely an historic matter.

Legal action is only one measure in a decolonization toolkit and is generally only undertaken when political measures have not been fruitful. Organized public dissent, similarly, is a tactic deployed when virtually all other measures have failed. The iconic social movement Idle No More emerged in 2012 in response to Canada's political intransigence on crucial matters vital to Indigenous human rights: failure to provide adequate housing, education, health care and implementation of treaty provisions, among others. Canada could have welcomed the political engagement of Idle No More activists. Yet, it has instead retreated to suspicion, spying and monitoring the movement for information for "detecting, preventing or suppressing subversive or hostile activities" (Ling 2014). It seems there is no acceptable way for Indigenous peoples to speak to the state about the conditions in their lives or about their unhappiness with Canada's historical and continuing mistreatment and its indifference to Indigenous suffering.

And ultimately, Indigenous peoples have signalled that assimilation into the settler state, or marginalization from its economic and political benefits, will not be accepted, especially by Indigenous youth. Like the international Occupy Movement, Idle No More represents the voice of the voiceless, the power of the marginalized and the aspirations of many people and communities. While it has been less evident in recent months than at its most prominent at the time of Chief Teresa Spence's fast to protest Canada's disregard of the needs in her community, it is a movement that could re-emerge. It is comprised of community members in cities, on reserves and in the hinterlands. It is an organization with many voices, a fairly flat structure and multiple strategists. It provides space for political debate and opportunities for leadership and activist development. It provides an important focus for settler media, thus helping to educate settler Canadians about the difficult political, social and economic realities in what is called Indian Country. It has led to solidarities with non-Indigenous activists, including through the Silent No More initiative, which speaks up about settler state violation of Indigenous human rights. Canada has not heard the last from Idle No More and its allies.

The international Indigenous movement is preparing for the United Nations World Conference on Indigenous Peoples in New York, on September 22–23, 2014. So, too, should settler states. The U.S.-based Indian Law Resource Center calls the conference "an historic opportunity to secure positive action in the U.N. to improve the lives of indigenous peoples around the world ... [and] to share perspectives and best practices on the realization of the rights of indigenous peoples and to pursue the objectives of the U.N. Declaration on the Rights of Indigenous Peoples" (ILRC Press Release 2014; http://indianlaw.org/worldconference).

Indigenous human rights are liberatory. Colonialism lies at the base of Indigenous dehumanization and oppression. The settler state citizen populations and its elites are the beneficiaries of these processes of racialization, oppression and denial by these now democratic (if also amnesiac) states. These states' policies have profoundly abused Indigenous peoples' human rights through forced relocations — an historical ethnic cleansing — and the forced family disintegration caused by residential schools, adoption and foster care of Indigenous children, Christian dogmas imposed by government policies and health catastrophes (Daschuk 2013). Other practices have included starvation as a means of domination, the destruction of Indigenous economies and imprisonment on meagre plots of land, enforced and monitored by the coercive force of the state. Settler states have used armed force, colonial bureaucratic institutions and racialized policing to dominate Indigenous peoples. States continue to subject Indigenous organizations and movements to constant surveillance and infiltration of police, security personnel and spy agencies of governments.

Indigenous human rights exist in law and in principle. They have achieved legitimacy at the United Nations, and the entire international community is now aware of the need to secure these rights on a state-by-state basis. It is time for these rights to be recognized, supported and implemented by the settler states. Only this can lead to the possibility of reconciliation with Indigenous peoples and to decolonization — the mutual imagining of a future that accommodates us all on terms we freely choose.

Notes

1   Both terms "Indigenous" and "Aboriginal" are used here. Indigenous is the accepted term in international law, as expressed in the *U.N. Declaration on the Rights of Indigenous Peoples*. The term "Aboriginal" is the accepted term in Canadian constitutional law and in the *Constitution Act, 1982*, s.35, which refers to "Indians, Inuit and Métis" and which recognizes and affirms the existing Aboriginal and treaty rights of the Aboriginal peoples of Canada.

2   A good examination of this history and its contemporary consequences may be read in Candace Savage's 2012 award-winning book *A Geography of Blood*.

References

Anaya, S. James. 1996. *Indigenous Peoples in International Law*. New York: Oxford University Press.

Brantlinger, Patrick. 1995. "'Dying races': rationalizing genocide in the nineteenth century."

In Jan Nederveen Pieterse and Bhikhu Parekh, eds., *The Decolonization of Imagination: Culture, Knowledge and Power*. London and New Jersey: Zed Books.

Brownlie, Robin Jarvis. 2012. "Others or Brothers?: Competing Settler and Anishinabe Discourses About Race in Upper Canada". In Robin Jarvis Brownlie and Valerie J. Korinek, eds., *Finding a Way to the Heart: Feminist Writings on Aboriginal and Women's History in Canada*. Winnipeg: University of Manitoba Press.

Comack, Elizabeth. 2012. *Racialized Policing: Aboriginal People's Encounters With the Police*. Halifax & Winnipeg: Fernwood Publishing.

Comack, Elizabeth, Lawrence Deane, Larry Morrisette and Jim Silver. 2013. *Indians Wear Red: Colonialism, Resistance, and Aboriginal Street Gangs*. Halifax & Winnipeg: Fernwood Publishing.

Cronlund Anderson, Mark, and Carmen L. Robertson. 2011. *Seeing Red: A History of Natives in Canadian Newspapers*. Winnipeg: University of Manitoba Press.

Daschuk, James. 2013. *Clearing the Plains: Disease, Politics of Starvation, and the Loss of Aboriginal Life*. Regina: University of Regina Press.

Falk, Richard. 2000. *Human Rights Horizons: The Pursuit of Justice in a Globalizing World*. New York: Routledge.

Flanagan, Tom. 2000. *First Nations? Second Thoughts*. Montreal: McGill-Queen's University Press.

Gordon, Todd. 2011. *Imperialist Canada*. Winnipeg: Arbeiter Ring Publishing.

Green, Joyce A. 2005. "Towards Conceptual Precision: Citizenship and Rights Talk for Aboriginal Canadians". In Gerald Kernerman and Philip Resnick, eds., *Insiders and Outsiders: Alan Cairns and the Reshaping of Canadian Citizenship*. Vancouver: UBC Press.

____. 2009. "From Stonechild to Social Cohesion: Anti-Racist Challenges for Saskatchewan". "*I Thought Pocahontas Was a Movie.*" In Carol Schick and James McNinch, eds., *Perspectives on Race/Culture Binaries in Education and Service Professions*. Regina: Canadian Plains Research Centre. Pp. 129-149.

Indian Law Resource Centre. 2014. Press Release, and "Recommendations for the World Conference on Indigenous Peoples". <http://indianlaw.org/worldconference>.

Kulchyski, Peter. 2013. *Aboriginal Rights are not Human Rights: In Defence of Indigenous Struggles*. Winnipeg: ARP Books.

Kuokkanen, Rauna. 2009. "Achievements of Indigenous Self-Determination. The Case of the Sami Parliaments in Finland and Norway." In Ed Beier, J. Marshall, eds., *Indigenous Diplomacies*. New York: Palgrave.

Ling, Justin. 2014. "Canada's spy agency helped prepare all-of-government approach in case Idle No More protests 'escalated': secret files" (*National Post* March 23 <http://news.nationalpost.com/2014/03/23/canadas-spy-agency-helped-prepare-all-of-government-approach-in-case-idle-no-more-protests-escalated-secret-files/>.

McNeish, John-Andrew and Robyn Eversole. 2005. "Overview: the right to self-determination". In Eversole, McNeish and Cimadamore, eds., *Indigenous Peoples & Poverty: An International Perspective*. London and New York: Zed Books.

Moreton-Robinson, Aileen. 2014. Personal Conversation, April 7, 2014.

____. 2001. "A Possessive Investment in Patriarchal Whiteness: Nullifying Native Title." In Paul Nursey-Bray and Carol Lee Bacchi, eds., *Left Directions: Is There a Third Way*. Perth: University of Western Australia Press.

Pieterse, Jan Nederveen, and Bhikhu Parekh. 1995. "Shifting imaginaries: decolonization, internal decolonization, postcoloniality." In Jan Nederveen Pieterse and Bhikhu Parekh, eds., *The Decolonization of Imagination: Culture, Knowledge and Power*. London and New Jersey: Zed Books.

Russell, Peter H. 2005. *Recognizing Aboriginal Title: The Mabo Case and Indigenous Resistance to English-Settler Colonialism*. Toronto: University of Toronto Press.

Savage, Candace. 2012. *A Geography of Blood: Unearthing Memory from a Prairie Landscape*. Vancouver: Greystone Books.

Smith, Andrea. 2005. *Conquest: Sexual Violence and American Indian Genocide."* Cambridge MA: South End Press.

Smith, Melvin H. 1996. *Our Home or Native Land? What Governments' Aboriginal policy Is Doing to Canada*. Toronto: Stoddard.

Star. 2013. "UN investigator urges inquiry for missing murdered Aboriginal women." <thestar.com/news/canada/2013/10/15/un_investigator_urges_inquiry_for_missing_murdered_aboriginal_women.html.

Thobani, Sunera. 2007. *Exalted Subjects: Studies in the Making of Race and Nation in Canada*. Toronto: University of Toronto Press.

Legal Cases

Calder v. *Attorney General of British Columbia* (1973) SCR 313 (Supreme Court of Canada).

Delgamuukw v. *British Columbia* (1997) 3 SCR 1010 (Supreme Court of Canada).

Mabo v. *Queensland* (No.2) (1992) 175 CLR 1 (High Court of Australia).

Wik Peoples v. *Queensland* (1996) 141 ALR 129 (High Court of Australia).

Part One

Theoretical and Political Context for Indigenous Human Rights

Chapter One

From Colonialism to Reconciliation Through Indigenous Human Rights
Joyce Green

Canada, a settler state with an imperial and colonial history, has accommodated Indigenous rights when necessary, broken its treaty promises when it could and used military, police, political and bureaucratic power to dominate, marginalize, delegitimate and assimilate Indigenous peoples. Like most bullies, Canada doesn't like being criticized for its treatment of Indigenous people. It diminishes its critics, preferring popular mythologies with respect to its goodness in the world. As a putatively democratic state with a now-universal franchise, Canada's political positions are the sum of the voting populations' dominant visions, within the limitations of the plurality electoral system (see, for example, Pilon 2007). The state does no more than it is allowed to do by those who control the economic and political apparatuses, including the economic and political elites, and enfranchised citizens. Thus, and regardless of personal awareness or intention, all Canadians are responsible for the violations of the particular and general human rights of Indigenous people by the state, done in citizens' collective name. These rights violations are essentially political problems with political solutions and, like all politics, are imbued with relations of dominance and subordination, and are amenable to analysis and transformation.

The results of the systematic practice of abrogating Indigenous rights are evident in what United Nations Special Rapporteur on Indigenous Peoples, James Anaya, calls "distressing socio-economic conditions of indigenous peoples" in Canada. "It is difficult to reconcile Canada's well-developed legal framework and general prosperity with the human rights problems faced by indigenous peoples in Canada that have reached crisis proportions in many respects," Anaya writes (CTV News 2014). He notes that "the well-being gap between aboriginal and non-aboriginal people in Canada has not narrowed over the last several years, treaty and Aboriginal claims remain persistently unresolved, indigenous women and girls remain vulnerable to abuse, and overall there appear to be high levels of distrust among indigenous peoples toward government at both the federal and provincial levels" (U.N. 2014: 1).

The lack of concern with and the denial of Indigenous human rights have been foundational to Canada's inception and development. Violence was "the necessary condition for the preservation of the colonial order" (Thobani 2007: 56). Imperial expansion historically brought flag-bearers for several European states to Turtle Island (the name a number of Indigenous nations used for all or parts of North

America), claiming chunks of it for sovereigns elsewhere. It also brought their commercial agents, for the search for territory was motivated by the classically colonial search for (other peoples') wealth. Thus, for example, the Hudson's Bay Company (HBC) obtained a trading monopoly from a British sovereign who presumed to both claim and distribute rights to territories that neither he nor they knew the extent of — and without regard to those whose territory it was. Moreover, and despite the recognition of Indigenous nations in the Royal Proclamation of 1763, the HBC was considered to bring British law and sovereignty to the territory, along with commercial interests and monopoly, in the process subjecting everyone, without their consent, to those legal and administrative regimes.

And after the 1867 Confederation event, now considered foundational to the contemporary Canadian state, then-Prime Minister John A. Macdonald initiated his much celebrated "National Policy" — a set of policies, actually — that structured the further expansion of the new settler state and necessarily the subordination of Indigenous peoples (Green 1995). Thobani writes that "nation building was steeped as much in the epistemic ejection of Aboriginal peoples from the category human as it was in the dispossession of Aboriginal peoples from their lands" (2007: 55). To be clear, then, the dehumanization of Indigenous peoples was necessary for dispossession and subsequent legislative oppression, in all of the state-sponsored and enforced violations of Indigenous human rights. The rest, as they say, is history: the mythology of Canada[1] (similarly with other settler states) elides the occasionally bloody and always coercive dispossession of Indigenous nations in favour of settlement myths about glorious white ancestors (Thobani 2007: 33–64).

Subsequent state policy either ignored Indigenous peoples or treated them as an impediment to be managed so that state development could proceed for non-Indigenous interests. Yet, Canada has also entrenched undefined "aboriginal and treaty rights" of the "Indians, Inuit and Métis" in s. 35 of the *Constitution Act 1982* and, despite the government's evident reluctance to do so, eventually adopted the United Nations *Declaration on the Rights of Indigenous Peoples* (hereafter UNDRIP or the Declaration). It is this contradictory history, with its vile and genocidal effects on Indigenous peoples and its potential for positive change, which preoccupies this chapter's analysis.

I use both "Indigenous," the accepted international term also used in the Declaration, and "Aboriginal" in reference to Indigenous peoples in Canada. "Aboriginal" is the accepted term in Canadian constitutional law and in the *Constitution Act, 1982*. The international discourse and legal regime in respect of Indigenous peoples applies to Indigenous peoples in Canada, and the Canadian state is bound both by international law and by the Canadian constitution to recognize and affirm these rights.

Colonialism as Context

In the formation of Canada, imperialism was initiated in the predatory economic and political activity of primarily European states, leading to the imposition of political and economic relationships on those they dominated. The process is the definition. As Said explains, "imperialism means thinking about, settling on, controlling land that you do not possess, that is distant, that is lived on and owned by others" (Said 1994: 7). The benefits accrue to the imperialist community at the expense of the colonized. Imperialism morphed into colonialism — the practice of creating permanent settlements with people from the imperial state. That produced permanent political frameworks, contested by Indigenous claims of sovereignty, and to state practices causing the marginalization and dispossession of the original inhabitants. The political economy of the Canadian state is underwritten by Indigenous dispossession. Canadian democracy is redolent with colonialism and has been largely meaningless to Indigenous people. As the late Oji-Cree political figure Elijah Harper said, "With your democratic state, you oppressed us, democratically" (Green 2012: 17).

The ideology for imperialism, according to Said, allowed decent folk to believe that "distant territories and their native peoples *should* be subjugated … [an] almost metaphysical obligation to rule subordinate, inferior, or less advanced peoples" (1994: 10, emphasis in original). Enacted through colonialism, imperialism was and is justified by racism, an ideology that assumes that those who are dominated represent vices or incapacities best remedied by the enforcement of colonial practices; by enforced civilization, Christianization, education and wardship or, if irremediable, by passive or active elimination. Those practices are essentially genocidal: they are intended to eliminate the cultural particularity and its political implications in favour of a homogeneous settler state culture, where rights are without distinction and history has no contemporary consequences.

In Canada, racism is now expressed in the language of intractable cultural differences between Indigenous and other people, or the need for specific forms of capitalist development to remedy the intergenerational suffering that plagues colonized Indigenous communities. There is virtually no consideration of the processes and consequences of colonialism in creating Indigenous immiseration, or in alleviating it. Joffe (2010: 74) proposes that "colonialism, dispossession and discrimination" are the basis of Indigenous peoples' poverty and intergenerational trauma, and constitute the denial of Indigenous human rights (see also Irlbacher-Fox 2009).

Moreover, colonial relationships are fraught with "pervasive structural and psychological" dimensions between colonizers and colonized (LaRocque 2010: 121; see also Fanon 1952, 1961; Coulthard 2007; Said 1979, 1994). Colonialism has damaged all Indigenous peoples, and it has been experienced by women differently than men (Green 2007; McKay and Benjamin 2010; Altamirano-Jiménez 2011; Kuokkanen; Brodsky; Eberts; Smith, this volume). Indigenous women suffer from the magnified impacts of the deterioration of community and culture because of gendered roles, the racist projection of sexual amorality onto Indigenous people and women's vulnerability to male violence in the home and in public spaces. Indigenous women in Canada are more likely to experience male violence than non-Indigenous women and they are more likely to be killed or imprisoned. Amnesty International has suggested that a toxic combination of racism and the vulnerabilities created by colonialism radically impairs Indigenous women's security (McKay and Benjamin 2010: 157–159). For example, there are several hundreds of missing and murdered Indigenous women in Canada, belatedly the subject of public consternation because of the advocacy of Indigenous women and other activists (Anderson et al. 2010). Acting Chief Commissioner David Langtry of the Canadian Human Rights Commission (CHRC) issued a statement in 2013 stating that the CHRC is "deeply concerned about the disproportionate number of Indigenous women and girls in Canada who are victims of violence and systemic discrimination" (CHRC 2013). McKay and Benjamin (2010: 157) argue that "the economic, social, and cultural rights of Indigenous women are indivisible from their right to be free from violence and discrimination." The federal government has refused to initiate an inquiry or commission on the matter despite being urged to do so by U.N. Special Rapporteur on Indigenous Peoples James Anaya (*Star* 2013).

The United Nations *Declaration on the Rights of Indigenous Peoples*

The effective constitutionalization of fundamental human rights emerged at international law, first through the United Nations Charter (Sambo Dorough 2001: 111), and then in the *Universal Declaration of Human Rights* and subsequent covenants. Respect for human rights is now a desired component of state legitimacy in the international community. Nakata (2001: 11) writes that the "fundamental freedom and human rights of all people has been considered an essential cornerstone in the maintenance of world peace." As is discussed in the Introduction to this book, Indigenous human rights are indivisible: it is not possible to separate what is human from what is Indigenous, and to attempt to do so would violate those same rights. For example, McKay and Benjamin write that "all human rights are universal, indivisible, interdependent, and interrelated … and the violation of one right puts others in jeopardy" and that the "principle of indivisibility" is a critical component of implementing the UNDRIP (2010: 160).

Yet no attention was paid to Indigenous peoples' rights for several decades after the adoption of the UNDRIP, though many states had dispossessed and otherwise oppressed Indigenous peoples in the primarily European imperial expansion. Perhaps this is unsurprising, as the United Nations is comprised of the same states that violated Indigenous rights (Sambo Dorough 2001: 110). The nature of this oppression as a violation by "white settler states, colonial administrations, and 'new world' governments" was little considered until after 1945 (Teeple 2004: 89).

After all, states had emerged into and then reinforced an international order that validated their existence and their sovereignty. This self-reinforcing order constitutes most of the corpus of international law and international relations currently framing the United Nations and its members' self-understanding. This positivist legal approach amounted to valorization of the rules of the rulers. Effectively, the foundational theorists of international law produced a framework in which states recognize law that affirms their sovereignty and legitimacy (Anaya 2004: 15–48). As Eide (2009: 32–33) writes:

> National sovereignty was the basic organizing principle. International law was considered to derive solely from state consent and state practice and to deal exclusively with relations between sovereign states. Conditions inside states were the exclusive concern of the colonizing power. Consequently, the treatment of Indigenous peoples was generally a matter of internal affairs.… Even treaties between colonial empires and Indigenous peoples were subsequently considered to fall under domestic, rather than international, jurisdictions.

Explained thusly, Indigenous peoples became, by definition, internal populations, even minority populations, of sovereign states, who were then insulated from international scrutiny and accountability for the nature of their relationships with Indigenous peoples.

Still, the sometimes problematic recognition of Indigenous peoples and rights was done without Indigenous participation, first in the 1957 International Labour Organization's Convention 107, modified substantially by Convention 169 in 1989 (Teeple 2004: 92–93). Thus, the development of the UNDRIP through a process which included Indigenous representation was unique and arguably confers a unique legitimacy on the result (Sambo Dorough 2001). Over forty years in the making, UNDRIP is the result of an innovative and unique process that began in the 1970s and is the first human rights instrument to include the participation of those affected — Indigenous non-governmental organizations representing Indigenous peoples from around the world (Willemsen-Diaz 2009; Eide 2009; Daes 2009; Henriksen 2009; Deer 2010; Joffe 2010). The Declaration is the first iteration of Indigenous peoples' human rights that emanates from Indigenous peoples acting in the international arena, under the aegis of the United Nations, adopted by the international community and having standing within the framework of international human rights law.

The Declaration was presented in draft form to the United Nations by the Working Group on Indigenous Peoples in 1993, the International Year of Indigenous Peoples. However, not until 2007 was there sufficient consensus among states to ensure passage of the UNDRIP by a vote of 143 in favour, 4 against (Canada, Australia, New Zealand and the U.S.) and 11 abstaining (Willemsen-Diaz 2009: 29). The UNDRIP was ratified by the U.N. General Assembly on September 13, 2007. It constitutes "the minimum standards for the survival, dignity and well-being" of Indigenous peoples (Article 43), and its provisions are to be "interpreted in accordance with the principles of justice, democracy, respect for human rights, equality, non-discrimination, good governance and good faith" (Article 46(3)).

The Declaration emerged as a response to profound state violation of inherent human rights of Indigenous peoples (Fontaine 2010: 8–11; Hartley, Joffe and Preston 2010: 12) and the rights guaranteed in it are a species of human rights (Anaya 2004; Green 2005: 230–31; Joffe 2010: 71). The Declaration is the gold standard in international and domestic law for state protection of Indigenous human rights and constitutes international human rights law (Charters and Stavenhagen 2009: 10). Its objectives represent "a standard of achievement to be pursued in a spirit of partnership and mutual respect" (John 2010: 51).

Human rights are abstract until they are abrogated and are "relative to present and past historical conditions" (Teeple 2004: 71). This contextual framework for human rights implies that rights are not always identical, nor are identical rights identical in their specific implementations because "human rights are not … homogeneous" (Teeple 2004: 71). For Indigenous peoples, colonialism frames the conditions under which rights are now claimed against settler states. Colonialism, a violent and coercive process inextricably linked to racism and dispossession, is the condition in which Indigenous human rights are claimed and in which they are to be implemented. The specific nature of rights implementation will depend on particular peoples' historical, cultural, gender and other contexts.

Canada and the Declaration

Canada's contemporary political record with respect to Indigenous rights is abysmal, and its non-compliance with the United Nations *Declaration on the Rights of Indigenous Peoples* impairs Canada's constitutional integrity regarding respect for the rule of law, for respect of human rights and for its relationship with the Indigenous peoples of Canada. The disparities between Indigenous people and other Canadians have resulted in criticism from the United Nations (CTV News 2014). Yet the Canadian government seems unwilling to hear such criticisms domestically or internationally, and shows no inclination to change its policy paths.

The Harper Government resisted adopting the Declaration and refused to take the advice of its own expert bureaucrats to do so. Indeed, Canada lobbied other states to reject the UNDRIP (Deer 2010: 25) and fomented dissention in the international community with regard to the United Nations adoption of the Declaration, voting against the resolution, for the first time opposing an international human rights instrument (Cosentino 2010; Deer 2010; Joffe 2010). At least some public commentators expressed consternation at the Canadian government's position. Salil Shetty, Director General of Amnesty International, rebuked Canada for its stand and expressed concern at the deteriorating climate for human rights and democratic expression in Canada (Sterling 2010). Amnesty's Canadian Secretary-General, Alex Neve, castigated the decision and warned that it "badly tarnishes" Canada's human rights reputation (Neve 2008; Neve and Benjamin 2011). Domestically, Indigenous organizations challenged the government's position. For example, on September 17, 2010, the Union of British Columbia Indian Chiefs (UBCIC) adopted Resolution 2010–33, "United Nations *Declaration on the Rights of Indigenous Peoples* and Canada's Intention to Endorse," and on October 20, 2010, the UBCIC wrote to the prime minister, saying: "On March 2010, your government announced in the Speech from the Throne that it would take immediate steps to endorse the UNDRIP in a manner that is fully consistent with Canada's Constitution and laws.... We strongly urge you to endorse the UNDRIP immediately and without qualification" (UBCIC 2010).

Other voices of concern include the U.N. High Commissioner for Human Rights, Louise Arbour (herself a Canadian and a former Supreme Court of Canada judge) (John 2010: 48); the U.N. Committee on the Elimination of Racial Discrimination; and Indigenous organizations and scholars and human rights advocates in Canada. Paul Joffe has argued that the Harper Government's opposition was based not on substantive legal and constitutional problems but on ideology and partisanship (Joffe 2010: 71). Moreover, in an undemocratic pique, the Harper minority government refused to accept the majority will of Parliament of April 8, 2008, which voted to endorse the UNDRIP and commit Canada to implement it (Joffe 2010: 76).

It was not until November 12, 2010, that Canada finally undertook an equivocal and conditional adoption of the UNDRIP. It was the second to the last state in the world to do so, trailed only by the U.S. (which adopted the UNDRIP in December 2010) (Cosentino 2010).

Contrary to the international consensus and to legal precedent with respect to international law (Charters and Stavenhagen 2009; Anaya 2004), and wrongly, according to Joffe (2010: 86; see also Nakata 2001: 12), the Harper Government claimed that the Declaration was aspirational and was not a legal obligation upon the state: "the Declaration is a non-legally binding document that does not reflect customary international law nor change Canadian laws" (AANDC 2010). This anaemic endorsement was accompanied by claims that the Canadian adoption was limited to the extent of any conflict with the Canadian constitution (a number of legal scholars say there are none) and by claims that the UNDRIP is not "law," which again contradicts most authoritative legal scholarship on the status of declarations (see for example Falk 2000; Anaya 2004; Joffe 2010). On November 16, 2010, twenty-nine Indigenous faith groups and other NGOs[2] issued a public joint statement urging the government to proceed with UNDRIP implementation "in a principled manner that fully respects their spirit and intent."

The Universality of International Law

The principle of international law is that it applies to all states: it cannot be conditional and is not merely aspirational. As Cosentino (2010) observed, "international human rights standards are essential in the promotion and protection of rights that states have failed to uphold. They are meant to assist the reform of laws, policies and guide state behaviour." By definition, then, international human rights law requires change from states rather than their status quo. The Declaration "imposes obligations on states" (Charters and Stavenhagen 2009: 13; Joffe 2010). Moreover, "domestic laws and policies do not prevail over international law" (Joffe 2010: 79; see also Gunn, this volume). The Declaration is part of international law. It may well be upgraded to the status of Convention in international law. The issue now is not whether it is law, but how it will be implemented. Canada has an obligation to revise existing and develop future legislation and policy in light of its obligations under the UNDRIP. Anaya notes the need for states to interpret other legal instruments in light of the provisions of the Declaration. "The Declaration, interpreted in conjunction with other international instruments, provided an authoritative normative framework for the full and effective protection and implementation of the rights of Indigenous peoples" (U.N. 2009).

The UNDRIP is part of the corpus of international law and legal norms that animates the human rights guarantees in the Canadian constitution. The UNDRIP recognizes the deleterious legacy of colonialism and affirms that states should guarantee the human rights and the collective rights of Indigenous peoples. It condemns all doctrines, policies and practices that are racist, false, unlawful, immoral and unjust. It affirms the right at international law of self-determination of all peoples, and the right of internal self-government. In Article 44 it guarantees all rights equally to male and female persons. Sakej Henderson calls the Declaration a "just document" that "expresses minimum standards of human rights" (2008: 75).

Indigenous and treaty rights arise from the historical and contemporary oppression by colonial states, which have usurped Indigenous lands, resources and sovereignty. They are a particular application of the guarantees in the Declaration, which is "comprehensive ... [and] covers the full range of civil, political, economic, social, cultural and environmental rights," recognizing these as inherent rights (Charters and Stavenhagen 2009: 13). Legal scholar James Anaya, now Special Rapporteur to the United Nations on the Rights of Indigenous Peoples, notes that these are not special rights, but a "contextualized elaboration of general human rights principles and rights as they relate to the specific historical, cultural and social circumstances of Indigenous peoples" (U.N. 2009).

The Declaration emerges from the foundation of international human rights law, beginning with the U.N. *Charter* in 1945 and including the U.N.'s *Declaration of Human Rights* (1948), the *Convention on the Prevention and Punishment of the Crime of Genocide* (1948), the *International Convention on the Elimination of All Forms of Racial Discrimination* (1965), the *Covenants on Civil and Political Rights* and *Economic, Social and Cultural Rights* (1966) (Willemsen-Diaz 2009: 17; Joffe 2010). It includes the optional protocol attached to the *Convention on Civil and Political Rights*, which permits individuals to take their states before the U.N. *Human Rights Committee* for alleged violations in the Convention. On this legal and philosophical basis, the international community has built additional rights guarantees relevant to Indigenous peoples, including the 1979 *Convention on the Elimination of All Forms of Discrimination Against Women,* the 1990 *Convention on the Rights of the Child* and, in 2007, the *Declaration on the Rights of Indigenous Peoples.*

In 2008 the United Nations celebrated the anniversary of the UNDRIP, as it has committed to do every August 9th, with U.N. Secretary-General Ban Ki-Moon saying:

> The fundamental motivation was the Assembly's recognition of the need to place the United Nations clearly and strongly behind the promotion and protection of the rights of Indigenous peoples, in order to put an end to their marginalization, their extreme poverty, the expropriation of their traditional lands and the other grave human rights abuses they have faced and continue to encounter. Indeed, the suffering of Indigenous peoples includes some of the darkest episodes in human history. (cited in Jurand 2008)

Equality and Indigenous Rights

Indigenous or Aboriginal rights are a species of human rights. They are vital for the survival of Indigenous peoples *as* Indigenous peoples; they are not assimilationist in their conception or implementation. All human rights are entitlements of Indigenous people. The UNDRIP Article 1 says: "Indigenous peoples have the right to the full enjoyment as a collective or as individuals, of all human rights and fundamental freedoms recognized in the Charter of the United Nations, the *Universal Declaration of Human Rights* and in international human rights law." Additionally, Indigenous peoples are entitled to those rights that guarantee the possibility of existence as Indigenous peoples.

The primary right protected at international human rights law and reiterated in the UNDRIP is the right to exist; it is closely followed (and is inextricable from) the right to self-determination. We exist as individuals. Our familial and social context gives meaning to our individuality. The right to self-determination is a collective one, belonging to "peoples" — culturally coherent, historically durable socio-political aggregates often referred to as "nations." This is a "relative right" that does not permit oppression of others or denial of others' right to self-determination (Sambo Dorough 2001: 118). The right includes land- and culture-based practices and "economic, cultural, spiritual, social and political dimensions" (116). The Declaration acknowledges that a range of international legal instruments provides the foundation for self-determination, and also recognizes the right of self-determination. Article 3 says: "Indigenous peoples have the right to self-determination." Article 8 asserts: "Indigenous peoples and individuals have the right not to be subjected to forced assimilation or destruction of culture."

For Indigenous peoples in Canada, "equality" has been both a stalking horse for assimilation and an unrealized state relative to the measures of quality of life of settler society. The only terms on which the state has offered equality to Indigenous peoples have been the adoption of dominant Canadian values, institutions and practices and the abandonment of Indigenous rights claims against the state. While most Indigenous people would welcome economic, social and political equality, those have been unavailable in the conditions of colonialism in Canada, as evidenced by the measurable disparity between most Aboriginal and non-Aboriginal lives. Essentially, achieving so-called equality has meant not being, in culturally and politically meaningful ways, Indigenous. Thus "equality" is both a normative aspiration and a political liability as offered by the state.

The UNDRIP makes clear the distinction between the objective of equality as inclusion in the social, political and economic order of states, and the objective of self-determination of Indigenous peoples existing in conditions of colonization and political non-dominance, with the loss of their territories and economies. Defining equality as inclusion has long been used to legitimate the colonial predations of settler states and their subsequent objectives of elimination of Indigenous peoples via assimilation. In conditions of colonization, equality is an unlikely benefit, measured against a standard determined by a regime hostile to the nations that were stigmatized, racialized and oppressed. Its assumptions, in particular the racist conception of Indigenous peoples and the glorification of the now dominant settler ones, are disrespectful, taking for granted the superior state of the dominant to that of the oppressed (for example, see Flanagan 2002). The form of equality is not chosen by Indigenous peoples exercising their right to self-determination and is not realized in any calculus by positive outcomes.

Equality, then, is an idealized abstraction always conceived in relation to an uninterrogated standard with which others are to be equal. Settler state assumptions have been that their economic, political and social frameworks contain the conditions to which Indigenous peoples are to be equal. This assumption also contains the *a priori* conclusion that Indigenous legal and philosophical frameworks and objectives are of relatively less value or are otherwise intolerable. A more difficult and nuanced conception of equality requires that the conditions of inequality be taken account of, and that those whose rights are under consideration choose their form. In Canada, equality must be conceptualized in the context of the historical and continuing violence inherent in colonization, and the will of the colonized to determine their contemporary conditions apart from or in resistance to colonial oppression. Thus equality inheres in implementation of self-determining visions, not only in including the colonized in the "one big tent" vision of the elites of the colonial state.

A History of Colonialism

During drafting and negotiations of the UNDRIP, some states were concerned with the use of the term "peoples" in relation to Indigenous nations, preferring the more anaemic term "populations" (Deer 2010). This dispute mirrors the distinction between assimilative equality and self-determination. At international law, "peoples" have a claim to territory, to self-determination and ultimately to sovereignty. As "populations" they can be conceptually and legally subsumed into existing states without regard for historical claims against the state: they become "minorities." At the core of state violation of Indigenous human rights is the continuing dispossession of Indigenous peoples of their land.

Histories of oppression, dispossession and genocide have been inflicted on Indigenous peoples in Canada by the colonial and then the Canadian governments. The legacies persist through intergenerational trauma and people's responses to those conditions (Comack et al. 2013; Irlbacher-Fox 2009). The denial of this reality exists at the highest level of the state and is diffused throughout its cultures via education, media entertainment and government propaganda. Perhaps the most astonishing manifestation of this was Prime Minister Harper's claim on the occasion of the G20 meeting in Pittsburgh, on September 25, 2009: "We are one of the most stable regimes in history ... we also have no history of colonialism" (Ljunggren 2009; see also Comack, this volume). This was met with a rebuttal from the Assembly of First Nations then-National Chief Shawn Atleo (cited in Hui 2009), who said:

> The effects of colonialism remain today. It is the attitude that fueled the residential schools; the colonial *Indian Act* that displaces traditional forms of First Nations governance; the theft of Indian lands and forced relocations of First Nations communities; the criminalization and suppression of First Nations languages and cultural practices; the chronic under-funding of First Nations communities and programs; and the denial of Treaty and Indigenous rights, even though they are recognized in Canada's Constitution.

However, to the dismay of some, there was no reaction from opinion leaders, opposition politicians or intellectuals in Canada about the prime minister's gratuitous misrepresentation of Canadian history, indicating that most Canadians are oblivious to the past and present reality of colonialism, as suggested by an editorial in the *Journal* of Queen's University (*Journal* 2009). Instead, most Canadians seem to cling to what John Ralston Saul (2008: 19) describes as "an imaginary special position inside the mythology of someone else's empire." And Canadian elites are (mis)educated in universities that "are not doing their job" (Saul 2008; see also Kuokkanen 2007; Smith 1999), that ignore the historical and contemporary functioning of colonialism, are blind to Indigenous knowledges and are consequently unable to engage with the reality of Indigenous struggles for measures of justice.

All of this frames the political conditions in which Indigenous peoples struggle against continual state violation of Indigenous human rights.

Self-Determination and Sovereignty

Self-determination is the foundational Indigenous right (Deer 2010: 27). In Canada, despite the protections of international law identifying self-determination's primacy and despite the protection of Indigenous and treaty rights in the Constitution, the dominant political discourse has been stalled in the framework of "self-government," a limited exercise more akin to self-administration of the regulatory and policy framework of the colonial state. The framing of self-government seems designed to avoid discussions of or implementation of self-determination. Moreover, Canada has historically blackmailed Indigenous nations by holding treaty rights, self-government agreements and land claims negotiations hostage to the agreement by the Indigenous participants to extinguish their general rights in return for limited codified rights (Green 1995; John 2010: 48–51). Article 10 of the UNDRIP says that "Indigenous peoples shall not be forcibly removed from their lands or territories." And yet agreeing to limited rights in return for signing away one's rights is effectively a form of removal: consider that recent treaties in British Columbia recognize only 10 percent of the traditional territory of Indigenous treaty signatories.

Despite the change of language in Canadian policy on Indigenous land claims from "extinguishment" to "certainty," the effect continues to be the extinguishment of Indigenous rights (John 2010: 48–51). Yet recognizing rights only so they can be minimized or extinguished is perverse. Moreover, the UNDRIP requires that any impingement on Indigenous territories must be done with "free, prior and informed consent" (see both Benjamin and Joffe, this volume). Further, agreements that impair future generations' rights are problematic. Aboriginal (or Indigenous) rights are both individual and collective, as well as intergenerational: they allow Indigenous cultures and communities to exist in the future in politically and materially viable ways. Efforts by governments to extinguish Indigenous rights effectively deprive future generations of their birthright.

People or Peoples?

During the UNDRIP negotiations between 1993 and 2007, some states were unwilling to account for the consequences of their origins in relation to Indigenous oppression. They feared economic, political and territorial implications, despite the explicit wording in the Declaration that it did not envision secession and the opinions of several noted legal scholars, including the current U.N. Special Rapporteur for Indigenous Peoples, James Anaya, that self-determination was not synonymous with statehood. Thus, recognizing the right to self-determination is not tantamount to secession from a state.

Indigenous peoples did and do not accept that they are minorities, insisting rather on the more muscular definition as "peoples." In the drafting of the Declaration, the focus of states' representatives was on Indigenous minorities while the focus of Indigenous peoples' representatives was on self-determination. The latter, according to Eide, shifted the focus onto "who should govern whom, and who should exercise authority and control over territory and natural resources" (Eide 2009: 36–37). Henderson (2008: 75) writes that the Declaration "clearly affirms that Indigenous peoples are peoples whom nation-states cannot arbitrarily deny the right of self-determination."

It was not until the adoption and normalization of the 1945 *U.N. Charter* that human rights became a subject of international concern. Notably, Article 27 of the *International Covenant on Civil and Political Rights* (ICCPR) guaranteed to "minorities" the right to culture, religion and language in community (Eide 2009: 33–35). "Minorities" are not viewed as "peoples" with the concomitant entitlements to self-determination and to recognition in international tribunals. Indigenous peoples, whose claims were primarily against states occupying their territories, stealing their resources and subjecting them to state sovereignty and genocidal practices, had few allies in the states represented at the United Nations, some of which did not even recognize Indigenous existence. While human rights were guaranteed equally to all human beings, states were charged with ensuring their realization. Thus, when the state was the violator of human rights, victims were at a disadvantage unless the international community was willing to raise concerns in an authoritative way; and for the most part, individual persons had no standing to raise issues in United Nations forums. The Optional Protocol attached to the ICCPR permits nationals to bring their states before the United Nations Human Rights Committee (UNHRC). Canada is signatory to the Optional Protocol, has been taken before the UNHRC successfully previously by Indigenous citizens and will likely be taken there in the near future by Sharon McIvor (see Brodsky, this volume, for a detailed discussion of the McIvor case). Are Indigenous peoples a challenge to the economic, social and political relationships within settler states? Almost certainly recognition as peoples infers countervailing claims to land, resources, political capacity and sovereignty — self-determination, as Henderson (2008) put it — and that has been the position of Indigenous nations since the moments of first colonial contact. In Canada, those countervailing claims were manifest in negotiated relationships and agreements such as treaties with Indigenous nations and political commitments to the Métis, honoured more in the breech by both the nascent and contemporary settler state. The Preamble to the UNDRIP states that treaties are both a means of improving state-Indigenous relationships, and can be matters of international concern (2007). Surely this must refer to good faith, good will and implementation by states party to Indigenous-state treaties.

Here, I turn to some specific rights and abrogations of rights to demonstrate the gap between situations Indigenous people in Canada experience relative to what human rights guarantees and the UNDRIP set as the rights minimums.

Education as Genocide; Education as Indigenous Right

In different ways, at different times and with some regional variation, the Canadian state has practised genocidal policies towards Indigenous peoples whose territory the state appropriated. These practices were framed by the goal of assimilation, which assumes cultural annihilation, and prosecuted with military, police and bureaucratic force and through education. Education, a superficially liberatory exercise, was implemented through the residential and day schools, sub-contracted to various Christian churches, which pursued assimilation, civilization, Christianization and education objectives in ways so violent that the Canadian state, through then-Prime Minister Harper, apologized for them on June 11, 2008, saying "this policy of assimilation was wrong, has caused great harm, and has no place in our country" (cited in John 2010: 53, CBC News 2014 for full text of the apology).

This grotesque historical approach to "education" deprived generations of Indigenous peoples of education and inflicted intergenerational suffering as a result of the social and psychological destruction consequent to the education policies. The Truth and Reconciliation Commission (TRC) was created out of the apology to attempt to both publicize the atrocity of the schools' practices and bring Canadian settler and Indigenous peoples into a reconciled relationship, according to its mandate (TRC n.d.). At the time of publication in 2014 the TRC is still holding hearings and commemorative events across Canada.

Despite this history, Indigenous peoples continue to insist on a right to education. That human right is first named in the *Universal Declaration of Human Rights*, in the *International Conventions on Civil and Political Rights* and *Economic, Social and Cultural Rights*, in the *Convention on the Rights of the Child* and enunciated specifically in relation to Indigenous peoples in the UNDRIP. Further support for Indigenous education in international law is found in the International Labour Organization (ILO) Convention 169, which requires Indigenous involvement and participation in education, including in its formulation and pedagogical methods (Graham 2010). Yet, federal policy and funding provides only modest support for some status Indian students — a fraction of the Indigenous student constituency — and does so not as an implementation of a right, but as a limited program. Additionally, the federal government generally spends less per student on on-reserve K–12 education, for which it recognizes a constitutional obligation, than provincial governments spend per student in provincial schools. For example, in 2012 in Saskatchewan, Education Minister Russ Marchuk estimates the funding gap there remained as high as 40 percent per student (*Maclean's* 2012). The UNDRIP addresses Indigenous control of and access to education:

> Article 14(1): Indigenous peoples have the right to establish and control their educational systems and institutions providing education in their own languages, in a manner appropriate to their cultural methods of teaching and learning.

Article 14(2): Indigenous individuals, particularly children, have the right to all levels and forms of education of the State without discrimination.

Article 14(3): States shall, in conjunction with Indigenous peoples, take effective measures, in order for Indigenous individuals, particularly children, including those living outside their communities, to have access, when possible, to an education in their own culture and provided in their own language.

The "Duty to Consult" and FPIC

Canadian judicial decisions, notably the Supreme Court of Canada in its decisions in the Haida, Taku and Mikisew Cree cases,[3] have held that the state has a "duty to consult" Indigenous peoples on matters affecting their lands, livelihoods and rights. The duty to consult has been restrictively interpreted by governments and industries, reframed as not much more than town hall meetings, with no consequent obligations on the consulters. This reality frames the power relations, the context in which Indigenous peoples in Canada must consult. Mary Eberts notes that the duty to consult does not go so far as recognizing a right of free prior and informed consent (FPIC), the right to say no to state action: "Supreme Court of Canada jurisprudence specifically says the government action required by the duty to consult varies with the circumstances, but in no case will it involve giving Indigenous peoples a veto over proposed action" (2014; see also Benjamin; Joffe; Gunn, this volume). The duty to consult is related to, though less robust than, the Declaration's protection of the right to FPIC on state and corporate developments affecting Indigenous lands. Article 19 reads: "States shall consult and cooperate in good faith with the Indigenous peoples concerned through their own representative institutions in order to obtain their free, prior and informed consent before adopting and implementing legislative or administrative measures that may affect them."

Sex Discrimination and Indigenous Women's Rights

The vexed matter of Indian status under the *Indian Act* provides a good example of how the UNDRIP should shape Canada's legislative approach. The status issue has been contested by Indigenous women especially since at least 1868. After 1982, the *Canadian Charter of Rights and Freedoms* was to eliminate legislative sex discrimination. However, the federal government's ham-handed amendments of the *Indian Act*, C-31 and then C-3 actually continued sex discrimination (see Brodsky and Eberts, this volume). The failure of Canada's political and legal processes to eliminate this discrimination is now about to land Canada before the U.N. Human Rights Committee, charged with persistent legislative violations of protected human rights of Indigenous peoples, however not for the first time. Sandra Lovelace, a Maliseet Indian exiled by the membership s. 12(1)(b), won a ruling by the UNHRC in 1977 that Canada was in violation of s. 27 of the *Convention on Civil and Political*

Rights, as the *Indian Act* deprived her and similarly situated persons of the right to reside and participate in her community and culture.

The UNDRIP addresses these matters especially in both Article 9: "Indigenous peoples and individuals have the right to belong to an Indigenous community or nation, in accordance with the traditions and customs of the community or nation concerned. No discrimination of any kind may arise from the exercise of such a right," and in Article 33: "1. Indigenous peoples have the right to determine their own identity or membership in accordance with their customs and traditions. This does not impair the right of Indigenous individuals to obtain citizenship of the States in which they live. 2. Indigenous peoples have their right to determine the structure and to select the membership of their institutions in accordance with their own procedures." The UNDRIP also prohibits sex discrimination in Article 44: "All the rights and freedoms recognized herein are equally guaranteed to male and female Indigenous individuals."

Métis Identity and Rights

Having made a multi-century mess with status Indian membership, in 2011 the federal government turned its sights to the Métis, floating suggestions through the civil service that it would assist with standardization of Métis membership (Green 2011). Currently, Métis identity is variously defined by several Métis organizations, by some communities and by individuals who self-identify. Formulae applied by various Métis organizations require "proofs," including multi-generational evidence of Métis ancestry, before they will issue "cards" to those who satisfy their criteria. Métis scholar Emma LaRocque carries no card, speaks Cree and English, and makes "a distinction between metis (or halfbreed) and Métis Nation peoples, the former meaning those individuals who are first-generation part Indian and part white; the latter referring to those peoples whose ancestors were originally white and Indian but who went on to develop as distinct peoples ... becoming a new race or ethnicity" (2010: 7) characterized by the experience of dispossession, colonization and racism (2010: 81, 100–104). Many Métis have not felt the need to obtain verification of their status, and identify without having the card in their pockets (or without participating in the political life of the organizations). Federal regulation of this diverse Métis diaspora would erase many, valorize some and complicate identities, families and politics as thoroughly as it has done for the status Indian constituency.

Reserve Lands and Treaty Rights

Other legislative initiatives that should have been framed with regard to the UNDRIP include the *Safe Drinking Water for First Nations Act* and *First Nations Accountability Act*, both of which suffered from a lack of consultation with Indigenous constituencies. Gina Cosentino (2010) argues that the *Accountability Act* "fails to meet even the most rudimentary tests of both international and domestic standards related to consultation and participation in decision-making," and certainly fails to meet the standards of FPIC. Both bills died when the 2011 federal election was called, but were re-introduced following the Conservative majority win in May 2012 and were passed in 2013 (AADNC 2012a, AADNC 2012b). More recently in 2013, the *Family Homes on Reserves and Matrimonial Interests or Rights Act* (SC 2013, c. 20) was passed. It implicitly denies that Indian governments in the form of band councils have the capacity to pass laws regarding matrimonial property on reserves (Eberts 2014). Eberts (2014) notes that the legislation "also gives non-Band members and non-status Indians prolonged rights of occupation on Band land."

The protection of the last remnants of Indigenous collective lands recognized by the state — Indian reserves — is under attack by those who argue it should be privately held and mortgageable, and thus could be sold by individuals in the private real estate market (see Flanagan et al. 2010). The federal Department of Indian Affairs is alleged by some researchers to be advocating "private ownership of reserve lands as the solution to First Nations economic and social development" in the form of the proposed *First Nations Property Ownership Act*, and is supported in this "by the First Nations Tax Commission, a federal agency whose chair and members are appointed by the Minister of Indian Affairs" (Four Arrows 2010). The Assembly of First Nations and many regional Indigenous organizations oppose any effort to transform the property regime on reserves. Arguing against the proposal to privatize reserve lands, Secwepemc leader Arthur Manuel notes: "Transforming Indian Reserve lands to Fee Simple would break up the Indian Reserve land base and take away the protection that the collective ownership of Indian Reserves by Indian Bands provides, making them inalienable and not subject to expropriation" (*First Nations Strategic Bulletin* 2010).

Manuel is not alone in his analysis. He notes that an overwhelming majority of chiefs, members of the Assembly of First Nations, which is Canada's national status Indian organization, passed a resolution rejecting the fee simple proposal, with only three opposing votes (Manuel 2010). It would seem, then, that state respect for, at minimum, Indian consensus, and perhaps for an expression of self-determination, requires deference to this rejection of the fee simple proposal.

Confronting Colonialism and Choosing Decolonization

The Canadian state is squatted on Indigenous lands and enjoys enviable first-world status from its resources. Most Indigenous peoples do not significantly share in this bounty. Manuel notes, "The big question facing us today is not how can we fit into the mainstream economy, but how the mainstream economy can fairly, honestly and justly manage the fundamental change that recognition of Indigenous Rights creates" (First Nations Strategic Bulletin 2010). He writes elsewhere:

> We are poor because we are systemically made poor because we are dispossessed of our land by federal and provincial laws that do not

recognize our Indigenous and Treaty Rights. Federal and provincial law irresponsibly ignores our Indigenous and Treaty Rights despite the fact they have been recognized by the Supreme Court of Canada (SCC) and protected by the Canada Constitution 1982.

And, the UNDRIP protects Indigenous territories and Indigenous development choices:

> Article 26 (1): Indigenous peoples have the right to the lands, territories and resources which they have traditionally owned, occupied or otherwise used or acquired.
> Article 26(2): Indigenous peoples have the right to own, use, develop and control the lands, territories and resources that they possess by reason of traditional ownership or other traditional occupation or use, as well as those which they have otherwise acquired.

The United Nations General Assembly's 2007 adoption of the *Declaration on the Rights of Indigenous Peoples* demonstrated at least two important facts. First, Indigenous peoples' rights are a concern of international law and attention for the entire international state community. Second, and despite the distinction between declaratory and covenant status, the UNDRIP assumes primacy at international law for protecting the fundamental human rights of Indigenous peoples: in effect, it becomes the norm for state practice. The passage of the Declaration is a "tipping point in international law and history" (Henderson 2008: 80) as it renders Indigenous peoples visible, self-determining and entitled to individual and collective human rights to be guaranteed by the very states that have subsumed Indigenous peoples.

The UNDRIP is now the international gold standard for state-Indigenous relations and for Indigenous human rights. Implementation of the Declaration would shift the colonial relationship towards a more mutually beneficial and potentially post-colonial one. Moreover, Canada's unwillingness to implement international human rights guarantees has negative implications for the state's respect for the human rights of all Canadians.

Canada has obligations at international and constitutional law requiring the state to guarantee the human and Indigenous rights of the Indigenous peoples now encapsulated in the Canadian state. Canada has been recalcitrant in acceding to international law on this point and has made haphazard, half-hearted and sometimes no efforts to bring its own practices, including its legislation, in line with international law. Yet Canada is regularly criticized in the international arena for the shocking disparity of quality-of-life indicators (see, for example, Statistics Canada 2006) for Indigenous and settler Canadians. In May 2013 Canada was criticized by Olivier de Schutter, the U.N. right-to-food envoy, for the inadequate food situation in many Indigenous communities, as well as for other poor Canadians (cited in Whittington 2012). In November 2013 Canada was criticized by one of

Canada's foremost constitutional scholars, Peter Russell (2013), for its failure to grant a visa to U.N. Special Rapporteur on Indigenous Peoples Dr. James Anaya, permitting him to visit Canada. The current federal government has an unfortunate and undemocratic pattern of dismissing critique of its practices and denying Canada's active politicking to frustrate Indigenous rights. Canada has been and will again be censured by the U.N. Human Rights Commission for egregious violation of Indigenous human rights. In May 2014 Anaya expressed "deep concern" with Canada's failure to improve Indigenous quality of life (CTV 2014).

Canada's constitutional law, too, has pointed the state in the direction of more consensual and beneficial relationships with Indigenous peoples. Foundationally, the obligation of the state, despite being squatted on Indigenous territories and claiming the entire portion of sovereignty, remains in the form of the duty to consult and the duty to respect and animate domestic and international human rights law.

Despite the reservations posed by the Harper Government, the obligations in the Declaration are neither optional nor detrimental to the body politic. Indeed, there are many positive implications for the settler state and for Indigenous nations, including the potential for the reconciliation of settler and Indigenous peoples in a common, mutually beneficial and mutually determined post-colonial future. Eberts argues that a commitment to reconciliation is inherent in the apology made by Prime Minister Harper on Canada's residential school policy. Chief Justice Murray Sinclair, Chair of the Truth and Reconciliation Commission, asserts that "Reconciliation is about forging and maintaining respectful relationships. There are no shortcuts" (TRC n.d.).

Despite the language of inclusion and the liberal assumptions of Canada's political culture, for many Indigenous peoples the state remains oppressive, both in its institutions and in the political culture that informs discussions about Indigenous peoples and their rights. Yet, the Declaration's Article 9 guarantees the right to belong to an Indigenous community or nation. Article 33(1) says that this does not preclude Indigenous citizenship in the state. Moreover, Article 15(2) requires states to take measures to "combat prejudice and eliminate discrimination." Article 34 guarantees the right to Indigenous structures, customs, traditions and juridical systems, in accordance with international human rights standards.

The history of Canadian citizenship demonstrates the evolution of an exclusive and exclusionary franchise to the present more inclusive formula. However, the politico-economic and legislative history of the Canadian state indicates that Indigenous people are welcome only when they effectively assimilate — when they adopt the assumptions and practices of the state and turn away from any criticism of the state's legitimacy. Yet the core of Indigenous rights is located in the historical realities of colonialism. This is the truth on which the Declaration is based. But for that, there would be no need to separately conceptualize Indigenous human rights. As declared in Article 46(2):

In the exercise of the rights enunciated in the present Declaration, human rights and fundamental freedoms of all shall be respected. The exercise of the rights set forth in this declaration shall be subject only to such limitations as are determined by law, in accordance with international human rights obligations. Any such limitations shall be nondiscriminatory and strictly necessary solely for the purpose of securing due recognition and respect for the rights and freedom of others and for meeting the just and most compelling requirements of a democratic society.

The occupation of Indigenous territories and peoples is sanitized by states through law, apologist scholarship and political culture of the dominant society, and Indigenous peoples are then invited to participate in the putatively egalitarian processes of the democratic settler state. Democratic settler states rely on profoundly contradictory assumptions: on the proposition that state sovereignty is unimpeachable, and on the proposition that all citizens, despite the colonial history and contemporary reality, are equal and equally empowered. Without a process for confronting the legacy of colonialism, settler states will never be able to offer meaningful citizenship or human rights protection to those whose ancestral communities and nations were subordinated by these same states. That process begins by acts of recognition of our relational past and of the human rights of Indigenous peoples. It begins with state recognition and animation of the guarantees of the UNDRIP. It continues with state deference to Indigenous rights, including in its own legislative and policy agenda. Without concrete implementation by the state it can be assumed that Canada continues to pay lip service to the notion of Indigenous peoples' human rights when it must and to use its judicial, political and economic power to continue the colonial practices of dispossession and domination when it can. When Canada is prepared to move from denial and repression to implementation of Indigenous human rights, it will also move into a new era of decolonization and justice, with state protection of the human rights of all.

Anaya writes in his 2014 Report on the Situation of Indigenous peoples in Canada that "it is necessary for Canada to arrive at a common understanding with indigenous peoples of objectives and goals that are based on full respect for their constitutional, treaty, and internationally-recognized rights" (U.N. 2014: 2). Canadians can and should insist that the state live up to domestic constitutional and international human rights guarantees of Indigenous peoples and animate these rights in public policy. Doing so is a necessary first step in a process that may yet permit reconciliation with the past and commitment to a shared future, thus shifting the historic relationship between Indigenous and settler peoples framed by racism and colonialism. And the benefits of recognition and implementation of Indigenous peoples' human rights is a benefit to all Canadians, as they are tied to and strengthen the fundamental principles of Canadian political culture and constitutional law: democracy, the rule of law and human rights.

Notes

This chapter is based on my 2011 article in *Prairie Forum*, "Canada the Bully: Aboriginal Human Rights" (Green 2011).

1. See, for example, Mikaere's (2001: 131–51) analysis of Pakeha racism and amnesia in Aotearoa/New Zealand.

2. The statement was signed by Amnesty International Canada, Amnistie internationale Canada francophone, Atlantic Policy Congress of First Nations Chiefs Secretariat, Canadian Arab Federation, Canadian Council on Social Development, Canadian Friends Service Committee (Quakers), Chiefs of Ontario, First Nations Child and Family Caring Society of Canada, First Nations Confederacy of Cultural Education Centers, First Nations Summit, First Peoples Human Rights Coalition, Front d'action populaire en réaménagement urbain (FRAPRU), Québec Grand Council of the Crees (Eeyou Istchee), Indigenous World Association, Innu Council of Nitassinan, Innu Takuaikan Uashat Mak Mani-Utenam, Institut Culturel Tshakapesh, International Organization of Indigenous Resource Development (IOIRD), Kanien'kehá:ka Onkwawén:na Raotitióhkwa Language and Cultural Center, KAIROS: Canadian Ecumenical Justice Initiatives, Louis Bull Cree Nation, National Association of Friendship Centres, Public Service Alliance of Canada, Quebec Native Women/ Femmes autochtones du Québec, RightOnCanada.ca, Samson Cree Nation, Treaty 4 Chiefs, Treaty 6 Medicine Chest Task Force and the Union of British Columbia Indian Chiefs.

3. *Haida Nation v. British Columbia* (Minister of Forests), 2004 SCC 73; *Taku River Tlingit First Nation v. British Columbia* (Project Assessment Director), 2004 SCC 74; *Mikisew Cree First Nation v. Canada* (Minister of Canadian Heritage), [2005] 3 S.C.R. 388, 2005 SCC 69.

References

AADNC (Aboriginal Affairs and Northern Development Canada). 2010. "Canada's Statement of Support on the United Nations *Declaration on the Rights of Indigenous Peoples.*" <http://www.aadnc-aandc.gc.ca/eng/1309374239861/1309374546142>.

____ . 2012a. "First Nations Financial Transparency Act." <aadnc-aandc.gc.ca/eng/13220 56355024/1322060287419>.

____ . 2012b. "Safe Drinking Water for First Nations Act." <aadnc-aandc.gc.ca/eng/1330 528512623/1330528554327>.

Altamirano-Jiménez, Isabel. 2011. "Settler Colonialism, Human Rights and Indigenous Women." *Prairie Forum* 36 (Joyce Green, ed.). Canadian Plains Research Centre, University of Regina.

Anaya, S. James. 2004. *Indigenous Peoples and International Law (2nd)*. New York: Oxford University Press.

Anderson, A. Brenda, Wendee Kubik and Mary Rucklos Hampton (eds.). 2010. *Torn from Our Midst: Voices of Grief, Healing and Action from the Missing Indigenous Women Conference, 2008*. Regina: Canadian Plains Research Centre Press.

Backhouse, Constance. 1999. *Colour-Coded: A Legal History of Racism in Canada 1900–1950*. Toronto: University of Toronto Press.

Canadian Broadcasting Corporation. 2014. "A long-awaited apology for residential schools." <http://www.cbc.ca/archives/categories/society/education/a-lost-heritage-canadas-

residential-schools/a-long-awaited-apology.html>.

Charters, Claire, and Rodolfo Stavenhagen (eds.). 2009. *Making the Declaration Work: The United Nations Declaration on the Rights of Indigenous Peoples.* Document No. 127. Copenhagen: International Working Group for Indigenous Affairs.

CHRC (Canadian Human Rights Commission). 2013. "CHRC Statement on Missing Indigenous Women." February 27. <www.chrc-ccdp.ca/eng/content/chrc-statement-missing-aboriginal-women>.

Comack, Elizabeth, Lawrence Deane, Larry Morrissette and Jim Silver. 2013. *"Indians Wear Red": Colonialism, Resistance and Aboriginal Street Gangs.* Winnipeg and Black Point: Fernwood Publishing.

Cosentino, Gina. 2010. "It's time to reconcile Indigenous rights and democracy in Canada." *Hill Times* December 6. <thehilltimes.ca/page/view/cosentino-12-6-2010>.

Coulthard, Glen. 2007. "Subjects of Empire: Indigenous Peoples and the 'Politics of Recognition' in Canada." *Contemporary Political Theory* 6.

CTV News. 2008. "Text of Stephen Harper's residential schools apology." <ctvnews.ca/text-of-stephen-harper-s-residential-schools-apology-1.301820>.

____. 2014. "UN Report on aboriginals warns of crisis in Canada." <http://www.ctvnews.ca/canada/un-report-on-aboriginals-warns-of-crisis-in-canada-1.1817505>.

Daes, Erica-Irene. 2009. "The Contribution of the Working Group on Indigenous Populations to the Genesis and Evolution of the UN *Declaration on the Rights of Indigenous Peoples." Making the Declaration Work: The United Nations Declaration on the Rights of Indigenous Peoples.* Document No. 127. Copenhagen: International Working Group for Indigenous Affairs.

Day, Shelagh, and Joyce Green. 2010. "Sharon McIvor's Fight for Equality." *Herizons* Summer.

Deer, Kenneth. 2010. "Reflections on the Development, Adoption, and Implementation of the UN *Declaration on the Rights of Indigenous Peoples."* In Jackie Hartley, Paul Joffe and Jennifer Preston (eds.), *Realizing the UN Declaration on the Rights of Indigenous Peoples: Triumph, Hope, and Action.* Saskatoon: Purich Publishing Ltd.

Dyck, Rand. 2004. *Canadian Politics: Critical Approaches (4th).* Scarborough: Thomson Nelson.

Eberts, Mary. 2010. "McIvor: Justice Delayed — Again." *Indigenous Law Journal* 9, 1.

____. 2014. Personal conversation with the author, May 15.

Eide, Asbjorn. 2009. "The Indigenous Peoples, the Working Group on Indigenous Populations and the Adoption of the UN *Declaration on the Rights of Indigenous Peoples." Making the Declaration Work: The United Nations Declaration on the Rights of Indigenous Peoples.* Document No. 127. Copenhagen: International Working Group for Indigenous Affairs. Pp. 32–47.

Falk, Richard. 2000. *Human Rights Horizons: The Pursuit of Justice in a Globalizing World.* New York: Routledge.

Fanon, Frantz. 1961 *The Wretched of the Earth* (1963 translation by Constance Farrington). New York: Grove Press).

____. 1952. *Black Skins, White Masks* (1967 translation by Charles Lam Markmann). New York: Grove Press.

First Nations Strategic Bulletin. 2010. Volume 8, Issues 4–8. <http://intercontinentalcry.org/wp-content/uploads/FNSB-Apr-Aug-10.pdf>.

Flanagan, Tom. 2002. *First Nations? Second Thoughts.* Montreal: McGill-Queen's University Press.

Flanagan, Tom, Christopher Alcantara and André Le Dressay. 2010. *Beyond the Indian Act: Restoring Indigenous Property Rights*. Montreal/Kingston: McGill-Queen's University Press.

Fontaine, Phil. 2010. "A Living Instrument." In Jackie Hartley, Paul Joffe and Jennifer Preston (eds.), *Realizing the UN Declaration on the Rights of Indigenous Peoples: Triumph, Hope, and Action*. Saskatoon: Purich Publishing.

Four Arrows. 2010. "The Government's Drive to Convert Reserves to Private Property: An Old Battle Cry Revived." November 9. <http://media.knet.ca/files/4-Arrows-Transfer-of-lands-on-reserve-Nov2010.pdf>.

Graham, Lorie M. 2010. "The Right to Education and the UN *Declaration on the Rights of Indigenous Peoples*." *Legal Studies Research Paper Series*, Research Paper 10–61, November 2. University of Suffolk Law School. Boston, MA.

Green, Joyce. 2011. "Don't Tell Us Who We Are (Not): Reflections on Métis identity."

____. 2011. University of Regina, Guest Contributor, Fedcan Blog-Equity Matters, Tuesday (15 March). At <blog.fedcan.ca/2011/03/15/don%e2%80%99t-tell-us-who-we-are-not-reflections-on-metis-identity/>; and on file with the author.

____. 2011. "Canada the Bully: Aboriginal Human Rights." *Prairie Forum* 36 (Joyce Green, editor). Canadian Plains Research Centre, University of Regina.

____. 2007. "Taking Account of Indigenous Feminism." In Joyce Green (ed.), *Making Space for Indigenous Feminism*. Halifax: Fernwood Publishing. Pp. 20–32.

____. 2005. "Toward Conceptual Precision: Citizenship and Rights Talk for Indigenous Canadians." *Insiders and Outsiders: Alan Cairns and the Reshaping of Canadian Citizenship*. Vancouver: UBC Press. Pp. 227–41.

____. 1995. "Towards a Detente With History: Confronting Canada's Colonial Legacy." *International Journal of Canadian Studies* 12 (Fall). Pp. 85–105.

Hartley, Jackie, Paul Joffe and Jennifer Preston (eds.). 2010. "Introduction." *Realizing the UN Declaration on the Rights of Indigenous Peoples: Triumph, Hope, and Action*. Saskatoon: Purich Publishing Ltd.

Henderson, James (Sa'ke'j) Youngblood. 2008. *Indigenous Diplomacy and the Rights of Peoples: Achieving UN Recognition*. Saskatoon: Purich Publishing Limited.

Henriksen, John B. 2009. "The UN *Declaration on the Rights of Indigenous Peoples*: Some Key Issues and Events in the Process." *Making the Declaration Work: The United Nations Declaration on the Rights of Indigenous Peoples*. Document No. 127. Copenhagen: International Working Group for Indigenous Affairs. Pp. 78–87.

Hui, Stephen. 2009. "Shawn Atleo criticizes Stephen Harper over 'no history of colonialism' remark." <queensjournal.ca/story/2009-09-29/opinions/where-was-outcry/>.

Irlbacher-Fox, Stephanie. 2009. *Finding Dahshaa: Self-Government, Social Suffering, and Indigenous Policy in Canada*. Vancouver: UBC Press.

Joffe, Paul. 2010. "Canada's Opposition to the UN Declaration: Legitimate Concern or Ideological Bias?" *Realizing the UN Declaration on the Rights of Indigenous Peoples: Triumph, Hope, and Action*. Saskatoon: Purich Publishing Ltd. Pp.70–94.

____. "UN *Declaration on the Rights of Indigenous Peoples*: Canadian Government Positions Incompatible with Genuine Reconciliation." *National Journal of Constitutional Law* 26, 10.

____. 2008. "UN Declaration: Achieving Reconciliation and Effective Application in the Context." Presentation to the Indigenous Law Conference, B.C. June.

John, Edward. 2010. "Survival, Dignity, and Well-Being: Implementing the Declaration in

British Columbia." In Jackie Hartley, Paul Joffe and Jennifer Preston (eds.), *Realizing the UN Declaration on the Rights of Indigenous Peoples: Triumph, Hope, and Action*. Saskatoon: Purich Publishing Ltd. Pp. 47–59.

Journal. 2009. "Where was the Outcry?" September 29. <queensjournal.ca/story/2009-09-29/opinions/where-was-outcry>.

Jurand, Deirdre. 2008. "UN celebrates adopting *Declaration on the Rights of Indigenous Peoples*." *The Jurist: Legal News and Research*, Saturday, August 09. <http://jurist.law.pitt.edu/paperchase/2008/08/un-celebrates-adopting-declaration-on.php>.

Kulchyski, Peter. 2013. *Aboriginal Rights Are Not Human Rights: In Defence of Indigenous Struggles*. Winnipeg: ARP Books.

Kuokkanen, Rauna. 2007. *Reshaping the University: Responsibility, Indigenous Epistemes, and the Logic of the Gift*. Vancouver: UBC Press.

LaRocque, Emma. 2010. *When the Other Is Me: Native Resistance Discourse 1850–1990*. Winnipeg: University of Manitoba Press.

Ljunggren, David. 2009. "Every G20 nation wants to be Canada, insists PM." <reuters.com/article/2009/09/26/columns-us-g20-canada-advantages-idUSTRE58P05Z20090926>.

Maclean's. 2012. <http://www.macleans.ca/news/canada/an-education-underclass/>.

Manuel, Arthur. 2010. Letter August 23, from Arthur Manuel, Indigenous Network on Economies and Trade. 11608 Palfrey Drive West, Coldstream, British Columbia, V1B 1A8, Canada.

McKay, Celeste M., and Craig Benjamin. 2010. "A Vision for Fulfilling the Indivisible Rights of Indigenous Women." In Jackie Hartley, Paul Joffe and Jennifer Preston (eds.), *Realizing the UN Declaration on the Rights of Indigenous Peoples: Triumph, Hope, and Action*. Saskatoon: Purich Publishing Ltd. Pp. 156–68.

Mikaere, Ani. 2001. "Racism in Contemporary Aotearoa: A Pakeha Problem." In Martin Nakata (ed.), *Indigenous Peoples, Racism and the United Nations*. Common Ground Publishing: Australia.

Moore, Margaret. 2010. "Indigenous Peoples and Political Legitimacy." In Jeremy Webber and Colin M. Macleod (eds.), *Between Consenting Peoples: Political Community and the Meaning of Consent*. Vancouver: UBC Press.

Nakata, Martin (ed.). 2001. *Indigenous Peoples, Racism and the United Nations*. Common Ground Publishing: Australia.

Neve, Alex. 2008. Presentation to the University of Regina. Unpublished paper on file with the author.

Pilon, Dennis. 2007. *The Politics of Voting*. Emond Montgomery Publications

Russell, Peter. 2013. "Canada Shamefully Shuns The UN's Scrutiny." <http://ontarionewswatch.com/onw-news.html?id=560>.

Thobani, Sunera. 2007. *Exalted Subjects: Studies in the Making of Race and Nation in Canada*. Toronto: University of Toronto Press.

Thompson, Debra. 2008. "Is Race Political?" *Canadian Journal of Political Science* 41, 3.

Said, Edward. 1979. *Orientalism*. New York: Vintage Books.

____. 1994. *Culture and Imperialism*. New York: Vintage Books.

Sambo Dorough, Dalee. 2001. "International Law, the United Nations and the Human Rights of Indigenous Peoples." In Martin Nakata (ed.), *Indigenous Peoples, Racism and the United Nations*. Common Ground Publishing: Australia.

Saul, John Ralston. 2008. *A Fair Country: Telling Truths About Canada*. Toronto: Viking

Canada.

Smith, Linda Tuhiwai. 1999. *Decolonizing Methodologies: Research and Indigenous Peoples.* London: Zed Books.

Star. 2013. "UN investigator urges inquiry for missing, murdered Indigenous Women." <thestar.com/news/canada/2013/10/15/un_investigator_urges_inquiry_for_missing_murdered_Indigenous_women.html>.

Statistics Canada. 2006. *Aboriginal Peoples, 2006 Census Aboriginal Peoples in Canada in 2006: Inuit, Métis and First Nations, 2006 Census.* Catalogue no. 97-558-XIE. <12.statcan.ca/census-recensement/2006/as-sa/97-558/pdf/97-558-XIE2006001.pdf>.

Sterling, Harry. 2010. "Opinion." *Edmonton Journal*, September 5. A14.

Teeple, Gary. 2004. *The Riddle of Human Rights.* Aurora: Garamond Press.

TRC (Truth and Reconciliation Commission). n.d. "Our Mandate." <trc.ca/websites/trcinstitution/index.php?p=7>.

UBCIC (Union of B.C. Indian Chiefs). 2010. October 20 letter to Prime Minister Harper regarding the UNDRIP.

United Nations. 2007. *United Nations Declaration on the Rights of Indigenous Peoples.*

_____. 2009. Human Rights Council, UN General Assembly. *Report of the Expert Mechanism on the Rights of Indigenous Peoples on its Second Session*, Geneva, 10–14 August. Reported 8 September, A/HRC/12/32.

_____. 2014. *Report of the Special Rapporteur on the Rights of Indigenous Peoples, James Anaya. Addendum.* The situation of indigenous peoples in Canada (advance unedited version). <http://unsr.jamesanaya.org/docs/countries/2014-report-canada-a-hrc-27-52-add-2-en-auversion.pdf>.

Webber, Jeremy, and Colin M. Macleod (eds.). 2010. *Between Consenting Peoples: Political Community and the Meaning of Consent.* Vancouver: UBC Press.

Whittington, Les. 2012. "UN food envoy blasts inequality, poverty in Canada." <http://www.thestar.com/news/canada/2012/05/16/un_food_envoy_blasts_inequality_poverty_in_canada.html>.

Willemsen-Diaz, Augusto. 2009. "How Indigenous Peoples' Rights Reached the UN." *Making the Declaration Work: The United Nations Declaration on the Rights of Indigenous Peoples.* Document No. 127. Copenhagen: International Working Group for Indigenous Affairs.

Chapter Two

The Race Bind
Denying Australian Indigenous Rights
Maggie Walter

The dominant discourses on the rights of Aboriginal and Torres Strait Islander peoples[1] have shifted and transformed since Australian colonization began two centuries ago. The current primary narrative interprets these changes as indicating an evolving discourse, moving from a paradigm of social Darwinism in the 1800s, adjusting and altering through the various eras to one that now reflects equal rights for all as a foundational tenet of what it is to be Australian. Evidence proffered for this conclusion includes: the extension of all voting rights to Aboriginal and Torres Strait Islander peoples in the 1960s; the official rejection of policies of Aboriginal assimilation and state support of the establishment of Indigenous organizations in the 1970s; the dismantling of the last of the "Aboriginal Protection" laws and the passing of anti-race discrimination legislation during the 1980s; and in the 1990s, the Mabo case, whereby Eddie Mabo and four other Merian people from the Murray Islands off North Queensland had their rights to their traditional lands upheld in the High Court of Australia. In doing so the High Court overturned colonization's justifying doctrine of *terra nullius* (empty land), making land rights at least a legal possibility (Chesterman and Galligan 1997; Peterson 1998; Attwood and Markus 1999).

Either alone or in sum these events do not represent an equalling of rights. Moreover, the narrative of egalitarianism is only accepted by the contemporary Euro-Australian majority. For Aboriginal or Torres Straits Islander peoples a different narrative of the history of Indigenous rights prevails, underscored by the lived reality of ongoing political, socio-economic and cultural marginalization. Evidence to support this alternative narrative includes damning national statistics on health and socio-economic inequality, broad white resistance to the concept of Indigenous rights and the ongoing disregard that permeates the non-Indigenous public and political discourse on Indigenous issues (Walter 2009; AIHW 2011; Watson and Venne 2012).

Juxtaposing these narratives of equal rights for all with embedded inequality presents an obvious contradiction. Yet, their contemporary co-existence within public and political debate remains largely unremarked. The explanation proposed here is that rather than evolving, the Australian discourse on Indigenous rights has merely changed shape. Yes, the discourse has been adapted in various ways to changing political and social landscapes, but never in a way that has threatened the status quo of non-Indigenous privilege and Indigenous disadvantage. The current version is underpinned by a concept termed here the "Australian race bind." While the discussion in this chapter is limited to the Australian context, readers from other Anglo-colonized first-world nations such as Aotearoa New Zealand, the United States and Canada will likely see parallels with the discursive positioning of Indigenous peoples in those countries.

This chapter uses the concept of the race bind to explore how the continuance of Indigenous social, cultural and political rights inequality is sustained alongside dominant narratives of egalitarianism and equal rights for all. The concept is used to demonstrate how Indigenous rights inequality is not an artefact of the past but is contemporary social and political practice. The two foci of the chapter are how social rights continued to be denied in the face of huge, long-term Indigenous socio-economic disparity and the denial of cultural and political rights through the refuting of the relevance of race to rights. In this discussion the race bind is first conceptualized.

The Australian Race Bind

This race bind concept encapsulates a racialized discourse that maintains the racial stratification system and its accompanying disparate access to social, economic, political and cultural resources while simultaneously denying the existence of race-based privilege or disadvantage. This discourse is achieved by merging newer discourses of individualism and free market capitalism with older colonial discourses on Aboriginal peoples as undeveloped culturally and morally and, therefore, undeserving. The resultant discursive paradox denies the concept of race itself, blaming or crediting racially differentiated life trajectories on individual choices, while contradictorily but simultaneously justifying racially differentiated social and political positioning. In doing so it achieves its discursive purpose. It allows the nation-state and its majority Euro-Australian population to perceive themselves as egalitarian, enlightened, educated twenty-first century first-world citizens while leaving largely undisturbed the social stratification of race and white privilege.

The race bind concept has theoretical similarities to and is influenced by Bonilla-Silva's (2010) notion of "colour-blind racism." Bonilla-Silva's theory forms part of the explanation of how newer versions of racism have replaced the now discredited theories of biological inferiority. These explanations include the work of Firebaugh and Davis (1988), who saw changing attitudes towards Blacks and minorities in the United States as sign of a genuine move to a more racially equal society. Others, such as Bobo (1997), use the term "*laissez faire* racism" to argue that racism previously attributed to biological inferiority has merely been recast as cultural inferiority. Kinder and Sears (1981) also argue that biological racism has merely been replaced, in their case by "symbolic racism." In this new form of racism, Sears and Kinder argue, racial resentment of programs such as affirmative action combines with traditional conservative moral values of individualism and the virtue of hard work. From this perspective, social problems such as welfare dependence, crime rates and drug abuse are attributed to the moral and behavioural traits of the racial group experiencing the problems.

These explanations resonate in the Australian context. In line with Firebaugh and Davis' work there has been an observable change in the racial attitudes of at least a portion of the non-Indigenous population. As shown by events such as the formal apology to the Aboriginal Stolen Generations by then-Prime Minister Rudd in 2008 and the work of many non-Indigenous people in organizations such as the Australians for Native Title and Reconciliation (ANTaR), a substantial number of Euro-Australians recognize the poor state of contemporary Aboriginal rights. But these are not the majority. Rather, race relations in Australia are largely marked by what Waleed Aly (2010) has called "high levels of low level racism." Attitudinal change doesn't necessarily always move in a positive direction. As demonstrated by Walter and Mooney (2007), the period of high support for the xenophobic One Nation political party was also a period of rising negative public sentiment towards Aboriginal issues. In what Hage (2003) refers to as "White Cultural Politics," One Nation's platform targeted what was seen as a decline in the rights of "ordinary Australians" because of the demands of minority groups, especially Aboriginal peoples. For example, a 1997 One Nation press release argued that Aboriginal Australians were deliberately cultivating "guilt in the minds of ordinary Australians" aimed at "raising the willingness to compensate the Aborigines" (One Nation 1997).

As per Kinder and Sears' (1981) concept of symbolic racism, the use of biological terminology to refer to Aboriginal racial inferiority has also been replaced with references to culture, built around the idea of behavioural and moral deficits. The social problems burdening Aboriginal peoples, including high levels of welfare receipt, low school attendance and alcohol and drug abuse, are increasingly attributed not to chronic poverty and marginalization, but to a lack of individual effort, low aspirations and poor attitudes and values. For example, an editorial in the national newspaper, the *Australian* (2005), blames welfare dependency for encouraging a sense of passivity and victimhood among Aboriginal people.

The race bind, as well as colour-blind racism, however, refutes the individualist lens that the Firebaugh and Davis (1988), Bobo (1997) or Kinder and Sears (1981) theories apply to racism. Instead, as argued by Bonilla-Silva (2010), a critical theoretical recognition is that the space where racism resides is not in the individual but in the way the social world is organized. The views of the social actors are correlated with their systemic raced location. For white people, the privilege of their race is obscured by their dominant position, as are the everyday disadvantages borne by those who are not white. It is, therefore, the system that needs to be explored to understand racism, not the individual social actor. The race bind also incorporates Bonila-Silva's (2010) understanding that this white/non-white divide on racism serves a discursive purpose. By restricting the gaze on race relations to racism and further restricting that gaze to individual acts of prejudice, white peoples can deny their own privileged position in their society's racial hierarchy and can deny that the benefits they derive arise from the racially disadvantaged position of others (Lipsitz 2011). Personal claims of racial liberalness valorize the racially privileged individual at the same time as minimizing the societal importance of race. Those who are not white, however, know only too well that race remains a central predictor of life chances. The insidious effects of the race hierarchy, race relations and racism are manifest, whether or not individuals regularly experience individual acts of prejudice. Those who are not white understand that taking an individualistic perspective on race and racism is itself a white privilege. It allows whites to develop "epistemologies of ignorance" (Mills 1997), which, in the Australian context, via their own social position, means they neither have to witness the effects of racial inequality on others nor accept that it even exists (Atkinson, Taylor and Walter 2010).

The individualism inherent in neoliberalism is a facilitating factor in how the race bind discourse operates on Aboriginal rights. As in other Anglo Western countries, neoliberalism has emerged as the dominant Australian economic and political discourse since the 1980s. This theory and accompanying political and economic practices posit that "human well-being can be best advanced by liberating individual entrepreneurial freedoms and skills within an institutional framework characterized by strong private property rights, free markets and free trade" (Harvey 2005: 2–3). Social good is seen as maximized by maximizing the reach of market transactions. Under this framework, the societal unit is reduced to the level of the individual, and, as individuals, we are all now individually responsible for our own life project (Beck and Beck-Gernsheim 2002). Individualization is hegemonically embedded in the way the rights position of the Indigenous and, as critically, the non-Indigenous are currently perceived, publically and politically. Individualism allows the further privileging of Western culture inherent within neoliberalism to be ignored while simultaneously allowing the trope of individual life choices to explain away the very different life trajectories of particular racial groups (Gale 2005).

Where the race bind rights discourse deviates from Bonilla-Silva's colour-blind racism is its engagement with the particular racism that emerges from colonizing settler states. Settler state racism combines the racism inherent in first-world nation-states with majority white populations towards those who are not white with the racial stratification system (and racialized discourses) that emerge from colonizer settler states towards the Indigenous peoples they have dispossessed and from whose lands and resources they now draw their wealth and identity. At the base of this racism is a deeply felt and wide-ranging resentment of Indigenous peoples. Most prominently, a continuing Indigenous presence undermines the nation's vision of itself as free, equal and egalitarian and casts a shadow over its legitimacy. Indigenous peoples' survival also reminds colonizing settler populations that Australia is a nation-state built on violent dispossession. It also increasingly contains tinges of what I refer to as "origins envy," a colonizing settler jealousy of

Aboriginality, of cultural traditions and heritage, of belongingness and connected-
ness to the varying Aboriginal nations and countries regardless of who now asserts
that these lands belong to them.

The race bind, therefore, is a particularly noxious mix: amalgamating older
discourses of racial inferiority, newer individualism-framed discourses of cultural
and moral deficiency, a discursive positioning of racism as limited to individual
acts and settler population racial antipathy to Aboriginal people.

"Equal Social Rights," Australian Style

Contemporary citizenship is a "bundle of entitlements and obligations which
constitute individuals as fully fledged members of a socio-political community,
providing them with access to scarce resources" (Turner and Hamilton 1994:
3). This definition with its attached set of rights is manifestly not applicable to
Aboriginal and Torres Strait Islander peoples in Australia. Most observably,
on the right to the prevailing standard of life and the social heritage of society
(Barbelet 1988), Indigenous life realities remain devastatingly disparate from
other Australians. It has been clear that Aboriginal and Torres Strait Islander lives
have been characterized by overwhelming poverty since the national census first
collected data on Indigenous Australians in 1971. Until amended by a national
referendum in 1967, the Australian Constitution excluded Aboriginal and Torres
Strait Islander peoples from being officially counted in the five-yearly national
censes. The 2011 national census yet again portrays the too familiar patterns of
socio-economic inequality between Australia's Indigenous and non-Indigenous
populations (ABS 2013).

National aggregate Indigenous data is a statistical convenience rather than a
social or political actuality. Aboriginal Australia comprises more than five hundred
Aboriginal nations spread across the continent, varying by country, culture, language, customs and traditions, as well as by histories of colonization and dispossession. While dominant mainstream perceptions of Aboriginal Australians remain
linked to remote, discrete Aboriginal or Torres Strait Islander communities, less
than 25 percent reside in such locations with the majority now resident in urban
settings, in cities or in regional towns (AIHW 2011). Yet, the embedded patterns
of inequality remain undisturbed regardless of where Aboriginal peoples live.

These embedded patterns of inequality are highlighted in Indigenous/non-
Indigenous socio-economic patterns from around Australia. Such comparisons,
as demonstrated in Figure 2-1, indicate that Indigenous and non-Indigenous
Australians exist within different socio-economic realms regardless of geographic
location, history or the broader population indicators of place. Figure 2-1, for
example, presents 2011 census data on Aboriginal populations from three diverse
sites. The first, Perth, is the capital city of the state of Western Australia, the
traditional country of the Nyungar people. The Nyungar people were dispossessed
of their lands by frontier violence and colonization from 1829 onwards. In 2006,

the legitimacy of their claim to the lands that make up the Perth region was upheld by the Federal Court (ABC 2006). Despite ongoing legal challenges by state and federal authorities the Nyungar are currently negotiating native title with their state government. The second is Dubbo, a large regional town in central New South Wales, the traditional country of the Tubbagah people, part of the Wiradjuri nation. Colonization and violent dispossession came earlier to the Tubbagah people, beginning the early 1800s. In 1995 the Tubbagah people lodged a native title claim over the sixteen-hectare Terramungamine reserve. This claim was contested by local and state authorities on the basis of public access and the presence of an historic stock trail. An agreement was finally reached in 2002 to protect the Aboriginal burial grounds as well as non-Indigenous historical sites (Native Title Tribune 2002). The third is Maningrida, a remote, predominantly Aboriginal town, the traditional lands of the Kunbidji people, who, by virtue of their location in remote Northern Territory, remained outside colonizing control into the 1900s. The Federal *Aboriginal Land Rights (Northern Territory) Act* 1976 gave the Kunbidji people inalienable freehold title to their lands (Maningrida Council Inc. 2008). Since 2007 these rights have been compromised when Maningrida became one of the seventy-three Aboriginal towns directly affected by the *Northern Territory National Emergency Response Act 2007*. This act, more commonly known as the NT Intervention, enabled the federal government to compulsorily acquire the town's lease for five years, restrict how residents spent

Figure 2-1: Unemployment, Rental Housing and Education to Year 12 Level for Indigenous and Non-Indigenous Residents of Dubbo, Perth and Maningrida

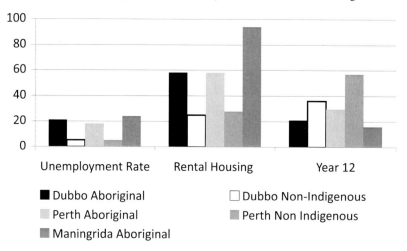

Note: Comparison figures for Maningrida not included as non-Indigenous residents are an employment-related population rather than permanent residents.
Source: Figures derived from Australian Census (ABS 2013) 2011 Community Profile Data

welfare payments and more latterly introduced (non-Indigenous) community managers (Hinkson 2007).

Similar patterns of Indigenous gross socio-economic inequality, regardless of location, exist between income levels, employment status, standard of housing and access to higher education. For example, despite very low levels of unemployment amongst the non-Indigenous populations in Dubbo and Perth, Aboriginal unemployment rates are all near, or above, 20 percent. Similarly, the proportion of the Indigenous population in Perth and Dubbo who are in rental accommodation is more than double those of their non-Indigenous co-residents. In Maningrida all housing is rental and characterized by limited, poor quality housing stock and very high rates of overcrowding. More than 72 percent of Aboriginal households have six or more residents, although none of the 240 non-Indigenous residents live in such conditions. Rates of education to Year 12 (the end of secondary schooling in Australia) vary more, with Aboriginal and Torres Strait Islander people in Perth reporting higher rates of Year 12 achievement than those in Dubbo or Maningrida. Yet, such rates still equate to just over half the rate of Year 12 achievement of the non-Indigenous population of Perth. Given that the Aboriginal peoples of Perth, Dubbo and Maningrida are very different culturally and geographically, how is it that they are so similar in their comparative socio-economic positions? The answer is that regardless of these differences, no matter where or how you live, Aboriginality and poor socio-economic outcomes are highly correlated. Inequality in Australia is strongly racialized.

These stark statistics sit uneasily alongside public understandings of Indigenous inequality. For example, the 2007 Australian Survey of Social Attitudes (AUSSA) finds only a bare majority (51 percent) of non-Indigenous Australians disagree with the statement: "Injustices towards Aboriginal people are now all in the past" (Walter 2012). This contradiction, between the discourse of discrimination no longer being widespread and the socio-economic realities, fits neatly into the concept of the race bind. Neither individualism nor neoliberalism has discursive space for either macro or historical forces, and, therefore, racism, discrimination, dispossession and intergenerational poverty are deemed historical. To sustain the relegation of injustice as a past phenomenon, any raising of inequality grievances tends to be immediately labelled as the deployment of a "victim" mentality. For example, recommendations from an expert panel to alter the Australian Constitution to recognize Aboriginal and Torres Islander peoples as the first Australians and remove the last vestiges of race-related provisions were branded in an opinion article in the national broadsheet, the *Australian*, as just the "grim legacy of compassion" and an attempt by Indigenous peoples to differentiate themselves from other Australians (McCauley 2012).

This present and future focus is also necessary to get the "right" answer to Bonilla-Silva's base question (and similar to the one asked above): "How is it possible to have this tremendous degree of racial inequality in a country where most whites claim that race is no longer relevant?" Combined with the individualism of neoliberalism, the rejection of the relevance of the past allows the embedded racial stratification system to be reclassified as a system of meritocracy that rewards individual effort. Contemporary Indigenous deprivation is framed under this discourse not as the failure of equal rights but the failure of Indigenous peoples to utilize those rights. Yet, within this discourse a paradox exists. Life trajectories and life chances are deemed related to individual choices and decisions, but there is little attempt to explain why so many of these individuals on the wrong side of the outcome ledger are Aboriginal, other than ones related to racial deficit.

Relabeling Disadvantage as Deficit

Inequalities previously blamed on Aboriginal biological inferiority have simply been shifted to racially aligned cultural and moral deficiencies. The flawed underpinnings of such a discourse are easily exposed. For example, Sutton (2005: 8), in his argument that Aboriginal health inequalities are related to Aboriginal culture, rolls under his label of "culture" individually experienced social issues such as poor diet, poor personal hygiene and substance misuse along with infrastructure issues such as domestic sanitation and housing density. He then adds in his own pejorative interpretation of Aboriginal norms of care of children and the elderly, conflict resolution, expression of emotion and attitudes to learning new information. Sutton's definition of culture, therefore, is just an ever-expandable category for any or all negative stereotypes and racially aligned constructs of deficit (Walter 2007).

The social problems identified by Sutton are not restricted to Aboriginal peoples, and nobody is suggesting that the incidence of these issues within the Euro-Australian population is due to Euro-Australian culture. Rather, laying the blame for contemporary inequality on Aboriginal culture allows the link between both Aboriginal disadvantage and Euro-settler privilege and unequal rights to be obscured. Aboriginal culture blaming also allows any link between contemporary disadvantage or privilege and unequal rights to be eschewed. Under this justification the extremes of overcrowding that exists in communities like Maningrida are tied to cultural deficiencies rather than the well-documented decades of neglect, underfunding and systemic overspending on bureaucracy for Indigenous services (see Yu 1994; Aikman 2012). Low levels of educational attainment at Maningrida can be despaired of as poor cultural attitudes to learning new information rather than the absence of a secondary school until 2003 despite a rapidly growing school population of over 500 children aged up to fourteen (Walter 2008).

Regardless, the broad public and political acceptance of race bind discourse of Aboriginal incapacity and deficit means policy "solutions" are similarly racially positioned. Within the dominant discourse, Aboriginal people are the problem. Official government reports reflect these elements. The primary policy addressing Indigenous socio-economic and health inequality is Closing the Gap, which sets the federal government six targets to achieve in reducing the disparity in Indigenous lives. These are: closing the life expectancy gap within a generation; halving the gap in mortality rates for Indigenous children under five; ensuring all four-year-olds in remote communities have access to early childhood education; halving the gap for Indigenous children in reading, writing and numeracy; halving the gap for Indigenous people aged twenty to twenty-four in Year 12 or equivalent attainment rates; and halving the gap in employment outcomes between Indigenous and non-Indigenous Australians within a decade. Some progress is being made in reduction of child mortality and access to early education, but the annual policy achievement reports make little mention of race and none of accumulative racially related social marginalization and economic disadvantage, past or continuing. Rather, Prime Minister Abbott, in his introduction to the 2014 Closing the Gap Report (2014: 1) states that "for the gap to close we must get kids to school, adults to work and the ordinary law of the land observed. Everything flows from meeting these three objectives." This introduction neatly moves the discourse from gross health and socio-economic inequality to the disparity being related to the poor, behavioural choices of Aboriginal people and communities.

The race bind is, therefore, a racially infused contradictory discourse that facilitates ongoing denial of social rights. On the one hand, Aboriginal people, as a named racial group, are stigmatized as problematically welfare dependent and therefore requiring racially restricted policy intervention. On the other hand, the atomized individualization of the dominant neoliberal paradigm denies the influence of race on the inequality hierarchy. As former Prime Minister John Howard asserted, there should be "no separate treatment of the First Australians" (cited in Hagan 2004). These sentiments are also reflected in national attitudinal data. As reported in the previous section, a bare majority of Australians responding to the 2007 AUSSA survey disagreed that Aboriginal people were now treated equally. But even fewer (45 percent) agreed with the statement, "Aboriginal people's levels of disadvantage justifies extra government assistance" (Walter 2012). The race bind, therefore, effectively makes Australian Aboriginals responsible not only for their current unenviable position at the bottom of the social and socio-economic gradient, but also for improving that position into the future.

Indigenous rights' achievements such as land rights have also been impacted by the discursive rationale of the race bind. As with most Indigenous people, land returned under native title legislation is held communally by traditional owners. It is now national Coalition policy (Liberal Party 2013) to support the replacement of communal land tenure with individual ownership. Influenced by neoliberal ideology, private home ownership is deemed a panacea for entrenched poverty, high levels of over-crowding and grossly inadequate infrastructure in most Aboriginal communities built on what is now native title land. In the words of the federal government the restrictive native title laws do not allow for private home ownership. The transfer control of the townships to the Commonwealth through the granting of ninety-nine-year leases will open up business and home ownership options for the Aboriginal residents. But as Altman (2013) writes:

> this latest land reform intervention is replete with contradictions ... while ostensibly about producing certainty for all land users and placing land tenure on a commercial footing ... this reform is fundamentally about extinguishing land rights in townships for a century in return for money.

The Racialization of Denying Race as Rights Denial

In 1882 a delegation of Aboriginal protestors from the Coranderrk Aboriginal reserve walked the forty miles to Melbourne to petition the Victorian colonial powers. The petition, demanding greater rights, was part of an ongoing campaign of activism against mismanagement and conditions on the reserve (Attwood and Markus 1999). The eventual response by the Victorian parliament was to not address grievances. Rather, the *Aborigines Act 1869* was amended to redefine Aboriginality to only include those deemed "pure Aboriginal" (Chesterman and Galligan 1997). This redefinition served two colonial purposes. First, reducing the reserve-eligible population reduced expenses. Second, most of those identified as troublemakers were now deemed non-Aboriginal and could be forcibly removed. Legal redefinition therefore allowed colonial authorities to punish the activists and control defiance of colonial rule. The new rigid line of Aboriginality was gazetted as law in May 1890. Those now legislatively "not Aboriginal" fell into a racial gap, separated from family but denied meaningful participation in the colonial society. The results were predictable. In response to a 1908 memorandum referring to a group of "half-castes" living in a "wretched state," state authorities replied, "the conditions under which they could be granted food and clothing terminated many years ago. Consequently when they were compelled to merge with the white population, they were obliged to provide for their own support" (cited in Chesterman and Galligan 1997: 29).

Since 2010 settler state attempts are again being made to redefine Aboriginality. Again, Indigeneity is simultaneously targeted and denied. The aim, as in 1890, seems to be to punish and remove the capacity of activist "troublemakers" to argue for Indigenous rights. The contemporary version, however, is built upon the racial resentment aspect of the race bind. This debate begins by discursively usurping the triple criteria of Australian Aboriginality, long accepted by Aboriginal organizations and state and federal government authorities: Aboriginal descent; public self-identification as Aboriginal; and acceptance as Aboriginal within the person's Aboriginal community. The conflict achieved national prominence in 2011 when a group of Aboriginal activists, artists and scholars took right-wing media commentator Andrew Bolt to the Federal Court, arguing that he had breached the *Racial Discrimination Act 1975*. In 2009 Bolt had written two opinion pieces in the best selling tabloid, the *Herald Sun*, suggesting these people had unfairly claimed Aboriginality to gain unearned honours and career benefits. The case against Bolt was successful, not only because many of his reported "facts" about the complainants he denounced were simply untrue, but also because Justice Bromberg upheld the complaint of vilification and the consequent *Racial Discrimination Act* breach. He noted in his ruling, "people should be free to fully identity with their race without fear of public disdain or loss of esteem for so identifying" (*Eatock v. Bolt* 2011).

The Bolt case has now become a *cause celebre* for conservative forces. Australian Prime Minister Tony Abbott is in the process of repealing the breached section of the *Racial Discrimination Act* (Kerr 2014). Even less militant commentators have accepted at face value Bolt's claim that Aboriginal identity is being used to opportunely garner unearned benefits (see Weiss 2012). As in 1890, the target of these claims are Aboriginal people who also have European forebears. The race bind frame for these arguments reflects whites' individualistic understanding of racism (Bonilla-Silva's 2010). From this perspective, if an individual is not manifestly "Aboriginal," s/he cannot have experienced race-related inequality. Thus, inherited intergenerational socio-economic marginalization and disadvantage, so evident in the socio-economic reality, or family, kin and community links are deemed immaterial.

The ensuing political and public debate on Aboriginality reflects other racialized discursive elements of the race bind. The first is a normed Western presumption that Aboriginal identity is something "chosen" by those with fairer skin. This presumption arises from the discourse of individualism whereby identity is fluid and aspects of identity can be selected and donned by the individual at will. This presumption is littered through the blog comments on the Bolt case. For example, when three prominent Aboriginal people wrote about their identity in an article for Crikey (Jamieson 2011), a relatively left wing e-journal, the blog comments were mixed, but in the majority, negative.

One blogger wrote:

> I really can't see what all the fuss is about. I am seven eighths Pom and one eight Swede and I call myself AUSTRALIAN [capitals in original].

Another commented:

> Is there some implication that one doesn't have a choice about identity if one was pushed in one direction by circumstances at an early age? If so, that is clearly BS.

Yet as Lipsitz (2006) argues, whiteness is a social condition not a race colour. The reverse is also true. Aboriginality is a social condition not a race colour. Indeed, "Aboriginal" is itself a racial construct invented by the colonists to conveniently group all the peoples who occupied an entire continent. It also reveals the contradictory tenets of the race bind discourse. The assumption that lighter skin colour indicates non-Aboriginality sits alongside the cultural deficit model whereby it is problematic Aboriginal culture, not biology, that sits at the base of continued Indigenous disadvantage. Also, just as in 1890, the discourse assumes that Euro-Australians have the right to make determinations about Aboriginality and that these trump the existing practice of Indigenous self, family and community-determined racial identity. For example, when Shane Mortimer conducted a "welcome to country" ceremony at Federal Parliament in November 2012, Professor Don Aitken wrote on his public blog that "he looked about as Aboriginal as I do," adding that his "constant references to his 'ancestors' make me scratch my head." Professor Aitken has since denied any insult was intended, claiming, "I am a supporter of the Aboriginal people in their struggle for respect" (cited in Hare 2012). The racial implication of his comment, however, is that anybody who had the option to pass as white, would naturally choose to do so.

The fourth highly racialized element of the discourse is the implicit assumption that Aboriginal people are unable to achieve success in almost any field without some special advantages not available to "ordinary" Australians. By this circular logic, the status of any successful Aboriginal person is assumed to rest on such "special measure" rather than merit. Or, more pejoratively, success is equated with the proportion of European heritage. As a blogger noted at the bottom of an unrelated story in *Tracker* magazine (Graham 2012):

> Well done to all the aboriginal people who have worked and studied hard and created a life for themselves without the "pity funds" from centrelink[2] ... I'm guessing you either had some with "white work ethics" in your midst ... stolen generation[3] or mixed race??

This blogger was later identified by the magazine as a bureaucrat employed to deliver programs to Aboriginal people in the New South Wales community of Toomelah (Graham 2012). This element of the discourse also taps into the "origins envy" aspect of the race bind. Pejoratively linking identity with opportunism creates a heavy social sanction against publicly identifying as Aboriginal. Under this discourse, Aboriginality becomes, yet again, the only Australian heritage that cannot be celebrated. The discursive strategy operationalized by origins envy seems to be intended to intimidate the increasing number of Australians with Aboriginal ancestry into silence or defensiveness, suppressing the resurgent discourses of Aboriginal pride and belonging to country. Just as in 1890, those now discursively deemed "not Aboriginal enough" are being politically compelled to merge with the white population, not on their own, but on Euro-Australian terms.

Yet, the current debate of Aboriginality is just as much a smoke screen now as it was in 1890. The real transgression of the targeted Aborigines was to threaten the status quo of Australia's racial hierarchy of privilege and disadvantage. By querying and challenging the terrain of race relations and the state of Indigenous rights, not from the position of supplicants or mendicants, but from prominent academic, political or organizational bases, they challenge the necessary positioning of the Indigene as deficient. Public challenges to Indigenous authenticity, therefore, are an attempt to delegitimize rights claims through targeted disparagement and, in doing so, frighten others from attempting to do the same. Fanning (2012) contends that the public denigration of Aboriginal identity is a particularly Australian form of racism. More properly it should be labelled a settler state form of racism. Indigenous peoples in other white settler states such as Aotearoa New Zealand and Hawai'i also experience versions of the same authenticity strategy (see Kukutai and Didham 2012 and Kauanui 2008, for example). This regular public questioning of Indigeneity is also at odds with the complete lack of public or political interrogation of the rather more dubious notion of "Australianness."

Under the ideology of a singular Australianness, albeit one where only those of European background get to use the term "Australian" without a racial identifier, calls for Indigenous rights are met with denial wrapped in public and political antipathy. At the centre of this resentment is a misunderstanding, sometimes deliberate, sometimes not. Again, individualism is the key. Since the 1980s human rights have been increasingly discursively positioned as the rights of the individual (Hokuwhitu 2010). Increasingly also, Indigenous rights are recast as "special" treatment. They are therefore, by definition, unfair and unequal and frequently labelled as a form of reverse racism. For example, the plans to include recognition of Australia's First Peoples in the Australian Constitution (as yet unrealised) were immediately labelled by Andrew Bolt as "racism" (Bolt 2008). Others, such as the conservative policy think tank, the Centre for Independent Studies (CIS), warns of the dangers to Australian society of treating Aborigines differently under the law. CIS researcher Sara Hudson (2012) writes in e-journal *Online Opinion*:

> Treating Aboriginal people differently causes more problems than it solves. It also sets a dangerous precedent that other ethnic groups could use to argue for different treatment by the courts. If we allow Aboriginal customary law should we also allow Sharia law, as some Muslim groups are asking for?

Yet, as shown repeatedly throughout this chapter, Aboriginal people are already being treated differently though their lack of access to the plethora of rights held solely by the Euro-Australian majority. As Lipsitz (2006) argues, the removal of racist legislation has not diminished the unearned and expected privileging of whites at all levels in society. Thus, Euro-Australians, by virtue of their dominant cultural status and control of all the institutions and resources of the state, exclusively possess and use rights withheld from the First Australians since colonization began. The above quote from CIS researcher Hudson (2012), for example, positions Aboriginal people as just another ethnic group to obscure the displacement of the existing system of Aboriginal law with imported English customary law, just

200 years ago. Thus, also, the Australian Constitution is the constitution of Euro-Australians. It was written by and for Euro-Australians to support the legitimacy of the settler state. Aboriginal and Torres Strait Islander peoples were absent except in only two clauses, both of which allowed racialized restrictions. More broadly, the United Nations 2007 *Declaration on the Rights of Indigenous Peoples* also reflects a set of rights already possessed, in exclusivity, by the Euro-Australian majority. These include the right to equality with other peoples, the right to strengthen culture, the right to not be forcibly removed from lands, the right to participate in policy or law making, the right to participate in decision-making, the right to citizenship, the right to their own justice systems and the right to collective and individual identity (United Nations 1994). Yet Australia was one of only four out of 154 nations to vote against the 2007 adoption of the Declaration. It was a reluctant signatory in 2009 following a change of government (AHRC 2008, 2009). Buttressed by the dominant frame of the race bind, arguments against "special" Indigenous rights sustain the long existing rights over-entitlement of the Euro-Australian majority.

Colonialism Continues

The race bind is the contemporary version of the Australian discourse on Indigenous rights. This discourse sustains Indigenous rights inequality via the linking of the disparity of social, economic, political and cultural rights to individualized but also racialized moral, behavioural and cultural deficit. This framework also allows claims for the recognition of Indigenous rights, even symbolically, to be regaled as unfair, while further embedding the denial of Indigenous rights and the outcomes of this inequality. As shown in this chapter, the dominance of the race bind discourse in relation to Indigenous social, cultural and political rights appears to be deepening, not retreating.

Notes

1. The preferred nomenclature of Australian Aboriginal peoples is "Aboriginal" or, when referring to all the continent's Indigenous peoples, "Aboriginal and Torres Strait Islander peoples." These terms are used here as well as the term "Indigenous" to refer to both Aboriginal and Torres Strait Islander peoples.
2. Centrelink is the national bureaucracy that delivers pensions and unemployment benefits.
3. The phrase "stolen generation" refers to those children, mostly of mixed Aboriginal and European heritage, forcibly removed from their families through the nineteenth and twentieth centuries.

References

ABC. 2006. "Nyoongar people win native title over Perth." ABC *On-Line*. <abc.net.au/nerws/newsitems/200609/s1744596.htm>.

ABS (Australian Bureau of Statistics). 2013. *Census*. <abs.gov.au/census>.

AHRC 2008. "Australia's Support of the Declaration on the Rights of Indigenous Peoples."

Australian Human Rights Commission. <humanrights.gov.au/social_justice/decla-ration/>.

____. 2009. "United We Stand — Support for United National Indigenous Rights Declaration a Watershed Moment for Australia." Australian Human Rights Commission. <human-rights.gov.au/about/medi/media_releases/2009> accessed 24/12/1012.

AIHW (Australian Institute of Health). 2011. *The Health and Welfare of Australia's Aboriginal and Torres Strait Islander People: An Overview.* Cat no. IHW 42.Canberra.

Aikman, A. 2012. "Remote indigenous funding 'spent on officials.'" *The Australian*, September 4: 8.

Altman, J. 2013. "Abbot Government Peddles De Soto on Arnhem Land Rights." *Crikey*, 4 December. <Crikey.com.au/2013/12/04/abbot-government-peddles-de-soto-on-Arnhem-land-rights/>.

Aly, W. 2010. *Race in America, Race in Australia: A Public Forum Featuring Glenn Loury, Waleed Aly and Bob Carr.* 7 June <http://ussc.edu.au/gallery/Race-in-America-race-in-Australia-A-public-forum-featuring-Glenn-Loury-Waleed-Aly-and-Bob-Carr>.

ANTAR (Australians for Native Title and Reconciliation). 2005. "The Native Title Act 1993." <http://www.antarvictoria.org.au/nta.html>.

Atkinson, R., E. Taylor and M. Walter. 2010. "Burying Indigeneity: The Spatial Construction of Reality and Aboriginal Australia." *Social and Legal Studies* 19, 3: 311–30

Attwood, B., and A. Markus. 1999. *The Struggle for Aboriginal Rights: A Documentary History.* Crows Nest: Allen and Unwin.

The Australian. 2005. "Welfare had failed." Editorial, Wednesday 12 August: 5.

Barbalet, J.M. 1988. *Citizenship.* Stratford: Open University Press.

Beck, U., and E. Beck-Gernsheim. 2002. *Individualization.* London: Sage Publications.

Bobo, L. 1997. "Race, Public Opinion, and the Social Sphere." *The Public Opinion Quarterly* 61, 1, Special Issue on Race (Spring): 1–15.

Bolt, A. 2008. "No to this racism." *Andrew Bolt Blog The Herald* Sun 13 July. <blogs.news.com.au/heraldsun/andrewbolt/index.php/heraldsun/comments/no_to_this_rac-ism/asc/P20/> accessed 10 December 2008.

Bonilla-Silva, E. 2010. *Racism Without Racists: Colour-Blind Racism and the Persistence of Racial Inequality in the United States.* 3rd edition. Maryland: Rowman & Littlefield Publishers.

Chesterman, B., and G. Galligan. 1997. *Citizens Without Rights, Aborigines and Australian Citizenship.* Cambridge: Cambridge University Press.

Closing the Gap Prime Minister's Report 2014. Australian Government, Commonwealth of Australia Liberal Party. 2013. "The Coalition's Policy for Indigenous Affairs." September. <http://www.liberal.org.au/our-policies>.

Eatock v. Bolt. 2011. FCA 1103 at [22], 28 September.

Fanning, E. 2012. "No, Andrew Bolt Did Not Have a Point." *The Global Mail.* August 9. <theglobalmail.org/feature/no-andrew-bolt-did-not-have-a-point/332/>.

Firebaugh, G., and K.E. Davis. 1988. "Trends in Antiblack Prejudice, 1972–1984: Region and Cohort Effects." *American Journal of Sociology* 94, 2: 251–72.

Gale, P. 2005. *The Politics of Fear: Lighting the Wik.* Frenchs Forest, NSW: Pearson Education Australia.

Graham, C. 2012. "'White trash mixed with black blood': Toomelah bureaucrat sacked." *Tracker,* July 5. <tracker.org.au/2012/07/g308>.

Hagan, S. 2004. "ATSIC must be replaced by a new body without 'flexible integrity." *On-Line*

Opinion. <http://www.onlineopoinion.com.au/view.asp?artcile=2169> accessed April 28, 2004.

Hage, G. 2003 *Against Paranoid Nationalism: Searching for Hope in a Shrinking Society.* Annandale, NSW: Pluto Press.

Hare, J. 2012. "Not fair: Indigenous identity back in court." *The Australian,* November 12. <http://www.theaustralian.com.au/national-affairs/policy/not-fair-indigenous-identity-back-in-court/story-fn9hm1pm-1226514765175>.

Harvey, D. 2005. *A Brief History of Neoliberalism.* Oxford: Oxford University Press

Hinkson, M. 2007. "Introduction: In the Name of the Child." In J. Altman and M. Hinkson (eds.), *Coercive Reconciliation.* North Carlton: Arena Publications Association.

Hokuwhitu, B. 2010. "A Genealogy of Indigenous Resistance." In B. Hokuwhitu, N. Kermoal, C. Andersen, A. Petersen, M. Reilly, I. Altamirano-Jimenez and P. Rewi (eds.), *Indigenous Identity and Resistance: Researching the Diversity of Knowledges.* Dunedin, NZ: Otago University Press.

Hudson, S. 2012. "Different justice?" *Online Opinion* <onlineopinion.com.au/view.asp?article=13949>.

Jamieson, A. 2011. "Aboriginal identity: 'I never had a choice.'" *Crikey,* 8 April. <http://www.crikey.com.au/2011/04/08/aboriginal-identity-i-never-had-a-choice/>.

Kauanui, J. K. 2008. *Hawiian Blood: Colonisalism and the Politics of Sovereignty and Indigeneity.* Durham: Duke University Press.

Kerr, C. 2014. "Race act set for radical reshaping." *The Australian,* March 18. http://www.theaustralian.com.au/national-affairs/race-act-set-for-radical-reshaping/

Kinder, D.R., and D.O. Sears. 1981. "Prejudice and Politics: Symbolic Racism Versus Racial Threats to the Good Life." *Journal of Personality and Social Psychology* 40, 3: 414–31.

Kukutai, T., and R. Didham. 2012. "Re-Making the Majority? Ethnic New Zealanders in the 2006 Census." *Ethnic and Racial Studies* 35, 8: 1427–46.

Lipsitz, G. 2011. *The Possessive Investment in Whiteness: How White People Profit from Identity Politics.* Philadelphia: Temple University Press.

Maningrida Council Inc. 2008. <http://www.maningrida.nt.gov.au/council/content/view/full/80>.

McCauley, P. 2012. "The Grim Legacy of Compassion." *The Weekend Australian,* January 14–15. <theaustralian.com.au/news/features/the-grim-legacy-of-compassion/story-e6frg6z6-1226243954814> accessed 29/12/2012.

Mills, C.W. 1997. *The Racial Contract.* Ithaca: Cornell University Press.

Native Title Tribunal. 2002. "Media Release: Strong commitment the Key to Terramungamine Agreement." 06 December. <http://www.nntt.gov.au/media/1039146342_532.html> accessed 5 September 2007.

One Nation. 1997. "Hanson, 'Aboriginal land grab was the object of a shameless PR campaign.' *Pauline Hanson's One Nation Press Releases.* <http://www.gwb.com.au/onenation/press/041297.html>.

Peterson, N. 1998. "Welfare Colonialism and Citizenship: Politics and Agency." In Nicholas Peterson and Will Sanders (eds.), *Citizenship and Indigenous Australians, Changing Conceptions and Possibilities.* Cambridge: Cambridge University Press.

Sutton, P. 2005. "The politicisation of disease and the disease of politicisation: Causal theories and the Indigenous health differential." Paper presented at 8th National Rural Health Conference, *Central to Health: Sustaining Wellbeing in Remote and Rural Australia,* Alice Springs, 10–13 March.

United Nations. 1994. *Draft Declaration on the Rights of Indigenous Peoples.* E/CN.4/1994/2/add.1.

Walter M. 2007. "Aboriginality, Poverty and Health: Exploring the Connection." In I. Anderson, F. Baum and M. Bentley (eds.), *Beyond Bandaids: Exploring the Underlying Social Determinants of Indigenous Health.* Darwin: CRC for Aboriginal Health.

____. 2008. "Lives of Diversity: Indigenous Australians." Occasional paper 4/2008, Census Series #2. Canberra: Australian Academy of the Social Sciences.

____. 2009. "An Economy of Poverty: Power and the Domain of Aboriginality." *International Journal of Critical Indigenous Studies.*

____. 2012. "Keeping Our Distance: Non-Indigenous/Aboriginal Relations in Australian society." In Juliet Pietsch and Haydn Aarons (eds.), *Australia: Identity, Fear and Governance in the 21st Century.* Canberra: Australian National University Press. <http://press.anu.edu.au/wp-content/uploads/2012/11/ch025.pdf>.

Walter, M., and G. Mooney. 2007. "Employment and Welfare." In Bronwyn Carson, Terry Dunbar, Richard Chenhall and Ross Bailie (eds.), *Social Determinants of Indigenous Health.* Sydney: Allen and Unwin.

Watson I., and S. Venne. 2012. "Talking up indigenous peoples' original intent in a space dominated by state intervention." In E. Pulitano (ed.), *Indigenous Rights in the Age of the UN Declaration.* Cambridge: Cambridge University Press.

Weiss, G. 2012. "So Did Andrew Bolt Have a Point?" *The Global Mail,* August 6. <theglobalmail.org/feature/so-did-andrew-bolt-have-a-point/273/>.

Yu, P. 1994 "The Kimberley: From Welfare Colonialism to Self-Determination." *Race and Class* 35, 4: 21–33.

Chapter Three

Colonialism Past and Present
Indigenous Human Rights and Canadian Policing
Elizabeth Comack

"We also have no history of colonialism." Prime Minister Stephen Harper made this remarkable assertion in responding to a question posed by a news correspondent during a press conference at the G20 Pittsburgh Summit in September 2009 (O'Keefe 2009). Harper's assertion is remarkable not just because it was delivered only fourteen months after he offered a formal apology (albeit without ever mentioning the word "colonialism") for Canada's role in the Indian residential school system (Harper 2008). The denial by the prime minister of the country's history as a settler colonial society also has profound implications for the prospects of realizing substantive equality for Aboriginal people. So long as Canadians are content (and privileged) in their denial of colonialism — and the damage created by that ongoing legacy — the likelihood of the Canadian state meeting its treaty and human rights obligations to the Indigenous population and complying with its international obligations, such as those spelled out in the United Nations' *Declaration on the Rights of Indigenous Peoples*, will be seriously diminished. Canadians — our Prime Minister included — need to be reminded of the historical record that colonialism has created.

At its core, colonialism involved, in the words of John McLeod (2000: 7), "a lucrative commercial operation, bringing wealth and riches to Western nations through the economic exploitation of others." Developing especially through the late seventeenth and early eighteenth centuries, McLeod notes that seizing "foreign" lands for settlement was in part motivated by the desire to create and control markets abroad for Western goods, as well as securing the natural resources and labour power of different lands and people at the lowest possible cost. As McLeod (2000: 7) emphasizes, colonialism "was pursued for economic profit, reward and riches. Hence, colonialism and capitalism share a mutually supportive relationship with each other." In the Canadian context, colonialism involved the process by which Europeans erected a new colonial society based on the seizure of the territories of the Indigenous population.

One of the enduring components of Canada's foundational narrative is that explorers and settlers arrived from Europe to a *terra nullius*, an "empty land" that could be claimed and used for their own purposes. Missing from this account is any recognition of the sophisticated trading and commercial exchanges, and customs and traditions practised by the various tribes that populated the space now known as Canada. Also missing is recognition of the forms of governance that prevailed.

As Aboriginal Justice Inquiry (AJI) commissioners Alvin Hamilton and Murray Sinclair (1991a: 54) note, "before the arrival of the Europeans, Aboriginal peoples had their own laws and customary practices for maintaining peace and stability within their communities — including the use of force and ostracism to enforce social norms and the role of elders in administering those norms."

While the appropriation of land was a key element of settler colonialism, this colonization process was decidedly racialized. As Patrick Wolfe (2006: 388) explains, "Indigenous North Americans were not killed, driven away, romanticized, assimilated, fenced in, bred White, and otherwise eliminated as the original owners of the land but *as Indians*." European colonizers aimed to eradicate Indigenous societies — what Wolfe (2006: 403) refers to as "structural genocide" in that elimination was not a one-time occurrence but an organizing principle of settler colonial society.

Settler colonization, as Wolfe points out, is "a structure rather than an event" and settler colonialism is "a specific social formation" (2006: 390, 401). As such, colonialism is not simply a historical artifact that has no bearing on contemporary events. Indeed, the racialization of Aboriginal people — "the process through which groups come to be designated as different and on that basis subjected to differential and unequal treatment" (Block and Galabuzi 2011: 19) — has continued into the present day. As Sherene Razack (2007: 74) notes: "As it evolves, a white settler society continues to be structured by a racial hierarchy."

One of the ways in which colonialism has been reproduced in Canada is through the role of the police. Police are the frontline enforcers of the colonial order — and of settler privilege. Police are entrusted to use force, including lethal force, to enforce the laws of the state — in this case a colonial state. In these terms, policing in Canada is "racialized": it is one of the projects through which race is interpreted and given meaning in a racially ordered society and the means by which that society is reproduced. This has been the case historically — as evidenced by the role played by the North West Mounted Police in the initial settlement of the Canadian West — as well as presently — in the role that modern police forces play in the containment and control of Aboriginal people. Understanding Canada's history of colonialism, therefore, requires attention to the strategic role that policing has occupied.

Colonialism Past

In the Canadian context the project of colonizing the Indigenous population and constructing a white settler society was a process that began in the seventeenth century. While Aboriginal peoples were initially valued for their skills and knowledge, as these were indispensable to the survival of the newcomers, this power balance began to shift as more and more Europeans arrived. "By the early 19th century, Eurocanadians had made Aboriginal people a minority in their own lands," Celia Haig-Brown (cited in Dion 2005: 36) states. "Acting through the power of organized religion and colonial governments, Canadians insisted that Aboriginal peoples should abandon their ways, languages, spiritual and economic systems, seasonal movement to hunting and gathering places and most importantly their lands."

This colonial project involved a number of strategies, one of which was signing treaties that the colonizers claimed transferred large tracts of land over to the government. As the Royal Commission on Aboriginal Peoples (RCAP 1996: vol. 1, chap. 8) notes, "Treaties and other agreements were, by and large, not covenants of trust and obligation but devices of statecraft, less expensive and more acceptable than armed conflict." Another colonial strategy was the passage of the *Indian Act* in 1876 — legislation that consolidated previous rulings and provided a national foundation "based unashamedly on the notion that Indian cultures and societies were clearly inferior to settler society" (RCAP 1996: vol. 1, chap. 8). The 1876 annual report of the Department of the Interior expressed the assimilationist and paternalistic philosophy that prevailed at the time:

> Our Indian legislation generally rests on the principle, that the aborigines are to be kept in a condition of tutelage and treated as wards or children of the State ... the true interests of the aborigines and of the State alike require that every effort should be made to aid the Red man in lifting himself out of his condition of tutelage and dependence, and that is clearly our wisdom and our duty, through education and every other means, to prepare him for a higher civilization by encouraging him to assume the privileges and responsibilities of full citizenship. (Cited in RCAP 1996: vol. 1, chap. 8)

The *Indian Act* defined in law who was an "Indian" and specified how someone could lose status as an Indian. An Indian was legally defined as "any male person of Indian blood reputed to belong to a particular band, and any child of such person and any woman who is lawfully married to such a person" (Gibbins and Ponting 1986: 21). Under this definition, an Indian woman who married a non-Indian man ceased to be an Indian in legal terms, and both she and her children lost all claims associated with that status (for example, residence on a reserve, ownership of reserve property, participation in band affairs and eligibility for the modest benefits provided by the government such as limited health care and minimal education). In contrast, a non-Indian woman who married an Indian man would gain legal status as an Indian, as would the children from that union. This provision in the *Indian Act* remained in effect until it was abrogated in 1985 (although, as Brodsky, Eberts and Kuokkanen in this volume emphasize, the negative impact of s. 12.1(b) of the *Indian Act* continues to affect the lives of Aboriginal women and their children). Indians were also denied basic political rights: they did not have a legal right to vote in provincial elections in British Columbia and Newfoundland until 1949, in Quebec until 1969 and in federal elections until 1960.

In addition to replacing traditional systems of governance by a restricted form of democracy in which only men had a voice and vote, the *Indian Act* gave considerable power to the Indian agents, who represented the Department of Indian Affairs. Hamilton and Sinclair state:

> Each agent had full authority to conduct trials anywhere in the country involving Indians charged with violating the *Indian Act* or with certain crimes under the *Criminal Code*. As a result, the Indian agent could direct the police to prosecute "troublemakers" and then sit in judgment. The agents effectively had power over all aspects of daily life. (1991a: 64–65)

Aboriginal[1] peoples governed under the *Indian Act* also experienced considerable restrictions on their mobility. With the loss of their land to the government under the treaty regime, most tribes were relegated to smaller tracts of land as part of the reservation system. A pass system was imposed as early as 1885 under which Indians were prohibited from leaving their reserve without first securing written permission from the local Indian agent. While the pass system had no legislative basis and therefore could not be legally enforced, Indian agents could withhold rations for those who refused to comply, and those found off the reserve without a pass could be prosecuted for trespass under the *Indian Act* or for vagrancy under the *Criminal Code of Canada* (Hamilton and Sinclair 1991; RCAP 1996).

To further the colonial project, the government also created a number of "status" offences. An 1884 amendment to the *Indian Act* outlawed the potlatch (a ceremonial gift-giving set of ceremonies) and *tamanawas* (a medicine or healing ceremony) and imposed sanctions of two to six months' imprisonment for those found in violation. In 1885 another amendment outlawed sun dances (religious ceremonies), providing for imprisonment of two to six months for violators. As Andrea McCalla and Vic Satzewich (2002) note, missionaries — who were tasked with the "civilizing mission" of the colonial project — saw the persistence of these cultural practices as "devil worship" (see also Pettipas 1995). Moreover, the giveaways associated with these cultural practices were inimical to the capitalist ethic — respect for private property and pursuit of individual accumulation — that the government was endeavouring to instill in Aboriginal peoples. As well, the hours taken to prepare for the ceremonies were considered to be time that could be better spent engaging in more "legitimate" economic pursuits. Yet Aboriginal peoples were not passive bystanders to these efforts to outlaw their culture. Resistance took the form of holding ceremonies in secret and altering the practices to make them seem more "acceptable" to European eyes.

One plank of the colonial project that was more difficult to resist was the residential school system, which was initiated in the 1880s with the specific objective of assimilating Aboriginal people into mainstream Canadian society. Aboriginal, primarily status Indian children, were forcibly removed from their homes and transported — often some distance away — to attend these large, racially segregated industrial schools. Attendance was compulsory. Indian agents were empowered to commit children under sixteen to these schools and to keep them there until they were eighteen. By way of contrast, non-Aboriginal children were not subject to compulsory schooling. Manitoba, for instance, did not introduce compulsory schooling until 1916. In addition, federal legislation passed in 1894 allowed for the arrest and conveyance to school of truant Aboriginal children, and for fines or jail terms for parents who resisted (Hamilton and Sinclair 1991). The government delegated this civilizing project of the residential school system to religious organizations and churches, which were given the task of transforming Aboriginal children from "savages" into "citizens" by inculcating the values of Christianity and industry so the youngsters could take up positions as "functioning" members of the emerging capitalist society. By the 1930s eighty residential schools were spread across the country, with children registered from every Aboriginal nation (RCAP 1996: vol. 1, chap. 2). Eventually, a total of 139 residential schools were in operation in Canada. Some 150,000 Aboriginal children — including First Nation, Inuit, and Métis — were forced to attend the schools.

Much has been written in recent times about the residential school system, especially in the wake of revelations by survivors as to the harsh treatment received at the schools (see, for example, York 1990; Hamilton and Sinclair 1991a; RCAP 1996; Milloy 1999; Knockwood 2001; Regan 2010). What we now know from this work is that conditions at the schools were abysmal; they were built with the cheapest materials, employed untrained staff and were overcrowded due to the government's financial inducements to increase enrolments (Blackstone and Trocmé 2004). The expressed goal was to produce educated graduates, but few of the children completed the full course of study. In 1945, for example, no students were enrolled beyond Grade 8 in any of the schools (RCAP 1996: vol. 1, chap. 2). Children were poorly fed and clothed; so many of them died from preventable diseases (such as malnutrition, smallpox and tuberculosis) that several of the schools even had their own graveyards. Physical punishment was the norm. Children were beaten for speaking their Indigenous languages; those who tried to run away were shackled to their beds. Suicide attempts by the children were common. Not only were physical abuse and neglect rampant, but so too was sexual abuse — something that was never cited in all of the major reports on the residential school system and only became public knowledge once survivors began to break the silence and tell their stories (RCAP 1996: vol. 1, chap. 2; Titley 1986).

Colonial Police

While the effort by the European colonizers to take control over the lives of Aboriginal people involved a number of strategies, including treaties, the *Indian Act* and the residential school system, the North West Mounted Police (NWMP) played an instrumental role in carrying out this "civilizing mission." The primary role of the NWMP — like that of other frontier police forces — was "to ensure the submission of Indigenous peoples to colonial rule" (Nettelbeck and Smandych 2010: 357).

The foundational narrative of the NWMP posits that the force was brought into being by a benevolent federal government intent on protecting the Aboriginal population of the North West in the wake of the Cypress Hills Massacre in May 1873, when U.S. whiskey traders murdered a number of Assiniboine people. Lorne and Caroline Brown (1978: 10), however, have a different view: "this is true only in the sense that the massacre hastened the organization of the Force. The establishment of the Force had been planned and officially authorized prior to this, and the primary reason for establishing it was to control the Indian and Métis population of the North West." Prime Minister John A. Macdonald had been making plans for the policing of the North West since 1869. His main concern was the containment of the Indigenous population so they would not impede western white settlement and economic development.

The plans for the NWMP were approved by an order-in-council on April 6, 1870. The force was to march west with the Canadian military in 1870, but this plan was shelved with the passage of the *Manitoba Act*, which left the administration of justice in the hands of the new province. Plans continued, however, for controlling that part of the North West outside of Manitoba, particularly because government officials worried that the Métis of Manitoba would ally themselves with Aboriginal nations further west and take a stand against the federal government. There were also concerns that any unrest would interfere with building the Canadian Pacific Railway and limit plans to settle the area with immigrants. A military presence was therefore increasingly seen as necessary.

Officially established by an act of Parliament in the spring of 1873, the NWMP was "to be a semi-military body directly controlled from Ottawa, and not by the local government officials in the North West" (Brown and Brown 1978: 13). While an earlier proposal had called for the inclusion of Aboriginal people on the force (similar to what had transpired under British colonial rule in India), the Act made no special provisions for this condition. The Red River Resistance of 1869, which began when Louis Riel and eighteen other Métis men confronted a survey crew that was staking out Métis land for the anticipated arrival of settlers, had "convinced the authorities that the native peoples were not likely to become loyal servants of their colonial masters" (1978: 13).

While the force was not intended to be put into effect until 1874, the Cypress Hills Massacre (see Savage 2012) caused the government to speed up its plans. The government's fear was that "the outrage in the Cypress Hills and other atrocities of this nature might provoke the Indians into open warfare against the whites" (Brown and Brown 1978: 13). Also of concern was the unrest generated by the prosecution of some of the activists by the provisional government of 1869–70, with fears raised about the whereabouts and activities of Louis Riel and "the fanaticism of the French Canadian Half-breeds" (cited in Brown and Brown 1978: 14).

The first years of the NWMP were not without controversy. Members of the force encountered severe hardships — poor food, deplorable living conditions, delays in receiving wages and bullying by officers — which led to a high rate of desertion. Concerns were raised about alcoholism and a high percentage of personnel suffering from venereal disease. In 1880 a Member of Parliament from Manitoba reported on the sexual exploitation of Aboriginal women. Prostitution was apparently rampant in the vicinity of NWMP posts, and the police were spreading venereal disease among the Aboriginal population (Brown and Brown 1978: 16)

As Sarah Carter (1999: 129) notes, the NWMP "had powers that were unprecedented in the history of police forces." In addition to the power to arrest, the NWMP were given magisterial powers, which meant that they were also able to prosecute, judge and jail an accused. The force was also charged with implementing the government's policies towards Aboriginal peoples. As AJI commissioners Hamilton and Sinclair (1991a: 592) note:

> Whenever an Indian agent felt the need for assistance in enforcing government policy regarding Indian people, he called upon the [NWMP]. Indian children who ran away from residential schools were sought and returned by NWMP officers. Indian adults who left their reserves without a pass from the Indian agent were apprehended by the Mounted Police.

Given that the historical record was written largely by the white colonizers, the standpoint of Aboriginal peoples during this period of history remains in the shadows — and especially because Aboriginal peoples used oral as opposed to written narratives to communicate and learn from their own past (see RCAP 1996: vol. 1, chap. 3). Nevertheless, we do know that factors such as the mass starvation caused by the virtual extinction of the buffalo, the profound impact of the infectious diseases that newcomers brought with them and the negative effects of the whiskey trade all took their toll on the Indigenous population (Daschuk 2013; Manuel and Posluns 1974). Due to these conditions, some of the people may well have welcomed the presence of the NWMP. Yet, as Brown and Brown (1978: 20) note, "a state of constant tension between the police and the Indian nations" was the norm, given that "the Force represented the interests who were rapidly destroying the Indian economy and way of life and was frequently called upon to protect those same interests."

This tension became even more pronounced during and after the Saskatchewan Rebellion of 1885. Under the leadership of Louis Riel, the Métis of the area rose up against the Canadian government for its failure to recognize and protect their rights, their land and their survival as a distinct people. While the NWMP was not the cause of the rebellion (and repeatedly warned the government that unrest was likely to occur), the force participated along with regular military forces in suppressing it. The NWMP was also instrumental in apprehending and meting out punishment to the rebels, including sentences of imprisonment and the execution of Métis leader Louis Riel and eight other First Nations leaders: Ikta, Little Bear, Wandering Spirit, Round-the-Sky, Miserable Man, Bad Arrow, Man-Without-Blood and Iron Body. Brown and Brown (1978: 22) write:

> The authorities punished Métis and Indians suspected of having sup-
> ported the rebellion regardless of whether they had been tried for specific
> offences. They virtually wiped out the Métis as a distinct national and
> political group. They burned and looted their homes and destroyed their
> property. They withheld annuities from those Indian bands that had par-
> ticipated in the rebellion and confiscated their horses and arms. From that
> time on they made greater efforts to restrict Indians to the reserves and
> strictly regulated the sale of ammunition to them. Most of these punitive
> measures were carried out by the [NWMP].

As Carter (1999: 161) notes, after 1885 a significant shift occurred in Euro-
Canadian attitudes towards Aboriginal people: "If there was a shred of tolerance
before, or the possibility of working towards a progressive partnership, it was
shattered in 1885, as thereafter Aboriginal people were viewed as a threat to the
property and safety of the white settlers." After 1885 government policies aimed
at controlling and monitoring the lives of Aboriginal people were "pursued with
great vigour" (1999: 162). During this period the pass system was implemented
(accompanying the outlawing of practices and ceremonies such as the potlatch
and sun dance). The number of NWMP officers was greatly increased to enhance
the effort to monitor and control the Indigenous population.

    A tradition of active, armed violence was missing from the Canadian experi-
ence, which was notably different from that of the United States. Between 1866
and 1885 the U.S. West saw 943 military engagements (Ennab 2010: 161). By
comparison, the Canadian North West saw only six or seven comparable clashes,
most of them taking place in the two years prior to the Métis resistance of 1885.
As Fadi Ennab (2010: 186) argues, overt physical violence was replaced with
compulsion and coercion:

> It was through intimidation and broken promises along with the larger
> colonial disciplinary system that was shaping the rationalities of the in-
> habitants that a few red-coated Mounties were able to coerce Aboriginal
> people to stay on reserves. If it was not for this, the NWMP would have
> needed more investment in the ongoing, armed engagements, which
> they could not afford, thus jeopardizing the entire colonial enterprise.
> Most Aboriginal people recognized that even if the NWMP were not able
> to "destroy" them, they were able to push them on the side to starve.

Historians have uncovered many instances where members of the NWMP acted
with fairness and concern towards Aboriginal people. But as Brown and Brown
(1978: 19) argue:

> That certain individuals in the Force sympathized with the plight of the
> Indians and attempted to carry out a disagreeable task in as humane a

manner as possible does not alter the nature of the Force and their work. Most police officials knew whose interests they served and knew that to be "too soft on Indians" endangered their career in the Force.

As such, even though the conquest of the Canadian West was not nearly so bloody an affair as it was in the Western United States, and violence by the frontier police against the Indigenous population was not as rife as it was in the Australian context (Nettelbeck and Smandych 2010), the NWMP did play a crucial role in implementing the colonial project. The NWMP, according to Brown and Brown, was "a crucial part of a conscious scheme by which powerful economic and political interests destroyed the economy and way of life of entire peoples and wrested a vast territory from its inhabitants for a pittance." Moreover, these authors argue, "Anyone who describes the role of the NWMP during this period as constituting the 'glorious foundations of a great tradition' must surely be either hopelessly naïve or lacking in moral sensitivity" (1978: 23).

In 1904 the North West Mounted Police was re-named the Royal North West Mounted Police (RNWMP) in recognition of its service to the Empire. As settlement of the West continued, with Saskatchewan and Alberta gaining provincial status in 1905, the RNWMP acted in the capacity of a provincial police force. The modern version of the force — the Royal Canadian Mounted Police — came into being in 1920 when the RNWMP was amalgamated with the Dominion Police. During the Great Depression of the 1930s, the RCMP expanded its scope, as some of the provinces and many smaller municipalities facing financial troubles disbanded their police forces and contracted the RCMP instead. This contractual relationship continues to the present day.

This history of the NWMP has a direct connection to contemporary relations between Aboriginal people and the police. As AJI Commissioners Hamilton and Sinclair note, memories of the treatment at the hands of the force "linger in many communities" and "the impact of past wrongs has been reinforced by the negative experiences of today" (Hamilton and Sinclair 1991a: 593). Those negative experiences include conflicts with police (as well as the Canadian army) over the appropriation of Indigenous land at Oka, Quebec, in 1990 and at Gustafson Lake, B.C., and Ipperwash Provincial Park, Ontario, in 1995.

Just as significant, the strategies of the colonial project laid down in the earlier period of Canadian history have had profound and long-lasting impacts. The *Indian Act* of 1876 — with its decidedly paternalistic and assimilationist bent — continues to constrain and shape the lives of First Nation peoples. Although the Act has been repeatedly amended, its fundamental provisions and intentions have remained intact. It "still holds a symbolic but powerful grip on the thinking of Canadians" towards Aboriginal peoples (RCAP 1996: vol. 1, chap. 8). Similarly, residential schools have had a profound and long-lasting impact. Although phasing out began in the late 1940s, it was not until 1996 that the last federally run residential school was shut down (DIAND 2003). The generations of children who attended the schools were cut off from their families, their communities and their cultural and spiritual teachings. Survivors were confronted with the difficult challenge of healing from years of abuse and neglect. Being deprived of healthy parenting role models also left many with diminished capacities as adults to raise and care for their own children. In the words of the AJI commissioners, "These policies have caused a wound to fester in Aboriginal communities that has left them diminished to this day" (Hamilton and Sinclair 1991: 505).

Colonialism Present

Colonialism — the construction of unequal relations of power between the colonizers and the colonized — has not disappeared in contemporary times. It has taken on new forms. One of the ways in which colonialism is perpetuated is through racialized discourse. While past discourses cast Aboriginal people as "savage," "inferior" and "child-like" (and therefore in need of a civilizing influence and the benevolent paternalism of the state), more contemporary discourses include the notions of the "welfare recipient," the "drunken Indian" and the "criminal Other" (and therefore in need of heightened surveillance and control). As with discourses generally, these racialized constructions have their basis in real material conditions. In contemporary times, social exclusion and poverty have dominated the lives of too many Aboriginal people.

Social exclusion, as Grace-Edward Galabuzi (2009: 253) notes, "is used to broadly describe the structures and the dynamic processes of inequality among groups in society, which, over time, structure access to critical resources that determine the quality of membership in society." These conditions define "the inability of certain subgroups to participate fully in Canadian life." Social exclusion is "also characterized by processes of group or individual isolation within and from Canadian societal institutions such as the school system, criminal justice system, health care system, as well as spatial isolation or neighbourhood segregation" (2009: 254).

Poverty is both a product and a cause of social exclusion, and it is also a racialized phenomenon in Canada. Being born Aboriginal means an increased likelihood of living in poverty. Almost 1.2 million people in Canada reported Aboriginal identity in the 2006 census, representing 3.8 percent of the total Canadian population (Statistics Canada 2008). In 2005, 18.7 percent of Aboriginal families and 42.8 percent of unattached individuals who identified as Aboriginal experienced low income, compared to 8.4 percent of families and 28 percent of unattached individuals who were non-Aboriginal (Collin and Jensen 2009). Children and youth account for just under half (48 percent) of the Aboriginal population, and some 35 percent of Aboriginal children live with a lone parent, which means that Aboriginal adults will often be on their own, providing for a larger group of dependants than non-Aboriginal adults (Smylie 2009: 291). The poverty gap is most pronounced in the Prairie Provinces. In Saskatchewan, for instance, where Aboriginal people make up 15 percent of the population, an Aboriginal person is about three and a half times more likely to be poor than a non-Aboriginal resident (Noël 2009: 8). While conditions vary by region, if we were to apply the United Nations Human Development Index to First Nations communities in Canada, they would rank 68 out of 174 nations. By comparison, Canada is in the eighth position (Graydon 2008).

Living conditions on many reserves have been defined as a matter of crisis proportions. Substandard and overcrowded housing is one pressing issue. In 2006, 28 percent of First Nations people were living in a home in need of major repairs, compared with just 7 percent of the non-Aboriginal population; First Nations people were five times more likely than non-Aboriginal people to live in crowded homes (Statistics Canada 2008). Access to potable water, adequate sanitation and waste disposal services are resources that many Canadians take for granted. Yet in November 2010, 117 First Nation communities were under drinking water advisories (Campaign 2000 2010). Many reserve communities still do not have running water or sewer lines. These living conditions undermine the health of a community. Aboriginal people have shorter life expectancy and a higher risk of suffering from infectious diseases such as tuberculosis and chronic illnesses such as diabetes. The Royal Commission (RCAP 1996; vol. 3, chap. 3) found that rates of tuberculosis infection were forty-three times higher among registered Indians than among non-Aboriginal Canadians born in this country, and the incidence rate for diabetes was at least two to three times higher among Aboriginal than among non-Aboriginal people. These impoverished conditions generate a sense of hopelessness and despair. While the suicide rates vary widely among First Nations communities, the youth suicide rate in these communities is still between three and seven times greater than in Canada overall (Campaign 2000 2010).

Deteriorating social and economic conditions in many First Nations communities have prompted increased migration between First Nations communities and urban centres. As John Loxley (2010) notes, remarkably few Aboriginal people were living in urban centres up to the 1950s. As of 2006, however, over half (54 percent) of the Aboriginal population of Canada now live in urban centres (Statistics Canada 2008). Conditions for Aboriginal people living in these urban settings are often no better than on reserves. Aboriginal residents of urban areas are more than twice as likely to live in poverty as non-Aboriginal residents. In 2000, for instance, 55.6 percent of urban Aboriginal people lived below the poverty line compared with 24.5 percent of non-Aboriginal urban residents (NCCAH 2009–10). In 2006, almost half (49 percent) of First Nations children living off-reserve and nearly one-third (32 percent) of Métis children were members of low-income families (Collin and Jensen 2009: 19).

The highest concentration of urban Aboriginal people is in the inner-city communities of major cities in the Western provinces. Of the major cities in

Canada, Winnipeg has the highest density of Aboriginal people — 68,385 in 2006 (United Way Winnipeg 2010: 40). While Aboriginal people make up 10 percent of Winnipeg's population, they constitute 25 percent of those living in poverty (MacKinnon, 2009: 30). Unemployment explains some of this disparity. As RCAP (1996) notes: "Aboriginal people living in urban centers fare somewhat better than reserve residents in gaining employment, but their unemployment rate is still two and a half times the unemployment rate of non-Aboriginal people, and their total annual income from all sources lags behind by 33 percent."

Jim Silver (2006: 17) has observed that "the spatial distribution of Aboriginal people in cities ... parallels their spatial distribution outside urban centres." That is, just as Aboriginal people have historically been confined to rural reserves, now in cities they are being set apart from the mainstream Canadian life. Their "move to the city is too often a move from one marginalized community to another" — creating what Razack (2000, 2002) refers to as the racialization of spaces inhabited by Aboriginal people. But colonialism has produced more than just the social and economic marginalization of Aboriginal people in contemporary Canadian society.

There is an inescapable connection between the colonial forces that have shaped Aboriginal communities and the criminalization and over-incarceration of Aboriginal people. Although Aboriginal people made up just 3 percent of the Canadian population in 2010–11, they accounted for 27 percent of admissions to provincial and territorial jails and 20 percent of admissions to federal prisons (Dauvergne 2012). This overrepresentation is most acute in the Prairie Provinces. In Saskatchewan, Aboriginal people made up 11 percent of the population and 81 percent of provincially sentenced custody admissions in 2007–8. In Manitoba, Aboriginal people made up only 15 percent of the population yet represented 69 percent of provincially sentenced custody admissions (Perrault 2009). As Michael Jackson (1989: 216) observes, prison has become for too many young Aboriginal people the contemporary equivalent of what the Indian residential school represented for their parents.

Colonial Police, Again

While it would be convenient to rest an explanation for the disproportionate incarceration rates of Aboriginal people on crime-producing conditions in their families and communities — that is, to simply frame the issue as a problem "of" Aboriginal people — such an explanation neglects the role of policing in the production of crime.

In his now classic study, Richard Ericson (1982) develops the argument that contemporary police forces "are essentially a vehicle for the 'reproduction of order.'" Their mandate is "to transform troublesome, fragile situations back into a normal or efficient state whereby the ranks of society are preserved." But as Ericson clarifies, "it is not the mandate of police to produce a 'new' order." Rather, "their sense of order and the order they seek to reproduce are that of the status quo." As well, Ericson specifies: "the term 'reproduction' implies that order is not simply transmitted in an unproblematic manner but is worked at through processes of conflict, negotiation, and subjection" (1982: 7).

Ericson's formulation has relevance for situating contemporary policing within its colonial context. Similar to the role played by the NWMP in the colonial project of creating the white settler society, contemporary police forces in Canadian society have been assigned a central role in the management and containment of Aboriginal people. This is especially the case in the urban centres of the Prairie Provinces. It falls to the police as "reproducers of order" to devote their considerable resources to the realization of that objective.

One event that has come to symbolize the colonial relationship between the police and Aboriginal people in contemporary times is the shooting death of Aboriginal leader John Joseph (J.J.) Harper by a Winnipeg police officer. Early on the morning of March 9, 1988, Harper was walking home along an inner-city street when he was approached by a police officer. The police had been looking for a suspect in a car theft. Despite the fact that the suspect was reported to already be in police custody, and that Harper was much older and of a stockier build than the young man police were looking for, the officer made the decision to stop Harper anyway. A struggle ensued and Harper was shot with the officer's revolver. Harper's tragic death became one of two incidents — the other being the murder of Helen Betty Osborne by four white men in The Pas, Manitoba, in 1971 — which led to the establishment of the Aboriginal Justice Inquiry of Manitoba in April 1989. In their report, commissioners Hamilton and Sinclair attribute Harper's death to the racism that existed in the Winnipeg police department (Hamilton and Sinclair 1991b: 93; see also Sinclair 1999; Comack 2012, chap. 4).

More recently, the freezing deaths of three Aboriginal men — Neil Stonechild, Rodney Naistus and Lawrence Wegner — and the experience of Darrel Night in Saskatoon set off a tidal wave of controversy revolving around the issue of "Starlight Tours" — a seemingly benign term that connotes the police practice of detaining people, driving them to another location and leaving them there to find their own way home (see Reber and Renaud 2005; Comack 2012, chap. 5). Stonechild's body was discovered on the outskirts of Saskatoon in November 1990. Some ten years later, in January 2000, the bodies of Naistus and Wegner were found within five days of each other. The day after Wegner's body was found Darrel Night told a police officer that he had encountered a similar experience. Night said that he had been taken out of town by two Saskatoon police officers and dropped off not far from where the bodies of Nastius and Wegner were discovered. Despite being dressed in only a jean jacket and summer shoes, Night managed to survive the bitterly cold weather by attracting the attention of a worker at a nearby power plant. The worker let him into the building to warm up and phone for a taxi. A commission to investigate the death of Neil Stonechild deemed the police investigation into his death to be "insufficient and totally inadequate" (Wright 2004: 212). The two officers who had Stonechild in their custody that night were subsequently dismissed from the

Saskatoon Police Service. While no one was ever held to account for the deaths of Naistus and Wegner, the two officers who had Night in their custody were found guilty of unlawful confinement and sentenced to eight months' imprisonment and were dismissed from the Saskatoon Police Service. Aboriginal activists and organizations, meanwhile, declared the practice of Starlight Tours to be evidence of the racism that was rampant on the Saskatoon police force (see also Green 2006).

Saskatoon is not the only Prairie city in Canada where troubling relations between Aboriginal people and the police prevail. Manitoba's largest urban centre, Winnipeg, is home to a large proportion of the province's Aboriginal population, many of whom reside in the inner city. While inner-city residents take pride in their community and see its many strengths and benefits (CCPA–MB 2007; Comack and Silver 2006; Silver 2006), these neighbourhoods are characterized by extreme poverty, inadequate housing, high unemployment and limited recreational and other resources (MacKinnon 2009; Deane 2006; Lezubski, Silver and Black 2000; Kazemipur and Halli 2000). As a result, very large numbers of inner-city people have been "raised poor" and have never known anything but poverty and joblessness.

Given such impoverished conditions, it is not surprising that crime and violence flourish in Winnipeg's inner city. This is particularly so when street drugs are readily available as a means of escape and can be bought and sold at prices and in volumes sufficient for the traffickers to earn a living beyond what they could earn from menial service-sector jobs. The illegal trade in drugs has become more and more insidious in Winnipeg over the last decade, with drugs such as crack cocaine and crystal methamphetamine being distributed on the street and via "crack houses" in inner-city neighbourhoods. For young — and disproportionately Aboriginal — women, working in the street sex trade is often their only recourse for getting by, which puts them at risk for violence and leads to drugging and drinking as a means for coping with the work (Brown et al. 2006; Seshia 2005). Tied up with the drug and street sex trades, street gangs have become a more prominent feature of life in Winnipeg's inner-city communities. Troubles at home, at school and on the street, as well as troubles that emanate from being taken into custody by the state and placed into foster and group homes or in detention centres have prompted some young Aboriginal people to resist their poverty and colonial condition by acting collectively (Comack et al. 2013). In the 1990s Winnipeg gained a reputation as the "gang capital of Canada," and the names Indian Posse, Native Syndicate and Manitoba Warriors became part of the public discourse. While only some people may choose this pathway, all those who reside in inner-city communities where the street gangs operate are tasked with negotiating the violence that pervades their social spaces. Because of the inner city's reputation as a disorderly and dangerous place in which crime, violence, gangs and the drug and street sex trades proliferate, police surveillance is heightened. Just being present in that space, therefore, means that Aboriginal people are at risk of being targeted as the "usual suspects."

In 2008 and 2009 I had the opportunity to interview seventy-eight Aboriginal people residing in Winnipeg's inner city about their encounters with police (see Comack 2012, Appendix). When interviewed, Aboriginal men report being regularly stopped by the police and asked to account for themselves. When the men ask, "What did I do wrong?" the typical response is "You fit the description" because the police are looking for an Aboriginal man as a suspect in a crime. In other words, the men are stopped precisely because they are Aboriginal. For many Aboriginal men living in Winnipeg's inner city, this experience has become all too normal an occurrence. One twenty-year-old man, for instance, reported that he is accustomed to being stopped by police "once a week, guaranteed. I can't even, like, count the number of times where I've been stopped just for walking down the street wearing, like, all black or something." When asked what the police say when they stop him he replied, "Nothing. Just, like, put some cuffs on me and say, 'Oh, we have a guy fitting your description. He's breaking into garages or throwing stuff at houses.' It makes me mad. But, like, there's nothing you can do." Another twenty-four-year-old man has had similarly frustrating experiences with police. Since the age of sixteen he has been stopped "at least twice a month" by police because he apparently fit the description of someone police were looking for.

One of the challenges confronting Winnipeg police officers in their endeavour to reproduce order is quelling the illegal trade in drugs that goes on in the inner city. Several men talked about how the police just assume they are involved in the drug trade. One thirty-year-old man, for instance, told of an incident when he had been standing in front of his house, "and my friend, my neighbour, he was giving me ten dollars so I can go get some beer for him. 'Cause I had a bike so I was going to the beer store for him." The police happened by and saw the exchange. "They grabbed me, searched me and everything, thinking I got drugs or something. I didn't have nothing." A nineteen-year-old man told of being pulled over by police "countless times." The police, assuming he was dealing drugs for a street gang, would ask him: "Who are you selling for?" "Who are you banging for?" "Where's the shit?" Another man in his thirties said that police would assume he was gang-involved when he wore a white track suit (associated with the Deuce gang) or a red one (Indian Posse). "They would beat you up and they would try to make you rat out where drug houses are and that. It was scary, scary growing up being Native in this neighbourhood."

While Aboriginal men are assumed by police to be involved in the drug trade and/or affiliated with a street gang, Aboriginal women encounter a different kind of stereotyping. Given the concerns with the street sex trade that operates in Winnipeg's inner-city neighbourhoods, police often assume than Aboriginal women found in those spaces are sex workers. As one woman noted: "They see a girl on a strip where prostitutes happen to roam, they automatically stereotype and think that they're, every girl out there is doing the same thing when, in reality, you know, half the girls that are out there aren't even working. They're just walking by or whatever."

For many Aboriginal people living in Winnipeg's inner-city communities, how the police chose to interact with them is a matter of importance. In particular, many people spoke of the way police officers put them down. As one woman queried, "Why do they have to treat us with such disrespect?" More often than not, this attitude shows up in the language they use. According to many of the people interviewed, police officers regularly use words like "squaw," "dirty Indian" or "fuckin' Indian" in their encounters with Aboriginal people. As one woman said, "I've heard it so many times from their mouths I just don't say anything anymore." The use of racist and sexist language by police obviously runs counter to the professional image of the police officer and the "core values" of honesty, integrity, trust, respect, accountability and commitment to excellence that the Winnipeg Police Service professes to uphold (Winnipeg Police Service 2009). While the use of such language may emanate from the effort to reproduce order, at its core it constitutes a power move that has the effect of silencing and marginalizing Aboriginal people. When such language is heard "so many times from their mouths" it becomes a routine part of the everyday life of Aboriginal people living in Winnipeg's inner city, thereby contributing to the perpetuation of a colonial order.

Even more concerning are the troublesome police practices reported by Aboriginal people. While the use of force by police officers is officially sanctioned, the conditions under which officers use force and whether the amount of force used is reasonable under the circumstances are contentious issues (Hoffman 2011). One of the ironies to emerge from the interviews with Aboriginal people is that police are tasked with the job of responding to the violence that occurs in the inner city, but, in the process, violence appears to have become one of the strategies that police themselves use in the reproduction of order.

People who are involved with street gangs appear to be especially prone to encountering violence from the police. One twenty-eight-year-old man, for instance, reported that he was part of a street gang when he was a teenager, and that brought him into conflict with the law. He acknowledged that his crimes were "pretty violent." So too was the response of the police. He told of one night when he was arrested and taken to the police station with two of his friends:

> They put us each in a cell and they confined us to three cells, side by side. And they started doing interviews? And the interviews, they were not interviews, there were five guys walking, five un-uniformed officers walking into the cell and beating the living daylights out of you to try to make you confess for what you did. And so I listened to the guy in the next cell. And he was just screaming and hollering. And then my turn came around and then I just gave up.

The young man said that he told the police "everything because I couldn't stand the assaults. I couldn't take it. So I just, whatever they said, I just agreed, and that was it." Participants also spoke of other troublesome police practices, including being subject to "the phone book treatment" (which involved placing a phone book against their head or body so that when they were hit it would not leave telltale bruises) and getting "red zoned" or banned from certain areas of the city. Similar to the events in Saskatoon, the matter of Starlight Tours emerged in thirteen of the seventy-eight interviews. While some of these "tours" had occurred several years previously, others were much more recent. One woman in her thirties, for instance, told of an experience that happened to her just a few months before our meeting. It was a minus-40 degree Celsius evening when the police came along and "grabbed" her. They drove her to the outskirts of the city, where they took her shoes and jacket and then abandoned her there to find her own way back. The woman managed to make it back to an inner-city homeless shelter, but didn't want to tell the staff about her experience "because I was scared they were going to call the cops and I'd get more harassed again. So I just left it at that and I didn't want to tell nothing to nobody."

The experiences of Aboriginal people with the policing of Winnipeg's inner-city communities suggest that racialization is deeply integrated into the routine practices of police officers. In reproducing order, police concentrate their attention and activity on the racialized space of the inner city. Not only is that space constituted as disorderly and dangerous, so too are the people who inhabit it. But the issue is more complicated than simply racial profiling or the stereotyping of Aboriginal people. Having defined (and experienced some) Aboriginal people as troublesome, the police respond with troublesome practices of their own — a response that clearly violates Aboriginal people's right to be afforded the protection of law, and to be treated with respect and dignity.

Over two decades ago AJI commissioners Hamilton and Sinclair (1991a: 593–94) came to a harsh conclusion about relations between Aboriginal people and the police in Winnipeg.

> We heard testimony that police-Aboriginal relations in the city of Winnipeg are not good. We heard complaints about the police refusing to follow up on allegations of assault. We heard of Aboriginal people being stopped on the street or in cars for no reason. Those arrested were afraid of the police and many reported being beaten by police officers. The large number of complaints which we received points to a problem of considerable magnitude concerning how Aboriginal people are treated by Winnipeg police.

Just as the AJI commissioners concluded two decades ago, more recent reports of Aboriginal people about their experiences with police provide a collective narrative that documents "a problem of considerable magnitude."

We *Do* Have a History of Colonialism

While Prime Minister Harper maintains that Canada has no history of colonialism, the historical record belies that assertion. Not only has colonialism been a defining feature of the Canadian landscape, when we enquire, as Patricia Monture (2006: 89) has done, "How was all of this delivered?" the answer is simple: "through law." The police have been the frontline enforcers of colonialism — both historically in terms of the strategic part played by the North West Mounted Police in ushering in the settler colonial society and in contemporary times in terms of the task assigned to police as reproducers of order in containing and controlling Aboriginal people. As Phillip Stenning and his colleagues (2009: 98, emphasis in original) remind us, "Police organizations are not commonly called 'police *forces*' for no reason."

Yet, just as our prime minister can state publicly that "we also have no history of colonialism," when confronted with the "problem of considerable magnitude" — the longstanding colonial relation between Aboriginal people and the police — the response is more often than not one of denial that the problem even exists. Aboriginal people who make public their negative experiences with police, such as in the Saskatoon case of Darrel Night, are readily cast as unbelievable. Aboriginal organizations and their spokespeople are regularly accused of "playing the race card" to advance their own political agenda when they name racism (see Comack and Bowness 2010). Journalists who write about the issue are chastised for engaging in "political correctness," and criminal justice officials who take action on incidents of racialized policing are criticized for being "too soft on crime" or acceding to the demands of "special interest groups" (McLean 2006).

Both the argument and the evidence for how racialization pervades policing practices have been mounted many times. The Ontario Commission on Systemic Racism in the Criminal Justice System (Ontario 1995: 106) concluded that "systemic racism, the social process that produces racial inequality in how people are treated, is at work in the Ontario criminal justice system." The Ontario Human Rights Commission (2003) found that the experience of being racially profiled by police has become routine for people of colour, and the impact of that experience has been profound. While the Aboriginal Justice Inquiry of Manitoba concluded that "Racism exists within the Winnipeg Police Department" (Hamilton and Sinclair 1991b: 93), the Royal Commission on the Donald Marshall, Jr. Prosecution deemed racism to be at work in the Sydney, Nova Scotia, police force, and that it was spawned from the "general sense in Sydney's White community at the time that Indians were not 'worth' as much as Whites" (Nova Scotia 1989: 3). Despite the combined weight of all of these pronouncements by government-sponsored commissions and inquiries, racialized policing practices persist.

As Joyce Green notes in her chapter in this volume, undermining Indigenous people's security and human rights in Canada is not happenstance. It seems that mainstream settler society is content to assign the job of reproducing a colonial order to the police. In that regard, recent conservative calls to "get tough" on crime by enhancing police powers of arrest and imposing harsher sanctions on those caught in the net of the criminal justice system carry a ready appeal (see Mallea 2011). Implicit in the public support for these "get tough" strategies is the assumption that they will not be directed at "Us" — the "ordinary citizen" — but only at "Them" — those deemed to be "trouble." So if aggressive policing strategies are directed at welfare recipients, the homeless, street sex trade workers, street gang members or other "troublesome" members of society, then so be it. If these strategies extend to include entire inner-city communities populated by Aboriginal people, then so be it. In these terms, the order that the police are reproducing is indeed one that privileges the colonizers.

The longstanding colonial history of Canada — and the denial of fundamental rights of Indigenous people that is integral to colonialism — raises doubts about the possibilities for realizing substantive change. Nonetheless, while colonialism has been delivered through law, and while police forces have been key players in that process, its future is not certain. Law is a contested terrain fraught with contradictions and inconsistencies. As historian E.P. Thompson (1975) suggests, for law to maintain its legitimacy, to live up to its appearance as fair and just, it must at times truly dispense justice. Exposing those inconsistencies and insisting that law lives up to its ideal can thereby open up the potential for change. Moreover, as Ericson (1982) notes, police may be tasked with the job of reproducing the order of the status quo, but that order is not simply transmitted in an unproblematic fashion. Resistance can take numerous forms, but a necessary first step is to acknowledge that we *do* have a history of colonialism — and that colonialism is an affront to the fundamental rights of Indigenous people.

Notes

Thanks are due to Joyce Green and Wayne Antony for their insightful feedback on an earlier version of this chapter. Much of what is produced here is drawn from my book *Racialized Policing: Aboriginal People's Encounters with the Police* (2012).

1. In Canada, "Aboriginal peoples" includes status and non-status Indians, Métis and Inuit peoples. While the *Indian Act* is concerned with status Indians only, primarily on reserves, all Aboriginal people have been racialized in the context of the colonial state. The preferred nomenclature for "Indians" is now First Nations, and most reserves incorporate that term into their names.

References

Blackstone, C., and N. Trocmé. 2004. "Community Based Child Welfare for Aboriginal Children: Supporting Resilience through Structural Change." <cecw-cepb.ca/sites/default/files/publications/en/communityBasedCWAboriginalChildren.pdf>.

Block, S., and G.-E. Galabuzi. 2011. *Canada's Colour Coded Labour Market: The Gap for Racialized Workers*. Ottawa and Toronto: Canadian Centre for Policy Alternatives and the Wellsley Institute.

Brown, J., N. Higgitt, C. Miller, S. Wingert, M. Williams, and L. Morrissette. 2006.

"Challenges Faced by Women Working in the Inner City Sex Trade." *Canadian Journal of Urban Research* 15, 1: 36–53.

Brown, L., and C. Brown. 1978. *An Unauthorized History of the* RCMP. Toronto: James Lorimer.

Campaign 2000. 2010. *Report Card on Child and Family Poverty in Canada: 1989–2010.* <campaign2000.ca/reportCards/national/2010EnglishC2000NationalReportCard.pdf>.

Carter, S. 1999. *Aboriginal People and Colonizers of Western Canada to 1900.* Toronto: University of Toronto Press.

CCPA–MB (Canadian Centre for Policy Alternatives–Manitoba). 2007. *Step by Step: Stories of Change in Winnipeg's Inner City.* <policyalternatives.ca/sites/default/files/uploads/publications/Manitoba_Pubs/2007/State_of_the_Inner_City2007.pdf>.

Collin, C., and H. Jensen. 2009. *A Statistical Profile of Poverty in Canada.* Ottawa: Library of Parliament. <parl.gc.ca/Content/LOP/ResearchPublications/prb0917-e.htm#a9>.

Comack, E. 2012. *Racialized Policing: Aboriginal People's Encounters with the Police.* Halifax and Winnipeg: Fernwood Publishing.

Comack, E., and E. Bowness. 2010. "Dealing the Race Card: Public Discourse on the Policing of Winnipeg's Inner-City Communities." *Canadian Journal of Urban Research* 19, 1: 34–50.

Comack, E., L. Deane, L. Morrissette, and J. Silver. 2013. *"Indians Wear Red": Colonialism, Resistance, and Aboriginal Street Gangs.* Halifax and Winnipeg: Fernwood Publishing.

Comack, E., and J. Silver. 2006. *Safety and Security in Winnipeg's Inner-City Communities: Bridging the Community-Police Divide.* Winnipeg: CCPA-MB.

Daschuk, James. 2013. *Clearing the Plains: Disease, Politics of Starvation, and the Loss of Aboriginal Life.* Regina: University of Regina Press.

Dauvergne, M. 2012. "Adult Correctional Statistics in Canada, 2010/2011." *Juristat* 85, 2.

Deane, L. 2006. *Under One Roof: Community Economic Development and Housing in the Inner City.* Halifax: Fernwood Publishing.

DIAND (Department of Indian Affairs and Northern Development). 2003. *Backgrounder: The Residential School System.* Ottawa: Indian and Northern Affairs Canada. <ainc-inac.gc.ca/gs/schl_e.html>.

Dion, S. 2005. "Aboriginal People and Stories of Canadian History: Investigating Barriers to Transforming Relationships." In C. James (ed.), *Possibilities and Limitations: Multicultural Policies and Programs in Canada.* Halifax: Fernwood.

Ennab, F. 2010. "Rupturing the Myth of the Peaceful Western Canadian Frontier: A Socio-Historical Study of Colonization, Violence, and the North West Mounted Police, 1873–1905." Master's thesis, Department of Sociology, University of Manitoba. <mspace.lib.umanitoba.ca/handle/1993/4109>.

Ericson, R. 1982. *Reproducing Order: A Study of Police Patrol Work.* Toronto: University of Toronto Press.

Galabuzi, G.E. 2009. "Social Exclusion." In D. Raphael (ed.), *Social Determinants of Health: Canadian Perspectives* (2nd ed.). Toronto: Canadian Scholars' Press.

Gibbins, R., and R. Ponting. 1986. "Historical Background and Overview." In R. Ponting (ed.), *Arduous Journey.* Toronto: McLelland and Stewart.

Graydon, J. 2008. "Canadian Aboriginal Reserves in Crisis: Long-Term Solutions Are Needed to Stop the Cycle of Poverty." <suite101.com/content/canadian-reserves-in-crisis-a78339>.

Green, Joyce. 2006. "From *Stonechild* to Social Cohesion: Anti-Racist Challenges for Saskatchewan." *Canadian Journal of Political Science* 39, 9.

Hamilton, A.C., and C.M. Sinclair (Commissioners). 1991a. *Report of the Aboriginal Justice Inquiry of Manitoba. Volume 1. The Justice System and Aboriginal People.* Winnipeg: Queen's Printer.

____. 1991b. *Report of the Aboriginal Justice Inquiry of Manitoba. Volume 2. The Deaths of Helen Betty Osborne and John Joseph Harper.* Winnipeg: Queen's Printer.

Harper, S. 2008. "Statement of Apology — To Former Students of Indian Residential Schools." <pm.gc.ca/eng/news/2008/06/11/pm-offers-full-apology-behalf-vsna-dians-indian-residential-schools-system>.

Hoffman, M.A. 2011. "Canada's National Use-of-Force Framework for Police Officers." *The Police Chief* (April). <policechiefmagazine.org/magazine/index.cfm?fuseaction=display_arch&article_id=1397&issue_id=102004>.

Jackson, M. 1989. "Locking up Natives in Canada." *University of British Columbia Law Review* 23: 215–300.

Kazemipur, A., and S.S. Halli. 2000. *The New Poverty in Canada: Ethnic Groups and Ghetto Neighbourhoods.* Toronto: Thompson.

Knockwood, I. 2001. *Out of the Depths: The Experiences of Mi'kmaw Children at the Indian Residential School at Shubenacadie, Nova Scotia* (3rd edition). Halifax: Rosewood.

Lezubski, D., J. Silver, and E. Black. 2000. "High and Rising: The Growth of Poverty in Winnipeg's Inner City." In Jim Silver (ed.), *Solutions that Work: Fighting Poverty in Winnipeg.* Halifax: Fernwood Publishing.

Loxley, J. 2010. *Aboriginal, Northern, and Community Economic Development: Papers and Retrospectives.* Winnipeg: Arbeiter Ring.

MacKinnon, S. 2009. "Tracking Poverty in Winnipeg's Inner City: 1996–2006." *State of the Inner City Report 2009.* Winnipeg: Canadian Centre for Policy Alternatives–Manitoba.

Mallea, P. 2011. *Fearmonger: Stephen Harper's Tough on Crime Agenda.* Toronto: James Lorimer.

Manuel, George, and Michael Posluns. 1974. *The Fourth World: An Indian Reality.* New York: Free Press.

McCalla, A., and V. Satzewich. 2002. "Settler Capitalism and the Construction of Immigrants and 'Indians' as Racialized Others." In W. Chan and K. Mirchandani (eds.), *Crimes of Colour: Racialization and the Criminal Justice System in Canada.* Peterborough: Broadview Press.

McLean, C. 2006. *When Police Become Prey: What Lies Behind Starlight Tours.* Video. Calgary: Silver Harvest Productions.

McLeod, J. 2000. *Beginning Postcolonialism.* New York: Palgrave.

Milloy, J. 1999. *A National Crime: The Canadian Government and the Residential School System, 1879 to 1986.* Winnipeg: University of Manitoba Press.

Monture, P. 2006. "Standing Against Canadian Law: Naming Omissions of Race, Culture, and Gender." In E. Comack (ed.), *Locating Law: Race/Class/Gender/Sexuality Connections* (2nd ed.). Halifax and Winnipeg: Fernwood Publishing.

NCCAH (National Collaborating Centre for Aboriginal Health). 2009–2010. *Poverty as a Social Determinant of First Nations, Inuit, and Métis Health.* <nccah-ccnsa.ca/docs/fact%20sheets/social%20determinates/NCCAH_fs_poverty_EN.pdf>.

Nettelbeck, A., and R. Smandych. 2010. "Policing Indigenous Peoples on Two Colonial Frontiers: Australia's Mounted Police and Canada's North-West Mounted Police." *The*

Australian and New Zealand Journal of Criminology 43, 2: 356–75.

Noël, A. 2009. "Aboriginal Peoples and Poverty in Canada: Can Provincial Governments Make a Difference?" Paper presented at the Annual Meeting of the International Sociological Association's Research Committee 19, Montreal, August 20. <cccg. umontreal.ca/RC19/PDF/Noel-A_Rc192009.pdf>.

Nova Scotia. 1989. *Royal Commission on the Donald Marshall, Jr., Prosecution: Digest of Findings and Recommendations.* (Chief Justice T. Alexander Hickman, Chairman). <gov.ns.ca/just/marshall_inquiry/_docs/Royal%20Commission%20on%20the%20 Donald%20Marshall%20Jr%20Prosecution_findings.pdf>.

O'Keefe, Derrick. 2009. "Harper in Denial at G20: Canada has 'No History of Colonialism.'" <rabble.ca/blogs/bloggers/derrick/2009/09/harper-denial-g20-canada-has-no-history-colonialism>.

OHRC (Ontario Human Rights Commission). 2003. *Paying the Price: The Human Cost of Racial Profiling.* Inquiry Report. Toronto: Ontario Human Rights Commission.

Ontario. 1995. *Report of the Commission on Systemic Racism in the Ontario Criminal Justice System.* (Margaret Gittens and David Cole, Co-Chairs). Toronto: Queen's Printer.

Perreault, S. 2009. "The Incarceration of Aboriginal People in Adult Correctional Services." *Juristat* 29, 3.

Pettipas, K. 1995. *Severing the Ties that Bind: Government Repression of Indigenous Religious Ceremonies on the Prairies.* Winnipeg: University of Manitoba Press.

Razack, Sherene. 2000. "Gendered Racial Violence and Spatialized Justice: The Murder of Pamela George." *Canadian Journal of Law and Society* 15, 2: 91–130.

____ (ed.). 2002. *Race, Space and the Law: Unmapping the White Settler Society.* Toronto: Between the Lines.

____. 2007. "When Place Becomes Race." In T. Das Gupta, C.E. James, R. Maaka, G.-E. Galabuzi and C. Andersen (eds.), *Race and Racialization: Essential Readings.* Toronto: Canadian Scholars' Press.

RCAP (Royal Commission on Aboriginal Peoples). 1996. *Report of the Royal Commission on Aboriginal Peoples.* Ottawa: Indian and Northern Affairs Canada. <ainc-inac.gc.ca/ch/rcap/sg/sgmm_e.html>.

Reber, S., and R. Renaud. 2005. *Starlight Tour: The Last, Lonely Night of Neil Stonechild.* Toronto: Random House Canada.

Regan, P. 2010. *Unsettling the Settler Within: Indian Residential Schools, Truth Telling, and Reconciliation in Canada.* Vancouver: UBC Press.

Savage, C. 2012. *Geography of Blood: Unearthing Memory from a Prairie Landscape.* Vancouver: Greystone Books.

Seshia, M. 2005. *The Unheard Speak Out.* Winnipeg: CCPA-MB.

Silver, J. 2006. "Building a Path to a Better Future: Urban Aboriginal People." In J. Silver (ed.), *In Their Own Voices: Building Urban Aboriginal Communities.* Halifax and Winnipeg: Fernwood Publishing.

Sinclair, G. 1999. *Cowboys and Indians: The Shooting of J.J. Harper.* Toronto: McClelland and Stewart.

Smylie, J. 2009. "The Health of Aboriginal Peoples." In D. Raphael (ed.), *Social Determinants of Health* (2nd ed.) Toronto: Canadian Scholars' Press.

Statistics Canada. 2008. *Aboriginal Peoples in Canada in 2006: Inuit, Métis and First Nations, 2006 Census.* <12.statcan.ca/census-recensement/2006/as-sa/97-558/pdf/97-558-XIE2006001.pdf>.

Stenning, P., C. Birkbeck, O. Adang, D. Baker, T. Feltes, L. Gerardo Gabaldón, M. Haberfeld, E. Paes Machado, and P. Waddington. 2009. "Researching the Use of Force: The Background to the International Project." *Crime, Law and Social Change* 52: 95--110.

Thompson, E.P. 1975. *Whigs and Hunters: The Origins of the Black Act.* Middlesex: Penguin.

Titley, E.B. 1986. *A Narrow Vision: Duncan Campbell Scott and the Administration of Indian Affairs in Canada.* Vancouver: UBC Press.

United Way Winnipeg. 2010. *Eagle's Eye View: An Environmental Scan of the Aboriginal Community in Winnipeg* (second edition). Winnipeg.

Wolfe, P. 2006. "Settler Colonialism and the Elimination of the Native." *Journal of Genocide Research* 8, 4: 387–409.

WPS (Winnipeg Police Service). 2009. *Annual Report.* <winnipeg.ca/police/annualreports/2009/2009_wps_annual_report_english.pdf>.

Wright, Justice D.H. (Commissioner). 2004. *Report of the Commission of Inquiry into Matters Relating to the Death of Neil Stonechild.* (October) <justice.gov.sk.ca/stonechild/finalreport/Stonechild.pdf>.

York, G. 1990. *The Dispossessed: Life and Death in Native Canada.* London: Vintage.

Chapter Four

Human Rights and Decolonization
Andrea Smith

Indigenous[1] activists have increasingly articulated their demands in terms of "human rights" given the limitation of "civil rights" frameworks. Civil rights are viewed under international law as rights derogable by states whereas human rights are not. Thus, in pursuing legal strategies that recognize the inherent sovereignty of Indigenous nations, it makes sense to articulate Indigenous rights as human rights — rights that cannot be abrogated by states. Furthermore, rather than seek redress primarily through the courts of the colonizer, it seems more appropriate for Indigenous nations to seek redress through those bodies that adjudicate disputes between nations, such as the United Nations. Framing Indigenous rights as human rights can be part of a larger political organizing strategy to challenge settler state rule over Indigenous nations. A human rights framework also provides an opportunity for Indigenous peoples to make transnational linkages with social justice movements globally. Of course, there is a limit to how well a human rights framework can challenge the power of a nation-state since the forums under which human rights laws are addressed, the United Nations et al., are also bodies of nation-states. But in the short term, the human rights framework seems another avenue to articulate rights in a way that could also challenge settler states such as the U.S. rather than reify state power and, implicitly, state sovereignty.

The human rights framework in turn has been critiqued by those who argue that "aboriginal rights are not human rights" (Kulchyski 2011: 33). Peter Kulchyski argues that the "human rights" framework presupposes a colonial and capitalist understanding of humans as distinct from their relationships to the rest of creation, which in turn is signified as property. Consequently, he argues that Aboriginal rights are fundamentally concerned with "cultural" rights that are not incorporated within human rights regimes. Of course "cultural rights" also presupposes a colonial and capitalist notion of "culture" that can be easily signified through the law. Thus, other scholars extend this critique by arguing that the proper framework is not "human rights" or even "cultural rights" but decolonization (Williams 2010). That is, should not the ultimate goal of Indigenous liberation to be to dismantle settler states rather than to seek recognition from them, either domestically or internationally? A human rights framework is still ultimately enforced by nation-states and hence this framework relies up on the continuation rather than the end of these states. In this chapter, I elaborate on the critiques of the human rights framework. However, I contend that while the ultimate goal of Indigenous liberation is decolonization rather than human rights protection, the human rights framework can potentially be used as part of a strategy for decolonization.

Human Rights versus Decolonization

In his germinal critique of human rights, Randall Williams argues that the human rights regime was developed as a strategy to keep decolonization struggles at bay (Williams 2010: xvii). He contends: "our starting point should be neither the law nor any desire for a 'progressive' appropriation of the law, but the mounting dead for whom the law was either a useless means of defense or an accomplice to their murder" (Williams 2010: xxxiii). China Miéville similarly contends that human rights are based on an international legal framework that is birthed out of colonialism. Utilizing the work of Antony Anghie, Miéville argues: "The beginnings of an international law of independent sovereign powers is thus predicated on a colonial disempowering of non-Western subjects. The 'darker history of sovereignty' ... is that the 'doctrine acquired its character through the colonial encounter'" (Miéville 2005: 175). There is thus a contradiction to utilizing a human rights framework when it is itself a colonial construction. Human rights theory tends to presume the law is neutral rather than constitutive of colonialism. "Where there is a problem of disorder or violence, it is deemed a *failure* of law: the main problem about law is that there is not enough of it" (Miéville 2005: 3). The reliance on human rights law tends to presuppose that it is based on fundamentally different logics than domestic law when in fact they both share the same colonial foundations.

It is for this reason that, as I have argued elsewhere (Smith 2008), many Indigenous peoples are calling not just for decolonization, but for the dismantling of nation-states as the appropriate form of governance for the world. One example would be the statements issued by Indigenous peoples' organizations at the 2008 World Social Forum (Smith 2012: 83). Those statements contended that the goal of Indigenous struggle was not simply for the survival of their particular peoples, but to transform the world so that it is governed through principles of participatory democracy rather than through nation-states. The nation-state has not worked for the last five hundred years, they argued, so it is probably not going to start working now. Their vision of nationhood required a radical re-orientation toward land. All are welcome to live on the land, they asserted, but we must all live in a different relationship to the land. We must understand ourselves as peoples who must care for the land rather than control it. Other scholars, such as Taiaiake Alfred, Glen Coulthard and Waziyatawin, have similarly made radical critiques of nation-states as inherently colonial and oppressive (Alfred 2005; Coulthard 2007; Waziyatawin 2008).

In addition, while ostensibly the human rights framework should be a check on state sovereignty, in fact human rights instruments presuppose the primacy of state sovereignty. For instance, Article 46 of the *Declaration on the Rights of Indigenous Peoples* states that "nothing in this Declaration may be interpreted as implying ... any right to engage in any activity or to perform any act contrary to the Charter of the United Nations or construed as authorizing or encouraging any action which would dismember or impair, totally or in part, the territorial integrity or political unity of sovereign and independent States." If state sovereignty of settler states remains supreme, then Indigenous nations remain subordinate to settler states. As Franceso Francioni argued at the U.N. Expert Seminar on Truth and Reconciliation Commission, ultimately the protection of Indigenous human rights necessarily requires an erosion of state sovereignty.[2] Otherwise, calls to protect the human rights of Indigenous peoples can strengthen rather than diminish nation-state sovereignty at the expense of Indigenous sovereignty.

For example, Elizabeth Povinelli (2006: 59) describes how, as a result of the publication of the *Little Children Are Sacred* report, which detailed the "problem" of child abuse in Aboriginal communities, the Australian government declared a national emergency in the Northern Territory. Under the guise of protecting the "human rights" of Indigenous children, the government seized control over Indigenous lands through military police action, began compulsory medical exams for children and seized control over the finances of all Indigenous programs. Through intense state surveillance, Aboriginal peoples could be monitored in terms of school attendance, purchasing choices and medical practices. Ironically, the report made an effort not to blame child abuse on Aboriginal "culture." Yet, as the report was used by the Australian government to justify its surveillance practices, Aboriginal culture was framed as the problem. Australia became the protector of Indigenous human rights through its attacks on Indigenous communities that were violating the rights of children. The fact that violence within Indigenous communities was itself the result of the gendered colonial policies that created child abuse in the first place disappeared from the analysis. Deemed unfit to parent and hence unfit to govern, Indigenous nations were once again subject to colonial domination in the name of human rights.

Human Rights as a Means to Advance Decolonization

All of the above critiques of human rights are valid. At the same time, a wholesale rejection of human rights can presuppose that there is a "pure" alternative framework that is also not implicated in capitalism. It also presupposes that decolonization can happen tomorrow without short-term strategies to improve the current conditions under which Indigenous peoples live. And as I will discuss later, it presupposes that Indigenous peoples are not capable of violating human rights. Scott Lyons (2010), in *X-Marks*, notes that those who call for decolonization often do not effectively engage in any short-term strategies that are viewed as reformist even though they may save the lives of Indigenous peoples who are currently under immediate attack. As a result, the immediate needs of people often get sacrificed in favour of articulating seemingly politically pure ideals. Conversely, those who do engage in short-term reform strategies often decry the goal of decolonization as "unrealistic." In doing so, they do not critique the manner in which these strategies often retrench rather than challenge the colonial status quo. Consequently, it is important to consider how human rights, no matter how implicated in colonialism, may be redeployed by Indigenous peoples to advance decolonization. Drawing from my experience working with the Boarding School Healing Coalition, I have found that human rights serve as important organizing and educative tools for Indigenous peoples, regardless of whether nation-states actually enforce the human rights documents they sign. Human rights can also be used to pressure nation-states into at least addressing some issues of concern for Indigenous peoples by using international pressure against domestic state interests and by educating state citizens about those rights abuses. In utilizing human rights, it is always important to be judicious and strategic — conscious of when strategies may be co-opted or deployed against us. And there may come a time when we might decide to no longer to use human rights as a strategy. Currently, human rights is a strategy worth considering. But before I focus on this, I will briefly discuss the human rights implication of American Indian boarding schools in the United States.

Human Rights Violations of Native Peoples in United States Boarding Schools

During the nineteenth century and into the twentieth century, American Indian children were taken from their homes to attend Christian and U.S. government-run boarding schools as a matter of state policy. The boarding school system became more formalized under President Grant's Peace Policy of 1869/1870. The goal of this policy was to turn over the administration of Indian reservations to Christian denominations. As part of this policy, Congress set aside funds to erect school facilities to be run by churches and missionary societies. Although they were run directly by the churches, the churches were acting under the auspices of the state. These facilities were a combination of day and boarding schools erected on Indian reservations.

Then, in 1879, the first off-reservation boarding school, Carlisle, was founded by Richard Pratt in Pennsylvania. He argued that as long as boarding schools were primarily situated on reservations, then 1) it was too easy for children to run away from school; and 2) the efforts to assimilate Indian children into boarding schools would be reversed when children went back home to their families during the summer. He proposed a policy where children would be taken far from their homes at an early age and not returned to their homes until they were young adults. By 1909, there were twenty-five off-reservation boarding schools, 157 on-reservation boarding schools and 307 day schools in operation. The stated rationale of the policy was to "Kill the Indian and save the man." Children in these schools were not allowed to speak Aboriginal languages or practise Aboriginal traditions. Physical, sexual and emotional abuse was rampant. Children were given inadequate education that only prepared them for manual labor and were also forced to work for no wages in order to maintain the school. Children were given inadequate food and medical care, and were overcrowded in these schools. As a result, children routinely died in mass numbers of starvation and disease. In addition, children were often forced to do grueling work to maintain the schools in order to raise monies for the schools and salaries for the teachers and administrators (Smith 2009).

While not all Aboriginal peoples see their boarding school experiences as negative, it is generally the case that much if not most of the current dysfunctionality in Aboriginal communities can be traced to the boarding school era. Today, most of the schools have closed down, although some boarding schools still remain. While the same level of abuse has not continued, because of my work with the Boarding School Healing Project (BSHP, later changed to Boarding School Healing Coalition), I still hear charges of physical and sexual abuse in currently operating schools that are not being addressed by the U.S. government.

In general, while other settler states, such as Canada, have at least acknowledged their histories of boarding school abuse, there has been no acknowledgement at all in the United States. A number of human rights violations have occurred and continue to occur in these schools. The U.S. has provided no recompense for victims of boarding schools, nor have they attended to the continuing effects of human rights violations. The Boarding School Healing Coalition has begun to document some of these abuses in South Dakota — violations that have targeted American Indians, constituting racial discrimination. In addition, Aboriginal communities continue to suffer effects from boarding schools that require redress from the U.S. government. The Boarding School Healing Coalition interviewed boarding school survivors in South Dakota.

The Boarding School Healing Coalition of South Dakota
Religious and Cultural Suppression

Aboriginal children were generally not allowed to speak their own languages or practise their spiritual traditions. As a result, many Aboriginal peoples can no longer speak their native languages. Survivors widely report being punished severely if they spoke Aboriginal languages. A survivor of boarding schools in South Dakota testified to these abuses:

> You weren't allowed to speak Lakota. If children were caught speaking, they were punished. Well, some of them had their mouths washed out with soap. Some of their hands slapped with a ruler. One of the ladies tells about how they jerked her hair, jerked her by the hair to move her head back to say "no" and up and down to say "yes." I never spoke the language again in public.

The continuing effect of this human rights abuse is that, of the approximately 155 Indigenous languages still spoken, it is estimated that 90 percent will be extinct in ten years. By 2050, there will be only twenty languages left, of which 90 percent will be facing extinction by 2060. However, the U.S. grossly underfunds language revitalization programs.

Malnutrition

Because boarding schools were run cheaply, children generally received inadequate food. Survivors testify that the best food was saved for school administrators and teachers: "Whenever we got the chore to clean the priest's dining room, everyone wanted that chore because they ate the best you know, the best food. I think Saturdays were the time when I went to bed hungry. That's when we only got a sandwich." Survivors today report that they continue to suffer the effects of this practice through eating disorders with associated diseases such as diabetes.

Inadequate Medical Care

Survivors report that they received inadequate medical care:

> There was a time when my little brother was sickly and he was in the hospital with a cold and I don't know what else was wrong. But they had the high beds in the hospital and he was little. And he fell out of bed during the night and got a nosebleed. He told them that he had a nose bleed, but they didn't believe him because they thought that everybody, Indians, had TB [tuberculosis]. So they sent him to Toledo, Ohio, to a TB sanatorium, where he spent about a year doing tests to see if he had TB. And he didn't have TB, but it took a year to find out that he didn't have TB. That was a whole year that he was sent away because they wouldn't believe him when he had nosebleeds.
>
> I just suspect, you know, that he must have been sick and had appendicitis. And he was thrown over the hood of a bed, the metal bedstead. And he was thrown over that and whipped. And he must have been sick. And so whatever it was, he wasn't doing or he got punished for it and got whipped and then he got sick and died from it. He had a ruptured appendix.

They also report that when they were sent to infirmaries, they were often sexually abused there.

Besides the continuing effects that arise from lack of proper medical treatment, survivors also report a reluctance to seek medical attention after they left schools, given the treatment they received.

Physical Abuses

Children report widespread physical abuse in boarding schools. They also report that administrators forced older children to physically and sexually abuse younger children. Children were not protected from the abuse by administrators or other children.

> If somebody left some food out and you beat the other one to it, they would be waiting for you. So there was a lot of fighting going on, a lot of the kids fighting with each other, especially the bigger kids fighting the littler ones. That is what you learned.

They used to send the boys through a whipping line. And we were not too far from there and the boys lined up, I don't know how many, in a line, and they all wore leather belts. They had to take off their leather belts and as the boy ran through, they had to whip them.

Sexual Abuse

Sexual, physical and emotional abuse was rampant. Many survivors report being sexually abused by multiple perpetrators in these schools. However, boarding schools refused to investigate, even when teachers were publicly accused by their students. In 1987, the FBI found that John Boone, a teacher at the Hopi Day School, run by the Bureau of Indian Affairs (BIA) in Arizona, had sexually abused over 142 boys, but the school's principal had never investigated any allegations of abuse. J.D. Todd taught at a BIA school on the Navajo Reservation before twelve children came forward with allegations of molestation. Paul Price taught at a North Carolina BIA school between 1971 and 1985 before he was arrested for assaulting boys. In all cases, the BIA supervisors ignored complaints from the parents before the arrests. And in one case, Terry Hester admitted on his job application that he had been arrested for child sexual abuse. He was hired anyway at the Kaibito Boarding School on the Navajo Reservation and was later convicted of sexual abuse against Navajo students. According to one former BIA school administrator in Arizona:

> I will say this ... child molestation at BIA schools is a dirty little secret and has been for years. I can't speak for other reservations, but I have talked to a lot of other BIA administrators who make the same kind of charges.

Despite the epidemic of sexual abuse in boarding schools, the Bureau of Indian affairs did not issue a policy on reporting sexual abuse until 1987, and did not issue a policy to strengthen the background checks of potential teachers until 1989. The *Indian Child Protection Act* in 1990 was passed to provide a registry for sexual offenders in Indian country, mandate a reporting system, provide rigid guidelines for BIA and Indian Health Services for doing background checks on prospective employees and provide education to parents, school officials and law enforcement on how to recognize sexual abuse. However, this law was never sufficiently funded or implemented, and child sexual abuse rates are dramatically increasing in Indian country while they are remaining stable for the general population (Hinkle 2003: 12–14). Sexual predators know they can abuse Indian children with impunity. According to the *American Indian Report*, "a few years ago ... a patient who had worked in a South Dakota-run facility where many of his victims were Indian children ... was caught and acquitted ... after [he] was released, he attacked three more kids and is now serving a 40-year sentence" (Hinkle 2003: 12–14). Survivors testify:

There was the priest or one of the brothers that was molesting those boys and those girls.

It seems like it was happening to the little ones. The real little ones. And that … I know that guy that they were accusing of that would always be around the little ones … the little kids … the little boys.

One of the girls, who was nine, nine or ten, jumped out the sixth floor window. The older girls were saying the nuns and the priests would take advantage of her and finally one of them explained to us younger ones what it was. And she finally killed herself. That was the most overt case that I can remember. There have been others that I have made myself forget because that one was so awful.

As a result of all this abuse, Aboriginal communities now suffer the continuing effects through increased physical and sexual violence, which was largely absent prior to colonization. As such, Aboriginal women are the women most likely to suffer domestic and sexual violence in the U.S. However, the U.S. fails to redress these effects by not providing adequate healing services for boarding school survivors.

Forced Labour

Children were also involuntarily leased out to white homes as menial labour during the summers rather than sent back to their homes. In addition, they had to do hard labour for the schools, often forced to do very dangerous chores. Some survivors report children being killed because they were forced to operate dangerous machinery. Children were never compensated for their labour.

We had to wash all the kids' clothes, and the priests' clothes, and iron them. The other thing that one of our nuns, she saved stamps. I remember she'd soak them, and we would get the stamps, put them in our hand, peel off the stamp, put it over here, and dry them … like you had to put them all in rolls. I don't know what she'd do with them.

Deaths in Schools

Thousands of children died in these schools, through beatings, medical neglect and malnutrition. The cemetery at Haskell Indian School alone has 102 student graves, and at least 500 students died and were buried elsewhere. These deaths continue today. On December 6, 2004, Cindy Sohappy was found dead in a holding cell in Chemawa Boarding School (Oregon) where she had been placed after she became intoxicated. She was supposed to be checked every fifteen minutes, but no one checked on her for over three hours. At the point, she was found not breathing, and declared dead a few minutes later. The U.S. Attorney declined to charge the staff with involuntary manslaughter. Sohappy's mother is planning to sue the school. A videotape showed that no one checked on her when she started convulsing or stopped moving. The school has been warned for past fifteen years from federal health officials in Indian Health Services about the dangers of holding cells, but these warnings were ignored. Particularly troubling was that she and other young women who had histories of sexual assault, abuse and suicide attempts were put in these cells of solitary confinement.

Two paraphrased testimonies:

> Two children died in school, and the administrators took the bodies home. However, the parents weren't there, so the administrators dumped the bodies on the parents' house floor with no note as to what happened to them.

> I used to hear babies crying in my school. Years later, the school was torn down, and they found the skeletons of babies in the walls.

Inadequacy of Domestic Legal Remedies

As mentioned previously, there are many valid critiques of utilizing human rights frameworks for addressing mass atrocities such as the U.S. boarding school system. At the same time, whatever the inadequacies of human rights, U.S. domestic legal remedies are even worse (Curcio 2006). The statute of limitations in federal court is very strict. Non-tort claims have a limitation of six years from the time the claim first accrues (28 U.S.C. § 2501). The Courts have construed this narrowly, as it is a suspension of sovereign immunity. The focus for the statute of limitations is "upon the time of the [defendant's] acts, not upon the time at which the consequences of the act became most painful" (*Fallini v. United States*, 56 F.3d 1378, 1383 (Fed. Cir. 1995) (quoting *Delaware State College v. Ricks*, 449 U.S. 250, 258, 101 S.Ct. 498, 66 L.Ed.2d 431 (1980)).

In order to claim ignorance of a claim, and thus extend this six year limitation, the claimant must show that the U.S. had concealed its actions so that the plaintiff was "unaware of their existence or that [plaintiff's] injury was 'inherently unknowable at the accrual date'" (*Japanese War Notes Claimants Ass'n v. United States*, 373 F.2d 356, 359, 178 Ct. Cl. 630 (Ct. Cl.), cert. denied, 389 U.S. 971 (1967)).

The statute of limitations for a tort claim under the *Federal Tort Claims Act* (FTCA) is even stricter. "A tort claim against the United States shall be forever barred unless it is presented in writing to the appropriate federal agency within two years after such claim accrues or unless action is begun within six months after the date of mailing, by certified or registered mail, of notice of final denial of the claim by the agency to which it was presented" (28 U.S.C. § 2401(b) (2010)). Many advocates who have tried to seek legal remedies for mass atrocities such as slavery have tried to argue that these atrocities create "ongoing harms" and hence the statute of limitations should not apply. However, this strategy, to the extent that it is recognized at all, is recognized in only very limited ways. For example, the ongoing harm must be a separate act committed by the wrongdoer and the wrongdoer is only responsible for acts that occur within that statute of limitations.

There is some possibility that those nations are covered under treaties with a "bad man clause" (this is a treaty provision that requires the U.S. to pay for any damages caused by a "bad white.") However, the courts have ruled that these cases must go through the Bureau of Indian Affairs first. The BIA, however, has no administrative process for addressing bad man claims, so they can just sit there indefinitely. This possibility also only works for individual claims and does not provide collective remedy. Thus, it can be difficult to fulfill the "exhaustion of remedies" requirement in court. In other words, if the BIA never decides on one's claim because of a lack of administrative process, how can one then prove one exhausted one's remedy through the BIA?

In addition, the damages recognized by courts are limited and currently do not include all the broader harms created by boarding schools, such as loss of language and loss of culture. While some court decisions have implied that the statute of limitations may not apply in cases involving property rights, it is not clear that cultural property will be recognized as property for such purposes. That is, one could argue that language is "cultural property" that has been lost because of the actions of the U.S. government. But there is no legal precedent for courts recognizing language as cultural property.

Furthermore, because Aboriginal peoples are such a small portion of the population, it is difficult for them to garner sufficient political support to pressure the U.S. government into providing legislative remedies, such as congressional inquiries into boarding schools or reparations for boarding school abuses. Thus, utilizing human rights approaches can be helpful as political organizing strategy to help build broad-based support for justice for boarding school survivors and their descendants. That is, by increasing public awareness about boarding school abuses through human rights mechanisms, it may be possible to increase public support for legislative remedies.

In addition, unlike other countries, such as Canada, which have engaged in at least some fact-finding missions to uncover the level of boarding school abuse, there have been no similar inquiries in the U.S. It is necessary for the U.S. to engage in a congressional inquiry into past and present boarding school abuses as well as the continuing effects of these abuses within Aboriginal communities. In the absence of such congressional action, fact-finding missions through international forums would benefit Aboriginal communities.

Finally, it is clear that the harms suffered from boarding schools are have impacted Aboriginal peoples on a collective level. Individual lawsuits are not sufficient to redress these harms, such as loss of language. Loss of language would need to be remedied through funding of community-based language revitalization programs. Other countries, such as Canada, have provided funds for collective remedies, such as healing services, truth and reconciliation commissions, the Aboriginal Healing Foundation and so on.[3] It is important that the United States do so as well.

Thus, despite the limitations of a human rights framework, it is certainly preferable to the U.S. legal system. International human rights law recognizes that states have a responsibility for addressing the ongoing effects of human rights violations, even when these violations occurred previous to the signing of relevant human rights documents. For instance, the U.S. has been found to be in non-compliance with human rights norms during its 2008 U.N. compliance review of the *Convention on the Elimination of Racial Discrimination* (CERD) when it had eradicated affirmative action policies. Even though the human rights violations perpetuated by slavery, for instance, happened prior to the formation of the human rights regime, it is recognized that the U.S. has a proactive responsibility to address the continuing effects of these human rights violations. Similarly, a human rights framework is capable of recognizing the responsibility of states to address the continuing effects of human rights violations perpetuated by boarding school policies. Under the *U.N. Declaration on the Rights of Indigenous Peoples*, there is also a clearer recognition of the collective and not just the individual rights of Indigenous peoples. The current legal system, to the extent that it can provide any remedy at all for boarding school abuses, is likely to only be able to provide remedy for individual survivors. Human Rights standards, however, provide a framework for providing collective remedy because they require governments to take positive action to eliminate discrimination and other human rights violations.

In addition, the institution of truth commissions provides another possibility for some redress. These commissions have been widely criticized for promoting the idea that colonizers should reconcile with their colonized without actually ending colonialism (Williams 2010: xvii). However, some advocates, such as Eduardo Gonzalez of the International Center for Transitional Justice, have argued that it is possible to promote truth commissions rather than truth and reconciliation commissions. In addition, these commissions do not necessarily have to be sponsored by the state (although this can also be beneficial). They can provide an opportunity for Indigenous peoples to organize, document the human rights abuses they have suffered and create coalitions with others interested in promoting justice, as has happened in Latin American countries, such as Argentina, Guatemala, Paraguay and Peru. In addition, truth commissions have more of a capacity to address mass atrocities and historic wrongs that domestic legal systems (particularly in the U.S.) are not set up to address. Thus, while the international legal instruments are limited, they are preferable to even more limited domestic legal remedies.

The Educative Function of Human Rights

Human rights legal strategies have value beyond functioning as a supplement to inadequate domestic legal regimes. They can function as important educative and organizing strategies to build political movements for decolonization. First, they can empower people by challenging the normalization of oppression. Second, they can be used to promote justice *within* Indigenous nations.

The Boarding School Healing Coalition, for example, conducted human rights workshops in Aboriginal communities in South Dakota. In these workshops, we demonstrated how the abuses boarding school survivors suffered were violations of international human rights standards. These workshops had a very visible effect on participants. One participant declared: "Wow! I didn't know I had human rights." For many others, they had normalized the abuse they had suffered in boarding schools. For instance, I would hear participants say they suffered no abuse while in boarding school and then proceed to detail all the beatings they had suffered there. Hearing that international law recognized that what they suffered were human rights violations changed the way they perceived their experience. These workshops also changed participants' sense of what they were entitled to. That is, rather than thinking of healing services as something the U.S. government might give Aboriginal peoples if it felt so inclined, participants recognized that the U.S. has an obligation to provide healing services in order to address the continuing effects of human rights violations perpetrated by boarding school policies and practices. Most of these participants did not have an interest in actually going to U.S. federal courts or pursing legal claims in international courts (at least at that moment) because these arenas were very unfamiliar to them. Nevertheless, the information itself had an important effect on how they perceived themselves and their communities.

In addition, human rights organizing can have a beneficial impact on promoting justice within Aboriginal communities. If all settler states disappeared tomorrow, Indigenous nations would not necessarily govern differently than the current system because of the internalization of colonialism through boarding/residential schools and other assimilationist policies. And as Joyce Green, Emma LaRocque and others have noted, Indigenous nations have also internalized heteropatriarchal values that require deconstruction (Green 2007; LaRocque and National Clearinghouse on Family Violence (Canada) 1994). Thus a human rights framework can be a helpful strategy to reverse the internalization of colonial logics within Indigenous nations so that there would actually be vibrant systems in a position to replace the current world order.

Joyce Green, Emma LaRocque and Joanne Barker, for instance, have contended that Indigenous nations should rely upon international human rights standards in order to challenge the internationalization of colonial gendered norms (Green 2005). LaRocque contends that concerns about gender justice should not be subordinated to Indigenous traditions, and that traditions themselves can be re-examined and critiqued from the framework of gender justice. She argues against Aboriginal peoples "living lives in the past lane," and instead calls on Indigenous women to take the roles of revolutionaries in their communities. She writes:

The challenge is, finally, to ourselves as Native women caught within the burdens and contradictions of colonial history. We are being asked to confront some of our own traditions at a time when there seems to be a great need for a recall of traditions to help us retain our identities as Aboriginal people. But there is no choice — as women we must be circumspect in our recall of tradition. We must ask ourselves whether and to what extent tradition is liberating to us as women. We must ask ourselves wherein lies (lie) our source(s) of empowerment. We know enough about human history that we cannot assume that all Aboriginal traditions universally respected and honoured women. (And is "respect" and "honour" all that we can ask for?) It should not be assumed, even in those original societies that were structured along matriarchal lines, that matriarchies necessarily prevented men from oppressing women. There are indications of male violence and sexism in some Aboriginal societies prior to European contact and certainly after contact. But, at the same time, culture is not immutable, and tradition cannot be expected to be always of value or relevant in our times. As Native women, we are faced with very difficult and painful choices, but, nonetheless, we are challenged to change, create, and embrace "traditions" consistent with contemporary and international human rights standards. (LaRocque 1996: 7)

As Joanne Barker similarly argues, the struggle over gender discriminatory policies in Canada's *Indian Act* became a pivotal moment in which sovereignty was cast in oppositional terms to gender justice. The Assembly of First Nations (AFN) resisted the attempts of Aboriginal women activists to reform the *Indian Act*, which denies status to Aboriginal women who marry outside their communities. She contends that on one hand, the AFN argued that Aboriginal women activists' demands were in opposition to "sovereignty," but at the same time, the AFN was refusing to comply with human rights standards on gender rights, which would be the responsibility of all sovereign nations (Barker 2006).

Wenona Singer further develops this analysis by proposing that Aboriginal nations set up an intertribal body to adjudicate human rights violations committed by Native nations. She contends that it is not only important for states to protect the human rights of Indigenous peoples, but that Indigenous nations themselves must respect human rights. Instead, argues Singer, Aboriginal nations have "effectively slipped into a gap in the global system of human rights enforcement" (Singer 2012: 568).

Thus, within a context where Aboriginal nations are often violating the rights of their citizens, many Aboriginal activists have argued that a human rights framework becomes a helpful starting point in calling for accountability to broader principles of justice beyond the immediate self interest of those in leadership roles. As Singer argues, a human rights framework does not necessarily mean Aboriginal nations have to adopt the same human rights framework as nation-states. Rather, it can be starting place to consider inter-tribal forms of governance and accountability.

A Strategy, Not an End

While "human rights" are often positioned as antithetical to decolonization, I argue that human rights can be a strategy in service of decolonization. Decolonization begins with where we are now, and hence short-term strategies are needed to address immediate concerns, build consciousness and create organizing opportunities. Of course, any strategy always runs the risk of being co-opted, but there is no pure strategy we can employ that we can be assured will never have any negative repercussions. As the journey to decolonization continues, we (Indigenous peoples) may find the human rights framework is no longer efficacious and we would adopt new strategies. But at this historical moment, it is a helpful means to supplement even more inadequate domestic state legal remedies. It also provides an occasion to build greater global consciousness about the gross human rights violations that continue to be perpetrated against Indigenous peoples. To quote theologian Emmanuel Martey (1994):

> Unlike Audre Lorde, who might be wondering whether the master's tools could indeed be used to dismantle the master's house, African theologians are fully convinced that the gun, in efficient hands, could well kill its owner.

Notes

1. Throughout this chapter I use the terms "Indigenous" and "Aboriginal" in order to remain consistent with the rest of the book's authors, although in the United States the term "Native" is much more commonly used.
2. Note: I attended this Seminar, which was held March 1–3, 2012, in New York City, so this an account based on my participation. This statement has not yet been published.
3. See <https://www.aadnc-aandc.gc.ca/eng/1332949137290/1332949312397>.

References

Alfred, Taiaiake. 2005. *Wasase.* Peterborough, ON: Broadview.

Barker, Joanne. 2006. "Gender, Sovereignty, and the Discourse of Rights in Native Women's Activism." *Meridians* 7: 127–61.

Coulthard, Glen. 2007. "Subjects of Empire: Indigenous Peoples and the 'Politics of Recognition' in Canada." *Contemporary Political Theory* 6: 437–60.

Green, Joyce. 2005. "Towards Conceptual Precision." In Gerald Kemerman and Philip Resnick (eds.), *Insiders and Outsiders: Alan Cairns and the Reshaping of Canadian Citizenship.* Vancouver: UBC Press.

____ (ed.). 2007. *Making Space for Indigenous Feminism.* London: Zed.

Hinkle, Jeff. 2003. "A Law's Hidden Failure." *American Indian Report* XIX: 12–14.

Kulchyski, Peter. 2011. "Aboriginal Rights Are Not Human Rights." *Prairie Forum* 36: 33–53.

LaRocque, Emma, and National Clearinghouse on Family Violence (Canada). 1994. *Violence in Aboriginal Communities*. Ottawa: National Clearinghouse on Family Violence, Family Violence Prevention Division, Health Programs and Services Branch, Health Canada.

Martey, Emmanuel. 1994. *African Theology*. Maryknoll: Orbis.

Miéville, China. 2005. *Between Equal Rights: A Marxist Theory of International Law*. Leiden: Brill.

Povinelli, Elizabeth. 2006. *Empire of Love*. Durham: Duke University Press.

Singer, Wenona. 2012. "Indian Tribes and Human Rights Accountability." *San Diego Law Review* 40: 567–626.

Smith, Andrea. 2012. "Indigenity, Settler Colonialism, White Supremacy." In David Martinez HoSang, Oneka LaBennett, and Laura Pulido (eds.), *Racial Formations in the Twenty-First Century*. Berkeley: University of California Press.

Waziyatawin. 2008. *What Does Justice Look Like?* St. Paul: Living Justice Press.

Wild, Rex, and Patricia Anderson. 2007. *Little Children Are Sacred*. Report of a Board of Inquiry into the Protection of Aboriginal Children from Sexual Abuse. Government of the Northern Territory, Australia.

Williams, Randall. 2010. *The Divided World*. Minneapolis: University of Minnesota Press.

Part Two

Aboriginal Human Rights:
Gender Matters

Chapter Five

McIvor v. Canada
Legislated Patriarchy Meets Aboriginal Women's Equality Rights
Gwen Brodsky

"Aboriginal women and their issues are always at the bottom of the totem pole." — Senator Sandra Nicholas Lovelace (Canada 2010a: 1450)

After more than twenty years of litigation in the constitutional sex equality challenge *McIvor v. Canada,*[1] in 2010 Parliament passed Bill C-3: *An Act to promote gender equity in Indian registration,* responding to the Court of Appeal for British Columbia decision in *McIvor* v. *Canada* (Registrar of Indian and Northern Affairs). The government estimates that because of this reform 45,000 previously excluded descendants of Aboriginal women are newly eligible for Indian status (Canada 2010b: 1040). From an advocacy perspective, this is a very significant victory, because it is not easy to compel any resistant government to make a shift of this magnitude. In light of the new legislation, some might wonder what is at stake in the McIvor petition to the United Nations Human Rights Committee, under the *International Covenant on Civil and Political Rights* (ICCPR).

Based on both personal reflection and knowledge gained through my history of advocacy work on behalf of Sharon McIvor and her son Jacob Grismer,[2] in this chapter I consider why appeal to an international treaty body is necessary. In a nutshell: the legislative criteria for Indian status continue to discriminate against Aboriginal women and their descendants. Furthermore, Canada's legal and governmental institutions have failed repeatedly and deliberately over an excessively long period of time to eliminate sex discrimination in the *Indian Act.* Consequently, the Human Rights Committee should step in, to recall Canada to its obligations to Aboriginal women under international human rights law. In the end, Canada must respect and ensure Aboriginal women's ICCPR-protected rights to equality, including their right to the equal enjoyment of Indigenous cultures, by eliminating sex discrimination from the *Indian Act* once and for all. A foundational aspect of an individual's right to enjoy his or her culture is the formation of a sense of identity and belonging to a group, and recognition of that identity and belonging by others in the group. The capacity to transmit one's cultural identity to one's descendants is also a key component of cultural identity. For the purpose of this chapter, Aboriginal women refers to women of First Nations descent, and does not refer to Inuit or Métis, in contradistinction to s. 35 of the Canadian *Constitution Act, 1982*, which includes all three groups.

The McIvor Petition

On November 24, 2010, I filed an official complaint under the Optional Protocol to the *International Covenant on Civil and Political Rights* (ICCPR), on behalf of Sharon McIvor and Jacob Grismer (McIvor and Grismer 2010). The McIvor petition to the U.N. Human Rights Committee reveals blatant, ongoing discrimination against Aboriginal women in the *Indian Act* criteria for determining entitlement to status registration. This discrimination under successive versions of the *Indian Act* has affected the totality of Aboriginal women's lives, including their identities as First Nations women, their relationships to their communities, their ability to transmit Indian status to their children and their access to certain social and economic programs.

Registration as a status Indian confers tangible and intangible benefits. The tangible benefits of status include things like entitlement to apply for some extended health benefits and some post-secondary education funding, among others. The intangible benefits of status relate to cultural identity, including the ability to transmit status, and a shared sense of legitimacy and belonging. For some people these are the most important aspects of status. There is an irony in all of this. The concept of "Indian" did not emanate from Aboriginal people. It was an artificial legal construct created by the colonists and imposed upon Aboriginal people. However, this does not mean that it lacks substance or meaning. Over a long period of time of being imposed, Indian status has become an important aspect of cultural identity for many individuals and Aboriginal communities alongside traditional concepts.

Support for the McIvor case has been overwhelming. This is exemplified by the solidarity that has been demonstrated by Aboriginal organizations, including the Assembly of First Nations, which, during the McIvor constitutional litigation, passed a resolution in support of the case; the Native Women's Association of Canada; the Congress of Aboriginal Peoples; the First Nations Leadership Council; the West Moberly First Nations; T'Sou-ke Nation; the Grand Council of the Waban-Aki Nation; the Band Council of the Abenakis of Odanak; the Band Council of the Abenakis of Wôlinak; and Aboriginal Legal Services of Toronto, all of which made supportive interventions in the McIvor constitutional litigation. Additionally, the Union of British Columbia Indian Chiefs is one of the organizations that made a submission in support of the McIvor petition to the U.N. Human Rights Committee. Other organizations and individuals too numerous to name have shown their support for the McIvor case, in various ways and at various times.

The immediate backdrop to the McIvor constitutional litigation is the federal government's breach of promise to eliminate sex discrimination from the *Indian Act* in the long-awaited reforms of 1985, which were supposed to bring the status provisions in line with women's constitutional equality rights. In the McIvor constitutional litigation, the British Columbia Supreme Court, followed by the British Columbia Court of Appeal, held that the criteria for status determination in the 1985 *Indian Act* discriminated, based on sex, contrary to the *Canadian Charter of Rights and Freedoms*.

When the McIvor U.N. petition was filed in November of 2010, amendments to the 1985 version of the *Indian Act* (also referred to as "Bill C-31"), were pending in the form of Bill C-3 (Canada 2010c). Bill C-3 was the federal government's legislative response to the culmination of the,McIvor litigation.

However, from its inception it was readily apparent that Bill C-3, if passed into law without further change, would not eliminate the sex discrimination from the registration scheme. For that reason, the petition was designed to anticipate the Bill C-3 amendments (McIvor and Grismer 2010). In December 2011, after Bill C-3 was passed into law, the McIvor petition was updated to explicitly challenge the continuation of sex discrimination in Bill C-3 (McIvor and Grismer 2011b).

In brief, Bill C-3 continues to relegate Aboriginal women like Sharon McIvor, to whom status was restored under the 1985 *Indian Act*, to an inferior category of status based on sex. It also continues the legislated exclusion of some Aboriginal people from status based on sex, because they are the female illegitimate children of a male Indian; because their status grandmother married a non-status man[3]; or because they are the grandchildren of a status woman who parented in a common-law relationship with a non-status man.

The claim of the McIvor petition is that the sex-based criteria for the determination of entitlement to Indian registration status introduced by the 1985 *Indian Act* and continued by Bill C-3 continue discrimination on the basis of sex and violate various provisions of the ICCPR:

- Article 26, which enshrines the right of all persons to equality before the law and to the equal protection of the law without any discrimination on the basis of sex.
- Articles 2(1), 3 and 27, which together guarantee the equal right of men and women to the enjoyment of their Indigenous culture, without discrimination based on sex.
- Article 2(3)(a), which guarantees the right to an effective remedy for violations of rights recognized in the ICCPR. (McIvor and Grismer 2010: para. 6)

The McIvor petition takes an integrated approach to the sex equality rights of Aboriginal women in relation to their rights to the enjoyment of Indigenous culture, illustrating the principle that human rights, including Indigenous rights, are indivisible. Of particular note for the purpose of this book's theme of indivisibility is the invocation of ICCPR Articles 27 and 3 together. Article 27 declares the right of Aboriginal people to enjoy their own culture. Article 3 obligates Canada to ensure the equal rights of men and women to their rights, under the Covenant. Article 27 is, on its own, somewhat of a crossover right in that it declares Indigenous cultural rights. As such, it is an Indigenous rights guarantee. However, it is worded in more universal terms (members of ethnic, religious, linguistic minorities shall not to be denied the right, in community with the other members of their group, to enjoy their own culture), which international human rights jurisprudence has interpreted as applying to Indigenous culture. As such, the ICCPR right to culture is both an Indigenous right and a human right. More deeply illustrative of the principle of indivisibility, and more central to what my chapter is about, is the insistence that Aboriginal women are entitled to the equal benefit and protection of rights to sex equality, and that rights to sex equality entitle Aboriginal women to the equal enjoyment of rights to Indigenous culture. Some conventional views of human rights, sex equality rights, Aboriginality and rights to Indigenous culture treat these as isolated compartments. Sex equality rights do not "talk" to rights to Indigenous culture. And sex is presumptively race neutral, but conceptually white, while Aboriginality and Indigenous culture are presumptively gender neutral, but in reality conceptually male. The McIvor petition resists these forms of compartmentalization. The patriarchal, racist, assimilationist character of *Indian Act* sex discrimination necessitates a sex equality analysis of Aboriginal women's human rights to such things as the enjoyment of Indigenous culture (whether cast as Indigenous rights, human rights or Indigenous human rights).

The intention of the petition is to secure eligibility for full status for Aboriginal women and all their descendants born prior to April 17, 1985, on the same basis as full status is granted to Indian men and their descendants born prior to April 17, 1985. Further, the petition not only challenges the continuing discrimination against status women who married non-status men: it challenges the full extent of the legislated preference for Indian men and male-line descendants in the status provisions of the *Indian Act*, including, for example, the ongoing discrimination against descendants of status women who had children with a common-law partner.

The federal government has argued that, for historic reasons, it is permissible to consign some Aboriginal women to a different, in reality a lesser, category of status than that accorded to their male Aboriginal counterparts. A fundamental premise of the McIvor case is that anything less than full equality for all Aboriginal women is discrimination and a violation of Canada's human rights obligations. This position should be unassailable. The principle that all human beings are inherently equal is allegedly the foundation of all human rights. For example, the *Universal Declaration of Human Rights*, which is generally agreed to be the foundation of international human rights law, begins, "recognition of the inherent dignity and of the equal and inalienable rights of all members of the human family is the foundation of freedom, justice and peace in the world" (UNDHR). By continuing to maintain and defend sex discrimination in the *Indian Act*, Canada refuses to recognize the inherent equality of Aboriginal women and their entitlement to benefit fully from the sex equality guarantees contained in the Charter, the ICCPR and numerous other international human rights treaties that are binding on Canada.

At the time of writing, a decision of the Human Rights Committee is still pending. A ruling favourable to McIvor could initiate a law reform process to finally eliminate *Indian Act* sex discrimination. Domestic legal avenues of redress have been exhausted, and time is running out for many Aboriginal people, particularly the older people, who are denied equal status recognition.

The Historical Context for Bill C-3

Canada's denial of equal Indian status to Aboriginal women has a long history rooted in patriarchy and colonization.[4] Since the early twentieth century the patriarchal, assimilationist regime for determining entitlement to Indian status has operated to deprive Aboriginal women and their descendants of Indian status and exile them from their communities; to undermine the equality and power of Aboriginal women in their communities; and to reduce the size of the First Nations population that the federal government feels obliged to recognize.

From 1857, when *An Act to Encourage the Gradual Civilization of Indian Tribes in the Province and to Amend the Laws Respecting Indians*[5] was passed, women were treated disadvantageously compared to men. Under that law, if an Indian man enfranchised or ceased to be Indian, his wife also ceased to be Indian.[6] The express purpose was assimilation of Aboriginal people. The Preamble of the 1857 Act identifies the assimilation of the Indian people as the purpose of the enactment:

> WHEREAS it is desirable to encourage the progress of Civilization among the Indian Tribes in this Province, and the gradual removal of all legal distinctions between them and Her Majesty's other Canadian Subjects, and to facilitate the acquisition of property and of the rights accompanying it, by such Individual Members of the said Tribes as shall be found to desire such encouragement and to have deserved it: Therefore, Her Majesty, by and with the advice and consent of the Legislative Council and Assembly of Canada, enacts as follows:

Section 1 of the 1857 Act provided that the 1850 Act would apply to:

> Indians or persons of Indian blood or intermarried with Indians, who shall be acknowledged as members of Indian Tribes or Bands residing upon lands which have never been surrendered to the Crown (or which having been so surrendered have been set apart or shall then be reserved for the use of any Tribe or Band of Indians in common) and who shall themselves reside upon such lands, and shall not have been exempted from the operation of the said section, under the provisions of this Act; *and such persons and such persons only shall be deemed Indians* within the meaning of any provision of the said Act or of any other Act or Law in

force in any part of this Province by which any legal distinction is made between the rights and liabilities of Indians and those of Her Majesty's other Canadian Subjects. (Emphasis added)

By means of this provision, the government assumed control over the determination of who was Indian. The *Gradual Civilization Act* instituted the policy that women who married men without Indian status lost their own status, and their children would not receive status.

A consequence of such legislation was the disruption of Aboriginal cultures through the imposition of colonial concepts of social organization and the introduction of patriarchal concepts, which did not exist before, into many Aboriginal societies. This was described by the Royal Commission on Aboriginal Peoples, which explained:

> In many cases, the legislation displaced the natural, community-based and self-identification approach to determining membership — which included descent, marriage, residency, adoption and simple voluntary association with a particular group — and thus disrupted complex and interrelated social, economic and kinship structures. Patrilineal descent of the type embodied in the *Gradual Civilization Act*, for example, was the least common principle of descent in Aboriginal societies, but through these laws, it became predominant.[7]

Under provisions known as the "marrying out" rules, introduced in 1869,[8] a status Indian woman who married a non-status man was stripped of her legal identity as an Indian and she and the children of the marriage lost the benefits that flowed from Indian status. In contrast, an Indian man who married a non-status woman did not lose his status, but rather conferred status on his wife. The Act also provided that when an Indian woman married an Indian man of a different tribe or band, she ceased to be a member of her own band or tribe and became a member of her husband's band or tribe. The children of the marriage became members of only the father's tribe or band. The legislation mirrored the colonial society's patriarchal practices and sexist attitudes toward women.

From 1876 onwards, an Indian was legislatively defined as a male Indian, the child of a male Indian or the wife of a male Indian.[9] For the most part, Aboriginal women could not transmit status. The 1876 Act continued the provision that any Indian woman marrying a non-Indian lost her Indian status and her band membership. The 1876 Act also continued the provision that an Indian woman marrying an Indian man who belonged to a different band or tribe would lose the membership in her band and become a member of her husband's band or tribe. These provisions continued, essentially unchanged, until the enactment of the *Indian Act*, S.C. 1951 c. 29 (the "1951 Act").

The scheme's bias in favour of male Indians and male descent was also reflected in the preferential treatment of the male descendants of unmarried male Indians. Under the version of the *Indian Act*[10] in force immediately prior to April 17, 1985, the sons, though not the daughters, of unmarried male Indians would always be Indian, whereas the children of unmarried female Indians were subject to disqualification on the grounds of non-Indian paternity (*McIvor* v. *Canada* 2007: paras. 8–34). Further, children whose paternity was not declared were assumed to have non-Indian fathers, and their status was qualified in accordance with the assumption.

A common misconception is that the notorious marrying out rules are the only instance of *Indian Act* sex discrimination. However, as indicated by the above illustrations, the scheme has always been characterised by multifaceted sex discrimination. This is simply the result of defining Indian-ness as male and imposing patriarchy. In the Victorian mind women, whether Aboriginal, Indian or not, were the property of men. And whereas over the last century law and policy in some other areas evolved to remove most instances of explicit discrimination against women in Canada, blatant legislated discrimination against Aboriginal women persists and to this day is vigorously defended by Canada.

It is not as though the problem of *Indian Act* sex discrimination has newly come to the attention of the federal government. Many Aboriginal women, some Indian leaders and many civil society organizations have objected to the sexist, racist operation of the *Indian Act* since its inception. An early example of protest noted by the Royal Commission on Aboriginal Peoples is that in 1872, the Grand Council of Ontario and Quebec Indians sent the Minister in Ottawa a strong letter that contained the following passage:

> They [the members of the Grand Council] also desire amendments to Sec. 6 of the Act of [18]69 so that Indian women may have the privilege of marrying when and whom they please, without subjecting themselves to exclusion or expulsion from their tribes and the consequent loss of property and rights they may have by virtue of their being members of any particular tribe. [11]

The protests have continued ever since. In the 1970s and 1980s public acknowledgement and criticism of *Indian Act* discrimination against women became widespread and included the following:

- the 1970 Report of the Royal Commission on the Status of Women called for reform (*Royal Commission on the Status of Women* (Government of Canada, 1970) at para. 106)[12];
- judicial recognition of Aboriginal women's equality rights violation by Laskin J of the Supreme Court of Canada, dissenting, in *Canada (Attorney General)* v. *Lavell* in 1973 (at 1386);
- the Government of Canada's own 1978 report titled *Indian Act*

Discrimination Against Sex, prepared for the Department of Indian Affairs and Northern Development, acknowledging the sex discrimination in the marrying out rule and other provisions of the *Indian Act*[13]; and

- the 1981 decision by the United Nations Human Rights Committee finding that the loss of Indian women's status pursuant to section 12(1)(b) of the 1951 *Indian Act* violated the right to enjoy cultural life under the ICCPR in *Lovelace* v. *Canada* (Human Rights Committee 1981).

In answer to the criticism, including the holding of the Human Rights Committee in Lovelace, and to bring the *Indian Act* into conformity with the Charter's new equality guarantees, Canada made amendments to the *Indian Act* in 1985. The amendments were expressly intended to ensure that henceforth status would be determined on a "totally non-discriminatory basis" and that sex and marital status would no longer affect an individual's entitlement to registration (Minister of Indian Affairs and Northern Development, David Crombie, Minutes of Proceedings and Evidence of the Standing Committee on Legal and Constitutional Affairs, March 7, 1985, para. 12:7–12:9.)

A crucial factor compelling the government to address *Indian Act* sex discrimination in 1985 was s. 15, the equality guarantee of the Charter. The wording of s. 15 was fought over, and buttressed, in response to a concerted civil society lobby intended to ensure that Aboriginal women would be fully protected from discrimination, and that governments and courts would give effect to Canada's obligations under international human rights law, like those flowing from the Lovelace decision.

Notwithstanding the acknowledged governmental awareness of *Indian Act* sex discrimination and strengthened commitments to women's equality, the government's approach to eliminating the discrimination was superficial.

The 1985 *Indian Act* amendment, also known as Bill C-31, was supposed to eliminate sex discrimination. However, there is a stark contrast between the constitutional and political promises and the reality of what the government delivered in Bill C-31. Furthermore, Bill C-31 was only slightly altered by subsequent *Indian Act* amendments with Bill C-3 in 2010. The bulk of the sex discrimination, initially carried forward by Bill C-31, has survived unscathed. Consideration of Bill C-31 reveals a lot about the persistence of government foot-dragging and is essential to understanding how the sex discrimination continues to operate.

Despite government promises, Bill C-31 continued to prefer descendants who trace their Indian ancestry along the paternal line over those who trace their ancestry along the maternal line. Bill C-31 also continued to prefer male Indians who married non-Indians and their descendants over female Indians who married non-Indians and their descendants.

Bill C-31 created three categories of status. First, s. 6(1)(a) accorded full status to those who were entitled to status under the previous patriarchal regime, including men who married non-status women, their wives and their children. Also included among those eligible for s. 6(1)(a) status are descendants of two generations of status men who married out. Pursuant to an *Indian Act* provision introduced in 1951, known as the double-mother rule, a legitimate child of a status Indian father, whose mother and grandmother only had status because of their marriages to status men, would lose status at the age of twenty-one. However, the double-mother rule was rarely applied. It operated for only thirteen years, from September 4, 1972, to April 17, 1985, and affected only two thousand individuals at most. It was inapplicable to the members of most bands because 311 of 580 bands were granted an exemption by order in council (Draft DIAND report, "The Potential Impacts of Bill C-47 on Indian Communities," November 2, 1984: 2).

Second, matrilineal descendants of status women who parented in common-law relationships, and women who were denied status under the former marrying out rule, became entitled to register but were granted a lesser status under a new s. 6(1)(c). S. 6(1)(a) status is superior to s. 6(1)(c) status with regard to the ability to transmit status to descendants, and in the social standing and legitimacy it confers in Indian communities. The significance of s. 6(1)(a) status within Aboriginal communities is exemplified by the evidence of Sharon McIvor and Jacob Grismer, highlights of which are set out later in this chapter. To this day, the women registered under s. 6(1)(c) of the 1985 Act are known as "Bill C-31 women," which has connotations of inferiority and illegitimacy.

Finally, s. 6(2) accorded partial status to persons who have only one parent registered under s. 6(1). This effectively created a "two-parent rule" because a child who has only one parent with s. 6(2) status is not entitled to any Indian status at all. This feature is known as the "second-generation cut-off," because the second generation of children with only one status parent lose all entitlement to status. Once status is lost, it can never be regained.

The children of Bill C-31 women who married out generally gained status under s. 6(2) rather than s. 6(1) even though the children were born before April 17, 1985. These children were consigned to s. 6(2) because their mothers married non-status men, and under the 1985 Act the children were considered to have only one Indian parent. The children of Indian men who married non-status women and conferred their Indian status on their wives were considered to have two Indian parents.

Children born before April 17, 1985, to Indian men who married non-status women were therefore entitled to status under the old discriminatory formula and had that right preserved under the 1985 Act. They were registered under s. 6(1)(a). Even if as adults they married non-status persons and had children born prior to April 17, 1985, those children were entitled to s. 6(1)(a) status. None of the male-line descendants born prior to April 17, 1985, were consigned to s. 6(1)(c) or s. 6(2). Under Bill C-31, the second-generation cut-off was thereby postponed for this group until at least the following generation. The lesser status accorded to women registered under s. 6(1)(c) as compared to those registered under s. 6(1)(a) imposed a legislated disadvantage on the ability of women with s. 6(1)(c) status to transmit status to their descendants, based on their sex.

Bill C-31 also continued discrimination against the descendants of status Indian mothers who, like McIvor's mother and grandmother, lived in and parented in common-law relationships with the non-status fathers of their children. It accorded preferential treatment to male descendants of status Indian fathers who parented in common-law relationships with non-status women, granting full Indian s. 6(1)(a) status to those male children. But, under Bill C-31, previously disqualified children of a status Indian mother who parented in a common-law relationship with a non-status man were not eligible for s. 6(1)(a) status (*McIvor v. Canada* 2007: para. 33).

The Court of Appeal decision in McIvor mistakenly states that the illegitimate child of a male Indian was non-Indian. Pursuant to Supreme Court of Canada jurisprudence, the male child of a male Indian would always be an Indian. "Illegitimate" female children of male Indians were not eligible for status (*Martin v. Chapman*, [1983] 1 SCR 365) and s. 11 of the 1951 *Indian Act*, SC 1951, c. 29).

Instead of eliminating sex discrimination as was promised and constitutionally mandated, Bill C-31 incorporated the pre-existing and longstanding legislative preference for male Indians and patrilineal descent. S. 6(1)(a) preserved the privileged position of male Indians and their descendants born prior to April 17, 1985.

Public criticism arose again soon after Bill C-31 came into effect, because of the sex discrimination that Bill C-31 continued, providing impetus for the British Columbia courts to rule in Sharon McIvor's favour in 2007 and again in 2009. In 1996, the Royal Commission on Aboriginal Peoples criticized the 1985 Act's continuation of sex discrimination. Various U.N. human rights treaty bodies — including the Human Rights Committee (Human Rights Committee 2006: para. 22); the Committee on Economic, Social and Cultural Rights (Committee on Economic, Social and Cultural Rights 2006: para. 17); and the Committee on the Elimination of Discrimination Against Women (CEDAW 2003: para. 361; CEDAW 2008: paras. 17–18) — criticized Canada for continuing discrimination against Aboriginal women.

The McIvor Constitutional Litigation

The McIvor constitutional challenge to the sex-based hierarchy for the determination of entitlement to Indian registration status contained in Bill C-31 was commenced in 1994. The constitutional claim rests on the equality guarantees of the Charter, contained in sections 15 and 28. S. 15 guarantees equality without discrimination based on the ground of sex. S. 28 guarantees all the rights in the Charter equally to men and women.

The McIvor constitutional challenge claims that the 1985 Act discriminated against matrilineal descendants born prior to April 17, 1985, and against Indian women who had married non-Indian men. McIvor, the child of a status mother and the grandchild of a status grandmother who had married a non-Aboriginal man, sought recognition of entitlement to full s. 6(1)(a) status for herself and all her children. McIvor's son Jacob Grismer, who is a co-petitioner to the United Nations Human Rights Committee, was also a plaintiff in the constitutional challenge because as the child of a "Bill C-31 woman," he too was — and remains — ineligible for full s. 6(1)(a) status.

At trial, the plaintiffs were entirely successful. In 2007, Judge Carol Ross of the British Columbia Supreme Court ruled that s. 6 of the 1985 Act, which determined entitlement to Indian registration status, violated sections 15 and 28 of the Charter in that it discriminated, on the grounds of sex and marital status, between matrilineal and patrilineal descendants born prior to April 17, 1985, and against Indian women who had married non-Indian men.

Justice Ross also concluded that the discrimination was not demonstrably justified as a reasonable limit under s. 1 of the Charter (*McIvor v. Canada*, BCSC: paras. 288, 342–343). She made an order requiring that the 1985 *Indian Act* be interpreted so as to entitle persons to registration for full status under s. 6(1)(a) who were previously not entitled to full status solely as a result of the preferential treatment accorded to Indian men over Indian women born prior to April 17, 1985, and to patrilineal descendants over matrilineal descendants, born prior to April 17, 1985. The clear implication of the decision was that McIvor and Grismer would be entitled to full s. 6(1)(a) registration status, notwithstanding that McIvor was a "Bill C-31 woman," as would other Aboriginal women and their descendants in situations similar to theirs.

However, Canada appealed the trial court decision to the British Columbia Court of Appeal, and was successful in significantly scaling back the McIvor trial-level victory in the British Columbia Supreme Court. In 2009, the Court of Appeal confirmed that s. 6 of the 1985 *Indian Act* discriminated, but on a much narrower basis. While the British Columbia Supreme Court dealt with the full scope of the McIvor challenge, the British Columbia Court of Appeal radically narrowed the analysis and the scope of the relief. In particular, the Court of Appeal found that much of the sex discrimination was justified based on the government's stated objective of preserving acquired rights. The only discrimination recognized by the Court of Appeal as unjustified was the preferential treatment given a small sub-set of descendants of male Indians affected by the obscure and rarely applied *Indian Act* provision known as the "double-mother rule," which I discussed earlier in this chapter. The Court of Appeal ruled that the discrimination against the female counterparts of the subset of male Indians was unjustified, because the rights of the sub-set of male Indians, acquired prior to 1985, were not only preserved by the 1985 Act, but improved. According to the Court, maintaining the sex-based hierarchy between s. 6(1)(a) and s. 6(1)(c) was justified, provided the privileged position of male-line descendants was simply preserved and not improved.

I will return to a discussion of the government's justificatory argument towards the end of this chapter. At this juncture, suffice it to say that Canada is urging the U.N. Human Rights Committee to adopt this rights-defeating line of reasoning.

In 2009, the Court of Appeal referred the question of how to remedy the discrimination back to the government and gave it a year to do its legislative repair work. A government committed to full equality for Aboriginal women would have introduced legislation that cured the sex discrimination completely. However, the Court's decision gave the government an out, one the government was eager to take. The government introduced amendments that were narrowly tailored to the Court of Appeal of decision, once again carrying forward sex discrimination into the current legislation.

Bill C-3: More Failed Remedial Legislation

The specific ingredients of Bill C-3 that ensured that the bulk of the sex discrimination retained by the 1985 Act was carried forward are these: it re-enacted the s. 6(1)(a) and s. 6(1)(c) sex-based hierarchy; it made no change to the discriminatory criteria for eligibility for full s. 6(1)(a) status; it preserved entitlement to s. 6(1)(a) status for those who were entitled to be registered under the pre-1985 discriminatory regime; it expressly recognized entitlements to be registered that existed under s. 6(1)(a) or (c) prior to Bill C-3; and it was narrowly tailored to merely extend inferior s. 6(1)(c) status to some individuals. The qualifications include:

(i) The registrant's mother must have lost status as a result of marriage under provisions related to marrying out dating from the 1951 Act through 1985, or under former provisions of the Act related to the same subject matter.

(ii) The registrant's father must be or have been, if deceased, not entitled to be registered under the Act in effect since the creation of the Indian Registry in 1951, or was not an Indian as defined in the pre-1951 Act.

(iii) The registrant must have been born after the marriage referred to in (i) and prior to April 17, 1985, when Bill C-31 came into force; persons born after that date are entitled to registration only if their parents married prior to it.

(iv) The registrant must have had or adopted a child on or after September 4, 1951, with a person not entitled to be registered. (Brodsky 2011b: para. 4)

The central question at issue in the McIvor petition is whether Bill C-3 fixed the sex discrimination in the *Indian Act*. Canada contends that it has. However, the following groups are still excluded:

- Aboriginal grandchildren born prior to September 4, 1951, who are descendants of status women who married non-status men, which is commonly referred to as "marrying out" (in contrast, comparable grandchildren of status men are eligible for status)[14];
- Aboriginal grandchildren, born prior to April 17, 1985, to status women who parented in common-law unions with non-status men (in contrast, comparable grandchildren of status men are eligible for status); and
- Aboriginal female children of male Indians, born prior to April 17, 1985, referred to in the legislation as "illegitimate" (in contrast, male "illegitimate" children of status men are eligible for status).

The current scheme not only determines who is and who is not entitled to status; it also continues to assign people to different categories of status based on sex. In particular, the current scheme continues to relegate Aboriginal women and their descendants to inferior categories of status. Women like McIvor can never have s. 6(1)(a) status. Consigning the women to inferior s. 6(1)(c) status devalues them, and it reduces the class of status they are able to transmit to their descendants.

For some, the effect of the Bill C-3 amendments has been to move the sex discrimination forward by one generation. The current scheme newly grants s. 6(2) status to the grandchildren born prior to April 17, 1985, of Aboriginal women who married non-status men and whose children married out. Under the 1985 Act those grandchildren were excluded. However, this does not eliminate the sex discrimination. Grandchildren born prior to April 17, 1985, to status men who married non-status women and whose children married out are eligible for full 6(1)(a) status. The effect of consigning the grandchildren of women who married non-status men to s. 6(2) status is still to exclude subsequent generations because of the sex of their Aboriginal ancestor.

Bill C-3: The Failed Parliamentary Process

For a bill to be enacted into law, it must pass through the Parliamentary process. In the House of Commons, this includes introduction and first reading, second reading and referral of the bill to committee, committee stage, report stage, third reading and passage of the bill. The Senate follows a similar process. On March 11, 2010, Bill C-3 was introduced. However, it was clear from the outset that the Harper minority government had no intention of remedying the full extent of the sex discrimination embedded in the status regime. On August 9, 2009, the government issued a discussion paper acknowledging that the *Indian Act* needed to be amended and explaining that the government intended to focus exclusively on remedying the "specific deficiency identified by the Court of Appeal."[15]

During the Parliamentary process there were repeated calls by individuals, groups and members of Canada's Parliament and Senate to amend Bill C-3 to eliminate the sex discrimination from the *Indian Act* registration scheme. For example, at the committee stage, when hearings were conducted by the Parliamentary Standing Committee on Aboriginal Affairs and Northern Development, numerous witnesses criticized the continuation of sex discrimination in Bill C-3[16] (Canada 2010c).

In light of criticisms by the witnesses, the Opposition members of the Committee became convinced that it was wrong to perpetuate the sex discrimination. On April 27, 2010, Todd Russell, Standing Committee member and the Liberal Critic for Aboriginal Affairs, moved a motion before the Committee that the Bill be amended to make s. 6(1)(a) status available to Aboriginal women and their descendants on the same basis that is available to Aboriginal men and their descendants (Canada 2010c). Conservative member of Parliament and Chair of the Committee Bruce Stanton ruled that the amendment was out of order. The Opposition members held the balance of power on the Committee and voted in favour of the amendment. On April 29, 2009, the Committee returned the bill to Parliament with the proposed amendment. However, the government moved swiftly to secure a ruling from the Speaker of the House disallowing the amendments (Canada 2010b).

Notwithstanding the Speaker's ruling, on May 25, 2010, during the Committee's report on Bill C-3 to the House of Commons, Todd Russell and other members of the Opposition parties urged the government to heed the calls for a comprehensive approach to the elimination of sex discrimination, including, for example, from Liberal Status of Women Critic Anita Neville; Larry Bagnell, a Liberal member of Parliament; Marc Lemay, a member of the Bloc Quebecois; and Jean Crowder, a member of the New Democratic Party (Canada 2010d: 1210). Neville explained: "We have heard a near unanimous call from Aboriginal women's organizations, individual Aboriginal women, including Sharon McIvor, Aboriginal governments and chiefs, academics and national organizations ... to amend or otherwise rewrite Bill C-3 to comprehensively and meaningfully end sex discrimination under the *Indian Act*" (Canada 2010d: 1210).

The government's primary strategy to keep the other parties in line was to threaten that the outcome of failing to meet a fixed deadline would be a legislative gap, an outcome which it attributed to the Court of Appeal decision in McIvor. The government's fear mongering started in its 2009 discussion paper to which I have referred, in which it warned that the registration process would be cast into doubt if the "tight deadline" was not met, such that no one would be able to be registered. Such warnings were made repeatedly. For example, at second reading, John Duncan the Minister of Indian and Northern Affairs, referred six times to the "deadline" for enacting Bill C-3 (Canada 2010b).

The spectre of legislative gap was a red herring. In reality, the only deadlines were of the government's making. The dates for legislative repair, referred to by the Court of Appeal in its directions to the government, were ones that the government itself had proposed: initially, April 6, 2010, with extensions July 5,

2010, and January 31, 2011. The Court would have allowed a further extension for a reasonable period of time, had the government requested it, to complete the Parliamentary process. At any point in the Parliamentary process the government could have introduced a bill that cured the sex discrimination, withdrawing Bill C-3 if necessary, but it refused to do that, preferring to rely on the flawed Court of Appeal decision that countenanced all but a fraction of the sex discrimination. At worst, a very small number of new registrations in British Columbia would have been temporarily delayed. However, the government's tactics unnerved the Opposition parties, which in the end could not maintain solidarity.

On December 10, 2010, Bill C-3 passed third reading, but with a number of opposition party members and senators holding their noses, because they objected to the sex discrimination and to the government's tactics. This is typified by the comments of Jean Crowder, who said during third reading in the House of Commons on November 22nd, 2010:

> All of us in the House are aware of the ongoing gender discrimination. However, in this particular situation, we are being forced to decide whether we disadvantage 45,000 people who could regain status under this narrow piece of legislation, or we tell them they need to wait for possibly a few more decades. Faced with this tough decision, a number of us will hold our noses and support the legislation knowing that it does not deal with all of the discrimination that still exists. (Canada 2010f: 1615. See also Todd Russell, Canada 2010f: 1555–615)

On December 6, 2010, at the hearings of the Senate Standing Committee on Human Rights, Committee members and senators Sandra Lovelace Nicolas, Mobina Jaffer and the Chair of the Committee, a Conservative Party member, all raised concerns about the continuation of sex discrimination in Bill C-3 (Canada 2010g, see also the comments of Senators Jaffer and Lovelace Nicolas, Canada 2010a). On December 7, 2010, the Committee took the somewhat unusual step of adding an addendum of observations to its report, stating: "Bill C-3 does not deal with all sex discrimination stemming from the Indian Act" (*Sixth Report of the Standing Senate Committee on Human Rights*, 7 December 2010).[17]

On December 8, during the Senate Debates, Senator Sandra Lovelace Nicolas — the petitioner in Lovelace the landmark 1977 complaint to the Human Rights Committee, the predecessor to the McIvor petition — stated:

> It is 25 years since Bill C-31 was passed, and we have another "take it or leave it" bill from the government with no amendments. Bill C-3 does not address all aspects of gender discrimination. It is unjust and irresponsible, and it is a bandage solution to an old existing problem for Aboriginal women in Canada … if Bill C-3 is passed, then Sharon McIvor will be forced to walk down the same long and lonely path that I once travelled

... where is the equality and justice for Canada's First People, Aboriginal women? ... I apologize to my people and their descendants that the Government of Canada will let Bill C-3 pass without amendments. As far as I can remember ... all Aboriginal women and their issues are always at the bottom of the totem pole (Canada 2010a: 1450).

On December 15, 2010, Bill C-3 received Royal Assent and took effect on January 31, 2011 (Royal Assent Statutes of Canada: 2010, c. 18 2010-12-15). The discrimination continues.

Ongoing *Indian Act* Discrimination Harms Aboriginal Women

Canada contends that Bill C-3 has provided a sufficient remedy to Sharon McIvor (Canada 2010e: paras. 52–54), but this is not convincing, based even on a simple comparison between Sharon McIvor and her brother Ernie McIvor. Although their lineages are identical, the scheme still treats Sharon McIvor adversely based on her sex.

Under the pre-1985 legislation, Sharon McIvor was completely ineligible for status because her claim to status was through the females in her family. Her grandmother, but not her grandfather, was a status Indian and a member of the Lower Nicola Band. If Sharon McIvor's grandfather, rather than her grandmother, had been a status Indian, Sharon McIvor would have been entitled to full status from birth. Because Sharon McIvor's grandmother could not transmit status, her daughter, that is, Sharon McIvor's mother, had no status, and Sharon had no status either.

Under the 1985 Act, initially Sharon McIvor was reinstated to s. 6(2) status. In 2006, on the eve of the McIvor constitutional trial, the government conceded, based on a revised interpretation of the legislation, that she was eligible for s. 6(1)(c) status, despite her matrilineal descent.[18] Up until this point Sharon McIvor and her brother Ernie McIvor had been both punished by the sex discrimination in successive versions of the scheme, based on their matrilineal descent. However, the consequence of this concession was to make the sex discrimination evident again in a different form, because the same legislative interpretation that gave Sharon McIvor s. 6(1)(c) status, gave her brother and all his children superior s. 6(1)(a) status, even though both Sharon McIvor and her brother had married out. For Ernie, marrying out did not lessen his status; for her, it did. That critical inequity has not been remedied by Bill C-3.

The Bill C-3 amendments improved the registration entitlement of Jacob Grismer somewhat, making him eligible for section 6(1)(c) status, and his children (Sharon McIvor's grandchildren) thereby newly eligible for s 6(2) status. However, Bill C-3 did not place Sharon McIvor on the same footing as her identically situated brother. Nor did it place Jacob Grismer on the same footing as his cousins. Despite her long litigation journey, she and her son remain consigned to the s 6(1)(c) subclass, whereas her brother and all his children are entitled to full s 6(1)(a) status.

Although Sharon McIvor and Jacob Grismer have the tangible benefits of status for themselves, unlike some others who, because of the continuation of sex discrimination, are categorically excluded from status, they do not enjoy all the intangible benefits of status on a basis of equality with their peers. In particular, they are denied the cultural legitimacy and social standing that full s. 6(1)(a) status confers.

Canada contends that differences between categories of status such s. 6(1)(a) and s. 6(1)(c) do not matter. Canada argues that the difference between s. 6(1)(a) and s. 6(1)(c), if any, is merely one of formal drafting or, in other words, writing style rather than substance; the Act only provides for one status, not degrees of status; and that Indian status is not a marker of cultural identity or legitimacy (Canada 2010e: paras 26, 82, 92, 100–105, 130). This is not persuasive.

One of the profound harms of the continuing legislated denial of s. 6(1)(a) status to First Nation women and their descendants is that the denial sends an invidious message that it is acceptable for First Nations communities to treat First Nations women and their descendants as though they are not equal, do not fully belong and are "less Indian." For example, consider the following, part of Sharon McIvor's testimony:

> Under the pre-1985 regime, as a matrilineal descendant Sharon McIvor was categorically ineligible for status. She suffered a form of banishment from the Aboriginal community that was hurtful and isolating, and excluded her from participating in important activities in her traditional territory, such as hunting, fishing, harvesting of berries, ceremonies, and community gatherings. The social and cultural exclusion extended to her children, and their access to community activities and events.
>
> The fact that her children were not automatically granted status in 1985 is a constant grief and indignity. She was unable to access the tangible benefits of status available under the 1985 Act for her children when they were growing up. It also made her feel inferior not to be able to transmit status to her children alone. For her, the implication was that her lineage was inferior. She is painfully aware that the lives of her children could have been different had they been granted status at the same time as her in 1987, particularly as regards Jacob Grismer's access to Aboriginal cultural and other community activities.
>
> Even though Jacob Grismer gained section 6(2) status in 2006, Sharon McIvor's sense of hurt and humiliation and the denial of respect for her inherent dignity and equality continued because the status that she was able to transmit was not equal to that which her brother can transmit. Up until 2011 she was only able to transmit inferior section 6(2) status to Jacob Grismer and no status to her grandchildren. And to this day she is not eligible for section 6(1)(a) status for herself, because of her sex.

Although she has experienced increased acceptance since gaining a form of status in 1987, she has found that within Aboriginal communities, after so many decades of state-imposed sex discrimination, there is an attitude that real Indians have section 6(1)(a) status. She has experienced stigma that is associated with being a "Bill C-31 woman," including the implication of the label that those women are inferior to and less Indian than their male counterparts. (McIvor and Grismer 2010a: paras. 103–105, 108)

Canada contends that the petitioners' Aboriginal community and families — not Canada — are to blame, if the petitioners feel that the legislated denial of s. 6(1)(a) status affects their equal enjoyment of their Aboriginal cultural identity (Canada 2010e: paras. 80–81, 104–108). This attempt to avoid responsibility for the impact of its legislated sex discrimination within Aboriginal communities has no credibility. Canada's contention that s. 6(1)(a) status is just a matter of legislative drafting fails to take into account the history of Canada's treatment of Aboriginal people. In particular, it fails to acknowledge that for First Nations women living under the *Indian Act* regime, Canada's long history of denial of their right to equal status is intertwined with the denial of the right to the equal enjoyment of their Indigenous culture. As Jane Gottfriedson, President of the Native Women's Association of Canada, said to the Standing Committee of Indian Affairs and Northern Development on September 9, 1982:

> The first concern of Indian women is that they have been denied their birthright. They have been denied the right to call themselves Indian. They have been denied their nationality. By birth and by blood, Indian women are a part of the First Nations of Canada. It is not so important how or in what manner they have been denied their nationality; what is important is that they have been denied this right. It so happens that Indian women have been systematically discriminated against on the basis of their sex in federal Indian Acts since 1869.
>
> However, Indian women are not merely saying that they do not want to be discriminated against on the basis of sex; what they have been saying is that they do not want to be denied their birthright for any reason. Indian women are as aware as Indian men that Indians are specifically mentioned in the *British North America Act,* now called the *Canada Act.* Indian women are as aware as Indian men that certain rights flow to Indians in Canada because of the Constitution of this country. They will not accept any recommendation which continues to deny Indian women the same rights enjoyed by Indian men. Equality of the sexes is an issue here because the federal government, through the *Indian Act,* chose to discriminate against Indian women and deny them their heritage because they married non-Indians. The bottom line for Indian women in the

country is that by birth and by blood they are Indians and will not accept any proposal which continues to deny Indian women this recognition. (Canada 1982: 2:37–2:38)

Sharon McIvor's and Jacob Grismer's evidence about the importance of registration status with respect to a sense of identity were echoed in the Report of the Royal Commission on Aboriginal Peoples (RCAP). RCAP noted that the Department of Indian and Northern Affairs' survey of 2,000 Bill C-31 registrants showed that almost two-thirds of those canvassed reported that they had applied for Indian status for reasons of identity or because of the culture and sense of belonging that it implied (*McIvor* v. *Canada*, BCSC: para 138).

It is completely unreasonable to blame the petitioners' communities and family for the esteem associated with s. 6(1)(a) status and the stigma associated with relegation to s. 6(1)(c) status. The affidavit of Grand Chief Stewart Philip, President of the Union of B.C. Indian Chiefs, submitted to the Human Rights Committee, slices through Canada's attempt to blame legislated discrimination on Aboriginal communities and families, explaining that it is a poorly disguised effort to pit the interests of Aboriginal individuals against Aboriginal collectives, that ignores the long history of the federal government imposing definitions of who is an Indian on Aboriginal people (Phillip 2011). Given Canada's historical role in regulating the life of First Nations peoples and the consequent link between status and cultural identity, it would be surprising if the exclusionary attitudes embedded in the status regime were not reflected in attitudes held by Aboriginal communities.

Grandfathering Sex Discrimination

Although Canada argues that any distinction between s. 6(1)(a) status and s. 6(1)(c) is justified because it preserves acquired rights, this argument is deeply flawed. The justificatory language in covenant jurisprudence is "based on reasonable and objective criteria." The Human Rights Committee has explained that not every distinction constitutes discrimination, in violation of Article 26, but that distinctions must be justified on reasonable and objective grounds, in pursuit of an aim that is legitimate under the Covenant.

Preservation of acquired rights cannot reasonably be regarded as the goal of the legislated distinction between s. 6(1)(a) status and s. 6(1)(c) status because both Bill C-31 and Bill C-3 do not just preserve existing legal entitlements; they preserve sex discrimination.

The continuation of *Indian Act* sex discrimination is not necessary to preserve previously acquired status registration. There is no way in which the full status of those registered under s. 6(1)(a) would be diminished by extending that same registration entitlement to Aboriginal women and their descendants.

The first step in analyzing any justificatory argument in favour of maintaining a discriminatory law is to assess the purpose of the discrimination. Preserving the acquired rights of male Indians and their descendants, whose enjoyment of historical privilege stems from systemic sex discrimination, cannot be regarded as a legitimate purpose under the ICCPR. If the Human Rights Committee were to accept this rationale, it could be advanced to justify a great many infringements of rights under the ICCPR, all over the world.

Canada's "preservation of acquired rights" defence rests on a thin and impoverished version of Aboriginal women's equality rights. It recalls to mind the 1915 case of *Guinn* v. *United States*, which concerned a literacy test prescribed by the government of Oklahoma as a condition of voting. Historically, "negro" citizens were not allowed to vote in Oklahoma. Pursuant to the Fifteenth Amendment of the United States Constitution it was impermissible to discriminate as to suffrage because of race. In response to the Fifteenth Amendment, in 1910 the State of Oklahoma adopted an amendment to its state constitution, which on its face was race-neutral. It excluded from voting persons who could not read or write.

Simultaneously, the government introduced a so-called "grandfather clause" which preserved the voting rights of those who had previously been entitled to vote, and descendants of such persons, prior to the enactment of the Fifteenth Amendment in 1866. Members of the grandfathered group were not subject to the literacy requirement. The State of Oklahoma argued that there was no discrimination based on race since everyone, whether "negro" or white was subject to the requirement. This argument was rejected. The United States Supreme Court said:

> We have difficulty in finding words to more clearly demonstrate the conviction we entertain that this standard has the characteristics which the Government attributes to it than does the mere statement of the text. It is true it contains no express words of an exclusion from the standard which it establishes of any person on account of race, color, or previous condition of servitude prohibited by the Fifteenth Amendment, but the standard itself inherently brings that result into existence since it is based purely upon a period of time before the enactment of the Fifteenth Amendment and makes that period the controlling and dominant test of the right of suffrage. In other words, we seek in vain for any ground which would sustain any other interpretation but that the provision, recurring to the conditions existing before the Fifteenth Amendment was adopted and the continuance of which the Fifteenth Amendment prohibited, proposed by in substance and effect lifting those conditions over to a period of time after the Amendment to make them the basis of the right to suffrage conferred in direct and positive disregard of the Fifteenth Amendment. (*Guinn* v. *United States* 1915: 364–65)

The Court in Guinn struck down the literacy requirement. But it would be easy to re-write Guinn to reach an opposite result, using "preservation of acquired rights" as a mask or justification for discrimination. Just as in Guinn, where the literacy rule combined with a grandfather clause created and perpetuated the race discrimination that the Fifteenth Amendment was intended to eradicate, so too, Bill C-3 simply extends the historical sex discrimination entrenched in section 6 of the 1985 *Indian Act* and is not justified.

Canada has tried to minimize the harm of the discriminatory regime by arguing that it is transitional, because by virtue of the 1985 amendments everyone born after April 17, 1985, will be subject to the two-parent rule: that is, they will be required to have two status parents to qualify for status (Canada 2010e: para 26).[19] This is an ugly argument. Although it is true that s. 6(1)(a) status and s. 6(1)(c) status are only granted to people born prior to April 17, 1985, for those who are directly affected by the continuing sex discrimination there is nothing about the scheme that is transitional. In its effects on people's lives, it is final. Each year that the discriminatory regime survives, more people die without having gained equal status and without having been able to pass status to their descendants. Furthermore, the discriminatory effects of the scheme will continue to be felt for generations to come.

The government's transitional scheme argument is all the more disturbing because it makes the trajectory of the second-generation cut-off seem benign, possibly even laudable. The scheme's adverse treatment of Aboriginal women has always been assimilationist. As we have seen, for female-line descendants, the assimilationist second-generation cut-off applies a generation sooner. The insidious threat of the second-generation cut-off, for all Aboriginal people, is that in the not very distant future, as the cut-off is applied to future generations in which there are families of mixed parentage, there will be no one who is eligible for Indian status. That is the true character of the "transition" that the second-generation cut-off seeks to bring about. The McIvor sex equality challenge has interfered with Canada's assimilationist agenda, temporarily.

The Only Effective Remedy

The time for ending more than 150 years of Canada's sex discrimination against Aboriginal women and their descendants is long overdue. For decades Aboriginal women in Canada have sought justice in the courts and remedial action by legislators in an effort to bring an end to the sex discrimination in the status registration provisions of the *Indian Act*. Yet, they have not yet succeeded in securing full recognition of their rights. Sex discrimination in the registration provisions continues to affect Aboriginal women and their descendants in generation after generation.

Canada has known of this problem for a long time and for decades has acknowledged that the criteria for status discriminate based on sex. Sharon McIvor has spent more than twenty years in the courts. At the close of the McIvor constitutional litigation, the government had the opportunity to completely eliminate the sex discrimination from the scheme. Instead it made amendments, but deliberately left the bulk of the sex discrimination untouched.

If Canada's legal and democratic institutions had taken the constitutional equality rights of Aboriginal women seriously, resort to the international human rights system would not be necessary. However, Aboriginal women in Canada do not yet enjoy full recognition of their constitutionally guaranteed equality rights, as the litigation journey of Sharon McIvor has demonstrated.

The intransigence of the federal government and its persistent failure to accord Aboriginal women the full protection of their constitutionally guaranteed sex equality rights has necessitated recourse, once more, to the international human rights system. In 1981 the U.N. Human Rights Committee was helpful to Aboriginal women in the case of *Lovelace* v. *Canada*, after the Supreme Court of Canada rejected the challenge of Jeanette Corbiere Lavell and Yvonne Bedard under the *Canadian Bill of Rights*.[20]

The Committee may be helpful once again, if it directs Canada to take effective remedial action. Respect for the equality rights of Aboriginal women requires that they and their descendants be made eligible for full Indian status on the same basis that full Indian status is granted to Indian men and their descendants. This is the only effective remedy for the discrimination.

In Canada's domestic courts the federal government has aggressively defended its policy of continuing sex discrimination in the *Indian Act*. However, the McIvor petition to the United Nations Human Rights Committee initiates a new post-Charter stage in Canada's engagement with Aboriginal women's equality rights. It gives Canada a fresh opportunity to revisit an egregious human rights violation and demonstrate its commitment to full equality for Aboriginal women. Ultimately, the goal of the McIvor petition is to spur Canada to action, to do the right thing.

Notes

1. *McIvor* v. *Canada* (2009) BCCA 153 rev'g, in part, 2007 BCSC 827, leave to appeal to SCC refused, No. 33201 (November 5, 2009). See also the supplementary trial court decision on the remedy ordered: *McIvor* v. *Canada* (2007).

2. I have been counsel to Sharon McIvor and Jacob Grismer over a long period of time. I wish to acknowledge the contributions that Sharon McIvor, Shelagh Day, Donna Sullivan and Robert Grant, my co-counsel in the McIvor constitutional litigation, have made to collaborative advocacy work in the McIvor case, in various ways and at various stages. They, as well as many others, have contributed intellectually to the McIvor case, and enriched my thinking about *Indian Act* discrimination and the importance and means of challenging it. I also thank the SSHRC Community University Alliance Programme; and the Centre for Feminist Legal Studies, the Indigenous Legal Studies Programme and the Visiting Scholar Programme, at the University of British Columbia Faculty of Law, for facilitating my work on this chapter. The opinions expressed are my own.

3. By virtue of what is commonly known as the second-generation cut-off introduced by the 1985 *Indian Act* and re-enacted in Bill C-3, these great-grandchilden born prior to April 17, 1985, are still excluded. Also still excluded are the grandchildren born prior to April 4, 1951, who are descendants of women who married out.

4. For discussions about the patriarchal nature of the *Indian Act*, the patriarchal and rac-

ist impulses in colonialism and the challenges of advocating Indian women's rights in the context of colonial and Aboriginal sexism, see Joyce Green 2007 and Kuokkanen, Rauna 2012.

5.   S. Prov. C. 1857, 20 Vict., c. 26.

6.   The 1857 Act provided for the enfranchisement of Indian men over the age of twenty-one who met certain specified criteria. Upon enfranchisement, the Indian men ceased to be Indians. So too did their wives and children.

7.   *Report of the Royal Commission on Aboriginal Peoples* (Ottawa: Supply and Services Canada, 1996) *Perspectives and Realities*, Vol. 4, p. 26. See also: See: *Corbiere v. Canada (Minister of Indian and Northern Affairs)* [1999] 2 S.C.R. 203 at para. 86; Public Inquiry into the Administration of Justice and Aboriginal People, *Report of the Aboriginal Justice Inquiry of Manitoba* (1991), vol. 1, *The Justice Systems and Aboriginal People*, at pp. 476–79.

8.   Parliament first defined Indian in *An Act providing for the organization of the Department of the Secretary of State of Canada, and for the management of Indian and Ordinance Lands*, S.C. 1868, c. 42 (31 Vict.), s. 15. The *1868 Act* was amended in 1869 by *An Act for the gradual enfranchisement of Indians, the better management of Indian affairs, and to extend the provisions of the Act 31st Victoria, Chapter 42*, S.C. 1869, c. 6. (32–33 Vict.). The 1869 Act amended the definition of Indian in s. 15 of the 1868 Act by adding a provision that any Indian woman marrying a non-Indian man lost her Indian identity. So too did the children of the marriage. The 1869 Act also provided that when an Indian woman married an Indian man of a different tribe or band, she ceased to be a member of her own band or tribe and became a member of her husband's band or tribe. The children of the marriage became members of only the father's tribe or band.

9.   The definition of Indian was modified in the *Indian Act*, S.C. 1876, c. 18 (39 Vict.). Pursuant to s. 3 of the 1876 Act the term Indian now meant:

(a)   any male person of Indian blood reputed to belong to a particular band;

(b)   the child of such person; and

(c)   any woman who is or was lawfully married to such person.

10.   *Indian Act*, S.C. 1951, c. 29, as amended.

11.   RCAP 1996.

12.   The *Royal Commission on the Status of Women* recommended that the *Indian Act* be amended "to allow an Indian woman upon marriage to a non-Indian to (a) retain her Indian status; and (b) transmit her Indian status to her children."

13.   The report stated in part:

INDIAN ACT: DISCRIMINATION AGAINST SEX

I.. INTRODUCTION

The Indian Act, it is alleged, discriminates on the grounds of sex and is, therefore, contrary to the provisions of the Human Rights Act. Sections 12(1)(b) and 11(1)(b) apply in particular.

II. PROPOSAL

The object of this paper is to propose that discrimination on the grounds of sex in the Indian Act be eliminated by the following formulation:

Indians who marry non-Indians would remain entitled to be registered; their non-Indian spouses would not be entitled to be registered. Their children would be entitled to be registered if the parents of the Indian parent were both Indian.

14.   Most such descendants did not lose status under a rule referred to as the double-mother

rule, either because they had not yet turned twenty-one in 1985, or their bands had obtained exemptions from the double-mother rule.

Pursuant to an *Indian Act* provision, introduced in 1951, known as the double-mother rule, a legitimate child of a status Indian father, whose mother and grandmother only had status because of their marriages to status men, would lose status at the age of twenty-one. The double-mother rule is exceptional in *Indian Act* history. It was the first and only occasion when a male Indian claiming Indian ancestry along the male line could lose status. However, the double-mother rule was rarely applied. The trial judge noted that only 2,000 individuals were affected by the double-mother rule (*McIvor v. Canada* 2009: para 246).

15. Indian and Northern Affairs Canada, *Discussion Paper: Changes to the Indian Act affecting Indian Registration and Band Membership: McIvor v. Canada* (Ottawa: Indian and Northern Affairs Canada, 2009) at 1, 8 [Indian and Northern Affairs Canada, *Discussion Paper*].

16. Including, for example: on April 13, 2010, Sharon McIvor and myself, Native Women's Association of Canada; Congress of Aboriginal Peoples; on April 15, 2010, Canadian Bar Association, Native Women's Association of Canada; on April 20, 2010, noted Indigenous scholar Pamela Palmater, Quebec Native Women's Association, Union of British Columbia Indian Chiefs.

17. The Committee's observation was noted by James Anaya, the U.N. Special Rapporteur on Indigenous Peoples, who stated in a May 7, 2014, Report to the Human Rights Council: "The enactment of the Gender Equity in Indian Registration Act remediated some of the ongoing discriminatory effects of historical provisions that revoked the Indian status of women — and all their descendants — who married non-status men, while granting status to non-aboriginal women — and their descendants — who married status Indians. Unfortunately, as acknowledged by the Senate Standing Committee on Human Rights, this legislation did 'not deal with all sex discrimination stemming from the Indian Act'; some classes of people continue to be excluded from status on the basis of the historic discrimination against matrilineal descent" (A/HRC/27/52/Add.2, para 55).

18. Prior to 2006, the government's position was that, under the 1985 Act Sharon McIvor was only entitled to s. 6(2) status, because her claim to status was through the female line, and her mother had been assigned s. 6(1)(c) status. Similarly, prior to 2006, Sharon's brother was also confined to section 6(2) status.

19. The government also tried to justify the registration scheme as transitional in the McIvor litigation (*McIvor v. Canada* 2009: paras. 9, 114, 122, 131).

20. *Canada (Attorney General)* v. *Lavell*. 1974. SCR 1349.

References

Canada. 1982. *Minutes of proceedings and evidence of the Sub-committee on Indian women and the Indian Act of the Standing Committee on Indian Affairs and Northern Development.* Parliament. House of Commons. Sub-Committee on Indian Women and the Indian Act of the Standing Committee on Indian Affairs and Northern Development, 32nd Parliament, 1st Session, Issue 2 (9 September).

———. 2010a. *Debates of the Senate.* Parliament. Senate. 40th Parliament, 3rd Session, No. 147 (8 December).

____. 2010b. *House of Commons Debates*. Parliament. House of Commons. 40th Parliament, 3rd Session, No. 018 (26 March).

____. 2010c. *Bill C-3. An Act to promote gender equity in Indian registration by responding to the Court of Appeal for British Columbia decision in McIvor v. Canada (Registrar of Indian and Northern Affairs)*. 40th Parliament, 3rd Session, 2010.

____. 2010d. *Gender Equity in Indian Registration Act*. Parliament. House of Commons. 40th Parliament, 3rd Session, No. 048 (25 May 2010).

____. 2010e. "Submission of the Government of Canada on the Admissibility and Merits of the Communication to the Human Rights Committee of Sharon McIvor and Jacob Grismer." <povertyandhumanrights.org/wp-content/uploads/2011/08/Canadas-Response-McIvor-Petition1.pdf>.

____. 2010f. *House of Commons Debates*. Parliament. House of Commons. 40th Parliament, 3rd Session, No. 101 (22 November).

____. 2010g. *Proceedings of the Standing Senate Committee on Human Rights*. Parliament. Senate. 40th Parliament, 3rd Session, Issue 8 (6 December).

Canadian Charter of Rights and Freedoms, Part I of the *Constitution Act, 1982*, being Schedule B to the *Canada Act 1982* (UK), 1982, c 11.

Committee on Economic, Social and Cultural Rights. 2006. *Concluding Observations of the Committee on Economic, Social and Cultural Rights*. UNGAOR, 36th Session, UN Doc E/C.12/CAN/CO/5.

CEDW (Committee on the Elimination of Discrimination against Women). 2003. *Report of the Committee on the Elimination of Discrimination against Women*. UNGAOR, 58th Session, Supp No 38, UN Doc A/58/38.

____. 2008. *Concluding Observations of the Committee on the Elimination of Discrimination Against Women*. CEDAWOR, 42nd session, UN Doc C/CAN/CO/7.

Green, Joyce. 2007. *Making Space for Indigenous Feminism*. Black Point, NS: Fernwood Publishing.

Human Rights Committee. 2006. *Concluding Observations of the Human Rights Committee*. CCPROR, 85th Session, UN Doc C/CAN/CO/5.

International Covenant on Civil and Political Rights. 1966. 16 December. 999 UNTS 171, Can TS 1976 No 47.

Kuokkanen, Rauna. 2012. "Self-Determination and Indigenous Women's Rights at the Intersection of International Human Rights." *Human Rights Quarterly* 34, 1.

McIvor and Grismer. 2010. "Sharon McIvor and Grismer v. Canada: Communication Submitted for Consideration under the First Optional Protocol to the *International Covenant on Civil and Political Rights*." <povertyandhumanrights.org/wp-content/uploads/2011/08/McIvorApplicantsPetition1.pdf>.

____. 2011. "Sharon McIvor and Grismer v. Canada: Petitioner Comments in Response to State Party's Submission on the Admissibility and Merits of the Applicants' Petition to the Human Rights Committee." <povertyandhumanrights.org/wp-content/uploads/2011/08/Mcivor-v.-Canada-Petitioner-Comments-December-5-2011.pdf>.

Phillip, Grand Chief Stewart. 2011. "*Sharon McIvor and Jacob Grismer v. Canada*: Affidavit of Grand Chief Stewart Phillip." <povertyandhumanrights.org/wp-content/uploads/2011/08/Grand-Chief-Stewart-Philip-Affidavit.pdf>.

RCAP (Royal Commission on Aboriginal People). 1996. *Report of the Royal Commission on Aboriginal Peoples, Perspectives and Realities* Vol. 4, p. 28. Ottawa: Supply and Services Canada.

____. 2006. *Report of the Royal Commission on Aboriginal Peoples.* Ottawa: Government of Canada.

Statutes

An Act to Encourage the Gradual Civilization of Indian Tribes in the Province and to Amend the Laws Respecting Indians, S Prov C 1857, 20 Vict, c 26.

Gradual Enfranchisement Act, SC 1869, c 6.

Indian Act, SC 1951, c 29.

Indian Act, RSC 1985, c I-5.

Legal Cases

Canada (Attorney General) v. *Lavell.* (1974). SCR 1349.

Guinn v. *United States.* (1915). 238 U.S. 347.

Lovelace v. Canada, Communication No. R.6/24, U.N. Doc. Supp. No. 40 (A/36/40) at 166 (1981).

McIvor v. *Canada (Registrar of Indian and Northern Affairs).* (2009). BCCA 153.

McIvor v. The Registrar, Indian and Northern Affairs Canada. (2007). BCSC 827.

Chapter Six

Confronting Violence
Indigenous Women, Self-Determination
and International Human Rights
Rauna Kuokkanen

In the past forty years, Indigenous peoples' self-determination has become a significant global human rights issue at both national and international levels. Indigenous
peoples' human rights have been recognized by the international community in
the adoption of the United Nations *Declaration on the Rights of Indigenous Peoples*
in 2007 (UNDRIP) (General Assembly 2007). Indigenous rights advocates have
been instrumental in redefining the concept of self-determination and advancing
collective human rights in international law. Indigenous peoples' human rights are
often regarded as part of the emerging "third generation human rights," centring on
collective rights and, in particular, the right to self-determination. "First generation
human rights" include civil and political rights, while "second generation human
rights" consist of rights related to equality. The third generation human rights
consist of rights usually articulated in aspirational declarations of international law
("soft law") and are often hard to enforce. The adoption of the U.N. *Declaration on
the Rights of Indigenous Peoples* signified an agreement (however uneasy) by the
international community that self-determination is the fundamental principle from
which Indigenous peoples' rights emanate. This has been the core of the Indigenous
peoples' claims — that without the collective right to self-determination, thereby
remaining distinct peoples, Indigenous peoples are not able to effectively exercise
their other human rights (Sambo Dorough 2009: 264–66). Importantly, the significance of collective rights for Indigenous peoples lies in the fact that "collective
rights claims are not just about protecting cultural attachment; they are also about
political voice and gaining access to the processes which affect the physical and
economic conditions under which one lives" (Holder and Corntassel 2002: 139).

Self-determination (both individual and collective) and gendered violence
are among the most important and pressing issues for Indigenous women worldwide. Existing Indigenous self-governance arrangements have often failed to protect women from social and economic dispossession and from the multilayered
violence they experience in their own communities and in society at large. It has
also become evident that current justice systems or existing structures do not adequately address violence against Indigenous women.[1] Therefore, there is a need
to extend the analysis from a legal framework to a political one. Without addressing the disadvantaged social and economic conditions of Indigenous women that
make them vulnerable to violence and often unable to escape from it, Indigenous

self-determination or self-governance will simply not be possible. Societies and communities afflicted by endemic levels of poverty, violence and ill-health are not in a position to take control of their own affairs. Although impoverishment and violence affect entire communities, they are particularly issues of women's human rights (broadly conceived including civil, political, social, economic and cultural rights) and of gender justice. Individual autonomy and agency strengthen Indigenous claims for self-determination by linking strong collective human rights (self-determination) to strong individual human rights. As "mutually interactive" sets of human rights, they contribute to the relational approach to Indigenous self-determination, which is reflected in many Indigenous women's views and perceptions of self-determination.

This chapter explores the interconnections between Indigenous self-determination, human rights and violence against women. It places both self-determination and violence against women within the international human rights framework and contends that Indigenous self-determination cannot be achieved without taking into account pressing issues involving Indigenous women's social, economic, civil and political rights. The chapter begins with a consideration of Indigenous self-determination as a collective human right and a critique of the standard, narrow interpretations of self-determination as state sovereignty and independent statehood. Second, it examines the question of Indigenous women's rights as human rights and the commonly assumed tension between collective Indigenous peoples' rights and individual rights. As the chapter demonstrates, this tension, however, is spurious and is imputed only to women's human rights. Otherwise, collective and individual rights in Indigenous communities are commonly considered "mutually interactive," or belonging to a holistic continuum. Finally, Indigenous women's human rights are linked to the question of violence against women and show how Indigenous self-determination is not achievable without taking account of the full scale of Indigenous women's human rights and addressing their violations.

Self-Determination as a Human Right

Rather than considering self-determination a right of sovereign states, it is increasingly regarded as a human right in international law. James Anaya holds that the widely shared opposition by states to the recognition of self-determination as applying to all peoples stems from the misconception that in its fullest sense, self-determination implies a right to independent statehood — a misconception "often reinforced by reference to decolonization, which has involved the transformation of colonial territories into new states under the normative aegis of self-determination" (Anaya 1996: 80). Anaya distinguishes between remedial (that is, decolonization) and substantive (that is, constitutional and ongoing) aspects of self-determination, the latter of which forms the principles defining the standard of self-determination.

Anaya is particularly critical of narrow conceptions of self-determination and peoples based on a post-Westphalian vision of the world divided into mutually exclusive territorial communities. This conception "ignores the multiple, overlapping spheres of community, authority, and interdependency that actually exist in the human experience" (Anaya 1996: 78). Hence, a more appropriate conception of self-determination arises within the human rights framework of contemporary international law such as the two 1966 international human rights covenants, the *International Covenant on Civil and Political Rights* (ICCPR) and the *International Covenant on Economic, Social and Cultural Rights* (ICESCR), both of which recognize that "all peoples have the right to self-determination" (General Assembly 1966a, 1966b). Importantly, this is a collective right applying to peoples rather than individuals — a reminder that challenges the polarized views arguing that all human rights are inherently individualistic — which, in the past decade, has also been applied to Indigenous peoples by the U.N. Human Rights Committee (see Koivurova 2008).

In the context of Indigenous peoples' rights, one of the most controversial issues has been the concept of "peoples." Anaya contends that in order to grasp self-determination as a human right, it is necessary to question the limited perception of "peoples" as "identified by reference to certain objective criteria linked with ethnicity and attributes of historical sovereignty" or "with the aggregate population of a state" and instead, to understand the term "in a flexible manner, as encompassing all relevant spheres of community and identity" (Anaya 2009: 186). He suggests:

> Understood as a human right, the essential idea of self-determination is that human beings, individually and as groups, are equally entitled to be in control of their own destinies, and to live within governing institutional orders that are devised accordingly ... under a human rights approach, attributes of statehood or sovereignty are, at most, instrumental to the realization of these values — they are not the essence of self-determination for peoples. (Anaya 2009: 187–88)

Feminist political theorists and Indigenous scholars view the recognition of the interdependence and overlapping character of human communities in the world as the foundation of theories and conceptions of relational self-determination. In her analysis of two conceptions of self-determination, Iris Marion Young (2007) argues that a relational interpretation of self-determination better reflects reality in general, and specifically Indigenous peoples' claims for the right to self-determination. In her view, the dominant understanding of self-determination as non-interference, separation and independence is misleading and also a dangerous fiction. She argues that the precept of non-interference "does not properly take account of social relationships and possibilities for domination" (Young 2007: 46). It also creates an illusion of independence that in fact is constituted by institutional relations and a system of domination. For Young, non-interference is neither desirable nor possible in today's interconnected and interdependent world. She contends:

> Insofar as outsiders are affected by the activities of a self-determining people, those others have a legitimate claim to have their interests and needs taken into account even though they are outside the government jurisdiction. Conversely, outsiders should recognize that when they themselves affect a people, the latter can legitimately claim that they should have their interests taken into account insofar as they may be adversely affected. Insofar as they affect one another, peoples are in relationships and ought to negotiate the terms and effects of the relationship. (Young 2007: 51)

While arguing for a relational approach and recognition of interdependence, Young makes an exception with regard to a people's "prima facie right to set its own governance procedures and make its own decisions about its activities, without interference from others" (Young 2007: 51). This understanding, which combines the group right to govern itself and to make decisions over its own affairs with the recognition of the relational nature of self-determination, is reflected in many Indigenous women's views and understandings of self-determination. These views recognize the interdependence and reciprocity between all living beings and often are articulated in terms of responsibilities rather than rights. Carried out through everyday practices as well as through ceremonies, self-determination is embedded and encoded in individual and collective responsibilities sometimes called the laws (or "customary law"[2]) that lay the foundation of Indigenous societies.[3] However, in the colonial context, cultural responsibilities have been forced into a framework of "Indigenous rights."

Indigenous Women's Rights

Women's rights have been formally codified as human rights in the *Convention on the Elimination of All Forms of Discrimination Against Women* (CEDAW) (General Assembly 1979). Indigenous peoples' human rights have been codified in UNDRIP, which, unlike CEDAW, is not a binding treaty. UNDRIP creates an instrument that recognizes and takes account of the specificities of Indigenous peoples' human rights (including collective human rights). In the same way as the global women's movement had argued earlier, the work leading to the UNDRIP was driven by the recognition that conventional or universal approaches to human rights had failed to adequately protect Indigenous peoples.

In spite of the adoption of these two key international human rights instruments, Indigenous women's rights remain a contentious and often neglected issue at both international and local levels. For Indigenous women, both women's rights and Indigenous rights movements have been problematic spaces due to colonization and ongoing colonial legacies (Parisi and Corntassel 2007: 81). The concern for Indigenous women has long been the lack of recognition of the ways in which "Indigenous women commonly experience human rights violations at the crossroads of their individual and collective identities" (FIMI 2006: 8). Environmental pollution and the destruction of ecosystems are good examples of such violations, as they undermine Indigenous peoples' control of and access to their lands and resources and often compromise women's ability to take care of their children and families due to health problems, contamination and displacement, which often leads to increased violence.

Feminist critiques have shed light on the way in which international human rights law has in many ways neglected women and their rights. Drawing on this criticism, I have argued elsewhere that international Indigenous human rights framework, most prominently represented by UNDRIP, reproduces and perpetuates similar exclusions and hierarchies toward Indigenous women. Like other international human rights instruments, it reflects the bias of prioritizing civil and political rights and the subsequent inferiority of rights violations taking place in the sphere considered private. It also renders Indigenous women inherently vulnerable, categorizing them with children and elders. Instead, the UNDRIP ought to have acknowledged that in most cases, women's vulnerability stems from the prevalent gender discrimination and subjugation in society. Moreover, it turns a blind eye to the intragroup difference and oppression that also exists in Indigenous communities (Kuokkanen 2014).

For the international women's movement, a problem with the conventional human rights framework has been the dichotomy between the private and the public spheres. For Indigenous women, the key issue is to pursue a human rights framework that not only simultaneously advances individual and collective rights, but also explicitly addresses gender-specific human rights violations against Indigenous women and does not disregard the continued practices and effects of colonialism. As indicated by Indigenous women's criticism of the Beijing Platform for Action (1995), the tension between the two movements is located in the international women's movement's "overemphasis on gender discrimination and gender equality which depoliticizes issues confronting Indigenous women" (Parisi and Corntassel 2007: 81) and does not recognize the special circumstances of Indigenous women (Sillett 2009). It has also been argued that a focus on gender discrimination tends to overemphasize individual equality and rights rather than explicating structural violence such as the oppression and dispossession by the state (Peterson 1990: 328–32).

UNDRIP recognizes both individual and collective human rights of Indigenous peoples and emphasizes that it applies equally to "male and female Indigenous individuals" (General Assembly 2007: art. 44). It also specifically mentions the obligation of both states and Indigenous nations "to ensure that Indigenous women and children enjoy the full protection and guarantees against all forms of violence and discrimination" (General Assembly 2007: art. 22, para. 2). Several other international documents have also recognized the significance of both individual and collective Indigenous rights. Thus, it has been argued that "Indigenous peoples generally recognize that collective and individual rights are *mutually interactive* rather than in competition" (Holder and Corntassel 2002: 129, emphasis in original). As an example, the Inuit Tapirisat of Canada "believe[s] in individual and collective rights as complementary aspects of an holistic human rights regime" (Commission on Human Rights 1994: para. 4).

In the quest for Indigenous self-determination, however, women's rights have been often considered divisive and disruptive. Indigenous women advocating their rights have been repeatedly charged of being disloyal to their communities, of being co-opted by "Western feminists" and of introducing alien concepts and thinking to Indigenous communities and practices. If not entirely disregarded, women's rights, concerns and priorities are commonly put on the back burner to be addressed "later," once collective self-determination has been achieved.[4] Many Indigenous women have confronted these views by contending that securing Indigenous women's rights is inextricable from securing the rights of their peoples as a whole (for example, Gutiérrez and Palomo 2000: 77–79; Smith 2005: 116, 129–30).

It has also been argued that without individual self-determination, meaningful and viable collective self-determination of Indigenous peoples is not possible. Val Napoleon argues that the Indigenous political discourse regarding self-determination would be more useful to communities if it incorporated an understanding of the individual as relational, autonomous and self-determining. That is, a developed perspective of individual self-determination is necessary to move collective self-determination beyond rhetoric to a meaningful and practical political project that engages Indigenous peoples and is deliberately inclusive of Indigenous women (Napoleon 2005: 31).

If Indigenous rights are widely regarded as both individual and collective, the issue in the continued opposition to or neglect of Indigenous women's rights is something other than the assumed irreconcilability between the two categories of human rights. Given the lack of adequate, sustained attention to the endemic levels of violence against Indigenous women in many countries by the Indigenous self-determination movement, Indigenous organizations and leadership, one can only conclude that prevailing and persistent gender injustice in both Indigenous and mainstream societies lies at the heart of the breaches of Indigenous women's human rights, not the conflict between individual and collective (or between universal and local) rights.

Violence Against Indigenous Women

Globally, gender violence is increasingly considered a serious human rights violation.[5] While direct physical and sexual violence are the most severe manifestations of the oppression of women, they cannot be fully understood outside the larger framework and ideologies of domination. As Catharine MacKinnon defines violence against women:

> By violence against women, I mean aggression against and exploitation of

women because we are women, systemically and systematically. Systemic, meaning socially patterned, including sexual harassment, rape, battering of women by intimates, sexual abuse of children, and woman-killing in the context of poverty, imperialism, colonialism, and racism. Systematic, meaning intentionally organized, including prostitution, pornography, sex tours, ritual torture, and official custodial torture in which women are exploited and violated for sex, politics, and profit in a context of, and in intricate collaboration with, poverty, imperialism, colonialism, and racism. (MacKinnon 2006: 29)

Violence against Indigenous women has reached endemic levels in many countries. This violence occurs at various levels and spheres: interpersonal, structural, public, private, state and non-state (such as multinational corporations) (see, for example, Amnesty International 2004, 2007; FIMI 2006, UNPFII 2012; Wirringa Baiya 2011). Indigenous women face violations of their civil and political rights when they are marginalized or excluded from their communities and when their membership is denied. They encounter abuses of their economic and social rights in the intersections of racism, sexism, poverty and discrimination, which lead to a lack of employment opportunities and access to health care and social services. They are confronted with violations of their personal integrity and human dignity in the form of, sometimes, extreme physical and sexual violence. Failure to recognize that Indigenous women's rights are violated not only as Indigenous people but also as women ultimately leads to a failure in promoting and protecting Indigenous rights in general.

Indigenous women and their organizations have long criticized mainstream approaches to violence against women for being too restrictive or for not taking Indigenous peoples' realities and specific circumstances, especially the consequences of colonialism, into account. For example, categories such as family, community and state may carry different meanings and relationships to Indigenous peoples than what is implied in standard research or in strategies addressing violence against women. According to Indigenous women's organizations, these studies and strategies fail to take account of the specific ways Indigenous women are targeted by various forms of violence — some of which may not apply to non-Indigenous women (for example, cross-border violence, ecological violence, spiritual violence) (FIMI 2006: 27–32).

The International Indigenous Women's Forum (FIMI) maintains that collective Indigenous rights are a key to anti-violence strategies and that the ability for Indigenous women to exercise their rights hinges on the legal recognition of Indigenous territories, governance and, ultimately, the right to self-determination. At the same time, collective Indigenous rights rely on the protection of Indigenous women's rights: "securing Indigenous women's human rights — in particular, the right to freedom from violence *as defined by Indigenous women themselves* — is integral to securing the rights of their Peoples as a whole" (FIMI 2006: 14, emphasis in original).

In its report *Mairin Iwanka Raya: Indigenous Women Stand against Violence* (2006), FIMI seeks to develop an Indigenous conception of violence against women in order to generate concrete and effective strategies to address the widespread problem. The report considers six broad categories of manifestations of violence against Indigenous women: neoliberalism and development aggression; violence in the name of tradition; state and domestic violence; militarization and armed conflict; migration and displacement; and HIV/AIDS. Under its category of "violence in the name of tradition" (a term which FIMI prefers over the widely used phrase "harmful traditional practices," which include female genital mutilation, bridal dowries and forced marriages), the report challenges the oft-proposed tension between universal human rights standards and local cultural practices, maintaining that "it is not 'culture' that lies at the root of violence against women, but practices and norms that deny women gender equity, education, resources, and political and social power" (FIMI 2006: 25). This echoes the criticism by Indigenous feminist scholars who have pointed out that traditions (including those claiming to respect women) do not necessarily protect women's individual rights or advance women's leadership but instead, have been employed to re-inscribe domination and patriarchal structures.[6]

However, a closer examination of FIMI's "Indigenous conception of violence against women" reveals a potential weakness in understanding violence against Indigenous women. Many of the manifestations of violence discussed by FIMI are not gender-specific in the sense that women are not specifically targeted by these forms of violence, although women may (and usually do) carry the disproportionate burden of the effects of these forms of violence due to their reproductive capacity and roles as primary caretakers of the children and families. In other words, FIMI's conception conflates gendered *forms* of violence with gendered *effects* of more general forms of violence that target Indigenous communities at large rather than specifically Indigenous women. This distinction (gendered forms vs. gendered effects of violence) is critical if we are to produce effective strategies to address gender-specific forms of violence against Indigenous women.

Conflating the forms with the effects obscures self-determination as an Indigenous women's issue and a gender justice issue. To ensure that the question of survival of Indigenous women is included in the question of survival of Indigenous communities, gender justice cannot be omitted from any discussion or project of Indigenous self-determination. In order to maintain gender justice as an inextricable part of Indigenous self-determination, gendered forms of violence need to be examined and addressed specifically and separately.

The way in which gendered violence among Indigenous peoples has been and continues to be a central tool of colonialism has been well established (Razack 2002; Smith 2005). What has been less examined is the politics of violence in Indigenous communities (Kuokkanen 2014a). The report of the U.N. Expert Group Meeting on Violence against Indigenous Women and Girls mentions a concern relating to "the overemphasis on colonization in conversations about addressing violence against Indigenous women and girls." The report argues:

> There is a stigma about talking about interpersonal violence within Indigenous communities. One reason for this is the imposed patriarchal societal practices that render interpersonal physical and sexual violence as belonging to the private domain and thus something that is not discussed in public. It is important to recognize the ways in which the private/public division of the colonizer has been adopted by Indigenous communities and how that affected the human rights of Indigenous women and girls. (UNPFII 2012, para. 23)

Elsewhere, I have argued that rather than dismissing the public/private dichotomy as a Western construct we need it to recognize how this dichotomy is employed to create, maintain and reproduce Indigenous women's subordination (Kuokkanen 2014). In another context, I have examined the danger of considering gendered violence as merely a consequence of discrimination against the entire Indigenous community. Recognizing how internalization and adoption of colonial policies and practices designed to regulate and discriminate against Indigenous women by Indigenous leadership and institutions has resulted in reluctance and refusal to deal with gendered violence, I examined the depoliticization of violence against women in Indigenous communities and argued that there is a need for an analysis of the scope and nature of gendered violence and forms of oppression in Indigenous communities (Kuokkanen 2014a).

International Human Rights Framework

The human rights framework and rights-based discourses are not without their critics. Inherently anti-relativist in its attempt to formulate fundamental moral and ethical norms for human behaviour and interaction, the human rights framework has long been criticized for its tendency to overlook cultural and regional differences and for representing a form of cultural imperialism in its attempt to universalize a Western liberal, individualistic rights framework. Feminist human rights scholars have also been critical of human rights' focus on male priorities, behaviour and interests while ignoring women's responsibilities and circumstances. However, the purpose of the U.N. *Charter* was never to replace national laws or impose homogeneity. There are numerous human rights bodies and instruments to recognize and accommodate group-specific and regional differences. The recognition of cultural diversity was also the starting point for UNDRIP, the ultimate objective of which was to create an instrument and framework for the realization of Indigenous peoples' human rights, including "a number of collective human rights specific to Indigenous peoples" (Sambo Dorough 2009: 265).

Rights-based discourses on Indigenous self-determination have been criticized for being too state-centric to be able to deliver viable Indigenous self-determination premised on community involvement and citizen participation.[7] Corntassel (2008: 108) contends: "Strategies that invoke existing human rights norms and that solely seek political and legal recognition of Indigenous self-determination will not lead to a self-determination process that is sustainable for the survival of future generations of Indigenous peoples." Corntassel is right to point out that appeals to human rights or calls for political and legal recognition of Indigenous self-determination either by states or intergovernmental organizations such as the U.N. will not deliver self-determination or even more limited forms of autonomy or self-government in Indigenous communities.[8] However, the role of international human rights discourse and Indigenous international advocacy in this process is important. They can — and already have, in the form of UNDRIP, for example — expanded conceptions and understandings of the scope and contents of Indigenous self-determination, not as non-interference and independent statehood as conceptualized in state-centric discourses, but as an internationally recognized and existing human right that belongs to people, not just nation-states. Historically, the exercise of self-determination has rarely taken place without negotiations and some kind of an agreement with the state or states within which borders the group or people has resided (Foster 2001: 143, 150). In today's interconnected and interdependent world, it would be unrealistic to assume future significant or sustainable achievements without some form of a dialogue or mediation. Also, considering how Indigenous peoples have transformed from being historical victims of international law into active participants and political actors in shaping international law (including the concept of self-determination), Indigenous peoples' active participation in rights-based discourses is not only appropriate, but necessary in realizing their very right to self-determination.

Indigenous rights advocates have deployed international human rights instruments in claims for self-determination and, more fundamentally, to be recognized as peoples as defined in Article 1(1) of the 1966 Human Rights Covenants (General Assembly 1966a). Although Indigenous rights advocates have acknowledged that international human rights discourse can be conceptually limiting and politically problematic, this discourse also has potential as one tool among several others, including a range of local, community-based processes rooted in culturally specific contexts and discourses. Moreover, the strategy of bypassing the states and going to international forums such as the United Nations indicates a preference for employing international, rather than nation-state, human rights instruments and thus avoiding subordination to the state and to its national legislation. As some have argued, UNDRIP in particular "reflects unified views of international human rights law that embrace cultural diversity and allow for a multiplicity of cultural contexts," and that the human rights standards of UNDRIP "provide the necessary framework for a human-rights based approach and for a new conceptualization of Indigenous and state relations" (Sambo Dorough 2009: 266).

In re-conceptualizing Indigenous and state relations, however, we need to bear in mind the inherent and unequal structures and relations of power and domination. States all too often use human rights discourses to circumscribe Indigenous peoples' attempts to exercise their local autonomy, demonstrating the ever-present potential for the politicization and misuse of human rights discourse. For example, in Chiapas, Mexico, the state has employed human rights to interfere in the affairs of Indigenous communities and "render Indigenous leaders vulnerable to state sanctions," for example by arresting "Indigenous leaders who (the government claims) have violated the human and constitutional rights of community members" (Speed and Collier 2000: 878). At the same time, these and other state interventions attest to the relative success of Indigenous peoples' struggles for greater self-determination. It appears governments view it necessary to manipulate rights discourses in order to curb Indigenous institutions and community leaders, which are seen as threatening to state power and authority.[9] Part of this success can be credited to Indigenous peoples redefining and making international human rights relevant and useful for their needs and purposes, while being fully aware of the foreign origins of the discourse and, at times, its inconsistency with Indigenous concepts and social norms. Indigenous actors involved in reconfiguring and redeploying human rights discourses to challenge existing power structures can be found in both local community struggles and international forums such as the United Nations (Hale 2002: 496). Thus, it would be incorrect to interpret Indigenous human rights-based discourses of self-determination as merely state-centric. Instead, the active engagement at local and international planes can and should be seen as the very exercise of autonomy and self-determination.[10] The emergence of various human rights discourses — some of which, in some contexts, seek to restrict the other — also indicates that they are constantly evolving and are not necessarily "products of the imposition of Western ideas [or] of specifically Indigenous or local concepts" (Speed and Solano 2008: 215, 218–21).

Further, Penelope Andrews maintains that the global human rights discourse, combined with local programs and initiatives, has the potential to create an effective framework to deal with violence against Indigenous women. Yet in order to do so, several serious obstacles must be overcome, such as complicated and distant enforcement mechanisms, lack of accessibility and a general unfamiliarity with the formal, legalistic paradigm of the international human rights framework (Andrews 1997; see also UNPFII 2012). She writes: "Although the pursuit of human rights through United Nations or regionally mandated procedures are theoretically possible, and symbolically positive, the enforcement procedures provided in various human rights instruments are constrained by lengthy time periods between initial reporting and final outcome" (Andrews 1997: 935).

While not specifically considering violence against Indigenous women,

Kerensa Johnston's analysis of employing CEDAW to end discrimination of Māori women in New Zealand sheds light on these issues. She distinguishes two categories of discrimination: internal discrimination stems from and is experienced in customary Māori contexts, while external discrimination refers to discrimination caused by sexist and colonial laws and practices. Johnston says a discrimination complaint under the Optional Protocol of the Convention could be an effective strategy. However, there are also potential drawbacks in pursuing an external discrimination complaint:

> There is no guarantee the New Zealand government will accept the recommendations [of the CEDAW Committee] in the current political climate. The government has a poor record of recognizing and protecting Māori rights and interests generally. In light of this, it is unlikely to be motivated to take steps to protect Māori women in particular from state-imposed discrimination, even though adverse attention from the Women's Committee is likely to cause embarrassment. (Johnston 2005: 57)

When it comes to internal discrimination in Māori customary contexts, Johnston argues against pursuing a complaint under international human rights instruments, for they "are not the right places to remedy discriminatory cultural practices that are arguably sourced in *tikanga* [that is, customary law]" (Johnston 2005: 20). The more appropriate place for solving internal disputes is the *marae*, the Māori meeting place. However, Johnston also recognizes the problem of leaving disputes unresolved, especially in internal discrimination cases involving Māori women who might feel silenced or alienated in their own communities and as a result, withdraw from participating in *marae* affairs.

While Johnston recognizes how Māori women, like many other Indigenous women and women of colour, are too often faced with the "your culture or your rights" ultimatum between aspirations for self-determination and women's rights, she appears to prioritize Māori self-determination:

> Although recourse to external bodies may be desirable in the short term because it provides an immediate solution to a pressing problem, the long-term benefits are not as clear. This is because the role of external bodies, and particularly the courts, is not to provide long-term, robust solutions for Māori communities that promote and develop Māori self-determination. (Johnston 2005: 60)

This, however, appears to be a false dilemma. Immediate, short-term solutions to the pressing problem of discrimination against Māori women will allow and enable Māori women to more effectively participate and get involved in developing and promoting the collective project of Māori self-determination. Further, while international human rights instruments might not be appropriate places to remedy discriminatory cultural practices, as Johnston argues, there is a need for caution when using culture as justification for certain sets of rights (and not others). Cultural practices and customary contexts are contested sites, especially in contemporary settings characterized by hierarchies of gender, power and status, as also recognized by Johnston (2005: 52–53).

Violence Is a Human Rights Issue

For many Indigenous women, self-determination is crucial at both individual and collective levels, and neither should be compromised in the name of the other. Individual self-determination is a condition for sustainable and strong collective self-determination. Survival, for Indigenous women, is both an individual and collective matter. Violence against Indigenous women is inseparable from the project of Indigenous self-determination. A human rights framework provides an intersectional analysis in a way that enables addressing both as explicitly human rights issues and anchoring gendered violence in the question of Indigenous self-determination.

Part of this framework is recognizing how the tension between collective and individual Indigenous rights is illusory, as those who argue against individual rights do so only when women's rights are in question. Put differently, those Indigenous individuals who object to women's human rights (often conceptualized as sex/gender equality rights) do not seem to oppose individual rights in general. It is, then, not individual rights per se that are being disputed, but rather gender justice and women's rights. The fact that both existing Indigenous self-governance arrangements and the international Indigenous self-determination movement have, thus far, paid inadequate attention to the question of Indigenous women's human rights in general, and violence against Indigenous women specifically, is also indicative of this.

Finally, conceptualizing Indigenous peoples' rights as human rights and as both individual and collective rights, exposes the double standard in the domestic politicized rhetoric that opposes Indigenous women's rights as individualistic and hence, in conflict with collective rights. Rather than separating them into different categories such as Indigenous rights vis-à-vis sex/gender equality rights, Indigenous peoples' rights and Indigenous women's rights are to be recognized as human rights existing in a continuum. Foregrounding the human rights framework also allows us to place gendered violence firmly in the broader context of rights and the violation of rights. The merit of such a framework is that it does not regard violence against women as only a criminal or social concern, nor does it separate the issue from the question of Indigenous self-determination. At the same time, there is a need to distinguish between gendered forms of violence against Indigenous women and gendered effects of violence that targets Indigenous communities as a whole. Collapsing gendered forms with broader effects obscures conceptualizing and understanding violence against Indigenous women explicitly as a question of gender justice, which cannot be considered merely as a consequence of oppression of Indigenous peoples in general.

Notes

This is a revised version of an article published in Human Rights Quarterly 34.1 (2012): 225, published with permission.

1. See Angela Cameron 2008: 170–75; Mary Crnkovich 1995; Jennifer Koshan 1998: 23, 35–38; Peter H. Russell 2008; Ann-Claire Larsen and Alan Petersen 2001: 121, 125–26.
2. The term "customary law" has been critiqued by many scholars. See, for example, Cunneen and Schwartz 2005; Val Napoleon 2006; Tim Schouls 2003: 131–32; and Gordon R. Woodman 2000.
3. See Rauna Kuokkanen 2011: 39, Patricia Monture-Angus 1999; Andrea Smith 2005: 116, 129; Sharon H. Venne 1999: 27; and Ingrid Washinawatok 1999: 23.
4. See Joyce Green, "Taking Account of Aboriginal Feminism," in Joyce Green 2007: 24–28; Kerensa Johnston 2005: 19, 41–47; Irma Otzoy 2008: 171, 181–82; Liesbeth van der Hoogte and Koos Kingma 2004: 47, 48–49; see also Andrea Smith 2005: 116, 121.
5. See, for example, Catharine A. MacKinnon 2006: 1–3; and Sally Engle Merry 2001: 39.
6. See Jennifer Nez Denetdale 2006: 9; Joyce Green 2001: 715, 726–28; Emma LaRocque 1997; Dawn Martin-Hill 2003: 107–14; Teressa Nahanee 1997: 95–100.
7. See Taiaiake Alfred 1999: 53–54; Jeff Corntassel 2007: 137, 150–51; Glen S. Coulthard 2007: 437, 438–39.
8. For criticism on current self-determination endeavors as state-centric to the detriment of local processes and engagement, see, for example, Rauna Kuokkanen 2009: 107–09.
9. See also Charles R. Hale, 2002: 485, 489–90.
10. Claire Charters 2010: 215, 218–21.

References

Alfred, Taiaiake. Peace, Power, Righteousness: An Indigenous Manifesto. Don Mills: Oxford University Press.

Amnesty International. 2004. "Stolen Sisters: A Human Rights Response to Discrimination and Violence Against Indigenous Women in Canada." <amnesty.ca/stolensisters/amr2000304.pdf>.

____. 2007. "Maze of Injustice: The Failure to Protect Indigenous Women from Sexual Violence in the USA." New York: Amnesty International.

Anaya, S. James. 1996. Indigenous Peoples in International Law. New York: Oxford University Press.

____. 2009. "The Right of Indigenous Peoples to Self-Determination in the Post-Declaration Era." In Claire Charters & Rodolfo Stavenhagen (eds.), Making the Declaration Work: The United Nations Declaration on the Rights of Indigenous Peoples. Copenhagen and New Brunswick: iwgia.

Andrews, Penelope. 1997. "Violence Against Aboriginal Women in Australia: Possibilities for Redress within the International Human Rights Framework." Alberta Law Review 60.

"Beijing Declaration and Platform for Action." 1995. Beijing: U.N. Fourth World Conference on Women.

Cameron, Angela. 2008. "R. v. Gladue: Sentencing and the Gendered Impacts of Colonialism." In John D. Whyte (ed.), Moving Toward Justice: Legal Traditions and Aboriginal Justice. Saskatoon & Regina: Purich & Saskatchewan Institute of Public Policy.

Castellino, Joshua, and Gilbert Jérémie. 2003. "Self-Determination, Indigenous Peoples and Minorities." Macquarie Law Journal 3.

Charters, Claire. 2010. "A Self-Determination Approach to Justifying Indigenous Peoples' Participation in International Law and Policy Making." International Journal on Minority and Group Rights 17, 2.

Commission on Human Rights. 1994. Information Received from Indigenous Peoples' and Non-governmental Organizations: The Inuit Tapirisat of Canada, A Comment on Article 3 of the Draft Declaration on the Rights of Indigenous Peoples, U.N. escor, Commission on Human Rights, U.N. Doc. E/CN.4/Sub.2/AC.4/1994/4/Add.1.

Corntassel, Jeff. 2007. "Partnership in Action? Indigenous Political Mobilization and Co-optation During the First U.N. Indigenous Decade (1995–2004)." Human Rights Quarterly 29, 1.

____. 2008. "Toward Sustainable Self-Determination: Rethinking the Contemporary Indigenous-Rights Discourse." Alternatives 33, 1.

Coulthard, Glen S. 2007. "Subjects of Empire: Indigenous Peoples and the 'Politics of Recognition' in Canada." Contemporary Political Theory 6, 4.

Crnkovich, Mary. 1995. The Role of the Victim in the Criminal Justice System — Circle Sentencing in Inuit Communities. Canadian Association of Sexual Assault Centres (casac). <casac.ca/content/role-victim-criminal-justice-system-circle-sentencing-inuit-communities-0>.

Cunneen, Chris, and Melanie Schwartz. 2005. Background Paper 11: Customary Law, Human Rights and International Law: Some Conceptual Issues, Law Reform Commission of Western Australia, 429, 431 <http://www.lrc.justice.wa.gov.au/094-bp.html>.

Denetdale, Jennifer Nez. 2006. "Chairmen, Presidents, and Princesses: The Navajo Nation, Gender, and the Politics of Tradition." Wicazo Sa Review 21, 1.

fimi (Foro Internacional de Mujeres Indigenas). 2006. Mairin Iwanka Raya: Indigenous Women Stand Against Violence. A Companion Report to the United Nations Secretary-General's Study on Violence against Women. New York: fimi/International Indigenous Women's Forum.

Foster, Caroline E. 2001. "Articulating Self-Determination in the Draft Declaration on the Rights of Indigenous Peoples." European Journal of International Law 12, 1.

General Assembly. 1966a. International Covenant on Civil and Political Rights [iccpr], adopted 16 Dec., G.A. Res. 2200 (XXI), U.N. gaor, 21st Sess., art 1, U.N. Doc. A/6316 (1966), 999 U.N.T.S. 171 (entered into force 23 Mar. 1976)

____. 1966b. International Covenant on Economic, Social and Cultural Rights [icescr], adopted 16 Dec., G.A. Res. 2200 (XXI), U.N. gaor, 21st Sess., art.1, U.N. Doc. A/6316 (1966), 993 U.N.T.S. 3 (entered into force 3 Jan. 1976).

____. 1979. Convention on the Elimination of All Forms of Discrimination Against Women, adopted 18 Dec. 1979, G.A. Res. 34/180, U.N. gaor, 34th Sess., U.N. Doc. A/34/46 (1980), 1249 U.N.T.S. 13 (entered into force 3 Sept. 1981).

____. 2007. Declaration on the Rights of Indigenous Peoples, G.A. Res. 61/295, adopted 13 Sep., U.N. gaor, 61st Sess., 107th plen. mtg., U.N. Doc. A/RES/61/295.

Green, Joyce. 1985. "Sexual Equality and Indian Government: An Analysis of Bill C-31 Amendments to the Indian Act." Native Studies Review 1, 2.

____. 2001. "Canaries in the Mines of Citizenship: Indian Women in Canada." Canadian Journal of Political Science 34, 4.

____. 2007. "Balancing Strategies: Aboriginal Women and Constitutional Change." In Joyce Green (ed.), Making Space for Indigenous Feminism. Halifax: Fernwood Publishing; London: Zed Books.

Gutiérrez, Margarita, and Nellys Palomo. 2000. "A Woman's Eye View of Autonomy." In Aracely Burguete Cal y Mayor (ed.), Indigenous Autonomy in Mexico. Copenhagen: iwgia.

Hale, Charles R. 2002. "Does Multiculturalism Menace? Governance, Cultural Rights and the Politics of Identity in Guatemala." Journal of Latin American Studies 34, 3.

Holder, Cindy L., and Jeff Corntassel. 2002. "Indigenous Peoples and Multicultural Citizenship: Bridging Collective and Individual Rights." Human Rights Quarterly 24, 1.

Jackson, Margaret A. 1994. "Aboriginal Women and Self-Government." In John H. Hylton (ed.), Aboriginal Self-Government in Canada: Current Trends and Issues. Saskatoon: Purich Publishing

Johnston, Kerensa. 2005. "Māori Women Confront Discrimination: Using International Human Rights Law to Challenge Discriminatory Practices." Indigenous Law Journal 4.

Koivurova, Timo. 2008. "From High Hopes to Disillusionment: Indigenous Peoples' Struggle to (re)Gain Their Right to Self-Determination." International Journal of Minority and Group Rights 15.1.

Koshan, Jennifer. 1998. "Aboriginal Women, Justice and the Charter: Bridging the Divide?" University of British Columbia Law Review 32, 23.

Kuokkanen, Rauna. 2009. "Achievements of Indigenous Self-Determination: The Case of the Sámi Parliaments in Finland and Norway." In J. Marshall Beier (ed.), Indigenous Diplomacies. New York: Palgrave Macmillan.

____. 2011. "Self-determination and Indigenous Women — 'Whose Voice Is It We Hear in the Sámi Parliament?'" International Journal on Minority and Group Rights 18.1: 39.

____. 2014. "Indigenous Women's Rights and International Law: Challenges of the U.N. Declaration on the Rights of Indigenous Peoples." In Corinne Lennox and Damien Short (eds.), Routledge Handbook of Indigenous Peoples' Rights. London: Routledge.

____. 2014a. ""Gendered Violence and Politics in Indigenous Communities: The Cases of Aboriginal People in Canada and the Sami in Scandinavia." International Feminist Journal of Politics (forthcoming).

LaRocque, Emma. 1997. "Re-Examining Culturally Appropriate Models in Criminal Justice Applications." In Michael Asch (ed.), Aboriginal and Treaty Rights in Canada: Essays on Law, Equality and Respect to Difference. Vancouver: ubc Press.

Larsen, Ann-Claire, and Alan Petersen. 2001. "Rethinking Responses to "Domestic Violence." Journal of Social Welfare & Family Law 23.

Lawrence, Bonita. 2004. "Real" Indians and Others: Mixed-Blood Urban Native Peoples and Indigenous Nationhood. Vancouver: ubc Press.

MacKinnon, Catharine A. 2006. Are Women Human? And Other International Dialogues. Cambridge, MA: Belknap Press of Harvard University Press.

Martin-Hill, Dawn. 2003. "She No Speaks and Other Colonial Constructs of 'The Traditional

Woman.'" In Kim Anderson and Bonita Lawrence (eds.), Strong Women Stories: Native Vision and Community Survival. Toronto: Sumach Press.

Merry, Sally Engle. 2001. "Rights, Religion, and Community: Approaches to Violence Against Women in the Context of Globalization." Law & Society Review 35, 1.

Monture-Angus, Patricia. 1999. Journeying Forward: Dreaming First Nations' Independence. Halifax: Fernwood Publishing.

Nahanee, Teressa. 1997. "Indian Women, Sex Equality, and the Charter." In Caroline Andrew and Sanda Rodgers (eds.), Women and the Canadian State. Montreal; Kingston: McGill-Queen's University Press.

Napoleon, Val. 2005. "Aboriginal Self Determination: Individual Self and Collective Selves." Atlantis 29, 2.

____. 2006. "Simple Law for Simple Cultures." Unpublished paper presented at the 5th Critical Race Conference, Regina, Saskatchewan.

Native Women's Association of Canada. 1999. "Aboriginal Women's Rights Are Human Rights." Canadian Human Rights Act Review Research Paper. <action.web.ca/home/narcc/attach/AboriginalWomensRightsAreHumanRights.pdf>.

Otzoy, Irma. 2008. "Indigenous Law and Gender Dialogues." In Pedro Pitarch, Shannon Speed, and Xochitl Leyva Solano (eds.), Human Rights in the Maya Region: Global Politics, Cultural Contentions, and Moral Engagements. Durham: Duke University Press.

Parisi, Laura, and Jeff Corntassel. 2007. "In Pursuit of Self-Determination: Indigenous Women's Challenges to Traditional Diplomatic Spaces." Canadian Foreign Policy 13, 3.

Peterson, V. Spike. 1990. "Whose Rights? A Critique of the 'Givens' in Human Rights Discourse." Alternatives 15, 3.

Razack, Sherene H. 2002. "Gendered Racial Violence and Spatialized Justice: The Murder of Pamela George." In Sherene H. Razack (ed.), Race, Space, and the Law: Unmapping a White Settler Society. Toronto: Between the Lines.

Russell, Peter H. 2008. "A Sustainable Justice System in Nunavut?" Paper presented at the VI International Congress of Arctic Social Sciences, Nuuk, Greenland.

Sambo Dorough, Dalee. 2009. "The Significance of the Declaration on the Rights of Indigenous Peoples and Its Future Implementation." In Claire Charters and Rodolfo Stavenhagen (eds.), Making the Declaration Work: The United Nations Declaration on the Rights of Indigenous Peoples. Copenhagen and New Brunswick: IWGIA.

Schouls, Tim. 2003. Shifting Boundaries: Aboriginal Identity, Pluralist Theory, and the Politics of Self-Government. Vancouver: ubc Press.

Sillett, Mary. 2009. "Ensuring Indigenous Women's Voices Are Heard: The Beijing Declaration of Indigenous Women." In Patricia A. Monture and Patricia D. McGuire (eds.), First Voices: An Aboriginal Women's Reader. Toronto: Inanna Publications and Education.

Silman, Janet. 1987. Enough Is Enough: Aboriginal Women Speak Out. Toronto: Women's Press.

Smith, Andrea. 2005 "Native American Feminism, Sovereignty, and Social Change." Feminist Studies 31, 1.

Speed, Shannon, and Xochitl Leyva Solano. 2008. "Global Discourses on the Local Terrain: Human Rights in Chiapas." In Pedro Pitarch, Shannon Speed, and Xochitl Leyva Solano (eds.), Human Rights in the Maya Region: Global Politics, Cultural Contentions, and Moral Engagements. Durham: Duke University Press.

Speed, Shannon, Xochitl Leyva Solano, and Jane F. Collier. 2000. "Limiting Indigenous Autonomy in Chiapas, Mexico: The State Government's Use of Human Rights." Human Rights Quarterly 22, 4.

unpfii (United Nations Permanent Forum on Indigenous Issues). "Report of the International Expert Group Meeting on Combating Violence Against Indigenous Women and Girls: Article 22 of the United Nations Declaration on the Rights of Indigenous Peoples (Advanced Unedited Version)." In U.N. Economic and Social Council (ed.), Permanent Forum on Indigenous Issues/Eleventh Session [Agenda Item 3]. New York: United Nations, 2012.

van der Hoogte, Liesbeth, and Koos Kingma. 2004. "Promoting Cultural Diversity and the Rights of Women: The Dilemmas of 'Intersectionality' for Development Organisations." Gender and Development 12, 1.

Venne, Sharon H. 1999. "The Meaning of Sovereignty." Indigenous Woman 6.

Washinawatok, Ingrid. 1999. "Sovereignty Is More Than Just Power." Indigenous Woman 2, 6.

Wilson, Richard Ashby. 2008. "Making Rights Meaningful for Mayas: Reflections on Culture, Rights, and Power." In Pedro Pitarch, Shannon Speed, amd Xochitl Leyva Solano (eds.), Human Rights in the Maya Region: Global Politics, Cultural Contentions, and Moral Engagements. Durham: Duke University Press.

Wirringa Baiya Aboriginal Women's Legal Centre. 2011. "Aboriginal Women Speaking Out about Violence: Is Anyone Listening?" Indigenous Law Bulletin 7, 23.

Woodman, Gordon R. 2000. Customary Law in Common Law Systems. Institute of Development Studies' International Workshop on Rule of Law and Development 2 (June). <http://www.vanuatu.usp.ac.fj/sol_adobe_documents/usp%20only/customary%20law/woodman.pdf>.

Young, Iris Marion. 2007. Global Challenges: War, Self-Determination, and Responsibility for Justice. Cambridge: Polity.

Chapter Seven

Victoria's Secret
How to Make a Population of Prey
Mary Eberts

Being Indian Is a High-Risk Lifestyle

"Indigenous women and girls are far more likely than other Canadian women and girls to experience violence and to die as a result" (HRW 2013: 25). Young Indigenous women are five times more likely than other Canadian women of the same age to die of violence, and between 1997 and 2000, the rate of homicide for Indigenous women was almost seven times higher than the rate for non-Indigenous women (NWAC and FAFIA 2013: 6). Indigenous women are more likely than non-Indigenous women to be killed by a stranger, and nearly half the murders are unsolved (NWAC 2010: ii).

The staggering violence against Indigenous women is a legacy of colonization (Kuokkenen, this volume, and HRW 2013). In this chapter, I examine how Canada's *Indian Act*, an instrument of colonization, makes Indigenous women legal nullities, places them outside of the rule of law and transforms them into prey for those who would harm and abuse them.

The Act's historic aim was the assimilation of "Indians." It segregated them from settler society and indoctrinated them until a satisfactory degree of "civilization" had been reached. Such civilization involved stripping Indigenous nations of name, language, culture and social organization (Cannon and Sunseri 2011: xvi, xviii), and re-creating them as small government-dependent polities of "Indians" meant to look like Victorian villages populated by Victorian families. The scheme discriminates on the basis of both race and gender. It rests on the view that the humanity of the Indian does not measure up to the humanity of the European. Its adoption of the Victorian patriarchal model of the family reflects the belief that the only proper place for women is under the dominion and control of men.

Women subject to the *Indian Act* are doubly diminished. If they fit within its Victorian confines, they have few or no rights. If they do not become (or seem to be) docile Victorian wives, as dictated by the Act, they are branded as deviants (often prostitutes) and considered fair game for mistreatment. The B.C. Human Rights Council found this branding to be discrimination on the combined grounds of race and gender. Valerie Frank of the Comox Indian Band had never experienced maltreatment when staying at a hotel with her family but was twice roughly evicted from her hotel room, and denied other services, when she visited there by herself (Frank 1993: paras. 6–12). In ruling against the hotel, the Council commented,

"What is particularly offensive ... is the assumption that she is a prostitute because she is a single Native woman in a hotel by herself" (Frank 1993: para. 31).

The Act's definition of "Indian" is conditioned by the reduction of Indigenous women's identity to primarily, if not exclusively, that of ungovernable sexual beings, appropriately treated as "sub-humans" (Oppal 2012, vol. IIA: 2). The *Indian Act* imports into the structure of Indian governance in Canada the widespread stereotypical portrayal of the Indigenous woman as "squaw," described by Métis scholar Emma LaRoque as a being with no human face who is lustful, immoral, unfeeling and dirty (AJI 1991 vol. 1: 479). This stereotype is applied to all Indigenous women, whether they are subject to the *Indian Act* or not.

Embedding that stereotype into legislation gives it the legitimacy of government approval, and in turn gives Canada an interest in its continued survival. The flourishing of this stereotype in the wider society is difficult, if not impossible, to curtail as long as it remains a centrepiece of official policy. The legislative scheme constructed on that stereotype drives women into exile, separates them from their families and impoverishes them and their children if they do not conform to the model of demure Victorian wife imposed upon Indigenous women.

Violence Against Indigenous Women in Canada

The patterns of violence against Indigenous women in Canada are endemic, pandemic and horrifying. Between 1997 and 2000, the rate of homicide for Indigenous women was 5.4 per 100,000, compared to 0.8 per 100,000 for non-Indigenous women (HRW 2013: 25, note 11). The Sisters in Spirit research program of the Native Women's Association of Canada (NWAC) found that between the 1960s and 2010, 582 Indigenous women and girls went missing or were murdered in Canada (NWAC 2010: 20–21). Two-thirds of the cases are murders, one-fifth are disappearances and the remainder are suspicious deaths or unknown (NWAC 2010: 18). The majority of the victims were under the age of thirty-one and many were mothers (NWAC 2010: ii). An updated report as of March 2013 found a total of 668 missing or murdered Indigenous women and girls (NWAC and FAFIA 2013: 7).

Further scrutiny has revealed even higher rates of murder and disappearance. Using the same type of public sources available to Sisters in Spirit, researcher Maryanne Pearce found 824 missing or murdered Indigenous women in the years 1990 to 2013 (Pearce 2013: 18, 28). In May 2014, the RCMP stunned observers by revealing, for the first time, statistics it had compiled across all federal, provincial and municipal police forces in Canada, showing that nearly 1,200 Indigenous women have been murdered or gone missing over the past thirty years (MacCharles 2014). About one thousand of these women are murder victims. This is the first time that official police statistics have been disclosed, and these numbers double those found by Sisters in Spirit. RCMP Commissioner Paulsen stated that although 4 percent of the women in Canada are Indigenous, 16 percent of Canada's murdered women and 12 percent of Canada's missing women are Indigenous, "clearly an overrepresentation." The same day these statistics were disclosed, the Government of Canada once again refused to hold a national inquiry into the murders and disappearances of Indigenous women (MacCharles 2014).

In 2004, Amnesty International Canada kicked off a period of intense international scrutiny of the violence against Indigenous women in Canada with the publication of its *Stolen Sisters* report (AIC 2004), characterizing violence against Indigenous women as a violation of their domestic and international human rights. Before that, attention had been drawn to the murder and disappearance of Indigenous women in various ways, including Ryga's 1967 play, *The Ecstasy of Rita Joe* (Ryga 1971), Amber O'Hare's database of missing and murdered women (Bronskill and Bailey 2005), the report of the Aboriginal Justice Inquiry of Manitoba into the murder of Helen Betty Osborne in The Pas in 1971 (AJI 1991) and individual cases like the conviction of two Regina university students for murdering Pamela George in 1995 (Razack 2002: 123–25) and the conviction of John Martin Crawford for the murder of three young Indigenous women in Saskatchewan in the 1990s (Goulding 2001).

With increased attention to incidents of violence against Indigenous women, long-buried historical cases came into public view, like the sexual assault of young women at the Cariboo Indian Residential School by Father (later Bishop) Herbert O'Connor in 1961, for which he was charged in 1991 (*R v. O'Connor* 1996), and the sexual assault of two teenage girls by Reform Party MP (and Justice critic) Jack Ramsay in 1969 when he was an RCMP constable in northern Saskatchewan (CBC News 2001).

The behaviour of the justice system in contemporary cases also came under scrutiny, including the decision-making of the Vancouver Police Department with respect to the numerous murders of women in the Downtown East Side of Vancouver (for many but not all of which Robert Pickton was later prosecuted and convicted) (Oppal 2012 vol. IIA: pt.2 and vol. IIB), and questioning of what was known locally, by whom and when about the abuse of young Indigenous women by sitting judge David Ramsay in Prince George, British Columbia (HRW 2013: 31–33). The perception grew that abuse of Indigenous women is more acceptable to the courts than abuse of non-Indigenous women. (AJI 1991 vol. 1: 482).

Despite the attention now focused on violence against Indigenous women in Canada, efforts to gather information have been frustrated by government actions. The Sisters in Spirit research program of NWAC was funded from 2005 until 2010, but the funding was not renewed (HRW 2013: 26). When a Commission of Inquiry was set up in British Columbia to study police decision-making with respect to the rash of murders in Vancouver's Downtown East Side, the government of British Columbia refused to fund Indigenous groups (including NWAC and the communities of the deceased women) to participate in the Inquiry. The Commission itself declared that it was not in the public interest to deny funding to these groups (Oppal 2012 vol. IV: 9–10). The Conservative majority on a Parliamentary Committee blocked it from recommending a national inquiry into the murders and disappearances in a report issued in 2014 after examining the phenomenon for several months (Special Committee on Violence Against Indigenous Women 2014).

Indigenous victims of violence are not seen as women with families and communities, or rounded human lives; they are all too often reduced to the stereotype of women who frequent bars or dangerous urban areas, engage in prostitution or have "high-risk" lifestyles. These characterizations are made by police (Project KARE 2012; Oppal 2012 vol. IIA: 2) and also by media and public commentary (Acoose 1995: 96–97; Goulding 2001: 209–19). In one case, the court attributed an adult level of sexual agency to a twelve-year-old Indigenous girl sexually assaulted by three white men in their twenties (Beyond Borders 2007: 7). By contrast, those accused of harming Indigenous women are sometimes portrayed as "normal," and a positive factor in their sentencing is the support they get from family and community (R. v. Edmonston 2005; R. v. Brown 1995: para. 97; Acoose 1995: 97; Razack 2002: 123–25). In some cases, the police, or the family or community of those eventually accused, may have known of the crime for some time before it came to light (AJI 1991, vol. 2: 1–2), or families may have helped to conceal it (Razack 2002: 139–40). Police may have been aware of practices endangering Indigenous women but done nothing about them (AJI 1991 vol. 2: 8; AIC 2004: 50; Oppal 2012 vol. IIB: 287).

Women disappear from or are found murdered in isolated areas, along highways or on vacant land outside cities, and also in urban areas where the most poor and marginal are forced to live. They may be missing for some time before their families are able to interest police in the disappearance. The Oppal Commission found that barriers in the reporting process contributed to delays in investigation. In some cases, families experienced degrading and insensitive treatment, and in a few, "the barriers were so pronounced as to amount to a denial of the right to make a report" (Oppal 2012 vol. IIB: 284–85). Women and their families do not, and perhaps cannot, expect help from the police, because of indifference, incompetence or even the involvement of police in misconduct of their own (AJI 1991 vol. 1: 482; HRW 2013: 29, 31–34; Oppal 2012 vol. IIB: 284–85). It has been suggested by a number of observers that if the missing or murdered woman were white instead of Indigenous, public and police interest would have been more forthcoming (HRW 2012: 37; Acoose 1995: 87; Goulding 2001: 211).

There have been many calls for a national commission of inquiry into the missing and murdered Indigenous women. Domestically, these calls come from groups as diverse as NWAC, Amnesty International and the Feminist Alliance for International Action, on the one hand (ICTMN 2013), and the premiers of Canada's provinces and territories on the other (Benzie and Brennan 2013: A6). Internationally, pressure has come from the U.N. Human Rights Council (in 2009 and 2013), the Committee to Eliminate All Forms of Discrimination Against Women (2008) and most recently by the United Nations Special Rapporteur on

Indigenous Issues, Dr. James Anaya, in the fall of 2013 (Canadian Press 2013). The Government of Canada repeatedly refuses to undertake an inquiry (Blanchfield 2013).

Foundations of the *Indian Act*

Canada is an example of "settler colonialism" (RCAP 1991: vol. 1, part 1, 105). Settler colonies practise "internal colonization," where "the dominant society coexists on and exercises exclusive jurisdiction over the territories and jurisdictions that indigenous peoples refuse to surrender" (Tully 2009: 39; see also Wolfe 1999: 1). Tully asserts that the colonizer aims to resolve this contradiction in the long term "by the complete … disappearance of the indigenous peoples as free peoples with the rights to their territories and governments" (Tully 2009: 40). One strategy for accomplishing this objective is that the Indigenous peoples would become "extinct in fact," through dying out, intermarriage, urbanization or extinguishing their will to resist assimilation (Tully 2009: 40).

The *Indian Act* has been preoccupied with extinction in fact. Deputy Superintendent of Indian Affairs Duncan Campbell Scott infamously proclaimed to Parliament in 1920, "Our objective is to continue until there is not a single Indian in Canada that has not been absorbed into the body politic, and there is no Indian question, and no Indian Department, and that is the whole object of this Bill" (Titley 1986: 50, note 55).

S. 91(24) of the *Constitution Act, 1867* gives the federal government jurisdiction over "Indians and lands reserved for Indians." Canada has sought to define "Indians" as narrowly as possible, so as to restrict the numbers for whom it is responsible. However, in the Eskimo Reference, the Supreme Court of Canada held that Inuit are included, and in 2014 the Federal Court of Appeal included Métis (*Canada* v. *Daniels* 2014) (the Canadian government is appealing this decision at the time of writing this chapter).

The major legislative enactment under s. 91(24) is the *Indian Act.* It establishes a comprehensive regime of governance directed at "lands reserved for Indians." The *Indian Act* provides for the existence of bands, which are composed of "Indians," and for allocation to a band of a reserve. Only members of that band may occupy or use the reserve. If the band ceases to exist, then the land is taken by the Crown. A band exists only so long as there are members of the band who are recognized by Canada as entitled to share in its land.

A narrow definition of "Indian" furthers Canada's own land ambitions in several ways: the fewer Indians it recognizes, the less land must be allocated as reserves in the first place; and the more people who are excluded from bands, the more quickly the Indian population will shrink. The faster the bands shrink and ultimately disappear, the more quickly the land may be taken by Canada. Beneficiary programs for Indians, such as education and health care, will also cost the federal government less to the extent that the number of Indians is reduced.

Although the *Indian Act* has never used the term "status," those recognized by Canada for purposes of the Act are commonly referred to as "status Indians" (Aboriginal Affairs and Northern Development Canada 2012a and 2012b). Indian status is seen by Canada as inferior to the full citizenship of the "normal" person. However, Indian status is also a form of privilege: as Palmeter (2011: 39) observes, "with regard to accessing programs and services, land, natural resources, and seats at self-government negotiating tables, the real question is not whether one is a citizen of the Mi'kmaq, Cree, or Mohawk, but whether one is an Indian and a band member." Sharon McIvor has argued that status confers cultural identity and belonging (McIvor and Grismer 2010: para. 22).

The Victorian view of woman and the family embedded in the *Indian Act* features the male as the patriarch and the female his dependent and obedient wife (Holcombe 1983: 33). The relationship between husband and wife paralleled that between master and servant (Chambers 1997: 10–11). By depriving married women of property, "the law deprived them of legal existence, of the rights and responsibilities of other citizens, and thus of self-respect" (Holcombe 1983: 35). While adopting these elements of the Victorian family, the *Indian Act* made one crucial exception. In Victorian settler society, the mother had responsibility in fact for rearing children, even though she had no legal authority to make decisions about them and no right to their custody. The *Indian Act*, by contrast, provided that Indian children would not be raised by their parents at all.

Nicholas Davin (1879: 10), architect of the residential school system, observed: "The Indian himself is a noble type of man, in a very early stage of development ... the race is in its childhood." Declaring that "one of the earliest things an attempt to civilize them does, is to take away their simple Indian mythology," he continued, "to disturb this faith, without supplying a better, would be a curious process to enlist the sanction of civilized races whose whole civilization, like all the civilizations with which we are acquainted, is based on religion" (Davin 1879: 14).

Davin (1879: 13) urged the government to utilize missionary schools and specified the role that religious women would play: "the influence of civilized women must be constantly present in the early years ... the plan is now to take young children, give them the care of a mother, and have them constantly in hand. Such care must go *pari passu* with religious training" (Davin 1879: 12). In this plan, Indigenous mothers would be replaced by *civilized white* mothers who would indoctrinate children in the practices and the faiths of the settler regime.

The residential schools run by Canada in conjunction with the major religious denominations had the twin goals of civilizing and Christianizing (TRC 2012: 10). The government considered that to achieve these goals, children had to be separated from their families (TRC 2012: title page). This policy tore the heart from Indigenous women's role in the family (Carter 2005: 139; Barman 2006: 286) as it tore the children from their families and communities.

Among the many reasons why the Indigenous mother was considered an inappropriate influence on her own children was the alleged hypersexuality of Indigenous women, a characterization that was essential to the justification of colonization. Indigenous women were "constructed as lascivious, shameless, unmaternal, prostitutes, ugly, and incapable of high sentiment or manners — the dark, mirror-image to the idealized nineteenth-century visions of white women" (Perry 2001: 49; also see Carter 1997: 161; Carter 1993: 148, 154; White 1991: 61). Aboriginal women represented "the wild" (Barman 2006: 279); they are almost wholly sexualized by settler society (Barman 2006: 277). They were rarely permitted any other form of identity (Barman 2006: 289). Barman attributes much of the white preoccupation with controlling Indigenous women's sexuality to a fear of their exercise of autonomy, the ultimate threat to the Victorian patriarchal family (Barman 2006: 277–86; Barman 2005: 208). Protecting the Victorian patriarchal family of the settler was, in effect, protecting the white race that was reproduced through that family.

White (1991: 61) says French observers "tended to select material that made the women seem merely a disorderly and lewd set of Europeans, not people following an entirely different social logic." One striking example of this is the refusal of colonial society, and the Canadian government, to acknowledge the Indigenous acceptance of divorce and remarriage, an omission that imparted an illicit characterization to any Indigenous conjugal union but the first (Carter 2005: 140; Carter 2008: 162; Sangster 2006: 312). This colonial characterization of Indigenous women was self-serving: it was used to deflect criticism from misbehaving government agents and from police who abused Indigenous women or did not protect them (Carter 1993: 150), or to allow settler men to abuse the women with impunity (Carter 1997: 165; Barman 2005: 205). This portrayal of Indigenous women as dangerously sexual helped justify the placing Indigenous peoples on remote reserves and introducing a pass system to confine residents there (Carter 1997: 187; Carter 2008: 152; Mawani 2009: 138).

Differentiating Indigenous women from white settler women was meant to reinforce the divide between Indigenous and white races. This practice emerged when the itinerant fur trade started giving way to established trading posts and with the upswing in settlement, both developments that brought more European women to Canada (Van Kirk 1980: 174; Brown 1980: 148–49; Mawani 2009: 87, 159). Unions between European men and Indigenous women had been a feature of the fur trade, though they were comparatively rare in the settled eastern part of Canada (VanKirk 2002: 3, 5), and they had underwritten the success of the fur trade by opening up valuable networks and skill sets to the European traders (Van Kirk 1980; Sleeper-Smith 2001: 19; McCormack 2011: 61).

However, such unions were seen to pose grave threats to the establishment of a land-based white settler society. If included in the white population the mixed-race children of such unions could have claims to land set aside for settlers; they could also challenge their white kin for possession of their father's property and estate, compromising whiteness as an entitling factor (Carter 2008: 152, 188; Carter 1993: 158; Mawani 2002: 50, 53). Including too many mixed-race children amongst the acknowledged Indian population could have required additional lands to be added to reserves (Mawani 2002: 65).

Inter-racial unions threatened not just whites' preferential access to land, but also the racial hierarchy itself. Perry observes that a white man who married an Indigenous woman was seen as "dangerously flirting" with relinquishing his place in the civilized race and becoming deracinated (Perry 2001: 70). Rather than upholding the superiority of the white race, the man became a "squaw man," corrupting and degrading the white race (Carter 1993: 154).

The answer to all of these challenges was a two-level enforcement by the *Indian Act* of the Victorian family ideal. Indians on reserve were to have conventional Victorian unions, with the husband as the controlling partner and the wife under his dominance. If an Indian woman married a white man, she would follow her husband off the reserve (and the Indian register) like a good Victorian wife (Green 2001: 723–27). In the words of the federal government, this would involve the woman's transition "from dependence upon the Indian community and its special position under our law to dependence upon her husband in the ordinary circumstances of the larger community" (Attorney General of Canada 1972: para 12).

This move from the reserve to the broader world was seen as the achievement of "civilization" (Mawani 2009: 138). For the federal government, "off-reserve residence has tended to carry an assumption that the integration process was proceeding satisfactorily" (Hawthorn 1966: 250). However, in the case of women who were forced off reserve for marrying a non-status man, the government was totally indifferent to whether they, and their children, were actually faring well in the new environment.

"To Be an Indian Is to Be a Man"

This opening sentence of Canada's White Paper sums up over one hundred years of Indian policy (RCSW 1970: para. 58). Under the rules for determining Indian status that endured in almost identical form until 1985 (see Brodsky; Kuokkanen in this volume for more complete description), it only took one Indian parent to make a person eligible for Indian status: the father. A status Indian would confer status on his children, and also on his wife if she were not already a status Indian. By contrast, an Indian woman who married a non-Indian (that is, "married out") would cease to be an Indian, and her children could not be registered as Indians. For purposes of this rule, Canada accepted the validity of marriages between Indigenous women and non-Indigenous men performed according to Indigenous custom: doing so meant that more women would be removed from Indian status (Carter 2008: 169).

Although it had been rare for a white woman to marry an Indian man (Van Kirk 2002: 2), by the 1960s the practice had become common enough to be cause for concern to Indian women (Standing Committee on Indian Affairs and Northern Development 1985, Issue 24: 24–33; Silman 1987: 11, 97, 186). The 1951 *Indian Act* introduced loss of Indian status at twenty-one for anyone whose mother and grandmother had both acquired status by marrying a status male ("the double-mother rule"). Starting in July 1980 the Minister of Indian Affairs offered bands the option of being exempted from the operation of this double-mother rule, and also from the rule that women who married a non-Indian would lose status (Standing Committee on Indian Affairs and Northern Development 1982, Issue 58: 10–11). By July 1984, 54 percent of bands had opted for exemption from the double-mother rule, while only 18 percent had asked to be excused from the operation of the marrying out rule (McIvor 2007: para. 61; McIvor 2009: para. 30). These were choices of a male leadership cadre in Indian bands that was becoming comfortable with the role of Victorian patriarch.

A woman who lost status upon marriage could not live on or visit the reserve, inherit reserve property or participate in the political and cultural life of the reserve. Mary Two-Axe Earley lamented that her marriage to a non-status man meant that she could not be buried on her reserve, although it had on its land a cemetery where outsiders could inter their pets (Sub-committee on Indian Women and the Indian Act 1982 Issue 4: 461). The women's children were similarly excluded. Even after widowhood or divorce, the woman could not regain her Indian status except by marrying a status Indian man.

We do not know how many women and children were excluded in this way, for Canada kept no statistics. However, it has been estimated that between 1985 and 1999, changes introduced by Bill C-31 increased the number of Status Indians by about 174,500 individuals (Clatworthy 2001: viii-ix). It is also estimated that about 40,000 people will move onto the Indian register as a result of the 2010 amendments to the Act contained in Bill C-3 (Indian and Northern Affairs Canada 2010). We can infer from the relatively large numbers of those still alive and seeking to regain status after 1985 that over the previous century the marrying out rule was responsible for a massive exile of women and children. Justice Laskin of the Supreme Court called the rule a "statutory excommunication" and a "statutory banishment" of Indian women who marry non-Indians (Lavell and Bédard 1974: 1386).

This exile heightened the vulnerability of women and children. Should an exiled woman be deserted, widowed or divorced, she could not return to her family and community. Should she lose the financial support of her husband, Canada would not resume its obligations to her. The marrying out rules, like the residential schools, fractured Indigenous families. Pearce has found that "the most striking" risk factor for violence against the Indigenous woman is being separated from her family (Pearce 2013: 256).

Women who did not lose status on marriage were also discriminated against by the *Indian Act*'s embrace of the Victorian family model. Indian women on reserve were legal nullities, having no right to vote or stand for election in band elections until past the middle of the twentieth century. Permission to occupy reserve land was granted preferentially to Indian men. A woman leaving an abusive marriage usually could not get her own reserve residence. Unless they could move in with another on-reserve family member, she and her children would have to leave the reserve, another instance of exile and family fragmentation being caused by the *Indian Act*.

The situation became even worse after the Supreme Court of Canada held in Derrickson (1986) and Paul (1986) that provincial family law dealing with occupation of the matrimonial home and division of matrimonial real property did not apply on reserve. These rulings left a legal gap, because there was no federal law dealing with these questions (Eberts and Jacobs 2004; Cornet and Lendor 2002, 2004). Not only were women left without substantive legal protection, they also suffered from "an equally significant ... gap in access to the court system, access to legal aid ... policing, enforcement of law ... and many other areas" (Grant-John 2007, Item 70: 5). Despite many calls for action (Canada House of Commons 2005; Canada Senate 2003), the gap persisted until the *Family Homes on Reserves Act* of 2013.

Although the *Indian Act* did not contain specific provisions allowing departmental officials to interfere with Indian women's sexual behaviour within their families, the Indian agent possessed broad discretion to do so. Sangster found that the Indian Affairs filing system had a whole category dealing with immorality on reserves (Sangster 2006: 313). In her study based on Agency records for Manitoulin Island and Parry Sound, Brownlie provides details of the Department's campaign between World Wars I and II to confine women to conventional patriarchal marriages. Indian agents used financial threats, like denying women treaty and interest payments on the ground of sexual transgression, and refusing or delaying provision of relief (Brownlie 2005: 163, 167). Agents might also send to residential school the children of a woman regarded as adulterous (Brownlie 2005: 169, 163). Ironically, in this same period, there are many stories of Indian agents and police coercing sex from Indian women in return for rations or other favours.

Indigenous women's activism in the 1960s and 1970s attacked both the *Indian Act*'s discrimination against status women on reserve (Silman 1987: 94, 99, 103–104, 175) and also the marrying out rules. Indian Rights for Indian Women organizations in Alberta and Quebec secured from the Royal Commission on the Status of Women a recommendation that women should not lose status for marrying a non-status man and should be able to pass status to their children (RCSW 1970: 237–38, 410). Jeanette Lavell from the Wikwemikong Unceded Territory on Manitoulin Island and Yvonne Bédard of Six Nations challenged their loss of status upon marriage under the *Canadian Bill of Rights* equality before the law guarantee.

The majority of the Supreme Court ruled against them. Mr. Justice Ritchie observed that rules about the status of Indian women who marry non-Indians were imposed as "a necessary part of the structure created by Parliament for the internal administration of the life of Indians on reserves and their entitlement to the use and benefit of Crown lands" (Lavell and Bédard 1974: 1359, 1369). Pointing out that these rules had been in effect for more than one hundred years, Justice Ritchie stated that any change to them had to be accomplished by specific, highly targeted legislation, and not by "broad general language directed at the statutory proclamation of the fundamental rights and freedoms of all Canadians" (Lavell and Bédard 1974: 1359–60).

Much the same reasoning had been used in the late 1920s when the "Five Persons" — white settler women from the Canadian establishment — argued in the Supreme Court that because "person" includes both male and female under modern-day *Interpretation Acts*, the term "Person" in the *Constitution Act, 1867* should be read to include women, thus permitting their appointment to the Senate. Chief Justice Anglin stated that it would be "dangerous to assume that by the use of the ambiguous term 'persons' the Imperial Parliament meant in 1867 to bring about so vast a constitutional change affecting Canadian women as would be involved in making them Privy Councillors" (Persons Case 1928: 287). This holding was almost immediately overturned by the Privy Council in London, which rejected the Supreme Court's protection of the discriminatory status quo (Persons Case 1930). However, this discredited reasoning was still used by the Supreme Court of Canada almost fifty years later to justify the legislated inequality of Indigenous women.

While Yvonne Bédard and Jeannette Corbière Lavell received support from women's organizations and from the Native Council of Canada (representing non-status Indians), major Indian groups like the National Indian Brotherhood and the Alberta chiefs opposed them. Indian leaders feared that a decision making the *Indian Act* subject to the *Canadian Bill of Rights* "would wipe out the *Indian Act* and remove whatever legal basis we had for our treaties" (Cardinal 1977: 110–11). To prevent this, the leadership decided to intervene in the Supreme Court against the women (Weaver 1981: 199). Despite the Act being upheld by the Supreme Court, Cardinal recounts that the case brought renewed attention to the political urgency of *Indian Act* revisions (Cardinal 1977: 115).

No revisions to the *Indian Act* resulted from the Lavell and Bédard case. What did result was exemption of the *Indian Act* from the *Canadian Human Rights Act* passed in 1977. The exemption was necessary, said the Justice Minister, because the government promised not to revise the *Indian Act* without consulting the National Indian Brotherhood and others (Standing Committee on Justice and Legal Affairs 1977, Issue No. 6A: 23; Cornet 2001: 125).

No amendments to the *Indian Act* resulted from this protected process (Cornet 2001: 125). However, the exemption stayed in the *Human Rights Act* for just over thirty years, in spite of widespread calls for its repeal and its inconsistency with Canada's international human rights obligations (Canadian Human Rights Act Review Panel 2000: 39–41, 127–33, and rec. 141; NWAC 2000; Canadian Human

Rights Commission 2005: 8–9). It was repealed with respect to federal government action in 2008 and with respect to band actions in 2011 (Statutes of Canada 2008).

This gap in the rule of law is profoundly unconstitutional, as was the gap in family law legislation on reserve. The *Universal Declaration of Human Rights* (General Assembly: 1948) states in its preamble that it is essential that human rights should be protected by the rule of law. The Supreme Court has held that "constitutionalism and the rule of law" is one of Canada's four foundational constitutional principles. Another is respect for minority rights, which the Supreme Court has interpreted as including the rights of Indigenous peoples. (Secession Reference 1998: paras. 49, 82) At its most basic, the rule of law "vouchsafes to the citizens and residents of the country a stable, predictable and ordered society in which to conduct their affairs. It provides a shield for individuals from arbitrary state action" (Secession Reference 1998: para.70). The rule of law requires the creation and maintenance of an actual order of positive laws (Secession Reference 1998: para. 71). These two prolonged gaps in the rule of law affecting Indigenous women are clearly contrary to Canada's constitutional imperatives and to its international human rights obligations.

Following the Supreme Court decision in Lavell and Bédard, activist Maliseet women took the marrying out rule to the U.N. Human Rights Committee under the Optional Protocol to the *United Nations Convention on Civil and Political Rights,* with Sandra Lovelace as the case's named complainant (Silman 1987: 74, 134–35, 176–77). Article 27 of the Convention provides that members of ethnic, religious or linguistic minorities shall not be denied the right, in common with other members of their group, to enjoy their own culture, to profess and practise their own religion or to use their own language. Ms. Lovelace, a fluent speaker of Maliseet, wanted to live on the Tobique reserve, with her son, after her marriage to a non-Indian broke up. She was prevented from doing so because of her loss of status. While holding that Article 27 does not guarantee her the right to live on reserve, the Committee found that her rights under Article 27 were interfered with because there is no place outside the Tobique reserve where she can access a like community. It ruled that to deny Sandra Lovelace the right to reside on the reserve does not seem "reasonable, or necessary to preserve the identity of the tribe" (Lovelace 1981 para. 17).

Finally Change, or Is It?

In 1985, after the Lovelace decision and coming into force of the Charter's equality guarantees, Canada passed legislation (Bill C-31) to change the registration provisions of the *Indian Act.* A new section, 6(1)(a), affirmed eligibility for status of all of those who had qualified for it under the old legislation. Women who had lost status when they married non-Indians were made eligible to return to status under s. 6(1)(c).

However, Bill C-31 worsened women's situation by replacing the one-parent rule for determining status. Instead of keeping that rule, and allowing either the mother or the father to confer full status on a child, Bill C-31 enacted a new two-parent rule. From 1985 on, under s. 6(1)(f), a person was registrable as an Indian only if both of his or her parents were eligible for status under s. 6(1). The only exception was the new s. 6(2), which allowed registration of those who had one parent registered or registrable under s. 6(1) of the Act. The children of women restored to status under s. 6(1)(c) acquired their status under s. 6(2), as they had only one Indian parent. However, this status was short-term; the section was nicknamed the "second-generation cut-off," because status derived under s. 6(2) did not count for purposes of the two-parent rule. Those restored to status under s. 6(2) would have to parent with a registered Indian in order to be able to pass along status.

Brownlie (2005: 167) tells us that by World War II, the Department of Indian Affairs had been forced to abandon its campaign to enforce European-style patriarchal marriage. However, the two-parent rule is actually the crowning achievement of this campaign: it compels an *Indian Act* family modelled after the monogamous patriarchal Victorian family, with two status Indian parents and no crossing of race lines in the production of offspring. It is deeply disturbing that this is the result of "reform" efforts driven by contemporary human rights instruments in Canada and at the international level.

The invidious effect of the two-parent rule is made worse by the way Canada applies the rule in cases where paternity is unstated or unacknowledged. Although nothing in Bill C-31 provided that this be done, Canada changed its policy to require the signature of the father on the birth form and other forms proving paternity. Without his signature, the child's registration would be determined solely on the basis of the mother's entitlement (Mann 2005: 1, 5–6). A mother who is herself registered under s. 6(2) is not able to register her child at all. A mother who is registered under s. 6(1) is able to register her child under s. 6(2), but that child will be unable to confer status on their offspring.

Many difficulties have been identified with this practice. If pregnancy was the result of abuse, incest or rape, the mother could be unwilling or unable to identify the father. A father may not want to acknowledge paternity because of concerns about being held financially responsible for the child. Where the relationship has been unstable or abusive, the mother may worry about the father asserting a right to custody or access. Privacy concerns may influence whether the father is willing to disclose paternity, or the mother is willing to ask that he do so, especially if the father is in a relationship with someone else (Mann 2005: 11–12). Difficulties also arise because of lack of knowledge about the requirements or other practical barriers to compliance, which mean that even where the father is prepared to acknowledge paternity, the paperwork may not reach the Registrar in time to permit the appropriate registration (Clatworthy 2004: 229–30; 234–43).

Most fundamentally, the policy on unstated or unacknowledged paternity is a retreat from previous versions of the Act. Until 1951, community acceptance of a child born out of wedlock would entitle the child to registration. After 1951, the mother's status was sufficient, unless there was actual proof that the father was not an Indian; the burden of proof was on the party seeking to disentitle the child. Now, the government presumes that the father is not a registered Indian if his identity is unknown. Moreover, under the present system, a mother registered under s. 6(2) has no right to transmit status. Under the old Act, any mother with status could pass it on to her child.

Once again, this time under the pretence of compliance with human rights guarantees, Canada has placed the Victorian yoke on the Indian woman's neck. It has done so despite the fact that by 2013, the disabilities imposed upon an "illegitimate" child (and the status of illegitimacy itself) have been removed from the common law and legislation in virtually all jurisdictions in Canada. By contrast, the *Indian Act* is making more severe the consequences for a child of having unmarried parents or an unknown father.

Between April 17, 1985, and December 31, 1999, 37,000 children with unstated paternity were born to women registered under s. 6(1), about 19 percent of the children born to s. 6(1) registered women during that period. About 30 percent of the children with unstated paternity were born to mothers under twenty years of age. It has been estimated that as many as 13,000 children born in this period to women registered under s. 6(2) may be ineligible for registration (Mann 2005: 8). By extrapolating this figure forward to 2012, Lynn Gehl (2012: 194) calculates that since 1985 as many as 25,000 such children have been unregistered. She describes the unstated paternity policy as genocide (Gehl 2013).

Sharon McIvor of the Lower Nicola Indian Band, and her son Jacob Grismer, challenged under the *Canadian Charter of Rights and Freedoms* the system of conferring status introduced in 1985. Their litigation is described in detail elsewhere in this volume (Brodsky), and has not yet been resolved at its final level of appeal. Importantly, both the British Columbia Court of Appeal and the Government of Canada responded to the narrowest possible construction of the McIvor/Grismer claim and of the Act's discriminatory history (Standing Committee on Aboriginal Affairs and Northern Development 2010, Issue 007: 3).

The desired change is straightforward and simple. Sharon McIvor, Jacob Grismer and Lynn Gehl all advocate affirmation of the status of all persons descended from either the male or the female line (Standing Committee on Aboriginal Affairs and Northern Development 2010, Issue 008: 3–4; Gehl 2006: 186). Instead of accepting this straightforward repair of past discrimination, Canada enacted Bill C-3, the *Gender Equity in Registration Act* in 2010 after the decision in the McIvor case. That law merely made one more generation eligible for status, while leaving in place the historical effects of preferring the male line of descent for over a hundred years and the exclusionary effect of the two-parent rule.

Creating a Population of Prey

The profile of violence against Indigenous women corresponds closely to the profile of the treatment accorded women under the *Indian Act*. Under the Act, women have experienced repeated exile, whether to residential school, to remote reserves or from their reserves when they marry non-Indian men or experience marital violence or breakdown. Children are exiled when their mothers deviate from narrowly prescribed norms. This statutory dispossession both causes and mirrors the dispossession of those who find themselves in urban enclaves of poverty. The theme of exile and dispossession under the Act echoes, as well, the remote and marginal sites where women are murdered, kidnapped or found; they wind up there in death, just as in life they had to pass through there on the way to, or from, their isolated reserves. The indifference toward missing and murdered women in today's Canada mirrors the official indifference to the fate of Indigenous women who were expelled from their families and communities upon marriage to non-Indians.

That missing and murdered Indigenous women are not seen as members of families by the press and public recalls to mind the strenuous efforts made by Canada to separate women from their extended and their immediate families by means of the *Indian Act*'s marrying out rules and the residential schools. The stereotype of "easy squaw" (Acoose 1995: 39), the "objects with no human value beyond sexual gratification" (AJI 1991: 52), attached to Indigenous women who have been assaulted or murdered is exactly the same as the stereotype of rampant sexuality upon which the *Indian Act*'s treatment of women is based, as part of colonization. While not the cause of the stereotype, the *Indian Act*'s affirmation of it as a basis for government policy has made it virtually immune from social influences that might change or erode it. Moreover, the constricting Victorian family model in the *Indian Act*, justified by the image of Indigenous women as needing control, has fractured families and impoverished and oppressed women for over a century, creating conditions of acute vulnerability.

Finally, given the history of the *Indian Act*, it should come as no surprise that Indigenous women are preyed upon in disproportionate numbers: they were expelled from the "rule of law" (however debased) that was the reserve system if they married a non-Indian, they were denied access to legal rights on the reserve right up until 2013, because Victorian wives do not have legal rights, and, for a substantial period, Canada withheld from them access to human rights law as a recourse against gender-based discrimination. Canada has demonstrated for over a century that it does not consider Indigenous women appropriate beneficiaries of the rule of law. Law is to be used only to control and confine them.

The treatment of women under the *Indian Act* is the archetype and model for the treatment of Indigenous women generally and has created of such women a population of prey. Women whose peoples have never been subject to the *Indian Act*, like the Métis and Inuit, suffer the same kinds of violation and oppression as do the women who have been ruled by the *Indian Act* for over a century. The

Act captured the racist and misogynist attitudes which Victorian-era settlers and colonial administrators had toward all Indigenous peoples, gave them a safe home and carried them forward through time. Decade after decade, application of the *Indian Act* validated those invidious ideas, which should have been subjected to the change processes of a maturing constitutional democracy. From their secure hideaway in the *Indian Act*, where they were refreshed and renewed year after year, these poisonous notions continued to infect our treatment of all Indigenous women, down to the present day, even though they should long ago have been thrown on the scrap heap. Until Canada signals a change in its official view of Indigenous women by changing the *Indian Act*, Indigenous women will continue to suffer violence to a disproportionate degree.

References

Aboriginal Affairs and Northern Development Canada. 2012a. *Secure Certificate of Indian Status (SCIS)*. <aadnc-aandc.gc.ca/eng/1100100032380>.

____. 2012b. *Terminology*. <aadnc-aandc.gc.ca/eng/1100100014642>.

Acoose, Janice. 1995. *Iskwewak-Kah' Ki Yaw Ni Wahkomakanak: Neither Indian Princesses Nor Easy Squaws*. Toronto: Women's Press.

AIC (Amnesty International Canada). 2004. *Stolen Sisters: A Human Rights Response to Discrimination and Violence Against Indigenous Women in Canada*. Ottawa: AIC.

AJI (Aboriginal Justice Inquiry of Manitoba). 1991. *Report: Vol. 1: The Justice System and Aboriginal People* and *Vol. 2: The Deaths of Helen Betty Osborne and John Joseph Harper*. Province of Manitoba.

Barman, Jean. 2005. "Aboriginal Women on the Streets of Victoria: Rethinking Transgressive Sexuality during the Colonial Encounter." In Katie Pickles and Myra Rutherdale (eds.), *Contact Zones: Aboriginal and Settler Women in Canada's Colonial Past*. Vancouver: UBC Press.

____. 2006. "Taming Aboriginal Sexuality: Gender, Power and Race in British Columbia, 1850–1900," in Mary-Ellen Kelm and Lorna Townsend (eds.), *In the Days of Our Grandmothers: A Reader in Aboriginal Women's History in Canada*. Toronto: University of Toronto Press.

Benzie, Robert, and Richard J. Brennan. 2013. "Premiers support demands for probe into missing aboriginal women." *Toronto Star,* July 25: A6.

Beyond Borders Inc. 2007. *Newsletter* No. 10 (Spring). Winnipeg.

Blanchfield, Mike. 2013. "Canada rejects U.N. call for review of violence against aboriginal women." *Globe and Mail,* September 13. <www.theglobeandmail.com/news/national/canada-to-reject-un-panels-call-for-revie>.

Bronskill, Jim, and Sue Bailey. 2005. "Aboriginal women fair game for predators amid public indifference." September 18. <http://cnews.canoe.ca/CNEWS/Canada/2005/09/18/pf-1222622.html>.

Brown, Jennifer S.H. 1980. *Strangers in Blood: Fur Trade Families in Indian Country*. Vancouver: UBC Press.

Brownlie, Robin Jarvis. 2005. "Intimate Surveillance: Indian Affairs, Colonization, and the Regulation of Aboriginal Women's Sexuality." In Katie Pickles and Myra Rutherdale (eds.), *Contact Zones: Aboriginal and Settler Women in Canada's   Colonial Past*.

Vancouver: UBC Press.

Canada. Department of Indian Affairs and Northern Development. 1969. *Statement of the Government of Canada on Indian Policy.* ["White Paper."] Ottawa: Queen's Printer.

Canada. House of Commons. Standing Committee on Aboriginal Affairs and Northern Development. 2005. *Report: Walking Arm-in-Arm to Resolve the Issue of On-Reserve Matrimonial Real Property.*

Canada. Senate. Standing Senate Committee on Human Rights. 2003. *Interim Report: A Hard Bed to Lie In: Matrimonial Real Property on Reserve.*

Canadian Human Rights Act Review Panel. 2000. *Promoting Equality: A New Vision.* Canada, Department of Justice. Ottawa.

Canadian Human Rights Commission. 2005. *A Matter of Rights: A Special Report of the Canadian Human Rights Commission on the Repeal of Section 67 of the Canadian Human Rights Act.* Ottawa.

Canadian Press. 2013. "James Anaya, U.N. Official, Backs Inquiry into Missing, Murdered Aboriginal Women." <huffingtonpost.ca/2013/10/15/james-anaya-united-nations-inquiry_n_410181>.

Cannon, Martin J., and Lina Sunseri. 2011. *Colonialism and Indigeneity in Canada: A Reader.* Toronto (Don Mills): Oxford University Press Canada.

Cardinal, Harold. 1977. *The Rebirth of Canada's Indians.* Edmonton: Hurtig Publishers.

Carter, Sarah. 1993. "Categories and Terrains of Exclusion: Constructing the 'Indian Woman' in the Early Settlement Era in Western Canada." *Great Plains Quarterly* 13: 147.

____. 1997. *Capturing Women: The Manipulation of Cultural Imagery in Canada's Prairie West.* Montreal, Kingston: McGill-Queens University Press.

____. 2005. "Creating 'Semi-Widows' and 'Supernumerary Wives': Prohibiting Polygamy in Prairie Canada's Aboriginal Communities to 1900." In Katie Pickles and Myra Rutherdale (eds.), *Contact Zones: Aboriginal and Settler Women in Canada's Colonial Past.* Vancouver: UBC Press.

____. 2008. *The Importance of Being Monogamous: Marriage and Nation-Building in Western Canada to 1915.* Edmonton: University of Alberta Press.

CBC News. 2001. "Ramsay sentenced to probation, community service." October 16. <cbc.ca/news/canada/ramsay-sentenced-to-probation-community-service-1.269551; and http://archive.today.M9iB>.

Chambers, Lori. 1997. *Married Women and Property Law in Victorian Ontario.* Toronto, Buffalo, London: Published for the Osgoode Society for Canadian Legal History by University of Toronto Press.

Clatworthy, Stewart. 2001. *Re-Assessing the Population Impacts of Bill C-31.* Four Directions Project Consultants.

____. 2004. "Unstated Paternity: Estimates and Contributing Factors." In Jerry P. White, Paul Maxim and Dan Beavon (eds.), *Aboriginal Policy Research: Setting the Agenda for Change,* Vol. II, Toronto: Thompson Educational Publishing.

____. 2010. *Estimates of Demographic Implications from Indian Registration Amendment — McIvor v. Canada.* Published under the authority of the Minister of Indian Affairs and Northern Development and Federal Interlocutor for Métis and Non-Status Indians, March.

Cornet, Wendy. 2001. "First Nations Governance, the *Indian Act* and Women's Equality Rights." In Status of Women Canada, *First Nations Women, Governance and the Indian Act: A Collection of Policy Research Reports.* Ottawa: November.

Cornet, Wendy, and Alison Lendor. 2002. *Discussion Paper: Matrimonial Real Property on Reserve*. Canada, Department of Indian and Affairs and Northern Development.

____. 2004. "Matrimonial Real Property Issues On-Reserve." In Jerry P. White, Paul Maxim and Dan Beavon (eds.), *Aboriginal Policy Research: Setting the Agenda for Change*, Vol. II, Toronto: Thompson Educational Publishing Inc.

Davin, Nicholas Flood. 1879. *Report on Industrial Schools for Indians and Half-Breeds*. Ottawa.

Eberts, Mary, and Beverly K. Jacobs. 2004. "Matrimonial Property on Reserve." In Marylea MacDonald and Michelle K. Owen (eds.), *On Building Solutions for Women's Equality: Matrimonial Property on Reserve, Community Development and Advisory Councils*. CRIAW/ICREF [*Voix feministes-Feminist voices*, No. 15] Ottawa.

Francis, Daniel. 2011 [1992]. *The Imaginary Indian: The Image of the Indian in Canadian Culture*. Vancouver: Arsenal Pulp Press (reissue).

Gehl, Lynn, Gii-Zhigaate-Mnidoo-Kwe. 2006. "The Queen and I." In Andrea Medovarski and Brenda Cranney (eds.), *Canadian Woman Studies: An Introductory Reader*, 2d ed. Toronto: Inanna Publications and Education Inc.

____. 2012. "Unknown and Unstated Paternity and *The Indian Act*: Enough Is Enough!" *Journal of the Motherhood Initiative [Motherhood, Activism, Advocacy, Agency]* 3, 2 (Fall/Winter): 199–99.

____. 2013. "Canada's unstated paternity policy amounts to genocide against Indigenous children." *rabble.ca*, January 29. <rabble.ca/news/2013/01/canadas-unstated-paternity-policy-amounts-cultural-genoci>.

Goulding, Warren. 2001. *Just Another Indian: A Serial Killer and Canada's Indifference*. Calgary: Fifth House Ltd.

Grant-John, Wendy. 2007. *Report of the Ministerial Representative, Matrimonial Real Property Issues on Reserve*. March. Ottawa: Minister of Public Works and Government Services Canada.

Green, Joyce. 2001. "Canaries in the Mines of Citizenship: Indian Women in Canada." *Canadian Journal of Political Science/Revue de science politique* 715, XXXIV: 4.

Hawthorn, H.B. (ed.). 1966. *A Survey of the Contemporary Indians of Canada: A Report on Economic, Political, Educational Needs and Policies in Two Volumes*. Volume 1. Indian Affairs Branch, IAND Publication No. QS-0603-020-EE-A-18.

Holcombe, Lee. 1983. *Wives and Property: Reform of the Married Women's Property Law in Nineteenth-Century England*. Toronto and Buffalo: University of Toronto Press.

HRW (Human Rights Watch). 2013. *Those Who Take Us Away: Abusive Policing and Failures in Protection of Indigenous Women and Girls in Northern British Columbia, Canada*. February. <http://www.refworld.org/docid/5209e6e94.html>.

ICTMN (Indian Country Today Media Network) Staff. 2013. "Open Letter Blasts Canada's Refusal to Convene National Missing-Women Inquiry." September 22. <indiancountrytodaymedianetwork.com/2013/09/22/open-letter-blasts-canadas-refusal>.

Indian and Northern Affairs Canada. 2010. *Estimates of Demographic Implications from Indian Registration Amendment McIvor v. Canada*. <www.ainc-inac.ca/br/is/eod.-eng.asp>.

Jamieson, Kathleen. 1978. *Indian Women and the Law in Canada: Citizens Minus*. Canadian Advisory Council on the Status of Women and Indian Rights for Indian Women. Ottawa: Minister of Supply and Services Canada.

MacCharles, Tonda. 2014. "1,200 native women murdered or missing." *Toronto Star*, May 2: A3.

Mann, Michelle M. 2005. *Indian Registration: Unrecognized and Unstated Paternity*. Ottawa:

Status of Women Canada.

Mawani, Renisa. 2002. "In Between and Out of Place: Mixed-Race Identity, Liquor and the Law in British Columbia, 1850–1913." In Sherene H. Razack (ed.), *Race, Space and the Law: Unmapping a White Settler Society*. Toronto: Between the Lines.

____. 2009. *Colonial Proximities: Crossracial Encounters and Juridical Truths in British Columbia, 1871–1921*. Vancouver: UBC Press.

McCormack, Patricia A. 2011. "Lost Women: Native Wives in Orkney and Lewis." In Sarah Carter and Patricia McCormack (eds.), *Recollecting: Lives of Aboriginal Women of the Canadian Northwest and Borderlands*. Edmonton: AU Press.

Native Women's Association of Canada. 2000. *Aboriginal Rights are Human Rights*: Research Paper Prepared [by Mary Eberts] for Canadian Human Rights Review. Ottawa.

____. 2010. *What Their Stories Tell Us: Research Findings from the Sisters in Spirit Initiative*. Ottawa.

Native Women's Association of Canada and Canadian Feminist Alliance for International Action. 2013. *Murders and Disappearances of Aboriginal Women and Girls in Canada: Information Update for the United Nations Committee on the Elimination of Discrimination Against Women*. Ottawa.

Oppal, The Honourable Wally T. 2012. *Forsaken: The Report of the Missing Women Commission of Inquiry*, Vols I through IV. Victoria and Vancouver.

Palmeter, Pamela D. 2011. *Beyond Blood: Rethinking Indigenous Identity*. Saskatoon: Purich Publishing Limited.

Pearce, Maryanne. 2013. "An Awkward Silence: Missing and Murdered Vulnerable Women and the Canadian Justice System." Doctorate in Laws thesis, Common Law Section, University of Ottawa, Ottawa.

Perry, Adele. 2001. *On the Edge of Empire: Gender, Race, and the Making of British Columbia, 1849–1871*. Toronto and Buffalo: University of Toronto Press.

Project KARE. 2012. *KARE Bulletin: Unsolved Homicides/High Risk Missing Persons*. April 12. <http://www.kare.ca/images/stories/Human%20remains%20identified%20as%20Annette%20Holywhiteman.pdf>.

Razack, Sherene H. 2002. "Gendered Racial Violence and Spatialized Justice: The Murder of Pamela George." In Sherene H. Razack (ed.), *Race, Space and the Law: Unmapping a White Settler Society*. Toronto: Between the Lines.

RCAP (Royal Commission on Aboriginal Peoples). 1991. *Report, Vol.1: Looking Forward, Looking Back*. Ottawa: Printed from For Seven Generations, published by Libraxus Inc.

RCSW (Royal Commission on the Status of Women in Canada). 1970. *Report*. Ottawa: Information Canada.

Ryga, George. 1971. *The Ecstasy of Rita Joe and Other Plays*. Introduction by Brian Parker. Toronto: New Press.

Sangster, Joan. 2006. "Native Women, Sexuality, and the Law." In Mary-Ellen Kelm and Lorna Townsend, *In the Days of Our Grandmothers: A Reader in Aboriginal Women's History in Canada*. Toronto and Buffalo: University of Toronto Press.

Silman, Janet. 1987. *Enough Is Enough: Aboriginal Women Speak Out*. Toronto: Women's Press.

Sleeper-Smith, Susan. 2001. *Indian Women and French Men: Rethinking Cultural Encounter in the Western Great Lakes*. Amherst: U. of Massachusetts Press.

Special Committee on Violence Against Indigenous Women. 2014. *Invisible Women: A Call to Action. A Report on Missing and Murdered Indigenous Women in Canada*. March 4.

1st Parliament, Second Session.

Titley, E. Brian. 1986. *A Narrow Vision: Duncan Campbell Scott and the Administration of Indian Affairs in Canada.* Vancouver: University of British Columbia Press.

TRC (Truth and Reconciliation Commission of Canada). 2012. *They Came for the Children: Canada, Aboriginal Peoples and Residential Schools.* Winnipeg.

Tully, James. 2000. "The Struggles of Indigenous Peoples for and of Freedom." In Duncan Ivison, Paul Patton and Will Saunders (eds.), *Political Theory and the Rights of Indigenous Peoples.* Cambridge U.K.: Cambridge University Press.

Vancouver Sun. 1998. "Bishop O'Connor Diverted." June 18. <www.rapereliefshelter.bc.ca/learn/news/bishop/oconnor_diverted>.

VanKirk, Sylvia. 1999 [1980]. *Many Tender Ties: Women in Fur Trade Society, 1670–1870.* Winnipeg: Watson, Dwyer Publishing Limited.

____. 2002. "From 'Marrying-In' to 'Marrying-Out': Changing Patterns of Aboriginal/Non-Aboriginal Marriage in Colonial Canada." *Frontiers* 23, 3: 1–11.

Weaver, Sally M. 1981. *Making Canadian Indian Policy: The Hidden Agenda 1968–1970.* Toronto: University of Toronto Press.

White, Richard. 1991. *The Middle Ground: Indians, Empires and Republics in the Great Lakes Region, 1650–1815.* Cambridge, U.K: Cambridge University Press.

Wolfe. Patrick. 1999. *Settler Colonialism and the Transformation of Anthropology: The Politics and Poetics of an Ethnographic Event.* London: Cassell.

Legal Cases

Attorney General of Canada v. Jeannette Vivian Corbière Lavell. [1972]. Supreme Court of Canada. *Factum* Attorney General of Canada.

Attorney General of Canada v. Lavell; Isaac et al. v. Bédard. [1974]. Supreme Court Reports 1349.

Canada v. Daniels, 2014, Federal Court of Appeal 101, partially overturning *Daniels v. Canada*, [2013] Federal Court 6.

Corbière v. Canada (Minister of Indian and Northern Affairs), [1999] 2 Supreme Court Reports 203.

Derrickson v. Derrickson, [1986] 1 Supreme Court Reports 285.

Frank v. AJR Enterprises [carrying on business as Nelson Place Hotel] [1993] 23 Canadian Human Rights Reporter D/228 (British Columbia Council of Human Rights).

McIvor v. Canada (Registrar of Indian and Northern Affairs), 2009 British Columbia Court of Appeal 153.

McIvor v. The Registrar, Indian and Northern Affairs Canada, [2007] British Columbia Supreme Court 827.

Paul v. Paul, [1986] 1 Supreme Court Reports 306.

R. v. Brown, [2005] Saskatchewan Court of Appeal 7.

R. v. Edmonston, [2005] Saskatchewan Court of Appeal 7.

R. v. O'Connor, [1996] CanLII 8458 (British Columbia Supreme Court), sentencing by Oppal J.

Reference as to the Meaning of the Word "Persons" in Section 24 of The British North America Act, 1867, [1928] Supreme Court Reports 276; on appeal to the Judicial Committee of the Privy Council, *Edwards v. Attorney General of Canada*, [1930] Appeal Cases 124 ("*Persons Case*").

Reference re Secession of Québec, [1998] 2 Supreme Court Reports 217 ("*Secession Reference*").

Reference Whether "Indians" includes "Eskimo," [1939] Supreme Court Reports 104 (*"Eskimo Reference"*).

Sandra Lovelace v. Canada, Communication No. R.6/24, U.N. Doc. Supp. No. 40 (A/36/40) at 166 [1981].

Sharon McIvor and Jacob Grismer v. Canada, Communication Submitted for Consideration under the First Optional Protocol to the *International Covenant on Civil and Political Rights*, before the U.N. Human Rights Committee, November 24, 2010; Submission of the Government of Canada on the Admissibility and Merits of the Communication to the Human Rights Committee of Sharon McIvor and Jacob Grismer, Communication No. 2020/2010 [August 21, 2010]; Petitioner Comments in Response to State Party's Submission on the Admissibility and Merits of the Applicants' Petition to the Human Rights Committee, Communication No. 2020/2010 [December 5, 2011].

Statutes

An Act to amend the Canadian Human Rights Act, Statutes of Canada 2008, c. 30.

An Act to Amend the Indian Act, Statutes of Canada 1956, c. 40.

An Act to amend the Indian Act, Statutes of Canada 1985, c. 27 (*Bill C-31*).

The Canadian Bill of Rights, Statutes of Canada 1960, c. 44.

Canadian Human Rights Act, Revised Statutes of Canada 1985, c. H-6 (1976-77, c.33).

Constitution Act, 1867, United.Kingdom., 30 & 31 Victoria, c.3.

Constitution Act, 1982, Schedule B to *Canada Act, 1982*, United Kingdom 1982, c.11.

Family Homes on Reserves and Matrimonial Interests or Rights Act, Statutes of Canada 2013, c. 20.

Gender Equity in Registration Act, Statutes of Canada 2010, c. 18.

Indian Act, 1876, Statutes of Canada 1876, c. 18.

Indian Act, 1880, Statutes of Canada 1880, c. 28.

Indian Act, Revised Statutes of Canada 1886, c. 43.

Indian Act, Revised Statutes of Canada 1906, c. 81.

Indian Act, Revised Statutes of Canada 1927, c. 98.

Indian Act, Statutes of Canada 1951, c. 29.

Indian Act, Revised Statutes of Canada 1985, c. I-5.

Parliamentary Hearings

Standing Committee on Aboriginal Affairs and Northern Development. March 1, 1985. *Minutes of Proceedings and Evidence ... Respecting Bill C-31, An act to amend the Indian Act.* House of Commons, Issue No. 24, March 26, 1985.

Standing Committee on Aboriginal Affairs and Northern Development. April 1, 2010. *Evidence.* AANO, Number 007.

Standing Committee on Aboriginal Affairs and Northern Development, April 13, 2010. Evidence. AANO, Number 008.

Standing Committee on Indian Affairs and Northern Development, September 20, 1982. *Minutes of Proceedings and Evidence*, Issue No. 58 (Includes Committee's Sixth Report to the House of Commons, i.e. First Report of the Sub-Committee on Indian Women and the Indian Act, Chair, Keith Penner).

Standing Committee on Justice and Legal Affairs, 1977, *Minutes of Proceedings and Evidence*, Issue No. 6A.

Sub-committee on Indian Women and the Indian Act of the Standing Committee on Indian

Affairs and Northern Development, September 17. 1982, *Minutes of Proceedings and Evidence,* Issue No. 4.

International Instruments

Convention on the Elimination of All Forms of Discrimination Against Women. Adopted and opened for signature, ratification and accession by General Assembly resolution 34/180 of 18 December 1979, entry into force 3 September 1981, in accordance with article 27(1).

International Covenant on Civil and Political Rights, Adopted and opened for signature, ratification and accession by General Assembly resolution 2200 A (XXI) of 16 December 1966, entry into force 23 March 1976, in accordance with article 49.

International Covenant on Economic, Social and Cultural Rights, Adopted and opened for signature, ratification and accession by General Assembly resolution 2200 A (XXI) of 16 December 1966, entry into force 3 January 1976 in accordance with article 27.

Optional Protocol to the International Covenant on Civil and Political Rights, Adopted and opened for signature by General Assembly resolution 2200 A (XXI) of 16 December 1966.

United Nations Declaration on the Rights of Indigenous Peoples, General Assembly Resolution 61/295 (Annex), UN GAOR, 61st. Sess., Supp.No. 49, Vol. III, UN Doc. A/49 (2008), 15.

Universal Declaration of Human Rights, Adopted and proclaimed by General Assembly Resolution 217 A (III) of 10 December 1948.

Part Three

International and Domestic Constitutional Law and Indigenous Human Rights

Chapter Eight

Free, Prior and Informed Consent
Defending Indigenous Rights in the Global Rush for Resources
Craig Benjamin

Faced with an onslaught of development projects targeting their lands, resources and territories, Indigenous peoples around the world are increasingly asserting their right to determine whether or not such development should take place on their lands and, if so, under what terms. The Forest Peoples Programme, which has been a leading advocate for the recognition of free, prior and informed consent (FPIC), describes this important international human rights standard in this way:

> Those who wish to use the customary lands belonging to indigenous communities must enter into negotiations with them. It is the communities who have the right to decide whether they will agree to the project or not once they have a full and accurate understanding of the implications of the project on them and their customary land. (Forest Peoples Programme n.d.)

FPIC, which is affirmed in the U.N. *Declaration on the Rights of Indigenous Peoples* (UNDRIP), and well-established in other international human rights law, means that Indigenous peoples must be *free* to engage in this process of negotiation, weighing alternatives without undue pressure, coercion or threat of retaliation. There must be sufficient time for an effective review of options *prior* to any actions that could affect Indigenous peoples' rights or predetermine the outcome of the decision-making process. FPIC requires transparency about the nature of what is being proposed and access to the means to independently evaluate the potential impacts, so that Indigenous peoples can make *informed* decisions about whether the plans need to be modified, or if they should be rejected altogether. FPIC means that the process by which Indigenous peoples come to this decision to grant or withhold their *consent* must be a process that is freely chosen by them, based on their own institutions, laws and procedures, rather than imposed by the state. If consent is granted, the principle of FPIC will also likely require ongoing engagement and review according to these same principles to ensure continued consent as new information emerges or if the circumstances significantly change.

Particularly since the adoption of the UNDRIP, Indigenous peoples' assertion of FPIC has been met with growing acceptance and support from other sectors of society, including human rights organizations, environmental movements and some significant voices within industry and investment. A major report on the business case for FPIC noted in 2010 that the standard "is rapidly gaining momentum" (Lehr and Smith 2010: 6). As one example, in 2012 the International Finance Corporation (IFC), the private financing arm of the World Bank, adopted a new lending policy requiring FPIC of Indigenous peoples under a range of circumstances, including if the proposed project would require the relocation of Indigenous peoples from lands subject to traditional ownership or use, or where "significant" and "unavoidable" impacts on "critical cultural heritage" are identified (IFC 2012: paras. 15, 16). The IFC's Performance Standard 7 also requires project proponents to document that consent has been obtained through a process acceptable to the affected peoples (IFC 2012: para. 12).

In contrast, the Government of Canada has, if anything, become more entrenched in its opposition to free, prior and informed consent. In interim guidelines released in 2008, the Government of Canada acknowledged that — at least in respect to "established" rights or title — the government *may* have a duty to obtain the consent of First Nations, Inuit or Métis peoples in decisions affecting their rights (Government of Canada 2008: 52). However the final version of these guidelines removed even this narrow acknowledgement. Instead, the guidelines offered the following comment on the FPIC provisions of the UNDRIP (which Canada had only recently endorsed):

> On November 12, 2010, Canada issued a Statement of Support endorsing the United Nations *Declaration on the Rights of Indigenous Peoples* (Declaration), an aspirational document, in a manner fully consistent with Canada's Constitution and laws. The Declaration describes a number of principles such as equality, partnership, good faith and mutual respect. Canada strongly supports these principles and believes that they are consistent with the Government's approach to working with Aboriginal peoples.
>
> However, Canada has concerns with some of the principles in the Declaration and has placed on record its concerns with free, prior and informed consent when interpreted as a veto. As noted in Canada's Statement of Support, the Declaration is a non-legally binding document that does not change Canadian laws. Therefore, it does not alter the legal duty to consult. (Aboriginal Affairs and Northern Development Canada 2011: 9)

These claims by the Government of Canada are both inaccurate and misleading. As has been argued elsewhere (Joffe 2010), and as will be addressed briefly in this chapter, the U.N. Declaration reflects standards of international human rights law that not only can but also must be used in the interpretation and application of Canadian domestic law (see Joffe, Green, Gunn, this volume). Furthermore, the Canadian government's characterization of FPIC as a "veto" is demonstrably at odds with the how the standard has been interpreted and applied by international human rights bodies. Rather than being in conflict with the principles of "equality, partnership, good faith respect," which the government claims to have embraced, FPIC is a crucial and necessary tool for realizing these ideals, as well as the protection of enjoyment of human rights.

In contrast to Canada's claims, domestic and international legal standards clearly affirm free, prior and informed consent not only as an aspirational standard, but as a legal requirement that can potentially be enforced in courts and regulatory processes. Furthermore, this obligation should not be narrowly interpreted as applying only to "established rights." Particularly in regards to resource development projects, which almost inevitably have the potential for significant impacts on the lives, cultures, economies and health of Indigenous peoples, FPIC should generally be required as an appropriate and necessary precautionary measure even when the rights of Indigenous peoples have yet to be formally recognized by the state.

Furthermore, while FPIC is a crucial legal standard for the protection of Indigenous peoples' human rights, its use is not limited to legal arenas. The right of Indigenous peoples to determine for themselves what forms of development are acceptable on their lands is a powerful and effective rallying call with the potential to unite diverse sectors of civil society in support of the rights of Indigenous peoples. The success of Asubpeeschoseewagong Netum Anishinabek (Grassy Narrows First Nation), a small and historically marginalized First Nation in northwestern Ontario, in halting large-scale industrial logging on their traditional territory illustrates the potential of FPIC.

Case Study: The De Facto Moratorium
on Clear-Cut Logging at Grassy Narrows

In December 2002, youth from Asubpeeschoseewagong Netum Anishinabek (Grassy Narrows First Nation) in northwestern Ontario blocked the main road by which logging companies were entering their traditional territory. That blockade, which was still continuing more than ten years later, drew widespread support both within the Grassy Narrows community and within Canadian civil society, including faith-based organizations, human rights groups and environmentalists (see Da Silva 2012).[1]

Significantly, this mobilization was focused not only on the protection of the lands of the Grassy Narrows reserve, but on an assertion of rights in respect to the much larger territory which the community continues to rely on to hunt, trap, fish, gather plant medicines and conduct ceremonies (Amnesty International 2009). While the provincial government had viewed these territories as Crown lands over which it had exclusive constitutional jurisdiction, the people of Grassy Narrows had long argued that they needed to be part of the management of the land in order to protect rights affirmed in their treaty with Canada and in the Canadian Constitution.[2] On January 17, 2007, the Chief and Council, the Clan Mothers of the community, the Elders Council, Trappers Council, Youth Council and the blockaders issued a joint statement declaring

> a moratorium on further industrial activity in our Traditional Territory until such time as the Governments of Canada and Ontario restore their honour and *obtain the consent of our community in these decisions that will forever alter the future of our people.* (Grassy Narrows Chief and Council et al. 2007, emphasis added)

Political pressure brought by the community and its allies through lobbying, demonstrations and media campaigns eventually resulted in an agreement with the provincial government, announced in September 2007, to hold high-level talks over the future management of the forest and other related issues (Ontario Ministry of Natural Resources 2007). Although this represented a significant breakthrough, potentially opening the door for the community to have a direct say in the management of their traditional territories, the province refused to stop logging while the talks proceeded or to take any other interim measures to protect the rights of the people of Grassy Narrows.

At the time, industrial logging at Grassy Narrows was being carried out by the Canadian transnational corporation Abitibi Consolidated. The hardwood trees were being sold to the U.S. company Weyerhaeuser for manufacture of construction materials and the softwoods turned into pulp, which was sold to the U.S. paper company Boise. In January 2008, the international environmental NGO Rainforest Action Network (RAN) organized a day of protests at OfficeMax stores in the U.S. and Grand & Toy stores in Canada to denounce the sale of paper which was being labelled as a "green" product but made with wood from Grassy Narrows.[3] Shortly afterward, Boise announced it would no longer deal with pulp from wood sourced in Grassy Narrows. Citing Amnesty International's analysis that logging without the consent of the people of Grassy Narrows constituted a violation of internationally protected human rights (Amnesty International Canada 2007), Boise stated that it was taking up Amnesty's recommendation that the companies involved should voluntarily suspend their operations (Earley 2008). Less than six months after Boise's decision, facing blockades, legal challenges, negative press and now the loss of a major purchaser, Abitibi announced that it was giving up its licence to log in the Grassy Narrows traditional territory, stating that it could not afford to wait for the province to resolve the dispute (Gorrie 2008).

Boise's decision, and the subsequent withdrawal of Abitibi, brought logging to a halt in the territory. Weyerhaeuser continued to press for renewed logging to support its particle board mill but five years later, in the absence of a company willing to process the rest of the wood for pulp, logging had still not resumed. In effect, the community's moratorium had been reinforced even without an agreement from province.

NGOs, including RAN and the Boreal Forest Network, continued to campaign against Weyerhaeuser for not having agreed to respect the right of the community to grant or withhold consent. In 2009, ongoing campaigning led to the international investment company Calvert Investments removing Weyerhaeuser from its list of sustainable and responsible companies and divesting Weyerhaeuser stocks from its own mutual funds (Earth Justice Initiative 2009).

While these events were taking place, Grassy Narrows trappers were also pursuing a legal challenge to the province's jurisdiction to issue logging licences that would interfere with their treaty-protected rights. In a decision that hinged on the fact that part of the territory was outside Ontario boundaries at the time that the province assumed jurisdiction over natural resources, the Ontario Superior Court ruled in 2011 that the province did not have the necessary jurisdiction (Keewatin 2011). Although that decision has since been overturned (Grassy Narrows First Nation 2014), the province took the unusual step of agreeing that, while the appeal was being heard, it would not issue further development licences on the lands covered by the decision unless it has the consent of the community (Talaga 2012). The agreement was given further force by a subsequent order by the Ontario Court of Appeal (Keewatin 2012). Lawyer Robert Janes, who represented the trappers in this case, stated in a press release:

> This is a big departure from the usual government insistence on business as usual during lengthy appeals. It speaks to the strength of Grassy Narrows' stand against unwanted clearcut logging from a legal perspective and also from a moral and political viewpoint. (Grassy Narrows 2012)

While the struggle for the rights of the people of Grassy Narrows is far from over, the victories that they have achieved are significant and offer important lessons for future organizing in defence of Indigenous rights. The people of Grassy Narrows have demonstrated the potential to establish common ground among a great diversity of organizations around a basic message of no development without consent. They have also shown that Indigenous peoples' right of free, prior and informed consent is enforceable through the mobilization of public opinion and consumer action and that such mobilization can complement and bolster the pursuit of FPIC through legal strategies. Community member J.B. Fobister said of Boise's decision to respect the right of free, prior and informed consent, and the subsequent withdrawal of Abitibi:

> People told us we were crazy to take on two of the largest logging companies in the world. We weren't crazy, we were just fed up with watching our livelihood, our culture, our medicine, our children's future — our forests — being carried off our land right before our eyes. We were tired after decades of letter writing, petitions, meetings, protests, speaking tours, legal challenges and rallies, but we refused to give up ... people need to hear about what we have done. Then people need to stand up

and do something for themselves and for the land too. If Grassy can do it, so can you. (Fobister 2008)

FPIC in the *U.N. Declaration on the Rights of Indigenous Peoples*

The *U.N. Declaration on the Rights of Indigenous Peoples* was adopted by the United Nations General Assembly on September 13, 2007, after more than two decades of deliberation within various U.N. human rights bodies. UNDRIP is the most comprehensive international human rights instrument setting out the collective rights of Indigenous nations and the individual rights of Indigenous women, men and children (Sambo Dorough 2009: 264–65). The lengthy and "robust" process of drafting, deliberation and adoption reinforces the Declaration's status as a highly authoritative source of human rights law (Charters 2009: 262). Although four states — Canada, the U.S., Australia and New Zealand — voted against the Declaration at the General Assembly, all four have since formally endorsed it, establishing it as a consensus instrument.

The Declaration includes numerous provisions that explicitly or implicitly set out free, prior and informed consent requirements. One of the broadest of these is Article 19:

> States shall consult and cooperate in good faith with the indigenous peoples concerned through their own representative institutions in order to obtain their free, prior and informed consent before adopting and implementing legislative or administrative measures that may affect them.

Article 32 of Declaration requires FPIC in respect to any use of the lands, territories and resources of Indigenous peoples, giving specific emphasis to the need for FPIC in respect to resource exploitation. The first clause in this article states the broader principle: "Indigenous peoples have the right to determine and develop priorities and strategies for the development or use of their lands or territories and other resources." The second clause requires that:

> States shall consult and cooperate in good faith with the indigenous peoples concerned through their own representative institutions in order to obtain their free and informed consent prior to the approval of any project affecting their lands or territories and other resources, particularly in connection with the development, utilization or exploitation of mineral, water or other resources.

This article also contains a third clause which requires states to provide "effective mechanisms" to ensure "just and fair redress" for the use of Indigenous lands and "appropriate measures" to mitigate any "adverse environmental, economic, social, cultural or spiritual" impacts.

The right of FPIC is also invoked in two other articles that likewise require redress for actions taken without the consent of Indigenous peoples. Article 28 states, in part:

> Indigenous peoples have the right to redress, by means that can include restitution or, when this is not possible, just, fair and equitable compensation, for the lands, territories and resources which they have traditionally owned or otherwise occupied or used, and which have been confiscated, taken, occupied, used or damaged without their free, prior and informed consent.

Article 28 goes on to state that the form of redress must be "freely agreed upon by the peoples concerned." Similarly, Article 11 requires redress whenever "the cultural, intellectual, religious and spiritual property of Indigenous peoples is taken without their free, prior and informed consent or in violation of their laws, traditions and customs."

Three other articles of the U.N. Declaration affirm the right of FPIC in relation to specific contexts. Article 10, which concerns the removal of Indigenous peoples from their lands and territories, states: "No relocation shall take place without the free, prior and informed consent of the indigenous peoples concerned." Article 29, on environmental protection, includes a provision that "States shall take effective measures to ensure that no storage or disposal of hazardous materials shall take place in the lands or territories of indigenous peoples without their free, prior and informed consent." Article 30 states that "Military activities shall not take place in the lands or territories of indigenous peoples, unless justified by a relevant public interest or otherwise freely agreed with or requested by the indigenous peoples concerned."

More broadly, the U.N. Declaration as a whole sets out a framework to enable Indigenous peoples to make their own decisions about what is best for their nations. Article 3 affirms Indigenous peoples' right of self-determination, by virtue of which "they freely determine their political status and freely pursue their economic, social and cultural development."[4] One of the preambular paragraphs that establishes the context and intent of Declaration states:

> Convinced that control by indigenous peoples over developments affecting them and their lands, territories and resources will enable them to maintain and strengthen their institutions, cultures and traditions, and to promote their development in accordance with their aspirations and needs.

The Preamble also states that "recognition of the rights of indigenous peoples in this Declaration will enhance harmonious and cooperative relations between the State and indigenous peoples, based on principles of justice, democracy, respect for human rights, non-discrimination and good faith."

Various provisions, such as Article 8 prohibiting forced assimilation, set clear limits on the power that the state can exercise over Indigenous peoples. Numerous other articles set out requirements that states act in conjunction or in collaboration with Indigenous peoples (for example, Article 14 on education and Article 22 on special measures to address the needs of, and prevent violence against, women, elders and other specific sectors of Indigenous society). Furthermore, the Declaration gives strong emphasis and weight to the state obligation to uphold those agreements it enters into with Indigenous peoples. The first clause of Article 37 states:

> Indigenous peoples have the right to the recognition, observance and enforcement of treaties, agreements and other constructive arrangements concluded with States or their successors and to have States honour and respect such treaties, agreements and other constructive arrangements.

Affirmation of FPIC in the Larger Body of International Law

The U.N. Declaration does not stand alone in affirming the right of free, prior and informed consent. The Declaration builds on decades of progressive development of international human rights law. The Declaration's provisions, including those setting out FPIC requirements, were accepted by states because they reflected standards of international law that had already been established through the interpretation of human rights treaties and the application norms of customary international law by regional and international human rights bodies and expert mechanisms. As James Anaya, the U.N. Special Rapporteur on the Rights of Indigenous Peoples, stated, the Declaration

> represents an authoritative common understanding, at the global level, of the minimum content of the rights of indigenous peoples, upon a foundation of various sources of international human rights law ... the Declaration reflects and builds upon human rights norms of general applicability, as interpreted and applied by United Nations and regional treaty bodies. (Human Rights Council 2008: paras. 85–86)

The larger body of international human rights norms and standards, which are consolidated in the Declaration, clearly includes the right of free, prior and informed consent. Ten years before the adoption of the Declaration, the United Nations expert committee responsible for the interpretation and oversight of the *Convention on the Elimination of All Forms of Racial Discrimination*, issued a general recommendation on protecting the rights of Indigenous peoples under that convention, calling on states to:

- Ensure that members of indigenous peoples have equal rights in respect of effective participation in public life and that no decisions directly relating to their rights and interests are taken without their informed consent

- Recognize and protect the rights of indigenous peoples to own, develop, control and use their communal lands, territories and resources and, where they have been deprived of their lands and territories traditionally owned or otherwise inhabited or used without their free and informed consent, to take steps to return those lands and territories. (Committee on the Elimination of Racial Discrimination 1997)

Other U.N. bodies have also applied the standard of free, prior and informed consent in assessing whether state actions are consistent with their obligations under binding human rights treaties. For example, in a 2009 decision the U.N. Human Rights Committee found that a Peruvian water project had violated an Indigenous Aymara community's right to culture (Article 24 of the *International Covenant on Civil and Political Rights*) by degrading the pasturelands on which they depended to practise their tradition of raisings llamas and alpacas. The Committee found that the Indigenous community's effective participation in the decision-making process required "not mere consultation but the free, prior, and informed consent of the members of the community" (Human Rights Committee 2008–9; para. 7.6).

Indigenous peoples' right of free, prior and informed consent has also been affirmed across a wide range of U.N. human rights mandates and in diverse contexts. For example, in a recent report on small-scale fisheries, the U.N. Special Rapporteur on the right to food concluded that "states should refrain from adopting any policy that affects the territories and activities of small-scale, artisanal and indigenous fishers unless their free, prior and informed consent is obtained" (General Assembly 2012b: para. 39).

Regional human rights bodies have also affirmed Indigenous peoples' right of free, prior and informed consent. For example, in a case concerning the forced eviction of an Indigenous Endorois community from their traditional lands in Kenya, the African Court on Human and Peoples Rights ruled in 2010 that the consultations which government claimed to have carried out were "not sufficient," concluding

> that any development or investment projects that would have a major impact within the Endorois territory, the State has a duty not only to consult with the community, but also to obtain their free, prior, and informed consent, according to their customs and traditions. (African Court 2010)

In the Saramaka decision, the Inter-American Court of Human Rights ruled that, in order "to preserve, protect and guarantee the special relationship that the members of the Saramaka community have with their territory, which in turn ensures their survival as a tribal people," the state must "must ensure the effective participation of the members of the Saramaka people, in conformity with their customs and traditions, regarding any development, investment, exploration or extraction plan ... within Saramaka territory" (IACtHR 2008: para. 129). The Court went on:

> In addition to the consultation that is always required when planning development or investment projects within traditional Saramaka territory, the safeguard of effective participation that is necessary when dealing with major development or investment plans that may have a profound impact on the property rights of the members of the Saramaka people to a large part of their territory must be understood to additionally require the free, prior, and informed consent of the Saramakas, in accordance with their traditions and customs. (IACtHR 2008: para. 137)

Taken together with the clear affirmation of FPIC in the U.N. Declaration, the consistent application of this standard by regional and international human rights bodies leaves no room for doubt about the relevance and applicability of FPIC as a standard of contemporary international human rights law.

The Purpose of FPIC in International Law

The principle of free, prior and informed consent has long been established in medical ethics as a fundamental protection against abuse of power and authority (Manson 2007). For Indigenous peoples, free, prior and informed consent is inseparable from the exercise of other established rights, including the right of self-determination and rights over lands and resources (Human Rights Council 2010), as well as more generally the right to full and effective participation in decisions affecting their rights (Human Rights Council 2009a). As in the field of medical ethics, Indigenous peoples' right of FPIC also serves as a safeguard against human rights violations, a measure necessitated by the power imbalance that often exists between Indigenous peoples and the state, the systemic discrimination that Indigenous peoples face in respect to national laws and institutions, and the heightened risk of human rights violations created by racism, marginalization, impoverishment and the unresolved legacy of past abuses.

The African Court of Human and Peoples' Rights has called FPIC a requirement of the "especially stringent" threshold for protection of Indigenous peoples' rights (African Court 2010: para. 226). The Inter-American Commission on Human Rights (IACHR) has described the requirement of free, prior and informed consent "as a heightened safeguard for the rights of indigenous peoples" (IACHR 2010: para. 333).

Critically, regional and international human rights bodies have identified free, prior and informed consent as the appropriate standard of protection for the rights of Indigenous peoples even when the exact nature and extent of these rights is the subject of unresolved court cases or negotiations with the state and thus not fully or conclusively defined. In the Maya Indigenous Communities of the Toledo

District case, the Inter-American Commission found that — until the Indigenous territories had been legally demarcated — the state must not grant logging and oil concessions within the disputed land except where there had been "effective consultations with and the informed consent of the [respective] people" (IACHR 2004: para. 194).

The IFC's performance standards, noted above, similarly identify FPIC as a precautionary measure necessitated by the high risk of further violation of Indigenous peoples' rights. The IFC states that its incorporation of FPIC requirements in Performance Standard 7

> recognizes that Indigenous Peoples, as social groups with identities that are distinct from mainstream groups in national societies, are often among the most marginalized and vulnerable segments of the population. In many cases, their economic, social, and legal status limits their capacity to defend their rights to, and interests in, lands and natural and cultural resources, and may restrict their ability to participate in and benefit from development. Indigenous Peoples are particularly vulnerable if their lands and resources are transformed, encroached upon, or significantly degraded. Their languages, cultures, religions, spiritual beliefs, and institutions may also come under threat. As a consequence, Indigenous Peoples may be more vulnerable to the adverse impacts associated with project development than non-indigenous communities. This vulnerability may include loss of identity, culture, and natural resource-based livelihoods, as well as exposure to impoverishment and diseases. (International Finance Corporation 2012: para. 1)

FPIC and the Private Sector

The widespread application of FPIC within the international human rights system has led to increasing engagement with this standard by influential organizations and corporations within finance and industry. As noted above, in 2012 IFC adopted a FPIC requirement for its lending. IFC performance standards are generally considered highly influential within the private sector (IPIECA 2012: 9). FPIC is increasingly used in screening for ethical investment (Ethical Funds Company 2008). A number of prominent voices within the extractive industries have also expressed formal support for the FPIC standard, although this support is often highly conditional.

For example, IPIECA, which describes itself as the global oil and gas industry association for environmental and social issues, encourages "good faith negotiation and decision-making with the objective of achieving agreements, seeking consent or broad community support." While IPIECA does not require its members to obtain FPIC, it characterizes processes for negotiating consent as "emerging good practice" for corporate relations with Indigenous peoples (IPIECA 2012: 17).

Similarly, in a 2013 position statement, the International Council on Mining and Metals (ICMM), an international industry body representing thirty-five national and regional industry associations and twenty-one member companies, committed its members to "work to obtain the consent of Indigenous communities for new projects (and changes to existing projects) that are located on lands traditionally owned by or under customary use of Indigenous Peoples and are likely to have significant adverse impacts" (ICMM 2013: Commitment 4).

Obtaining consent has clear benefits for industry (Sohn 2007). A study commissioned by the Canadian oil and gas company Talisman Energy notes that obtaining free, prior and informed consent provides greater certainty for long-term investments, reduces the potential for conflict and protects against harm to the corporation's reputation by demonstrating a "social licence" to operate (Lehr and Smith 2010).

However, even companies that are willing to seek Indigenous consent are often reluctant to make any formal commitment that their projects will go ahead only if consent is granted. For example, ICMM, while calling on its members to "work to obtain the consent" of Indigenous peoples, leaves open the door to projects going ahead regardless. The position statement says that if, "despite the best efforts of all parties," consent is not granted,

> in balancing the rights and interests of Indigenous Peoples with the wider population, government might determine that a project should proceed and specify the conditions that should apply. In such circumstances, ICMM members will determine whether they ought to remain involved with a project. (ICMM 2013)

Such an interpretation of FPIC falls below the standard of international law. National laws, however regressive, and the will of national governments, whatever their record of treatment of Indigenous peoples, are allowed to trump human rights standards in determining whether or not Indigenous peoples' own decisions are respected. As a consequence, while taking a positive step to encourage the negotiation of FPIC, the ICMM position statement still denies Indigenous peoples the rigorous safeguard for their rights that FPIC is intended to provide.

More than Consultation, but Not a "Veto"

Taken in isolation, some of the provisions in the U.N. Declaration could be interpreted as supporting a weakened interpretation of FPIC, in which consent may be sought, but only the act of consultation is actually required. For example, Article 32 says "states shall consult and cooperate in good faith with the indigenous peoples ... in order to obtain their free and informed consent." The provision does not explicitly state that governments can proceed only if consent is obtained. Some observers have interpreted this article as meaning that while governments are obliged to make a good faith effort to obtain consent, there is no further constraint on government decision-making if Indigenous peoples withhold their consent. However, by leaving government and industry with a free hand to ignore Indigenous peoples' rights, such an intepretation would run contrary to the Declaration's fundamental purpose of setting minimum standards for the "survival, dignity and well-being" of Indigenous peoples (Article 43). Critically, such an interpretation is also clearly refuted by other provisions in the Declaration.

As noted above, Article 32 also includes a requirement for redress for use of land where FPIC has not been obtained. Similarly, Article 19 requires redress for confiscation, use or damage of Indigenous lands, territories and resources without FPIC. There would be no such duty to provide redress if the only requirement was to try to obtain consent. These redress provisions clearly establish that acting without FPIC is a violation of Indigenous peoples' rights.

In addition, the provisions of the Declaration must be interpreted in relation to the broader body of international law of which it is part. Even at the time of the Declaration's adoption, international and regional human rights bodies had clearly affirmed a state obligation to not only seek consent, but to proceed with projects only if such consent is granted.

This does not mean, however, that FPIC is a form of absolute veto, as opponents, including the Government of Canada, often suggest. Human rights are rarely absolute (Joffe 2010b: 82). In application, rights often need to be reconciled with contending rights. The U.N. Declaration includes explicit provisions setting out the intention of achieving an appropriate balancing in which the "human rights and fundamental freedoms of all shall be respected" (Article 46), as well as a requirement for "a fair, independent, impartial, open and transparent process" to "adjudicate the rights of indigenous peoples pertaining to their lands, territories and resources" (Article 27).

The jurisprudence of regional and international human rights bodies clearly establishes that FPIC is not an absolute right, but a measure that is applied in relation to a careful assessment of the rights at stake and the harm that would result from their violation. As noted above, critical factors informing the application of FPIC by regional and international human rights bodies include the vital importance of lands, territories and resources to the cultures and well-being of Indigenous peoples, and the situation of extreme disadvantage that has resulted from historic and ongoing discrimination against Indigenous peoples.

This was also the approach taken by Amnesty International when it decided to support the people of Grassy Narrows in campaigning for a moratorium on clear-cutting logging in their territory. Amnesty's first brief on the issue, submitted to the Government of Ontario in 2007, documented the ongoing health and social impact of massive mercury contamination of their river system in the 1960s, the current state of impoverishment and ill-health affecting much of the community, the government's failure to respect rights protected by treaty and the Canadian

Constitution, and the continued critical importance of the forest to the economy, culture and spiritual life of the community (Amnesty International Canada 2007). Amnesty's analysis was cited by Boise in its decision to stop purchasing pulp from wood logged at Grassy Narrows without consent (Earley 2008).

The IACHR has found that the impacts of certain actions are so inherently prejudicial to the rights of Indigenous peoples, that free, prior and informed consent will always be required. Three examples cited by the Commission are permanent relocation of Indigenous peoples from their traditional lands, storage or disposal of hazardous materials in Indigenous peoples' lands or territories, and activities that would deprive Indigenous peoples of "the capacity to use and enjoy their lands and other natural resources necessary for their subsistence" (IACHR 2010: para. 334).

More broadly, resource extraction projects on the lands of Indigenous peoples are seen as potentially so disruptive that FPIC will almost always be required. During his term as U.N. Special Rapporteur on the Situation of Human Rights and Fundamental Freedom of Indigenous People, Rodolfo Stavenhagen wrote that when large-scale economic activities are carried out on the lands of Indigenous Peoples,

> it is likely that their communities will undergo profound social and economic changes that are frequently not well understood, much less foreseen, by the authorities in charge of promoting them. Large-scale development projects will inevitably affect the conditions of living of indigenous peoples. Sometimes the impact will be beneficial, very often it is devastating, but it is never negligible. (Commission on Human Rights 2003)

This statement was cited by the Inter-American Court as part of its reasoning for applying the standard of free, prior and informed consent in the Saramaka decision (IACtHR 2008: para. 135).

More recently, James Anaya, who was appointed Special Rapporteur after Rodolfo Stavenhagen, stated that it is "a general rule that extractive activities should not take place within the territories of indigenous peoples without their free, prior and informed consent" (Human Rights Council 2013: para. 27). While there may be exceptions to this general rule, such exceptions must be consistent with the principle of international law that potentially restricting human rights must serve "a valid public purpose within a human rights framework" (Human Rights Council 2013: para. 35) and that the resulting limitations on human rights be "necessary and proportional to that purpose" (Human Rights Council 2013: para. 36). The Special Rapporteur went on to caution:

> This requirement will generally be difficult to meet for extractive indus-tries that are carried out within the territories of indigenous peoples without their consent. In determining necessity and proportionality, due

account must be taken of the significance to the survival of indigenous peoples of the range of rights potentially affected by the project. Account should also be taken of the fact that in many if not the vast majority of cases, indigenous peoples continue to claim rights to subsurface resources within their territories on the basis of their own laws or customs, despite State law to the contrary. These factors weigh heavily against a finding of proportionality of State-imposed rights limitations, reinforcing the general rule of indigenous consent to extractive activities within indigenous territories. (Human Rights Council 2013: para. 36)

Consent in Canadian Law

Ten years before the adoption of the *U.N. Declaration on the Rights of Indigenous Peoples* the Supreme Court of Canada recognized that there are instances in which the consent of Indigenous peoples is required to fulfill the Constitutional protection of Aboriginal and Treaty rights. In *Delgamuukw v. British Columbia* (1997), a case concerning provincial authorization of logging on land subject to an unresolved assertion of Indigenous title, the Supreme Court ruled that the "honour of the Crown" necessitates "the involvement of aboriginal peoples in decisions taken with respect to their lands" (para. 168). The Court went on to specify that Indigenous peoples' involvement in decision-making must be meaningful, requiring consultation "in good faith, and *with the intention of substantially addressing* the concerns of the aboriginal peoples whose lands are at issue" (para. 168, emphasis added). The Court also stated that, depending on the potential for harm to the rights of Indigenous peoples, the substantial accommodation "may even require the *full consent* of an aboriginal nation" (para. 168, emphasis added).

The framework of substantial accommodation set out in Delgamuukw should have provided a powerful tool for Indigenous peoples, like the Grassy Narrows First Nation and other nations across Canada, to play a decisive role in decisions about what development should take place on their lands. In Delgamuukw the court gave as an example of when accommodation may require "full consent" the enacting of "hunting and fishing regulations in relation to aboriginal lands" (para. 168). This example suggests that the threshold at which consent may be required is one that should frequently come into play in respect to decisions about the development and use of Indigenous lands.

In the years since the Delgamuukw decision, there has been a substantial body of court decisions further elaborating on the duty of consultation and accommodation. The frequency with which Indigenous peoples in Canada have had to go to court to seek enforcement of this duty is some indication of the degree of government resistance. While there is now widespread acknowledgement of a "duty to consult" with Indigenous peoples, government practice generally does not meet the standards set out in the Delgamuukw decision. In practice most consultation does not promote meaningful involvement of Indigenous peoples in the actual decision-making or ensuring the substantial accommodation of their concerns. Federal guidelines on implementing the "duty to consult" claim that government departments and agencies are implementing a "wide array of consultation practices" (Aboriginal Affairs and Northern Development Canada 2011: 7). However, the primary example provided in the guidelines is that of environmental assessments — processes in which Indigenous peoples are treated as one stakeholder among many and which serve only to provide recommendations for decisions that will ultimately be made by government without the participation of Indigenous peoples (Aboriginal Affairs and Northern Development Canada 2011: 39). Environmental assessments under federal jurisdiction were drastically curtailed as part of two omnibus budget bills passed in 2012, with the anticipated result that independent public assessments would be come even rarer, and the scope of such assessments would be much more limited than before. The curtailing of federal environmental impact assessments was one of the developments that helped catalyze the Idle No More movement for Indigenous rights.

As noted above, federal guidelines on consultation no longer even acknowledge the possibility that consent may be required as part of the process of consultation and accommodation. In rejecting the concept of free, prior and informed consent, governments in Canada have relied on a second Supreme Court decision, which also concerned development on the unceded lands of Indigenous peoples in British Columbia. In the Haida Nation (2004) decision the Court stated that the duty of consultation "does not give Aboriginal groups a veto over what can be done with land pending final proof of the claim" (para. 48). This phrase has been frequently quoted by governments and project proponents to justify their intent to ignore Indigenous opposition to a project. For example, during the environmental assessment of the proposed New Prosperity Mine, which would have impacted Indigenous peoples' traditional territories in British Columbia, the project proponent submitted a series of excerpts from Court decisions in which this phrase about Indigenous peoples not having a veto was cited (Taseko Mines 2013). It's important to understand, however, that in the Haida Nation decision the Court was rejecting the notion that either party in an unresolved dispute can exercise arbitrary and absolute decision-making power. The Court goes on to state that "what is required is a process of balancing interests, of give and take. This flows from the meaning of 'accommodate'" (paras. 48–49).

It is clear that the right of free, prior and informed consent in international law is not an absolute veto. Rather, it is a measure that is applied based on an understanding of the importance of the rights at stake and an analysis of the potential for serious harm to these rights. Contrary to the way the case is often cited, the Supreme Court in the Haida Nation decision did not preclude the application of such a concept of consent (Amnesty International 2013). In fact, while the Haida Nation decision is potentially ambiguous, the decision actually lends further support to FPIC, as it sets out a need for effective protection for the rights of Indigenous peoples even when these rights are the subject of unresolved litigation and negotiation:

> The Crown, acting honourably, cannot cavalierly run roughshod over Aboriginal interests where claims affecting these interests are being seriously pursued in the process of treaty negotiation and proof. It must respect these potential, but yet unproven, interests. (para. 27)

The Haida Nation decision also makes clear that the preferred means to resolve outstanding disputes over Indigenous lands and title is through the negotiation of mutual agreements:

> Put simply, Canada's Aboriginal peoples were here when Europeans came, and were never conquered. Many bands reconciled their claims with the sovereignty of the Crown through negotiated treaties. Others, notably in British Columbia, have yet to do so. The potential rights embedded in these claims are protected by s. 35 of the *Constitution Act, 1982*. The honour of the Crown requires that these rights be determined, recognized and respected. This, in turn, requires the Crown, acting honourably, to participate in processes of negotiation. (para. 25)

The ambiguity of the Haida Nation decision lies in its comments on the measures needed to protect the rights of Indigenous peoples pending such a negotiated resolution. The Court stated "the 'consent' spoken of in Delgamuukw is appropriate only in cases of established rights, and then by no means in every case" (para. 48). However the Court also presented the following seemingly contradictory analysis,

> The Court's seminal decision in Delgamuukw, in the context of a claim for title to land and resources, confirmed and expanded on the duty to consult, suggesting the content of the duty varied with the circumstances: from a minimum "duty to discuss important decisions" where the "breach is less serious or relatively minor"; through the "significantly deeper than mere consultation" that is required in "most cases"; to "full consent of [the] aboriginal nation" on very serious issues. These words apply as much to unresolved claims as to intrusions on settled claims. (para. 24)[5]

Although Canadian courts have subsequently cited the Haida Nation decision to restate that Indigenous peoples do not have a "veto" over unresolved claims, there has been no further elaboration of what is meant, or not meant, by "veto." The Supreme Court has also not substantively addressed the issue of Indigenous consent since the Haida Nation decision. However, other decisions by Canadian courts clearly suggest that there is still room for the elaboration of the right of free, prior and informed consent within Canadian law.

In the 2005 Mikisew Cree First Nation decision, the Supreme Court again repeated the statement from Delgamuukw that within the spectrum of accommodation required of the state, "some cases may even require the full consent of an aboriginal nation" (para. 61). Although stating that "consultation will not always lead to accommodation, and accommodation may or may not result in an agreement" (para. 66), the court was clear that the outcome of the consultation and accommodation process could not be pre-determined and thus presumably could not rule out the possibility of proceeding only on the basis of such "full consent." The Court stated, "The contemplated process is not simply one of giving the Mikisew an opportunity to blow off steam before the Minister proceeds to do what she intended to do all along" (para. 54).

This line of argument was taken up by lower courts in the 2010 West Moberly case. The B.C. Superior Court found that a mining company's plans were "irreconcilable" with the environmental protection sought by the First Nation. The Court ruled that the consultation that had been carried out over the planned mineral development "was not sufficiently meaningful, and the accommodation put in place was not reasonable" (para. 144) because provincial officials never considered the possibility that the project should be rejected, as the affected First Nation wished. The Court argued that to "commence consultations" with the view that the project would proceed regardless of the concerns expressed by the affected First Nation "does not recognize the full range of possible outcomes, and amounts to nothing more than an opportunity for the First Nations 'to blow off steam'" (para. 144).

The West Moberly decision was upheld on appeal. In 2012, the Supreme Court denied the province and the project proponent leave to further appeal the decision. The West Moberly decision now stands as a powerful reminder that under Canadian law any good faith process of consultation and accommodation, however narrowly interpreted, must at least give serious and meaningful consideration to the possibility that Indigenous peoples' rejection of a project may be the preferred and necessary outcome.

In a landmark 2014 decision recognizing the Tsilhqot'in title to 1700 square kilometres in the heart of their traditional territory in British Columbia (*Tsilhqot'in Nation v. British Columbia* 2014), the Supreme Court explicitly stated that such title "means that governments and others seeking to use the land must obtain the consent of the Aboriginal title holders" (para. 76). Although the unanimous decision makes a dozen references to consent, it never uses the word "veto." The judgment, in fact, is clear that the requirement of consent is not absolute, but could potentially be infringed, if such infringement meets established tests, including the existence of "a compelling and substantial public interest," and that the infringement is consistent with the Crown's fiduciary duty (para 88). That fiduciary duty, the Court said, "infuses an obligation of proportionality" into the determination of whether an infringement can be justified: "Implicit in the Crown's fiduciary is the requirement that the incursion is necessary to achieve the government's goal (rational connection); that the government go no further than necessary to achieve it (minimal impairment); and that the benefits that may be expected to flow from that goal are not outweighed by adverse effects on the Aboriginal interest (proportionality of impact)" (para 87).

While the judgment addresses consent in the context of the Court having now recognized Tsilhqot'in title, Chief Justice McLachlin made a point of offering this piece of broader advice: "I add this. Governments and individuals proposing to use or exploit land, whether before or after a declaration of Aboriginal title, can avoid a charge of infringement or failure to adequately consult by obtaining the consent of the interested Aboriginal group" (para. 97).

Clarifying Consent: International Law and Canadian Law

There is clearly need for continued evolution of the standard of protection of Indigenous rights required under Canadian law. One critical aspect of such an evolution is to bring together international and domestic legal standards, to clarify and bolster the requirement of Indigenous consent in Canada.

The Supreme Court of Canada has long affirmed "the important role of international human rights law" in interpreting Canadian law (*Baker v. Canada* 1999: para. 70). Former Supreme Court Chief Justice Brian Dickson characterized "the various sources of international human rights law" as "relevant and persuasive sources" for the interpretation of human rights in Canada (*Reference re Public Service Employee Relations Act* 1987: para. 57). Among these relevant and persuasive sources, the Chief Justice included "declarations, covenants, conventions, judicial and quasi-judicial decisions of international tribunals, customary norms" (*Reference re Public Service Employee Relations Act* 1987: para. 57).

In addition, Canadian legal tradition assumes that, unless there is clear and explicit intent to do otherwise, laws and regulations passed in Canada are meant to comply with "the values and principles of customary and conventional international law" and with "Canada's obligations as a signatory of international treaties and as a member of the international community" (*R v. Hape* 2007: Para 53; see also Gunn, this volume). Accordingly, the Supreme Court has held that any interpretation of domestic law that would put the government in violation of these international obligations must be strictly avoided. The only possible exception allowed in Canadian law is when there is "an unequivocal legislative intent to default on an international obligation" (*R v. Hape* 2007: para. 53).

International standards for the protection of Indigenous rights are not an exception to these principles of interpretation. This was confirmed in 2012 in a case before the Federal Court. The Court ruled that the Canadian Human Rights Tribunal had erred when it failed to adequately consider international human rights standards in interpreting and applying the *Canadian Human Rights Act* in a discrimination complaint concerning First Nations children. The decision stated:

> The Supreme Court has recognized the relevance of international human rights law in interpreting domestic legislation ... the Court has held

that in interpreting Canadian law, Parliament will be presumed to act in compliance with its international obligations. As a consequence, where there is more than one possible interpretation of a provision in domestic legislation, tribunals and courts will seek to avoid an interpretation that would put Canada in breach of its international obligations.

International instruments such as the UNDRIP and the *Convention of the Rights of the Child* may also inform the contextual approach to statutory interpretation.

As a result, insofar as may be possible, an interpretation that reflects these values and principles is preferred. (*First Nations Child and Family Caring Society of Canada v. Canada* 2012: paras. 351–54)

This decision has been subsequently upheld by the Federal Court of Appeal (*Canada v. Canadian Human Rights Commission* 2013) and has not been further appealed.

To date, no Canadian court has yet explicitly considered the applicability of the standard of free, prior and informed consent as set out in international human rights law. This may only be a matter of time. Given the established principles of application of international law in Canada, there is considerable potential to bring the standard of free, prior and informed consent to bear in any forum where decisions are being made that affect the rights of Indigenous peoples, including environmental impact assessments and the permitting processes for resource extraction projects (Amnesty International Canada 2013).

In fact, in 2013, an independent, federally appointed panel assessing the potential impact of a proposed gold-copper mine on traditional Tsilhqot'in territory in central British Columbia not only considered the interaction of international human rights law and domestic law, but also said that the fact that Tsilhqot'in had not given their consent was a significant factor in its findings that the project would cause "severe" harm to their rights that could not be mitigated (Review Panel 2013: 212–13). The review was carried out prior to the 2014 Supreme Court decision recognizing Tsilhqot'in title over a large area of territory near the proposed mine site (*Tsilhqot'in Nation v. British Columbia* 2014). The review was further constrained by terms of reference that specifically precluded making findings on the probable existence of Aboriginal title, or whether the Crown had adequately discharged its duty of consultation and accommodation. Nonetheless, the Panel did reach the conclusion "that displacement of Tsilhqot'in from this sacred site, and the practical impediments to conducting cultural and spiritual ceremonies at and around Fish Lake (Teztan Biny) (e.g., loss of pristine environment to mine-related noise, blasting, light, dust, activity and other sensory disturbance) would amount to a severe infringement of Tsilhqot'in Aboriginal rights [Review Panel 2013: 212]." In its discussion of these findings, the panel summarized submissions from the Tsilhqot'in National Government, MiningWatch Canada, a local advocacy coalition (Fish Lake Alliance) and Amnesty International, all of which had raised the *U.N. Declaration on the Rights of Indigenous Peoples* and FPIC. The Panel's summary of the Amnesty International submission included:

> A very high and strict standard of precaution is always required in any decision that has the potential to infringe, limit or undermine human rights ... especially... in any context where: a particular group such as indigenous nations had already been marginalized, impoverished or disadvantaged by the historic violation of their human rights; or ongoing serious human rights violations such as the denial of their land rights have yet to be addressed and where systemic discrimination continues to bar families and communities from enjoying a standard of living and quality of life comparable to other communities around them. (Review Panel 2013: 210–11)

During the hearings, the project proponent had tried to portray the Tsilhqot'in as being unreasonable for having taken the position that the proposed mine was unacceptable under any circumstances. The proponent also claimed that any assertion of a need for FPIC was contrary to Canadian legal standards as reflected in Supreme Court judgements. The proponent's arguments were implicitly and explicitly refuted in the panel report. The Panel concluded, "the Tsilhqot'in cultural attachment to Fish Lake (Teztan Biny) and the Nabas areas is so profound that they cannot reasonably be expected to accept the conversion of that area into the proposed New Prosperity Mine or to accept other areas as an adequate replacement" (Review Panel 2013: 197). The panel went on to cite as factors "particularly relevant to its findings":

> Amnesty International submitted that free, prior and informed consent as it is understood and has been applied in international law, is consistent with the leading Supreme Court of Canada decisions in *Delgamuukw* and *Haida Nation*, which identify consent as being within the spectrum of substantial accommodation required by the constitutional protection of Aboriginal rights. (Review Panel 2013: 213)

The panel's report provides a clear example of the way that FPIC in international law can be used to clarify and bolster the legal framework for Indigenous rights in domestic law. As noted earlier, under federal legislation the conclusions of environmental assessment panels provide only recommendations that the government can take into account or ignore in its final decision about whether or not to approve a proposed project. In early 2014, the federal government announced its decision to reject the New Prosperity Mine proposal. Speaking to the Prospectors and Developers Association of Canada about his government's decision to reject the project, Prime Minister Stephen Harper is quoted as saying that the proposal was "in an area where there's unresolved land claim issues, and local aboriginal groups ... do not approve the project" (Koven and Penner 2014).

The Ongoing Struggle for FPIC

The federal government's Economic Action Plan predicts that more than six hundred new, large-scale resource development projects will get under way across Canada in this decade (Treasury Board of Canada 2012). As has already happened with existing resource development projects, the scale of planned development would inevitably affect the lands and waters of continued vital importance to First Nations, Inuit and Métis peoples and the enjoyment of their human rights. Due in part to new trade agreements, a similar rush for resources is threatening the lands of Indigenous peoples throughout the world.

In this context, a rigorous framework of human rights safeguards are needed both to prevent further harm to Indigenous peoples and to ensure that Indigenous peoples have the opportunity to advance their own visions of how their lands and resources should be used and protected. Free, prior and informed consent as affirmed in UNDRIP and elaborated within the international human rights system is necessarily central to this framework of safeguards.

For the immediate future, governments in Canada are likely to continue to oppose the recognition and application of free, prior and informed consent. Despite this, the legal basis for FPIC is clear and persuasive. Furthermore, as demonstrated by the people of Grassy Narrows' successful defence of their lands, and by the conclusions of the New Prosperity Gold-Copper Mine Review, the tide of legal opinion, corporate standards and even public sentiment are already turning in this direction. Enforcement of FPIC does not have to depend on the goodwill of government: the potential to advance this right both through legal advocacy and public campaigning is considerable but will necessarily require continued collaboration and concerted effort by Indigenous peoples and civil society.

Notes

My appreciation to Paul Joffe for his insights into international and domestic legal standards for the rights of Indigenous peoples, and to David Sone for his help with the case study included in this chapter.

1. For an account of this mobilization from the perspective of the one of key community leaders, see Da Silva 2012.
2. Letters to government from the Band Council, individual trappers and others in the community dating back to 1998 have been posted <http://freegrassy.net/learn-more/resources/official-correspondence/#c1863>.
3. For an account of this campaign, and other work by RAN to support the people of Grassy Narrows, see Rainforest Action Network, "The Old Growth Campaign Victory — How we did that," <http://understory.ran.org/2008/06/20/the-old-growth-campaign-victory-how-did-we-do-that/>.
4. Article 3 of the U.N. Declaration mirrors common Article 1 of the *International*

Covenant on Civil and Political Rights and the *International Covenant on Economic, Social and Cultural Rights.*

5.   This spectrum, including consent, is restated at paras. 30 and 40.

References

Aboriginal Affairs and Northern Development Canada. 2011. *Aboriginal Consultation and Accommodation — Updated Guidelines for Federal Officials to Fulfill the Duty to Consult — March 2011.* <aadnc-aandc.gc.ca/eng/1100100014664>.

African Court for Human and Peoples' Rights. 2010. *Centre for Minority Rights Development (Kenya) and Minority Rights Group International on behalf of Endorois Welfare Council v Kenya.* 276 /2003.

Amnesty International. 2009. *"A Place to Regain Who We Are": Grassy Narrows First Nation in Ontario.* <amnesty.org/en/library/info/AMR20/001/2009/en>.

Amnesty International Canada. 2007. *The law of the land: Amnesty International Canada's position on the conflict over logging at Grassy Narrows.* <http://www.amnesty.ca/sites/default/files/grassynarrowsamnestyreport2007.pdf>.

_____. 2013. *Submission to the New Prosperity Gold-Copper Mine Review.* <www.amnesty.ca/sites/default/files/ai_canada_15_july_2013_submission_new_prosperity_review.pdf>.

Charters, Claire. 2009. "The Legitimacy of the U.N. *Declaration on the Rights of Indigenous Peoples."* In Claire Charters and Rodolfo Stavenhagen (eds.), *Making the Declaration Work: The United Nations Declaration on the Rights of Indigenous Peoples.* IWGIA Document No. 127. Copenhagen.

Commission on Human Rights. 2003. *Report of the Special Rapporteur on the Situation of Human Rights and Fundamental Freedoms of Indigenous People.* E/CN.4/2003/90, January 21.

Committee on the Elimination of Racial Discrimination. 1997. "General Recommendation XXIII concerning Indigenous Peoples." CERD/C/51/Misc.13/Rev.4 (adopted by the Committee on August 18).

_____. 2012. "Consideration of reports, comments and information submitted by States parties under article 9 of the Convention (*continued*): *Nineteenth and twentieth periodic reports of Canada* (continued)." Summary record of 1242nd meeting on 23 February 2012, UN Doc. CERD/C/SR.2142, 2 March.

Da Silva, Judy. 2012. "Grassy Narrows: Advocate for Mother Earth and its Inhabitants." In Lynne Davis (ed.), *Alliances: Re/Envisioning Indigenous-non-Indigenous Relationships.* Toronto: University of Toronto Press.

Doyle, Cathal, and Jill Cariño. 2013. "Making Free Prior and Informed Consent a Reality: Indigenous Peoples and the Extractive Sector." *Indigenous Peoples Links* (PIPLinks) Middlesex University School of Law, and the Ecumenical Council for Corporate Responsibility.

Earley, Stephen. 2008. Letter from Region Woodlands Manager, Boise, dated February 27. <understory.ran.org/wordpress/wp-content/uploads/2008/02/boises-letter.pdf>.

Earth Justice Initiative. 2009. "Calvert Divests Weyerhaeuser: Indigenous Land Rights Conflict with Grassy Narrows Ontario Cited." Press release. June 15. <freegrassy.org/wp-content/uploads/2010/03/Calvert-Divests-Weyerhaeuser-June-15-2009.pdf>.

Economic and Social Council. 2003. *Human rights and indigenous issues: Report of the Special*

Rapporteur on the situation of human rights and fundamental freedoms of indigenous people, Rodolfo Stavenhagen, submitted in accordance with Commission resolution 2001/65. E/ CN.4/2003/90, 21 January.

Ethical Funds Company. 2008. *Winning the Social License to Operate Resource Extraction with Free, Prior, and Informed Community Consent.*

Fobister, JB. 2008. "Message from JB Fobister in Grassy Narrows." Rainforest Action Network. <understory.ran.org/2008/06/05/message-from-jb-fobister-in-grassy-narrows/>.

Forest Peoples Programme. n.d. "Free, prior and informed consent (FPIC)." Webpage. Accessed 16 August 2013. <www.forestpeoples.org/guiding-principles/free-prior-and-informed-consent-fpic>.

General Assembly. 2010. *Situation of human rights and fundamental freedoms of indigenous people: Note by the Secretary-General.* Interim report of the Special Rapporteur on the situation of human rights and fundamental freedoms of indigenous people. U.N. Doc. A/65/264, 9 August.

____. 2012a. *Rights of indigenous peoples: Note by the Secretary-General.* U.N. Doc. A/67/301, 13 August (report of the Special Rapporteur on the rights of indigenous peoples, James Anaya).

____. 2012b. *Interim Report of the U.N. Special Rapporteur on the right to food.* UN Doc. A/67/268, 8 August.

Gorrie, Peter. 2008. "Protest prompts Abitibi pullout: One of the world's biggest logging companies has pulled out of a Northern Ontario forest because of opposition from a small local Indian community." *Toronto Star,* June 5.

Government of Canada. 2008. *Aboriginal consultation and accommodation: Interim guidelines for Federal officials to fulfill the legal duty to consult.*

Grassy Narrows Chief and Council, Environmental Committee, Blockaders, Trappers, Clan Mothers, Elders, Youth. 2007. "Open Letter Re: Moratorium on industry in our Traditional Territory, and opposition to MNR tender process." January 17. <freegrassy.org/wp-content/uploads/GrassyMoratorium%20Jan%2007%20signed%20copy.pdf>.

Grassy Narrows First Nation. 2012. "ON Court of Appeal orders no logging without consent on Grassy Narrows Territory north of the English River during appeal of landmark legal victory." Press release. <freegrassy.net/2012/03/23/on-court-of-appeal-orders-no-logging-without-consent-on-grassy-narrows-territory-north-of-the-english-river-during-appeal-of-landmark-legal-victory/>.

Human Rights Committee. 2008–09. *Poma v. Peru.* Case No. 1457/2006. *Report of the Human Rights Committee,* GAOR, 64th Sess., Supp. No. 40, Vol. I, UN Doc. A/64/40.

Human Rights Council. 2008. *Report of the Special Rapporteur on the situation of human rights and fundamental freedoms of indigenous people, S. James Anaya.* UN Doc. A/ HRC/9/9, 11 August.

____. 2009a. *Report of the Special Rapporteur on the situation of human rights and fundamental freedoms of indigenous people, James Anaya.* U.N. Doc. A/HRC/12/34, 15 July.

____. 2009b. *Report of the Special Rapporteur on adequate housing as a component of the right to an adequate standard of living, and on the right to non-discrimination in this context, Miloon Kothari: Addendum — Mission to Canada.* UN Doc. A/HRC/10/7/Add.3, 17 February.

____. 2010. *Report of the Special Rapporteur on the situation of human rights and fundamental freedoms of indigenous people, James Anaya: Addendum: Cases examined by the Special*

Rapporteur (June 2009 — July 2010). U.N. Doc. A/HRC/15/37/Add.1, 15 September.

_____. 2011. *Final report of the study on indigenous peoples and the right to participate in decision-making.* U.N. Doc. A/HRC/18/42, 17 August, Annex (Expert Mechanism advice No. 2).

_____. 2012. Follow-up report on indigenous peoples and the right to participate in decision-making, with a focus on extractive industries. A/HRC/21/55, 16 August.

_____. 2013. *Report of the Special Rapporteur on the rights of indigenous peoples, James Anaya: Extractive industries and indigenous peoples.* A/HRC/24/41, 1 July.

IACHR (Inter-American Commission on Human Rights). 2004. *Maya Indigenous Communities of the Toledo District (Belize).* Report No. 40/04, Case 12.053, October 12.

_____. 2010. *Indigenous and Tribal Peoples' Rights Over Their Ancestral Lands and Natural Resources: Norms and Jurisprudence of the Inter-American Human Rights System.* OEA/Ser.L/V/II. Doc. 59/06.

IACtHR. 2008. *Case of the Saramaka People v. Suriname. Interpretation of the Judgment of Preliminary Objections, Merits, Reparations and Costs.* Judgment of August 12. Series C No. 185.

ICMM (International Council on Mining and Metals). 2013. "Indigenous Peoples and Mining Position Statement." May.

IFC (International Finance Corporation). 2012. "Performance Standards on Environmental and Social Sustainability." January 1. <ifc.org/wps/wcm/connect/115482804a0255 db96fbffd1a5d13d27/PS_English_2012_Full-Document.pdf>.

IPIECA. 2012. "Indigenous Peoples and the oil and gas industry: Context, issues and emerging good practice."

Joffe, Paul. 2010. "*U.N. Declaration on the Rights of Indigenous Peoples*: Canadian Government Positions Incompatible with Genuine Reconciliation." *N.J.C.L.* 26: 121.

_____. 2010b. "Canada's Opposition to the U.N. Declaration: Legitimate Concerns or Ideological Bias?" In Jackie Hartley, Paul Joffe, and Jennifer Preston (eds.), *Realizing the U.N. Declaration on the Rights of Indigenous Peoples: Triumph, Hope, and Action.* Purich Publishing.

_____. 2012. "*U.N. Declaration on the Rights of Indigenous Peoples*: Not Merely 'Aspirational,'" September 16. <quakerservice.ca/wp-content/uploads/2012/09/UN-Decl-Not-merely-aspirational-.pdf>.

Koven, Peter, and Derrek Penner. 2014. "Stephen Harper comes down hard on Taseko mine proposal: PM cites environment, aboriginal issues among reasons to not approve project." *Vancouver Sun*, March 4. <http://www.vancouversun.com/technology/Step hen+Harper+comes+down+hard+mine+proposal/9574570/story.html>.

Lehr, Amy K., and Gare A. Smith. 2010. *Implementing a Corporate Free, Prior, and Informed Consent Policy: Benefits and Challenges.* Foley Hoag Ltd.

Manson, Neil C. 2007. "Consent and Informed Consent." In Richard Ashcroft, Angus Dawson, Heather Draper and John McMillan (eds.), *Principles of Health Care Ethics* (2nd ed), London: John Wiley.

Ontario Ministry of Natural Resources. 2007. "Ontario Enters into Forestry Discussions with Grassy Narrows." Press release, September 8. <www.mnr.gov.on.ca/mnr/csb/news/2007/sep7nr_07.html>.

Review Panel Established by the Federal Minister of the Environment. 2013. *Report of the Federal Review Panel — New Prosperity Gold-Copper Mine Project.* Canadian Environmental Assessment Agency. CEAA Reference No. 63928. 31 October. <http://

www.ceaa-acee.gc.ca/050/document-eng.cfm?document=95631>.

Sambo Dorough, Dalee. 2009. "The Significance of the *Declaration on the Rights of Indigenous Peoples* and Its Future Implementation." In Claire Charters and Rodolfo Stavenhagen (eds.), *Making the Declaration Work: The United Nations Declaration on the Rights of Indigenous Peoples.* IWGIA Document No. 127. Copenhagen.

Sohn, Jonathan (ed.). 2007. *Development Without Conflict: The Business Case for Community Consent.* World Resources Institute.

Talaga, Tanya. 2012. "English River logging suspended during court battle." *Toronto Star,* 22 March.

Taseko Mines. 2013. "Taseko's position regarding Canada's endorsement of the U.N. *Declaration on the Rights of Indigenous Peoples* (UNDRIP) and its implications with respect to the question of 'free, prior and informed consent.'" Submitted to the New Prosperity Gold-Copper Mine Review, July 26. <www.ceaa-acee.gc.ca/050/documents/p63928/92200E.pdf>.

Treasury Board of Canada. 2012. *Canada's Economic Action Plan.* <actionplan.gc.ca/en/page/r2d-dr2/overview>.

United Nations Declaration on the Rights of Indigenous Peoples. 2007. GA Res. 61/295 (Annex), U.N. GAOR, 61st Sess., Supp. No. 49, Vol. III, U.N. Doc. A/61/49.

Legal Cases

Baker v. Canada (Minister of Citizenship and Immigration). 1999. 2 S.C.R. 817, Para. 70.

Canada (Attorney General) v. Canadian Human Rights Commission. 2013. FCA 75.

Delgamuukw v. British Columbia. 1997. 3 S.C.R. 1010.

First Nations Child and Family Caring Society of Canada v. Canada (Attorney General). 2012. FC 445.

Grassy Narrows First Nation v. Ontario (Natural Resources). 2014. Supreme Court of Canada 48.

Haida Nation v. British Columbia (Minister of Forests). 2004. 3 S.C.R. 511.

Keewatin v. Minister of Natural Resources. 2011. ONSC 4801.

Keewatin v. Minister of Natural Resources. 2012. ONCA.

Mikisew Cree First Nation v. Canada (Minister of Canadian Heritage). 2005. 3 SCR 388.

R v. Hape, 2007. 2 S.C.R. 292.

Reference re Public Service Employee Relations Act (Alberta). 1987. 1 S.C.R. 313.

Tsilhqot'in Nation v. British Columbia, 2014 Supreme Court of Canada 44.

West Moberly First Nations v. British Columbia (Chief Inspector of Mines). 2010. BCSC 359.

West Moberly First Nations v. British Columbia (Chief Inspector of Mines). 2011. BCCA 247.

West Moberly First Nations v. British Columbia (Chief Inspector of Mines). 2012. SCC 8361.

Chapter Nine

Getting It Right
The Canadian Constitution and International Indigenous Rights
Brenda L. Gunn

S. 35(1) of the *Constitution Act, 1982* states "the existing aboriginal and treaty rights of the aboriginal peoples of Canada are hereby recognized and affirmed." The hope for many Aboriginal people in constitutionalizing Aboriginal[1] and treaty rights under s. 35(1) was to recognize the unique place of Aboriginal people in Canada as founding nations (Boldt and Long 1985: 14). Entrenching Aboriginal and treaty rights in the Constitution has the potential to recognize Aboriginal peoples as "peoples" in Canada with rights sourced from their own laws, customs and traditions. As "peoples," Aboriginal peoples have the right to self-determination, including the right to determine their own political, economic, social and cultural development. The potential of s. 35(1) is limited by the current interpretations given it by the Supreme Court of Canada. The *United Nations Declaration on the Rights of Indigenous Peoples* (UNDRIP) presents a framework for which the Canadian courts can now turn to fully realize this potential.

Tracing the evolution of the Supreme Court's interpretation shows that current standards do not allow s. 35(1) to achieve its full potential. However, there are rules of interpretation and general principles that exist within the s. 35(1) jurisprudence that must be resurrected to ensure that the constitutional entrenchment of Aboriginal and treaty rights promotes reconciliation based on the recognition of Aboriginal peoples as the original nations in Canada. The role of the UNDRIP in Canada remains debated. The arguments have ranged from the UNDRIP having no legal relevance but being merely aspirational (Canada's position when endorsing the UNDRIP), to the UNDRIP reflecting customary international law, which would be directly applicable and binding in Canada. While pushing for the UNDRIP to be recognized as customary international law and binding would allow the UNDRIP to be justiciable on its own accord, the exact scope of customary international law is often difficult to ascertain. Such arguments may meet considerably more resistance and may not be necessary to achieve the goal of expanding the scope of protection of Indigenous peoples' rights in Canada. The UNDRIP is the most recent articulation of the international standards on the rights of Indigenous peoples and works together with other human rights instruments. These other binding international instruments, including the *U.N. Charter*, the *International Covenant on Civil and Political Rights* (ICCPR) and the *International Covenant on Economic, Social and Cultural Rights* (ICESCR), may also provide useful guidance on s. 35(1), or be justiciable in their own right.

Despite some uncertainties that exist in Canadian jurisprudence on the role of international law in Canada, this chapter takes the modest position of arguing that at a minimum, the standards set out in the UNDRIP can provide a framework to reinterpret Aboriginal and treaty rights under s. 35(1). This argument provides a middle ground to the all or nothing debate on the role of the UNDRIP in Canada. Using the UNDRIP to interpret s. 35(1) promotes the UNDRIP's legal effect in Canada and provides greater protection to Indigenous peoples' rights. The presumption of conformity, which requires Canadian law to be interpreted in conformity with international law, can be invoked to expand the scope of s. 35(1) in line with the UNDRIP.

Realizing Aboriginal Rights

Early relations between Aboriginal peoples and Britain were nation to nation (Borrows 1997a: 171). This relationship quickly deteriorated through Crown assertion of sovereignty and ownership over lands in Canada, as well as its failure to uphold treaty promises and provide protection to Aboriginal peoples' lands. Canada also took actions to undermine Aboriginal peoples, including passing the *Indian Act* and all the related restrictions, as well as the military repression of the Manitoba and Saskatchewan Métis. The 1930 Natural Resource Transfer Agreements included a limitation of Indians' rights to hunt.[2] Canada's action to undermine Aboriginal peoples included the 1969 White Paper, which proposed termination both of treaties and legislative recognition of Indians. Aboriginal peoples have always resisted these impositions, asserting their nationhood.

When Canada began the process of patriating the Constitution, Aboriginal peoples across Canada mobilized to ensure that their rights and their place in Confederation were secured (Sanders 1983: 321; Green, this volume). Including Aboriginal peoples' rights in the Constitution was one of the most challenging issues in the patriation process (Sanders 1983: 315). However, with assistance of some opposition parties, s. 35(1) was inserted into the draft Constitution (Waddell 2003: 18). In an effort to gain the support of the Prairie Provinces for the new Constitution, the provision was removed in November 1981. However, after "intensive lobbying and public demonstrations," s. 35(1) was reinstated with the word "existing" inserted (Slattery 1984: 364). The effect was to allow Canadian courts to decide what rights were existing.

When s. 35(1) was included in the Constitution, Aboriginal people cautiously celebrated, believing "aboriginal peoples were elevated to a special constitutional status" (Boldt and Long 1985: 11). Aboriginal people believed that the constitutional entrenchment of their rights meant that Aboriginal peoples' place in confederation, as founding nations, was recognized (Boldt and Long 1985: 13–14). Sakej Henderson argues that there was hope that s. 35(1) would provide for

the displacement of and remedy for colonial law that had institutionally segregated First Nations from wealth and power, institutionalized and stigmatized them by their "race" and denigrated their heritage, humanity, dignity, and rights. The constitutional reform sought to eliminate the injustices of colonization and racial discrimination suffered by First Nations, which had become so habitual as to be invisible to most Canadians. (Henderson 2006: 34)

Arguably, constitutional entrenchment recognizes Aboriginal peoples' pre-existing sovereignty. Thus, patriation was a time of hope, when Aboriginal people believed a new framework was created in which the relationship between Aboriginal people and the Crown could be defined (Boldt and Long 1985: 11). These hopes were quickly dashed with the failed constitutional negotiations to flesh out the scope of s. 35(1) rights (Asch and Macklem 1991: 504) and the limited interpretation given to s. 35(1) by the courts.

As far back as 1923, Aboriginal peoples have tried to use the international arena to protect their rights. Travelling on an Iroquois Nation passport, Haudenosaunee hereditary Chief Deskaheh went to Geneva to submit a complaint to the League of Nations against Canada. His goal was to "defend the right of his people to live under their own laws, on their own land and under their own faith" (UNPFII n.d.). More recently, Aboriginal peoples from Canada have been active in the international Indigenous movement since at least the 1970s (Sanders 1983: 323) pursuing similar goals of gaining recognition of their inherent sovereignty, sometimes articulated as the right to self-determination. When the spirit and intent of their treaty was not being honoured, Treaty 6 people turned to the United Nations in 1977 to seek "recognition and justice from the international community" (Littlechild 2009: 373). Over the next forty years, Indigenous peoples participated in international processes to gain recognition of their rights as peoples as well as other human rights. During this forty-year process, several significant gains were made in the international human rights system, including the entering into force of International Labour Organizations Convention 169 and the progressive interpretations of general human rights instruments to better account for Indigenous peoples' specific concerns, notably the interpretation of property rights in the Inter-American System of Human Rights. Indigenous peoples successfully persuaded these systems to adapt existing ideas of human rights to better reflect Indigenous peoples' rights, including the idea of collective rights. Many international human rights bodies, including human rights treaty monitoring bodies, began to recognize the failure of the human rights system to protect Indigenous peoples' rights in a way that properly reflected their particular circumstances. Treaty monitoring bodies also recognized a need to interpret their instruments with particular understandings of rights specific to Indigenous peoples (for example, the Committee on the Elimination of Racial Discrimination's 1997 General Comment 23 on Indigenous Peoples). The broader international human rights system supported Indigenous peoples' international activism at the United Nations, and culminated in the U.N. *Declaration on the Rights of Indigenous Peoples* in September 2007.

While there is limited acknowledgement in the s. 35(1) jurisprudence that Aboriginal and treaty rights stem from and are grounded in Aboriginal peoples' own legal systems, this recognition is more explicit in international human rights instruments such as the UNDRIP. This recognition is key because

> Aboriginal legal traditions are derived from relationships, experiences, and reflections with families and ecosystems. They are conceptually self-sustaining and dynamically self-generating aspects of the knowledge system; they have never required an absolute sovereign, the will of a political state, or affirmation or enactment by a foreign government to be legitimate. (Henderson 2010: 34)

Thus grounding Aboriginal peoples' rights in their own legal traditions recognizes that these are inherent rights, not contingent upon recognition from any state or court (Asch and Macklem 1991: 501–02). While Aboriginal peoples' rights stem from their own legal systems, recognition of these rights is also a critical tool to make claims against colonial states.

New Directions:
The *U.N. Declaration on the Rights of Indigenous Peoples*

When the vast majority of the United Nations General Assembly voted in favour of Resolution 61/295 in 2007, the *United Nations Declaration on the Rights of Indigenous Peoples* (UNDRIP) became part of the body of international law that recognizes and protects Indigenous peoples' rights. The results were overwhelming with 144 countries voting in favour, 11 abstaining, and only 4 voting against (Australia, Canada, New Zealand and the United States). Subsequently, all states that voted against the UNDRIP have indicated their support as have many of the states that originally abstained — it is arguable that there is now consensus on the UNDRIP (Wiessner 2010: 253). The UNDRIP represents a major turning point for the recognition and protection of Indigenous peoples' rights.

Canada's endorsement of the UNDRIP came with some caveats. Canada argued that the UNDRIP did not have legal effect in Canada, but was rather aspirational. However, Canada's statement of endorsement reflected a political position, rather than one founded in legal principle. The UNDRIP has legal effect in Canada and had effect since at least the majority vote of the General Assembly. The UNDRIP formally became a legal international human rights instrument once the majority of the General Assembly voted in its favour, adding to the scope of member states' human rights obligations. As a declaration annexed to a General Assembly resolution, there is no need for a state to ratify the UNDRIP for it to have domestic legal effect. Given its legitimacy, in part due to international consensus, the UNDRIP provides a framework to protect the inherent rights of Aboriginal peoples in Canada, as recognized and affirmed in s. 35(1).

A Brief Overview of the UNDRIP

Indigenous peoples fought for decades in the international arena for recognition and protection of their inherent rights as they understood them. This struggle culminated in the UNDRIP, which now explicitly includes Indigenous peoples' rights within the larger system of international human rights protections. The UNDRIP represents a major turning point for the way in which the human rights of Indigenous peoples are recognized and protected within the United Nations system. Over the thirty-year negotiation process, Indigenous advocates negotiated with member-states and the U.N. to articulate the scope of their inherent rights according to their own laws. Today, there is almost universal support for those rights (Weissner 2010: 253).

The UNDRIP did not create new rights for Indigenous peoples. It expanded upon and clarified the application of existing human rights standards to protect Indigenous peoples' inherent rights (Anaya 2008: para. 41). As a declaration, the UNDRIP "represent[s] the dynamic development of international legal norms and reflect the commitment of states to move in certain directions, abiding by certain principles" (UNPFII n.d.). As the UNDRIP is the most recent articulation of Indigenous peoples' rights, it is now recognized as the principal international instrument to understand Indigenous peoples' rights (see Green, Joffe, this volume).

The persistent denial of basic human rights of Indigenous peoples despite the existence of general human rights treaties was the main impetus for the UNDRIP (Hartley, Joffe and Preston 2010: 12). Special Rapporteur James Anaya explains: "the U.N. Declaration aims at repairing the ongoing consequences of the historical denial of the right to self-determination and other basic human rights affirmed in international instruments of general applicability" (Anaya 2009: para 36).

The UNDRIP is monumental because through the use of the term "peoples" it explicitly recognizes that Indigenous peoples' rights are collective (Anaya 2004: 100). As indicated above, the UNDRIP confirms that Indigenous peoples are "peoples" in international law and thus entitled to the right to self-determination, which does not, however, automatically equate to a right to secede (Anaya 2009: 189). As Victoria Tauli-Corpuz (2007), Chair of the U.N. Permanent Forum, stated, "This is a Declaration which makes the opening phrase of the U.N. Charter, 'We the Peoples...' meaningful for the more than 370 million indigenous persons all over the world."

The UNDRIP sets the floor for Indigenous peoples' rights, the minimum international human rights standards, not a ceiling. The articulation of Indigenous peoples' rights in the UNDRIP is broad and covers almost all aspects of Indigenous peoples' lives. Because of the ongoing violation of Indigenous peoples' rights by colonial governments and other non-state actors, the starting point for the UNDRIP is the principles of equality and non-discrimination articulated in Article 1. The UNDRIP celebrates the distinctiveness of Indigenous peoples and provides protection for these differences, ensuring Indigenous peoples and their cultures the international legal framework to thrive. A contextual approach recognizes and appreciates that differences are necessary when determining Indigenous peoples' rights, which is a critical aspect of domestic implementation (Allen 2011: 234–35).

The UNDRIP also recognizes self-determination as a foundational right (Article 3), without which Indigenous peoples' rights cannot be fully realized (Anaya 2009: para. 41). Its wording mirrors the wording of the right to self-determination found in common Article 1 of the ICCPR and ICESCR. For Anaya (2008: 187), "the essential idea of self-determination is that human beings, individually and as groups, are equally entitled to be in control of their own destinies, and to live within governing institutional orders that are devised accordingly." The right to self-determination does not mean that every group that can be identified as a people has a free standing right to form its own state or to dictate any one particular form of political arrangement. Rather, "self-determination means that Indigenous peoples are entitled to participate equally in the constitution and development of the governing institutional order under which they live and, further, to have that governing order be one in which they may live and develop freely on a continuous basis" (Anaya 2009: 189). Self-determination means that Indigenous peoples, like other peoples, are entitled to determine their relationship with the state and be involved in setting up the state's governing structures. Indigenous peoples also have the right to maintain their own political systems and institutions (Article 5).

Kenneth Deer, Mohawk and former co-chair of the Indigenous Peoples' Caucus, puts it this way:

> All our rights either flow from or are linked to our right of self-determination. These include our right to land, our right to natural resources, our right to our language and culture, our right to our songs … "free, prior and informed consent" (FPIC) also flows from the right to self-determination. (Deer 2010: 27)

Thus, the UNDRIP provides recognition of a broad range of political, civil, economic, social and cultural rights. The UNDRIP articulates rights to life, liberty and security of the person; rights to culture, religious and linguistic identity; rights to education, public information and employment; rights to participate in decision-making and free, prior and informed consent; economic and social rights; rights to lands, territories and resources; rights to fulfillment of treaties, agreements and other constructive arrangements; and women's rights, especially to be free from violence. The articulation of these rights specifically acknowledges that these rights are based in and determined by Indigenous peoples' own legal traditions.

Even if the UNDRIP is not technically "binding" in and of itself, or justiciable on its own in Canada, it does have legal relevance in Canada. The UNDRIP is not merely aspirational, it sets out obligations that Canada and all other states are expected to achieve as part of their broader commitments to uphold human rights, in connection with their obligations under the *U.N. Charter*. Conforming the interpretation of s. 35(1) to the UNDRIP is one way to explicitly recognize its legal effect in Canada.

Promoting Conformity: The UNDRIP and S. 35(1)

Canadian courts have hesitantly embraced international law (Brunnee and Toope 2002: 4). Canadian courts have not always explicitly explained how or why international law applies in a particular situation. This uncertainty is used to support an erroneous belief that international and domestic law exist in separate realms, having nothing to do with one another. However, international human rights law has long been part of Canadian law. Certain provisions of the UNDRIP may reflect customary international law (ILA Committee 2012); those provisions could arguably be directly incorporated into Canadian law as binding obligations. As the most recent statement by the international community of the minimum standards for Indigenous peoples' rights, this chapter takes a moderate position arguing that as a minimum starting point, the UNDRIP should be used to interpret Canadian law, including the scope of rights protected under s. 35(1). This proposition is not as radical as some may believe; Canadian courts have often invoked the presumption of conformity to cite international law when interpreting domestic law, especially when interpreting the Constitution.

The Presumption of Conformity

In *Canadian Foundation for Children, Youth and the Law* v. *Canada (Attorney General)* (2004), the court cited *Ordon Estate* v. *Grail* (1998) to highlight that the presumption of conformity requires that Canadian law be interpreted consistent with Canada's international obligations. The presumption has been used by the courts to "inform the interpretation of the content of Charter rights, the interpretation of what constitutes a s.1 justification, the interpretation of quasi-constitutional text, statutory and common law interpretation, and judicial review (Weiser 2004: 134–35). For example, in *R* v. *Hape* (2007: para. 53), LeBel J wrote:

> It is a well-established principle of statutory interpretation that legislation will be presumed to conform to international law. The presumption of conformity is based on the rule of judicial policy that, as a matter of law, courts will strive to avoid constructions of domestic law pursuant to which the state would be in violation of its international obligations, unless the wording of the statute clearly compels that result.

The presumption of conformity has been used as far back as 1968. In *Daniels* v. *White* (1968: para. 541), Pigeon J began his concurring opinion with reference to the presumption of conformity, writing that "Parliament is not presumed to legislate in breach of a treaty or in any manner inconsistent with the comity of nations and the established rules of international law." In the decision, the *Migratory Birds Convention Act*, which implements the international *Migratory Birds Convention*, was critical to the interpretation of the Indian hunting provisions in the *Natural Resource Transfer Agreement* (*British North America Act, 1930*).

The presumption is also used to interpret statutes. In *Ordon Estate* v. *Grail* (1998), Justices Iacobucci and Major used the presumption of conformity referencing Canada's international obligations on maritime actions when deciding between two possible limitation periods provided in two conflicting statutes. Justices Iacobucci and Major held that "a court must presume that legislation is intended to comply with Canada's obligations under international instruments and as a member of the international community. In choosing among possible interpretations of a statute, the court should avoid interpretations that would put Canada in breach of such obligations" (*Ordon Grail* 1998: para. 137). To support invoking the presumption of conformity, Justices Iacobucci and Major cited *Driedger on the Construction of Statutes*:

> The legislature is presumed to respect the values and principles enshrined in international law, both customary and conventional. These constitute a part of the legal context in which legislation is enacted and read. In so far as possible, therefore, interpretations that reflect these values and principles are preferred. (Sullivan 1994: 330)

Moreover, in Charter litigation, courts have used international law, in particular international human rights law, to inform the scope of a constitutional guarantee and to inform what might be an acceptable limitation of a right (Weiser 2004: 135–36). In *Slaight Communications Inc* v. *Davidson* (1989: par 23), when considering whether an infringement of s. 2(b) of the Charter was justified, Chief Justice Dickson stated "the fact that a value has the status of an international human right, either in customary international law or under a treaty to which Canada is a State Party, should generally be indicative of a high degree of importance attached to that objective."

The Supreme Court of Canada has also used various binding and non-binding sources of international law to interpret the Charter. Justice LeBel notes that the presumption of conformity can rely on at least two categories of international law: signed international treaties and "the values and principles of customary and conventional international law" (*Hape* 2007: para. 53). In *Reference Re Public Service Employee Relations Act (Alta)* (1987: para. 57), when determining whether legislation was consistent with the Charter, Chief Justice Dickson considered the relevance of various international human rights laws: "the various sources of international human rights law — declarations, covenants, conventions, judicial and quasi-judicial decisions of international tribunals, customary norms — must, in my opinion, be relevant and persuasive sources for interpretation of the Charter's provisions." He continued: "[international norms] provide a relevant and persuasive source for interpretation of the provisions of the Charter" (*Hape* 2007: para. 59).

In *Baker* v. *Canada (Minister of Citizenship and Immigration)* (1999), L'Heureux Dubé J, writing for the majority, considered whether the *Convention on the Rights of the Child*, which had been ratified, but not yet transformed into Canadian law, was relevant to the appeal at hand. She held that "the values reflected in international human rights law may help inform the contextual approach to statutory interpretation and judicial review" (*Baker* 1999: para. 70). Using the presumption of conformity, L'Heureux Dube identifies the relevant international human rights principles without focussing on the binding nature of the instrument.

The Court has also used other non-binding obligations to interpret domestic legislation. In *114957 Canada Ltee (Spraytech, Societe d'arrosage)* v. *Hudson (Town)* [2001] 2 SCR 241, the Court considered the precautionary principle, an international legal principle, when interpreting the Quebec *Cities and Towns Act*. Justice L'Heureux Dubé, writing for the majority, concluded that "reading s. 410(1) to permit the Town to regulate pesticide use is consistent with principles of international law and policy" (*Spraytech* 2001: para. 30).

In *Canadian Foundation for Children, Youth and the Law* v. *Canada (Attorney General)* (2004), the Foundation sought a declaration that the exemption from criminal sanctions for parents and teachers who use force to discipline children violates the Charter. In making her determination on whether the exemption was reasonable, McLachlin CJ considered several international human rights treaties, reports of human rights monitoring bodies, including European instruments, and jurisprudence to identify the international standard for which to judge the domestic law. The breadth of material considered indicates that the presumption of conformity is not limited to so-called binding obligations, but rather is focused on identifying and applying human rights norms. Karen Knop argues that the Supreme Court's decision in *Baker* v. *Canada* (1999) is indicative of the Supreme Court of Canada's shift from a focus on the dichotomy of bindingness/non-bindingness to a focus of persuasiveness of the international principle for the determination of Canadian law (Knop 2000: 501). This shift and the jurisprudence cited here supports the need to reconsider s. 35(1) jurisprudence in light of the standards set out in the UNDRIP.

Failed Promise of Section 35(1)

As s. 35(1) is encompassed within the *Constitution Act, 1982* it is reasonable to use international human rights norms at least to interpret its scope. S. 35(1) is broadly and vaguely worded. Where such an ambiguity exists or clarification is needed, the presumption of conformity demands that international standards such as the UNDRIP be used to interpret Canadian law. This approach promotes the development of Canadian law to uphold Canada's international obligations. Using the UNDRIP to interpret s. 35(1), the application of the presumption of conformity is also consistent with the interpretation principles identified by Dickson CJ and LaForest J in Sparrow, especially given the need to flesh out the broad wording of the provision.

Even if s. 35(1) is not judicially held to be ambiguous, it is still appropriate to consider the UNDRIP in its delineation. Citing several cases, including *National Corn Growers v. Canada* (1990), *Reference Re Public Service Employee Relations Act (1987) and Slaight Communications* (1989), Irit Weisner argues that the ambiguity requirement has been eliminated before the consideration of international law to interpret domestic law (Weitner 2004: 119). In the Canadian context, Stefan Beaulac also contends that international norms should be used in the contextual approach to interpreting domestic law (Beaulac 2003: 259).

As Sparrow directs a purposive and contextual approach, the UNDRIP provides important context for the current state of Aboriginal rights and thus a framework for modern interpretation of Aboriginal and treaty rights protected under s. 35(1). Chief Justice McLachlin (2002) has acknowledged the significance of international law when determining Aboriginal rights: "Aboriginal rights from the beginning have been shaped by international concepts … whether we like it or not, aboriginal rights are an international matter."

The Federal Court of Canada recently used the UNDRIP to interpret domestic law in *Canada (Human Rights Commission) v. Canada (Attorney General)*, 2012 FC 445. In this case, Madam Justice MacTavish held that "international instruments such as the UNDRIP and the *Convention on the Rights of the Child* may also inform the contextual approach to statutory interpretation" (*Canada v. Canada* 2012: para. 353). She cited with approval the positions brought forth by Amnesty International and the Assembly of First Nations that the UNDRIP is "an important indication of the Government of Canada's commitment to treating First Nations peoples fairly and equitably. They further submit that UNDRIP also reflects emerging norms in international law regarding the rights of indigenous peoples" (*Canada v. Canada* 2012: para. 350).

The presumption of conformity is beneficial because it focuses less on whether or not Canada is bound by a specific instrument, and considers the normative developments within international law on the rights of Indigenous peoples. Using the presumption also helps move past debates on the precise legal status of the UNDRIP in Canada. The UNDRIP now synthesizes the international human rights standards and thus should be used to interpret s. 35(1). The next sections discusses the limitations of the current interpretation of s. 35(1) and contrasts those with the standards set out in the UNDRIP.

Addressing the Limits of Section 35(1)

S. 35(1) has been viewed as an act of reconciliation (Vermette 2011: 64). It was to be a new beginning for the relations between Aboriginal people and Canada: "the choice to recognize and affirm aboriginal rights in s. 35(1) established a path towards balancing the needs, wants and expectations of colonial society while at the same time protecting Aboriginal interests from the domination which accompanies the habituations of colonialism" (Vermette 2011: 62). Reconciliation continues to resonate in Canada. Reconciliation has been recognized as a fundamental component necessary to remedy the abuses of colonialism in the mandate and processes of the Truth and Reconciliation Commission, for example, whose focus is on the abuse of Indian children by government-mandated residential schools. Unfortunately, the direction taken by the Courts seriously limits the potential of s. 35(1) to provide constitutional reconciliation and protection of Aboriginal peoples' inherent rights. By returning to first principles articulated in early cases and using the UNDRIP to expand the protected activities, there is still a chance for s. 35(1) to live up to its potential to facilitate reconciliation.

The Supreme Court of Canada has limited the great potential of s. 35(1) in losing the original interpretive approach. The foundational principles of these limits are set out in *R v. Sparrow* (1990). In *R v. Van der Peet* (1996) Chief Justice Lamer develops the "central and integral" test, which limited the scope of s. 35(1) protection to activities that are central and integral to distinctive Aboriginal cultures, greatly limiting the potential of s. 35(1) to truly promote reconciliation in Canada. There are, however, some minority decisions such as those of McLachlin J and L'Heureux Dube J in Van der Peet (1996) that better accord with the original vision of s. 35(1), provide some direction to get back to the original purpose and better align with the principles and norms now articulated in the UNDRIP.

R v. Sparrow

In *R v. Sparrow* (1990: para. 53), the Supreme Court recognized "that s. 35(1) of the *Constitution Act, 1982*, represents the culmination of a long and difficult struggle in both the political forum and the courts for the constitutional recognition of aboriginal rights." The Court wrote, "s. 35(1) is a solemn commitment that must be given meaningful content" (*Sparrow* 1990: para. 60). This strong statement of the significance of s. 35(1) aligns with the hopes and aspirations of Aboriginal people, as well as governments, when the provision was originally framed (Waddell 2003).

After setting this purpose, the Court then identified several principles to guide s. 35(1) analysis, including flexibility to permit rights to evolve over time, applying general principles of constitutional interpretation, applying principles relating to Aboriginal rights and considering the purposes behind the constitutional provision itself (*Sparrow* 1990). Chief Justice Dickson and Justice LaForest explained these principles include a "generous, liberal interpretation," with any doubtful expressions being resolved in favour of the Aboriginal claimants and upholding the special, trust-like and non-adversarial, relationship (*Sparrow* 1990: para. 56). These principles have shaped subsequent judicial decisions and formed new terrain for litigation. These principles can also be interpreted to support the use of the UNDRIP to ensure the necessary flexibility for the continued evolution of rights.

There are several important purposes set out in the Preamble of the UNDRIP which should also guide the interpretation of s. 35(1): that the injustices Indigenous peoples experience prevent them from exercising their rights in accordance with their own needs and interests; that recognizing Indigenous peoples' rights will enhance harmonious and cooperative relations "based on principles of justice, democracy, respect for human rights, non-discrimination and good faith"; and that the standards set out in the UNDRIP should "be pursued in a spirit of partnership and mutual respect" (UNDRIP: Preamble). These purposes emphasize the need to ensure s. 35(1) is interpreted to address injustices and for the Canadian government and Aboriginal peoples to work together to realize Aboriginal peoples' rights.

Despite the absence of an express limitation in s. 35, the Court interpreted the words "recognize and affirm" to include a limitation to the protected rights. The Court held that the "federal power must be reconciled with federal duty and the best way to achieve that reconciliation is to demand the justification of any government regulation that infringes upon or denies aboriginal rights" (*Sparrow* 1990: para. 62). This led the Court to require a valid legislative objective to justify interferences with Aboriginal rights. The government must attain its legislative objective in a way that upholds the honour of the Crown and upholds the unique contemporary relationship between the Crown and Aboriginal peoples, a relationship grounded in history and policy. The Court concluded: "suffice it to say that recognition and affirmation requires sensitivity to and respect for the rights of aboriginal peoples on behalf of the government, courts and indeed all Canadians" (*Sparrow* 1990: para. 83). The notions of the "honour of the Crown" and of "valid legislative objectives" have become key concepts in subsequent Aboriginal rights jurisprudence. These doctrines highlight the continuation of federal power and explicitly assume the validity of Crown sovereignty.

In setting out the justifiable infringement test, the Court understood s. 35(1) to have a reconciliatory purpose. Initially, the concept of reconciliation was used to limit federal government actions and protect Aboriginal rights from unchecked federal power (Vermette 2011: 59). In this initial approach s. 35(1) protects Aboriginal people from government interference, which was part of Aboriginal peoples' motivation in pushing for constitutional protection of their rights.

The ability to justify interferences of Aboriginal rights on such a broad basis as set out in Sparrow differs from the UNDRIP, where the limits are set out in Article 46, but sets a higher threshold for interferences, including the requirement that international human rights law be upheld. Further, Article 46 states that "any such limitations shall be non-discriminatory and strictly necessary solely for the purpose of securing due recognition and respect for the rights and freedoms of others and for meeting the just and most compelling requirements of a democratic society." However, Article 46 needs to be read with Article 38 to understand the allowable limitations. The UNDRIP explicitly requires states to "take appropriate measures, including legislative measures, to achieve the ends of this Declaration" (Article 38), which again emphasizes the need to fulfill the rights as a primary obligation. The restrictions must also be understood in light of the broader rights of Indigenous peoples to participate in decision-making where their rights or interests may be impacted, found throughout the UNDRIP (see Articles 3–5, 10–12, 14, 15, 17–19, 22, 23, 26–28, 30–32, 36, 37, 38 and 40–41). Therefore restrictions should not occur through unilateral government action. Such an approach is different from the Canadian jurisprudence that justifies interferences when only minimal consultation has occurred, as discussed in more detail below.

R v. Van der Peet

In Van der Peet, the next major decision on s. 35(1), the right to sell fish was vigorously contested by the Crown (*Van der Peet* 1996). It was in this case that the Court had its first opportunity to consider the scope of protected rights under s. 35(1). In this decision, the court was no longer unanimous in its approach, Chief Justice Lamer wrote the majority decision and Justices McLachlin and L'Heureux Dube each wrote their own dissenting opinions.

While Chief Justice Lamer started by reiterating the Sparrow interpretive principles, the approach he took does not accord with the Sparrow principles. According the Lamer, s. 35(1) only protects activity if it is an "element of a practice, custom or tradition integral to the distinctive culture of the aboriginal group claiming the right" (*Van der Peet* 1996: para. 46). In creating this test, Chief Justice Lamer highlighted a new purpose to s. 35(1):

> s. 35(1) ... provide(s) the constitutional framework through which the fact that aboriginals lived on the land in distinctive societies, with their own practices, traditions and cultures, is acknowledged and reconciled with the sovereignty of the Crown. ... the aboriginal rights recognized and affirmed by s. 35(1) must be directed towards the reconciliation of the pre-existence of aboriginal societies with the sovereignty of the Crown. (*Van der Peet* 1996: para. 31)

John Borrows (1997: 28) points out the inherent contradiction in this purpose: "If Aboriginal peoples have prior right to land and participatory governance, how did the Crown and Court gain their right to adjudicate here." The Court attempts to resolve this potential dilemma by simply stating that Crown sovereignty is assumed and becomes the point at which to define "Aboriginal" (Borrows 1997: 28). This newly stated purpose assumes the validity of Crown sovereignty.

Lamer CJ then used this new purpose to justify interference with Aboriginal peoples' constitutionally protect rights for the benefit of other Canadians (McNeil 2003: 17). According to Lamer CJ, s. 35(1) does not have a remedial purpose to address the ongoing historical injustices that continue to occur through the colonial process in Canada and provide a new foundation for the relationship, as stated in Sparrow and the UNDRIP. Barsh and Henderson are particularly pointed in their criticism: "The Lamer Court's naïve imperialism betrays the efforts of the Dickson

Court to bring a degree of accountability and self-restraint to Crown dealings with Aboriginal nations" (Barsh and Henderson 1997: 1002). Moreover, as McNeil critiques, "Aboriginal rights, even though they are constitutionally protected, might have to give way to the interests of other Canadians in order to achieve vague goals like 'economic and regional fairness'" (McNeil 2003: 9). Lamer CJ's approach uses s. 35(1) as the final act to perfect and legitimize Crown sovereignty (Vermette 2011: 72; Borrows 1997: 31–32). Again, subjecting Aboriginal peoples' rights to the unilateral power of the Canadian government runs contrary to ideas of participation, partnership and the realization of rights as primary purposes of recognizing rights in the UNDRIP.

To support his approach, Chief Justice Lamer cites the U.S. case *Johnson v. M'Intosh* (1823) (*Van der Peet* 1996: para. 36). Lamer CJ omits to mention that Chief Justice Marshall's decision in M'Intosh was justified based on the "savage" nature of the Indian tribes whose "occupation was war" (*Johnson v. M'Intosh* 1823: para. 590). Reliance on *Johnson v. M'Intosh* (1823) without acknowledging the basis of those principles allows Lamer CJ to "adopt language and propose concepts that appear enlightened on their face but that actually are limited to formalizing the process of colonization" (Vermette 2011: 56). Reliance on such racist doctrines in the delineation of rights is explicitly rejected in the UNDRIP Preamble.

When identifying the interpretative principles for s. 35(1) rights, Lamer CJ stated that the perspective of the Aboriginal claimant needed to be considered and that the rights must be identified by considering both Aboriginal and common law legal systems. However, Lamer CJ does not consult Aboriginal law when defining the scope of s. 35(1) (Borrows 1997: 31), again contrary to the right to participate in decision-making recognized in the UNDRIP.

The test set out in Van der Peet puts the Court in the position to define what is Aboriginal. According to Lamer CJ, "Aboriginal is retrospective. It is about what was, 'once upon a time,' ... Aboriginal means a long time ago; pre-contact" (Borrows 1997: 28–29). The test proposed by Lamer CJ further restricts s. 35(1) to rights "of a certain vintage" (Slattery 2000: 216). S. 35(1) only protects rights which originate from practices, customs and traditions that existed at contact (Slattery 2000: 216). If the goal of s. 35(1) is reconciliation, then the protected practices under s. 35(1) should not exclude those practices that allow Aboriginal people to survive as contemporary communities (Borrows 1997: 32). The effect of Van der Peet is to freeze Aboriginal peoples as historic anomalies and to prevent them from expressing themselves through contemporary cultures and practices.

As discussed above, the rights set out in the UNDRIP are premised on the right to self-determination, which emphasizes Indigenous peoples' right to freely determine their own political, economic, social and cultural development (Article 3), which is contrary to the restrictive scope set out for Aboriginal rights under the Lamer approach in Van der Peet, where the Court set the limit for the protected activities and determines whether the particular activity is "central and integral" to the Aboriginal people. As part of the right to self-determination, "Indigenous peoples have the right to maintain and strengthen their distinct political, legal, economic, social and cultural institutions, while retaining their right to participate fully, if they so choose, in the political, economic, social and cultural life of the State" (Article 5).

This approach of trying to identify practices that are central and integral to the distinctive societies has led the Court to only accept specific rights rather than broad or generic rights (Slattery 2000: 211). For example, s. 35(1) only protects self-government on a case-by-case consideration of each specific aspect of asserted jurisdiction. In *R* v. *Pamajewon* (1996), s. 35(1) would only protect the right to self-government if it met the Van der Peet test because self-government was viewed as no different from a claim to any other Aboriginal right (*Pamajewon* 1996: para. 24). Again, this approach to self-government under s. 35(1) is more restrictive than the broader right recognized under the UNDRIP in Article 4: the right to self-government and autonomy over internal and local affairs, as well as the means for financing those functions.

The s. 35(1) approach to self-government fails to allow s. 35(1) to protect Aboriginal peoples as distinct and contemporary peoples whose cultures evolve, as do all cultures, within the Canadian constitutional framework. Further losing the focus on the context of colonialism and s. 35(1) as recognizing the unique place of Aboriginal people as founding nations in Canada, in *Mitchell* v. *Canada (Minister of National Revenue — MNR)* (2001: para. 164), Binnie J expressed his opinion that s. 35(1) ought to focus on "national interests that all of us have in common rather than to distinctive interests that for some purposes differentiate an aboriginal community. In my view, reconciliation of these interests in this particular case favours an affirmation of our collective sovereignty." This understanding of s. 35(1) is particularly problematic because "behind such a statement lurks the assumption that the colonial government is better positioned to manage the Aboriginal claim as part of 'our collective sovereignty' than Aboriginal people are at managing their constitutional rights" (Vermette 2011: 63). This approach emphasizes assimilation of Aboriginal peoples within mainstream Canadian "sovereignty," and not Aboriginal peoples as having a distinct place within Canada. This approach is further contrary to Canada's obligation to promote and protect Aboriginal peoples' right to self-determination as set out in the UNDRIP.

Court's Application of Sparrow and Van der Peet

The Sparrow and Van der Peet tests have had negative impacts on treaty rights as well. Despite appearing to take a progressive approach to treaty rights in *R* v. *Marshall* (1999), s. 35(1) has overall failed to fully protect treaty rights. These rights are now more vulnerable because they are subject to interferences through the application of the Sparrow justification test, which amount to unilateral amendment to the scope of treaties. Here again, the UNDRIP provides useful direction.

Article 37 recognizes Indigenous peoples' "right to the recognition, observance and enforcement of treaties." Article 37 also requires states to "honour and respect" treaties. The UNDRIP Preamble further notes that in some situations, treaties are "matters of international concern, interest, responsibility and character." As such, the scope of protection given to treaty rights under s. 35(1) also needs to be re-examined to better align with the UNDRIP.

In Van der Peet, Lamer CJ noted that the test for Aboriginal rights, which required protected activities to be traced back to the point of colonial contact, would not work for Métis people, one of the three constitutionally protected Aboriginal peoples. This recognition that the test could not universally apply to all Aboriginal people, despite one common constitutional provision, is yet another indication of the flawed nature of Lamer CJ's analysis. The test for Métis peoples' rights under s. 35(1) was determined in R v. Powley (2003). In Powley, under the leadership of Chief Justice McLachlin, the Court created a legal definition of Métis and modified the Van der Peet test to accommodate the post-contact ethnogenesis of the Métis peoples. Powley is yet another example where the Court placed itself in the position to define Métis people. Métis culture is also viewed as historical: Métis peoples' rights must be traced back to a period post-contact but pre-Canadian control. Contrarily, the UNDRIP recognizes Indigenous peoples' "right to determine their own identity or membership in accordance with their customs and traditions" and "to determine the structures and to select the membership of their institutions in accordance with their own procedures" (Article 33), rather than the Court determining identity.

Building upon the Sparrow approach to justifying infringements based on considerations of consultation, the Court has developed the doctrine of the "duty of consultation and accommodation," which applies to proven and unproven rights. Haida Nation v. British Columbia (Minister of Forests) (2004) was the first case where the Court applied the duty of consultation and accommodation to asserted, but unproven, rights. Unfortunately, the Court's application of this doctrine emphasizes consultation, and has not yet provided any real guidance as to what is necessary to meet the standard for accommodation, confirming federal power to interfere with Aboriginal peoples' protected rights provided there is some minimal discussion beforehand. Most decisions on the duty of consultation and accommodation only consider whether consultation was fulfilled and have not considered whether there has been sufficient accommodation of Aboriginal peoples' rights (Haida Nation 2004). The scope given to the duty of consultation and accommodation fails to fulfill Aboriginal peoples' right to participate in decision-making according to the standard of free, prior and informed consent as required in international law set out in the UNDRIP (see also Joffe, Benjamin, this volume).

The Van der Peet–based approach limits economic rights. In Lax Kw'alaams Indian Band v. Canada (Attorney General) (2011: para. 5), the Supreme Court rejected the Lax Kw'alaams' claim to "commercial harvesting and sale of 'all species of fish' within their traditional waters" because,

> when it comes to "evolving" the *subject matter* of the Aboriginal right, the situation is more complex. A "gathering right" to berries based on pre-contact times would not, for example, "evolve" into a right to "gather" natural gas within the traditional territory. The surface gathering of copper from the Coppermine River in the Northwest Territories in pre-contact times would not, I think, support an "Aboriginal right" to exploit deep shaft diamond mining in the same territory. While courts have recognized that Aboriginal rights must be allowed to evolve within limits, such limits are both quantitative and qualitative. A "pre-sovereignty aboriginal practice cannot be transformed into a different modern right." (*Lax Kw'alaams* 2011: para. 51, emphasis in original)

This statement exemplifies the Court's view of Aboriginal identity and culture as historic and static, refusing to recognize that cultures and economies evolve.

In making his determination in Lax Kw'alaams, Binnie J held:

> The Lax Kw'alaams live in the twenty-first century, not the eighteenth, and are entitled to the benefits (as well as the burdens) of changing times. However, allowance for natural evolution does not justify the award of a quantitatively and qualitatively different right. (*Lax Kw'alaams* 2011: para. 8)

Binnie J's statement indicates the underlying racist assumptions that infiltrated Chief Justice Lamer's approach in Van der Peet: s. 35(1) protects practices, customs and traditions of Aboriginal peoples as historical and stereotypical "Indians." If Aboriginal peoples want to engage in "modern" forms of economic development, they cannot do so with s. 35(1) protection. This approach again fails to allow s. 35(1) to have any remedial scope for the ways in which colonization has negatively impacted Aboriginal peoples. It further fails to consider Aboriginal laws when determining the scope s. 35(1).

The UNDRIP has several broad and robust provisions relating to economic rights, including the right to determine their own economic development under self-determination (Article 3); the right to maintain and develop their economic systems, the right to be secure in "their own means of subsistence and development, and to engage freely in all their traditional and other economic activities" (Article 20); the right to the improvement of their economic conditions (Article 21); and the right to development including to determine and develop their own priorities and strategies (Article 23). These provisions recognize that Indigenous peoples' economic rights include rights to traditional economic activities and modern economic activities, which is significantly broader than the limited economic rights protected under s. 35(1).

In these decisions, the Court negates its obligation to be a neutral arbiter between the Crown and Aboriginal peoples. For example, in *Delgamuukw* v. *British Columbia* (1997), Chief Justice Lamer refused to grant a declaration of title for failure to meet the newly created test and encouraged the issue to be resolved through negotiation. Vermette claims:

> The Court seems to be divesting itself of the responsibility to reconcile competing claims and, instead, placing this responsibility solely on the Crown. The problem with such an approach is that the Crown is not in a position to make such a determination with any degree of neutrality and objectivity." (Vermette 2011: 67)

This push away from litigation and toward negotiation moves Aboriginal peoples' fight out of the legal arena and back into the political arena. This obfuscates the reason Aboriginal people fought for constitutional recognition of their inherent rights: the political arena failed to provide recognition of inherent rights or sufficient protection against state action (see Green, this volume). The UNDRIP recognizes the need for "just and fair procedures for the resolution of conflicts and disputes with States" as well as "effective remedies for all infringements of their individuals and collective rights" (Article 40). Article 40 continues to recognize the need for such decision to give due consideration to Indigenous peoples' customs, traditions, rules and legal systems, as well as international human rights law.

While the "central and integral to the distinctive culture" test adopted by Lamer CJ in Van der Peet has been heavily critiqued, there are some aspects of the decision that deserve greater emphasis and that better accord with the UNDRIP. Henderson argues that "the Court's trans-systemic approach to constitutional law developed innovative principles of adjudication that create a unique reorientation of Canadian constitutional jurisprudence" (Henderson 2010: 25). As part of the implicit recognition that s. 35(1) protects the rights of Aboriginal peoples as peoples, in McLachlin J's dissent, the Court has recognized that Aboriginal and treaty rights are based on Aboriginal peoples' own laws, customs and traditions (*Van der Peet* 1996: para. 247). In particular, Justice McLachlin's dissenting opinion in Van der Peet laid out another approach for s. 35(1) based on the recognition of a prior legal regime that gives rise to these rights (*Van der Peet* 1996: para. 230). As noted above, several provisions of the UNDRIP recognize that Indigenous peoples' rights are grounded in Indigenous peoples' own legal traditions.

In addition to the inference to Aboriginal legal systems in McLachlin's dissent, it is arguable that through the use of the doctrine of *sui generis*, which recognizes that Aboriginal rights are unique and call for interpretation that accords with their unique status, the majority of the Court realized that "the extraordinary sources of Aboriginal legal traditions and jurisprudence were beyond their [the Court's] legal training" (Henderson 2010: 31). The reference to the ongoing relevance of Aboriginal legal systems was also discussed in Mitchell where Chief Justice

McLachlin noted "the doctrine of continuity, which governed the absorption of aboriginal laws and customs into the new legal regime upon the assertion of Crown sovereignty over the region" (*Mitchell* 2001: para. 62).

Justice L'Heureux Dube's dissenting opinion in Van der Peet recognized that the inclusion of Aboriginal and treaty rights in the Constitution is based on the fact that Aboriginal people are "peoples" (*Van der Peet* 1996: para. 30), which may be an important step to recognizing Indigenous peoples' right to self-determination as recognized in the UNDRIP. While a dissenting opinion does not reflect the current law, it can be used as persuasive authority when trying to point out flaws in the current state of the law, encouraging the Court to rethink the law. In Van der Peet, L'Heureux Dube's opinion criticized Lamer CJ's approach for impoverishing the understanding of Aboriginal cultures because "an approach based on a dichotomy between aboriginal and non-aboriginal practices, traditions and customs literally amounts to defining aboriginal culture and aboriginal rights as that which is left over after features of non-aboriginal cultures have been taken away" (*Van der Peet* 1996: para. 154). L'Heureux Dube advocated for an approach which focused on the significance of the activity to Aboriginal people and not merely the activity itself (*Van der Peet* 1996: para. 157). Her approach focused on the goal of preserving the Aboriginal peoples and thus s. 35(1) should protect "all practices, traditions and customs which are connected enough to the self-identity and self-preservation of organized aboriginal societies" (*Van der Peet* 1996: para. 162), which better aligns with the UNDRIP standards of allowing Indigenous peoples' to articulate their rights. She would also not have restricted rights to pre-contact activities, recognizing that Aboriginal societies would evolve and thus s. 35(1) should protect those practices, traditions and customs that "maintain a continuing relevance to the aboriginal societies as these societies exist in the contemporary world" (*Van der Peet* 1996: para. 173). Her approach allows s. 35(1) to ensure the ongoing recognition and protection of Aboriginal peoples as distinct peoples within Canada as contemporary, not historic, peoples, which again accords with the purposes of protecting Indigenous peoples' rights under the UNDRIP.

To ensure that s. 35(1) fulfills the goal of reconciliation, the interpretation of s. 35(1) rights must not blindly rely on colonial legal principles and thus perpetuate colonial injustices (Slattery 2000: 206). To avoid such an approach, it is critical that the scope of s. 35(1) should take into account the perspective of Aboriginal peoples themselves (*Van der Peet* 1996: para. 49). This includes better appreciation of Aboriginal peoples' own laws and the rights that stem from their legal systems. The UNDRIP provides a framework on how to apply these broad principles and thus should at a minimum be used to reinterpret the scope of s. 35(1).

Aboriginal Laws are the Source of S. 35(1) Rights

Renewing the interpretation of s. 35(1) based on the UNDRIP lends real recognition to the source of the protected rights as Aboriginal peoples' own customs, laws and traditions. Recognizing the inherent nature of Aboriginal peoples' rights "would begin to reverse the historical pattern of systemic exclusion of Canada's First Nations from constitutional discourse and acknowledge the importance of native difference in the constitution of Canada" (Asch and Macklem 1991: 517). This approach promotes true reconciliation and leads to greater social harmony. Recognizing Aboriginal laws as the source of s. 35(1) rights requires real consideration be given to these laws when defining the scope of s. 35(1). Given that Indigenous peoples articulated the rights in the UNDRIP as understood according to their own laws, the UNDRIP presents a useful framework for this approach.

Connected to giving effect to Aboriginal peoples' own laws is the recognition that Aboriginal peoples are distinct peoples within Canada. A renewed approach to s. 35(1) requires a more robust protection of self-government. While political negotiations may still be the primary means for achieving self-government, there is an important role for the court to play in arbitrating the inevitable disputes. In such instances, the specific rights approach in Van der Peet is especially inappropriate for self-government. As recognized in the UNDRIP, self-determination includes the right to self-government and is the foundation from which all other rights flow. S. 35(1) must be interpreted in a fashion that permits self-government to flourish.

Part of a renewed interpretation of s. 35(1) must allow Aboriginal peoples' cultures to continue evolving, including their practices, customs and traditions. As Henderson states, "Aboriginal traditions are not comprehensive, they are always becoming. They are open, ongoing, renewing processes of lifelong learning. They were never static forms of social order" (Henderson 2010: 33; see also Borrows 1997: 32). Approaches based on racist notions of Aboriginality as historic cultures like those found in museums must be rejected. This renewed interpretation of s. 35(1) that draws on the standards and framework of the UNDRIP "will enhance harmonious and cooperative relations between the State and indigenous peoples, based on principles of justice, democracy, respect for human rights, non-discrimination and good faith" (UNDRIP Preamble).

Notes

1. In this article, the terms "Aboriginal" and "Indigenous" are used: Aboriginal is the umbrella term used in the Canadian constitution, Indigenous is an umbrella term used in the international discourse.
2. *British North America Act*, 1930, c 26.

References

Allen, Stephen. 2011. "The U.N. *Declaration on the Rights of Indigenous Peoples* and the Limits of the International Legal Project." In Stephen Allen and Alexandra Xanthaki (eds.), *Reflections on the U.N. Declaration on the Rights of Indigenous Peoples*. Portland: Hart Publishing.

Anaya, S. James. 2004. *Indigenous Peoples in International Law*. 2nd edition. New York: Oxford University Press.

____. 2009. "The Right of Indigenous Peoples to Self-Determination in the Post-Declaration Era." In Claire Charters and Rodolfo Stavenhagen (eds.), *Making the Declaration Work*. Copenhagen: IWGIA.

Anaya, S. James, Human Rights Council. 2008. "Report of the Special Rapporteur on the Human Rights and Fundamental Freedoms of Indigenous Peoples." A/HRC/9/9, August 11.

____. 2009. *Report of the Special Rapporteur on the situation of human rights and fundamental freedoms of indigenous people.* UN Doc. A/HRC/12/34, 15 July.

Asch, Michael, and Patrick Macklem. 1991. "Aboriginal Rights and Canadian Sovereignty: An Essay on *R. v. Sparrow*." *Alberta Law Review* 29, 2: 498.

Barsh, Russel Lawrence, and James Youngblood Henderson. 1997. "The Supreme Court's Van der Peet Trilogy: Naive Imperialism and Ropes of Sand." *McGill Law Journal* 42: 994.

Beaulac, Stephane. 2003. "National Application of International Law: The Statutory Interpretation Perspective." *The Canadian Yearbook of International Law* 41: 225.

Boldt, Menno, and Anthony Long. 1985. *The Quest for Justice: Aboriginal Peoples and Aboriginal Rights*. Toronto: University of Toronto Press.

Borrows, John. 1997. "The Trickster: Integral to a Distinctive Culture." *Constitutional Forum* 8, 2: 27.

____. 1997a. "Wampum at Niagara: The Royal Proclamation, Canadian Legal History, and Self-Government." In Michael Asch (ed.), *Aboriginal and Treaty Rights in Canada: Essays on Law, Equality, and Respect*. Vancouver: UBC Press.

Brunnée, Jutta, and Stephen J. Toope. 2002. "A Hesitant Embrace: The Application of International Law by Canadian Courts." *Canadian Yearbook of International Law* 3.

Committee on the Elimination of Racial Discrimination. 1997. *General Recommendation No. 23: Indigenous Peoples*, UN Doc A/52/18, annex V.

Deer, Kenneth. 2010. "Reflections on the Development, Adoption, and Implementation of the U.N. *Declaration on the Rights of Indigenous Peoples*." In Jackie Hartley, Paul Joffe, and Jennifer Preston (eds.), *Realizing the U.N. Declaration on the Rights of Indigenous Peoples: Triumph, Hope and Action*. Saskatoon: Purich Publishing.

Hartley, Jackie, Paul Joffe and Jennifer Preston. 2010. "From Development to Implementation: An Ongoing Journey." In Jackie Hartley, Paul Joffe, and Jennifer Preston (eds.), *Realizing the U.N. Declaration on the Rights of Indigenous Peoples: Triumph, Hope and Action*. Saskatoon: Purich Publishing.

Henderson, James Youngblood. 2006. *First Nations Jurisprudence and Aboriginal Rights*. Native Law Centre, Saskatoon.

____. 2010. "Constitutional Vision and Judicial Commitment: Aboriginal and Treaty Rights in Canada." *Australian Indigenous Law Review* 14, 2: 24.

ILA Committee (International Law Association, Rights of Indigenous Peoples Committee).

2012. "Sofia Conference Report." <http://www.ila-hq.org/en/committees/index. cfm/cid/1024>.

Knop, Karen. 2000. "Here and There: International Law in Domestic Courts." *International Law and Politics* 32: 501.

Littlechild, Wilton. 2009. "When Indigenous Peoples Win, the Whole World Wins." In Claire Charters and Rodolfo Stavenhagen (eds.), *Making the Declaration Work*. Copenhagen: IWGIA.

McLachlin, Beverly, Chief Justice Canada. 2002. "Statement at the Order of Canada Luncheon."

McNeil, Kent. 2003. "Reconciliation and the Supreme Court: The Opposing Views of Chief Justices Lamer and McLachlin." Indigenous Law Journal 2, 1.

Sanders, Douglas. 1983. "Aboriginal Rights." Canadian Bar Review 61: 315.

Slattery, Brian. 1984. "The Hidden Constitution: Aboriginal Rights In Canada." *American Journal of Comparative Law* 32: 361.

____. 2000. "Making Sense of Aboriginal and Treaty Rights." *Canadian Bar Review* 79: 197.

Sullivan, Ruth. 1994. *Driedger on the Construction of Statutes*, 3rd ed. Toronto: Butterworths.

Tauli-Corpuz, Victoria. 2007. "Statement of Victoria Tauli-Corpuz, Chair of the U.N. Permanent Forum on Indigenous Issues on the Occasion of the Adoption of the U.N. *Declaration on the Rights of Indigenous Peoples*." Delivered to the United Nations General Assembly, New York.

UNPFII (United Nations Permanent Forum on Indigenous Issues). n.d. "History of Indigenous Peoples and the International System." <undesadspd.org/ IndigenousPeoples/AboutUsMembers/History.aspx>.

____. n.d. "Indigenous Peoples, Indigenous Voices: Frequently Asked Questions on the United Nations *Declaration on the Rights of Indigenous Peoples*." <un.org/esa/socdev/ unpfii/documents/faq_drips_en.pdf>.

Vermette, D'arcy. 2011. "Dizzying Dialogue: Canadian Courts and the Continuing Justification of the Dispossession of Aboriginal People." *Windsor Yearbook of Access to Justice* 29, 1: 54.

Waddell, Ian. 2003. "Building a Box, Finding Storage Space." In Ardith Walkem and Halie Bruce (eds.), *Box of Treasures or Empty Box? Twenty Years of Section 35*. Vancouver: Theytus Books.

Weiser, Irit. 2004. "Undressing the Window: Treating International Human Rights Law Meaningfully in the Canadian Commonwealth System." UBC *Law Review* 37, 1: 113.

Wiessner, Siegfried. 2010. "Re-Enchanting the World: Indigenous Peoples' Rights as Essential Parts of a Holistic Human Rights Regime." UCLA *Journal of International Law and Foreign Affairs* 15, 1: 239.

Legal Cases

114957 Canada Ltee (Spraytech, Societe d'arrosage) v Hudson (Town). 2001. 2 SCR 241. (Supreme Court of Canada).

Baker v Canada (Minister of Citizenship and Immigration). 1999. 2 SCR 817. (Supreme Court of Canada.

Canada (Human Rights Commission) v Canada (Attorney General). 2012. FC 445. (Federal Court of Canada).

Canadian Foundation for Children, Youth and the Law v Canada (AG). 2004. 1 SCR 76. (Supreme Court of Canada).

Daniels v White. 1968. SCR 517. (Supreme Court of Canada).

Delgamuukw v. British Columbia. 1997. 3 SCR 1010. (Supreme Court of Canada).

Haida Nation v British Columbia (Minister of Forests). 2004. 3 SCR 511. (Supreme Court of Canada).

Johnson v M'Intosh. 1823. 21 U.S. (8 Wheat.) 543. (United States Supreme Court).

Lax Kw'alaams Indian Band v. Canada (Attorney General). 2011. 3 SCR 535. (Supreme Court of Canada).

Mitchell v Canada (Minister of National Revenue – MNR). 2001. 1 SCR 911. (Supreme Court of Canada).

National Corn Growers v Canada. 1990. 2 SCR 1324.

Ordon Estate v. Grail. 1998. 3 SCR 437. (Supreme Court of Canada).

R v Hape. 2007. 2 SCR 292. (Supreme Court of Canada).

R v Marshall. 1999. 3 SCR 533.

R v Pamajewon. 1996. 2 SCR 821. (Supreme Court of Canada).

R v Powley. 2003. 2 SCR 207.

R v Sparrow. 1990. 1 SCR 1075. (Supreme Court of Canada).

R v Van der Peet. 1996. 2 SCR 507. (Supreme Court of Canada).

Reference Re Public Service Employee Relations Act (Alta). 1987. 1 SCR 313. (Supreme Court of Canada).

Slaight Communications Inc v Davidson. 1989. 1 SCR 1038. (Supreme Court of Canada).

Statutes

Cities and Towns Act, CQLR c C-19.

Constitution Act, 1982, Schedule B to the Canada Act 1982 (UK), 1982, c 11, s. 35(1).

Convention on the Rights of the Child, 20 November 1989, UNTS 1577 at 3.

GA Res 61/295 (Annex), UN GAOR, 61st Sess, Supp No 49, Vol. III, UN Doc A/61/49 (2008)

Indian Act, RSC 1985, c I-5.

International Covenant on Civil and Political Rights, 16 December 1966, UNTS 999 at 171.

International Covenant on Economic, Social and Cultural Rights, 16 December 1966, UNTS 993 at 3.

International Labour Organization Convention 169, 27 June 1989.

Migratory Birds Convention Act, RSC 1952, c 179.

Migratory Birds Convention, Canada-US, 16 August 1916.

Chapter Ten

Undermining Indigenous Peoples' Security and Human Rights
Strategies of the Canadian Government
Paul Joffe

In myriad ways, the Government of Canada undermines the rights of Indigenous peoples, which include First Nations, Inuit and Métis. This includes government actions relating to Indigenous peoples' rights to land and resources, food security, environment and climate change, free trade, essential services and children's rights. In so doing, the government repeatedly casts aside its constitutional and international obligations. Since the federal election in 2006, the government has refused to even discuss the nature and scope of its obligations.

Indigenous peoples' issues and rights are increasingly addressed in diverse international processes and forums. The federal government often takes positions that adversely affect Indigenous peoples' rights. At the international level, the government appears to proceed on the assumption that it has no obligation to consult and accommodate Indigenous peoples on their concerns. The Supreme Court of Canada has ruled that the duty to consult arises when a Crown actor "has knowledge, real or constructive, of the potential existence of Aboriginal rights or title and contemplates conduct that might adversely affect them" (*Taku River Tlingit First Nation* 2004: para. 25). The high end of the spectrum of consultation requires "'full consent of [the] aboriginal nation on very serious issues" (*Haida Nation* 2004: para. 24).

The Canadian government cannot undermine Indigenous peoples' constitutional rights or circumvent its constitutional duties — such as its duty to consult and accommodate — simply because it takes such actions in international forums. Canada also has international obligations to respect and protect human rights, including those of Indigenous peoples.

Indigenous peoples' collective rights constitute human rights. By adversely affecting these human rights, the federal government is also undermining the security of Indigenous peoples. Security and human rights are interrelated and entail international responsibilities. The U.N. High Commissioner for Human Rights has emphasized: "Respecting human rights is not only a legal obligation. It is also a precondition for our societies to grow and prosper in peace and security" (General Assembly 2006: para. 52).

One expects a more honourable approach from the Government of Canada. The *United Nations Declaration on the Rights of Indigenous Peoples* (UNDRIP) was adopted by the General Assembly in 2007. It constitutes a major and historic step towards addressing the persistent human rights violations against Indigenous peoples worldwide.

The UNDRIP is the most comprehensive universal international human rights instrument explicitly addressing the rights of Indigenous peoples. It affirms a wide range of political, civil, economic, social, cultural, spiritual and environmental rights. The UNDRIP is a consensus instrument for justice and reconciliation. It provides a principled and normative legal framework for achieving reconciliation between Indigenous and non-Indigenous peoples around the world.

The Preamble of the UNDRIP calls for "harmonious and cooperative relations" between states and Indigenous peoples. It was proclaimed by the General Assembly as a "standard of achievement to be pursued in a spirit of partnership and mutual respect."

Since the federal election in 2006, the Canadian government has opposed the adoption and implementation of the UNDRIP at home and abroad. It aligned itself with states with poor human rights records and "with histories of brutal repression of Indigenous rights advocates" (Amnesty International Canada 2007: 7).

Despite its endorsement of the UNDRIP in November 2010, the Canadian government continues to devalue this human rights instrument by ignoring its significance and legal effects. The UNDRIP affirms the right to security of Indigenous peoples and individuals (section 7).

Within the Canadian constitutional context, the right to "security of the person" is included in the *Canadian Charter of Rights and Freedoms* (section 7). While rights to collective and individual security have not been sufficiently elaborated in the Indigenous context, such rights contribute to and are interrelated with the protection of Aboriginal and treaty rights. If the guarantees in s. 35 of the *Constitution Act, 1982* are to be effective, the security of Aboriginal peoples and individuals must be a key result.

In relation to Aboriginal rights, the Supreme Court has spoken in terms of "cultural security and continuity" (*R. v. Sappier* 2006; *R. v. Gray* 2006: para. 33). In regard to Indigenous peoples' treaties with states, the Federal Court referred to their "economic security" (*Samson Indian Nation and Band* 2006: para. 511). It is clear from the content of treaties that a key objective was and continues to be to ensure the collective and individual security of Indigenous peoples and individuals.

Canadian government actions relating to Indigenous peoples must be consistent with the principles of justice, democracy, equality, non-discrimination and respect for human rights and the rule of law. The rights, security and well-being of present and future generations of Indigenous people must be ensured.

In Canada, undermining Indigenous peoples' security and human rights is not happenstance. Nor is it the unintended effect of misguided government policy. It is the ongoing result of conceived strategies of the government that are implemented internationally and domestically. In the context of Indigenous peoples, the government has shown little regard for their human rights and security or the rule of law.

Double Standards on Human Rights, Security and the Rule of Law

In August 2012, Foreign Affairs Minister John Baird (2012) declared: "Canadian values are the envy of the world. We support freedom, democracy, and respect for the rule of law, and we don't apologize for it ... these values are universal." In an October 2012 address to the General Assembly, the minister underlined the relationship between security and human rights:

> The world's security is closely linked to ... protecting the dignity and worth of every person by upholding and protecting fundamental freedoms ... protecting human rights and human dignity is an obligation that each state owes its citizens, and a mutual obligation of all members of the international community. (Canada: 2012)

Yet the Canadian government applies a different and lesser standard on democracy, human rights, security and the rule of law when addressing the rights of Indigenous peoples. The government refuses to acknowledge that Indigenous peoples' collective rights are human rights.

Such actions are inconsistent with the practice within the U.N. system for the past thirty years. The Canadian Human Rights Commission (2008: 8) confirms: "Human rights have a dual nature. Both collective and individual human rights must be protected; both types of rights are important to human freedom and dignity."

The UNDRIP (Article 1) affirms: "Indigenous peoples have the right to the full enjoyment, as a collective or as individuals, of all human rights and fundamental freedoms as recognized in the Charter of the United Nations ... and international human rights law." As affirmed in the *Vienna Declaration* and countless other international instruments: "All human rights are universal, indivisible, interdependent and interrelated" and "it is the duty of States ... to promote and protect all human rights" (*Vienna Declaration* 1993: para. 5).

Canada's ongoing failure to address Indigenous peoples' collective rights as human rights constitutes racial discrimination. Simply because Indigenous cultures hold their property and other rights collectively, for example, does not mean such rights are stripped of their human rights quality. As affirmed in the 2001 Durban *Declaration and Programme of Action* (para. 41), "full realization by indigenous peoples of their human rights ... is indispensable for eliminating racism, racial discrimination." The UNDRIP affirms that Indigenous peoples and individuals have the "right to be free from any kind of discrimination, in the exercise of their rights, in particular that based on their indigenous origin or identity" (Article 2).

Discriminatory Approaches on Indigenous Land Rights

Throughout Canada's history, in virtually every court case relating to Aboriginal and treaty rights, the Government of Canada has acted as an adversary. No other people in Canada are automatically subjected to such consistently adverse and discriminatory treatment. In litigation within the United States, it is common for the federal government to act as *amicus curiae* (friend of the court) in support of an Indigenous nation or individual (Joffe 2010: note 114).

In August 2002, the U.N. Committee on the Elimination of Racial Discrimination (para. 16) expressed concern that "to date, no Aboriginal group has proven Aboriginal title" and recommended that Canada examine ways and means to facilitate the establishment of such proof. Yet no affirmative measures have been implemented.

Upon completion of his October 2013 visit to Canada, Special Rapporteur James Anaya cautioned that "Canada faces a crisis when it comes to the situation of indigenous peoples ... overall there appear to be high levels of distrust among aboriginal peoples toward government at both the federal and provincial levels" (OHCHR 2013). In particular, Anaya encouraged the federal government to "re-think available claims processes" and "take a less adversarial, position-based approach in which it typically seeks the most restrictive interpretation of aboriginal and treaty rights possible."

The Canadian government is especially aggressive in opposing Indigenous peoples' rights to lands and resources. In *Tsilhqot'in Nation* v. *British Columbia* (2012), Canada and British Columbia insisted that only small site-specific areas may be subject to title claims. In the same case, the B.C. Court of Appeal (para. 219) agreed, viewing "broad territorial claims to title as antithetical to the goal of reconciliation." The Court ruled that respect for the traditional rights of First Nations must not place "unnecessary limitations on the sovereignty of the Crown or on the aspirations of all Canadians." However, in a landmark decision, the Supreme Court rejected all such views and confirmed that "regular use of definite tracts of land for hunting, fishing or otherwise exploiting its resources" could suffice to establish Aboriginal title based on a territorial approach (*Tsilhqot'in Nation* v. *British Columbia* (2014: para. 44). The Court (para. 73) added that Aboriginal title confers ownership rights including "the right to decide how the land will be used; the right of enjoyment and occupancy of the land; the right to possess the land; the right to the economic benefits of the land; and the right to pro-actively use and manage the land."

The Court of Appeal (*Tsilhqot'in Nation* v. *British Columbia* 2012: para. 166) invoked the "principle of discovery," in the context of the doctrine of discovery: "European explorers considered that by virtue of the 'principle of discovery' they were at liberty to claim territory in North America on behalf of their sovereigns." Yet international law rejects the doctrine of discovery as "racist" and legally invalid, since it is largely based on European and Christian superiority over Indigenous peoples (Williams, Jr. 2012: 228; Miller 2011: 849, 854; Newcomb 1993).

The Preamble of the *International Convention on the Elimination of All Forms of Racial Discrimination* affirms that: "any doctrine of superiority based on racial differentiation is scientifically false, morally condemnable, socially unjust and dangerous, and that there is no justification for racial discrimination, in theory or in practice, anywhere" (see also UNDRIP: Preamble; and *Declaration and Programme of Action* 2001: Preamble and para. 7). The U.N. Human Rights Council by consensus "condemned" doctrines of superiority "as incompatible with democracy and transparent and accountable governance" (Human Rights Council 2011d: para. 5).

An element of the doctrine of discovery is the discredited notion of *terra nullius* ("lands belonging to no one") (Miller 2011: 900). Both were used to colonize Indigenous peoples — that is, to dehumanize, exploit and subjugate Indigenous peoples and dispossess them of their most basic rights. The General Assembly (1970: para. 1) has called the continuation of colonialism "a crime which constitutes a violation of the Charter of the United Nations."

In *R. v. Van der Peet* (1996: para. 38), the Supreme Court of Canada accepted the repudiation of *terra nullius* as racially discriminatory, as explained in the High Court of Australia ruling in *Mabo* v. *State of Queensland* (1992). In *Tsilhqot'in Nation* v. *British Columbia* (2014), the Supreme Court ruled that the doctrine of *terra nullius* "never applied in Canada" (para. 69) and that once Aboriginal title is confirmed, the lands are "vested" in the Aboriginal group and "the lands are no longer Crown lands" (para. 115).

A new study on the doctrine of discovery issued by the U.N. Permanent Forum on Indigenous Issues underlined that state reliance on "discovery" and denial of Indigenous peoples' sovereignty and self-determination are "incompatible with the principles of justice, democracy, respect for human rights, equality, non-discrimination, good governance and good faith, which are the core principles for interpreting and applying indigenous peoples' rights and the related State obligations affirmed in the Declaration" (Permanent Forum on Indigenous Issues 2014: para. 8). In *Tsilhqot'in Nation* v. *British Columbia* (2014), the Supreme Court did not address the doctrine of discovery, but included elements of self-determination or self-government in relation to Aboriginal title land (para. 73).

Denial of the UNDRIP's Legal Effects

Both prior to and after the adoption of the UNDRIP, the Canadian government did not consult Indigenous peoples on its significance but declared it had "no legal effect in Canada" (Joffe 2010: 198). Similarly, at the time of its endorsement, it described this historic instrument as "an aspirational document ... the Declaration is a non-legally binding document that does not reflect customary international law nor change Canadian laws" (Aboriginal Affairs and Northern Development Canada 2010). Such interpretation is erroneous and inconsistent with international law (Joffe 2012). A norm of customary international law has binding effect when: (i) most countries adhere to the norm in practice, and (ii) those countries follow the norm because they feel obligated to do so by a sense of legal duty (*opinio juris*).

In 1962, the U.N. Office of Legal Affairs clarified that "in United Nations practice, a 'declaration' is a solemn instrument resorted to only in very rare cases relating to matters of major and lasting importance where maximum compliance is expected" (Economic and Social Council 1962: para. 105). Special Rapporteur on the Rights of Indigenous Peoples James Anaya affirmed: "even though the Declaration itself is not legally binding in the same way that a treaty is, the Declaration reflects legal commitments that are related to the Charter, other treaty commitments and customary international law" (General Assembly 2010: para. 62).

Examples of customary international law in the UNDRIP include, *inter alia*: the general principle of international law of *pacta sunt servanda* ("treaties must be kept"); the prohibition against racial discrimination; the right of self-determination; the right to one's own means of subsistence; the right not to be subjected to genocide; the *Charter of the United Nations* obligation of states to promote the "universal respect for, and observance of, human rights and fundamental freedoms for all"; and the requirement of good faith in the fulfilment of the obligations assumed by states in accordance with the *U.N. Charter*. Some prominent jurists have highlighted that the rule banning gender discrimination is also now customary international law (Joffe 2010: 206–7).

Anaya has also concluded that the claim by Canada that the UNDRIP does not include any customary international law is "a manifestly untenable position" (Human Rights Council 2010: para. 112).

In 2011, when the Federal Court of Canada was assessing the significance of the UNDRIP, the government conceded that it can have legal effect: "Non-binding international law may provide legal context that is of assistance in interpreting domestic legislation" (Canada Factum 2011: para. 71). Similarly, in regard to the UNDRIP, Canada indicated to the U.N. Committee on the Elimination of Racial Discrimination: "Canadian courts could consult international law sources when interpreting Canadian laws, including the Constitution" (2012: para. 39).

The refusals of the Government of Canada to consult Indigenous peoples on its positions on the UNDRIP violate the rule of law under Canadian constitutional and international law. Such actions can be especially damaging in international forums or processes, such as the Convention on Biological Diversity, Food and Agricultural Organization and climate change, where new standards are being negotiated. Special Rapporteur James Anaya indicated that the duty to consult "derives from the overarching right of indigenous peoples to self-determination and from related principles of democracy and popular sovereignty … the right of self-determination is a foundational right, without which indigenous peoples' human rights, both collective and individual, cannot be fully enjoyed" (Human Rights Council 2009a: para. 41).

Canada's highest court has ruled on the Crown's constitutional duty: "The duty to consult arises when a Crown actor has knowledge, real or constructive, of the *potential* existence of Aboriginal rights or title and contemplates conduct that *might* adversely affect them" (*Taku River Tlingit First Nation* 2004: para. 25, emphasis added). The UNDRIP (para. 38) affirms a general duty: "States, in consultation and cooperation with indigenous peoples, shall take the appropriate measures, including legislative measures, to achieve the ends of this Declaration."

This added requirement of "cooperation" goes beyond "consultation" and includes negotiation and even partnership in accordance with the circumstances. Special Rapporteur Anaya emphasized: "Consulting with indigenous peoples on the very elements of the consultation procedure to be employed not only helps to ensure that the procedure is effective, it is also an important, necessary confidence-building measure" (Human Rights Council 2009a: para. 68).

Use of International Processes to Undermine Indigenous Rights

Virtually every issue relating to Indigenous peoples is increasingly being addressed at the international level. New international instruments and standards are being negotiated on such key matters as food security, biodiversity, genetic and other resources, traditional knowledge, environment, development, climate change and intellectual property.

Under existing procedures of international organizations, such as the Convention on Biological Diversity, Food and Agriculture Organization and World Intellectual Property Organization, Indigenous peoples have no effective means of safeguarding their rights. When Indigenous representatives raise concerns that the positions of states are inconsistent with the *Charter of the United Nations* and international human rights law, such concerns are generally not addressed by the parties (GCCEI 2012a).

The Government of Canada repeatedly uses international processes and forums to undermine Indigenous peoples' rights and the UNDRIP, based on narrow self-interest. Such government actions are inconsistent with its international obligations. Yet the "rule of law applies to all States equally, and to international organizations ... and ... respect for and promotion of the rule of law and justice should guide all of their activities" (*Declaration of the High-level Meeting of the General Assembly on the Rule of Law at the National and International Levels* 2012).

Within such bodies and processes, the practice is often to seek consensus. Canada and other states are exploiting such practice to the detriment of Indigenous peoples. The state with the lowest position most often prevails. These unfair procedures are undermining principles of justice, democracy, non-discrimination and respect for human rights and the rule of law.

The U.N. Expert Mechanism on the Rights of Indigenous Peoples recommended in its 2011 *Final Report of the Study on Indigenous Peoples and the Right to Participate in Decision Making*: "Reform of international and regional processes involving indigenous peoples should be a major priority and concern" (Human Rights Council 2011a: para. 26). Special Rapporteur James Anaya has also highlighted the need for reforms: "Potential reforms within international institutions and platforms of decision-making that affect indigenous peoples' lives should be closely examined" (General Assembly 2010: para. 52).

These prejudicial approaches by states are not honourable. They fail to respect and protect Indigenous human rights and serve to weaken the United Nations system. The misuse of international processes is clearly at work in approaches to genetic resources, food security and environment and climate change.

Discriminatory Approach on Genetic Resources

Negotiations on the Nagoya Protocol on access and benefit sharing should have resulted in respect and protection of the rights of Indigenous peoples. Both the Convention on Biological Diversity and Nagoya have identical objectives that include "fair and equitable sharing of the benefits arising from the utilization of genetic resources ... *taking into account all rights over those resources*" (Article 1, emphasis mine). This objective calls for a culturally sensitive, rights-based approach.

Genetic resources refer to genetic material of actual or potential value. Examples include "material of plant, animal, or microbial origin, such as medicinal plants, agricultural crops and animal breeds" (World Intellectual Property Organization 2014).

In regard to genetic resources and traditional knowledge, the Expert Mechanism on the Rights of Indigenous Peoples concluded that it is "imperative that United Nations institutions and related entities take a human rights-based approach to the development of international legal standards and policies" and "ensure that they conform" to the UNDRIP (Human Rights Council 2012a: para. 28). Article 31(1) of the UNDRIP affirms:

> Indigenous peoples have the right to maintain, control, protect and develop their cultural heritage, traditional knowledge and traditional cultural expressions, as well as the manifestations of their sciences, technologies and cultures, including human and genetic resources

Genetic resources are especially critical for Indigenous traditional medicines. In Canada and other countries, Indigenous peoples face biopiracy — which refers to the unauthorized commercial or other use by third parties of genetic resources and traditional knowledge without sharing the benefits.

During the negotiations of the Protocol, Canada played a lead role in undermining the rights of Indigenous peoples to genetic resources (GCCEI 2012c). Canada insisted that the Protocol only recognize "established" rights of Indigenous peoples "in accordance with domestic legislation" (Articles 5(2), 6(2)).

"Established" rights might only refer to those affirmed by domestic legislation, agreement or judicial ruling. Should the term "established" be interpreted in such a restrictive manner, most Indigenous peoples worldwide could be denied their rights to genetic resources — regardless of how strong the evidence that such rights exist. Indigenous peoples' inherent rights are not dependent on national legislation for their existence. Thus all genetic resource rights based on customary use would not be recognized. In 2011, the Permanent Forum on Indigenous Issues (para. 27) raised discrimination concerns and urged states that "all rights based on customary use must be safeguarded and not only 'established' rights."

In 2011, the Canadian government prepared a draft Domestic Policy that may only recognize rights related to genetic resources for those Indigenous peoples that have "completed land-claim and self-government agreements" (GCCEI 2011). Those peoples facing possible dispossession of their customary rights to genetic resources may include Indigenous peoples with numbered treaties or specific claims agreements or uncompleted land-claim and self-government agreements.

Failure to affirm all customary rights could lead to massive dispossessions of Indigenous peoples' inherent rights to genetic resources (GCCEI 2011). Third parties may gain access to and use of genetic resources in the territories of Indigenous peoples without their free, prior and informed consent.

Not affirming customary rights is incompatible with Canada's obligations in the *Charter of the United Nations* (Articles 1(3), 2(2), 55 c and 56), the *Convention on Biological Diversity* (Article 3) and international human rights law.[1] It could deprive Indigenous peoples of their rights to self-determination, culture and resources contrary to principles of equality and non-discrimination.

As indicated by the U.N. Independent Expert in the field of cultural rights: "The right of peoples to self-determination protects the right of peoples to freely pursue their cultural development, and dispose of their natural wealth and resources, which has a clear link with cultural heritage" (Human Rights Council 2011c: para. 45). The U.N. Special Rapporteur on the right to food has added: "Control over and preservation of plant and animal genetic resources is today crucial for the economic interests of indigenous peoples and their long-term food security" (General Assembly 2005: para. 30).

The restrictive "established" rights approach is incompatible with the jurisprudence of the Committee on the Elimination of Racial Discrimination (2006: para. 15). The Canadian government has been unsuccessful in its attempts to restrict its constitutional duty to consult Indigenous peoples to situations where their rights were already "established." In this regard, the Supreme Court of Canada rejected Canada's approach as "not reconciliation" and "not honourable" (*Haida Nation*: paras. 27, 33).

Prejudicing Food Security and Related Rights

In May 2012 the U.N. Special Rapporteur on the right to food visited Canada, yet Cabinet ministers were not prepared to meet with him. Prior to his departure, Special Rapporteur Olivier De Schutter emphasized that "rates of food insecurity are unacceptable" in Canada (Whittington 2012). Government ministers scoffed at his concerns and questioned his focus on such a wealthy country as Canada (Scoffield 2012). His final report on the mission to Canada elaborated on the serious food insecurity among Aboriginal households; the need for a "comprehensive rights-based national food strategy"; and the importance of Indigenous peoples' human rights affirmed in the UNDRIP (Human Rights Council 2012b: paras. 55, 66 and 69(a)).

It is wrong to suggest that developed countries, including Canada, should not be scrutinized by the U.N. for human rights violations relating to food. As a High Level Panel of Experts on Food Security and Nutrition concluded, "food insecurity is reported even in the richest countries" (FAO 2012: para. 4).

The U.N. Permanent Forum (2012: para. 56) underlines that Indigenous peoples' "right to food depends on access to and control over their lands and other natural resources in their territories." In view of the Canadian government's aggressive policies in favour of oil sands, minerals and other resource development, it is likely that issues of food and water security will continue to arise. The Office of the High Commissioner for Human Rights (2010: 12) has affirmed: "Water is essential for life, but is also key to food security, income generation and environmental protection."

Within the Food and Agriculture Organization (FAO), Canada joined with other states to undermine Indigenous peoples' rights. In May 2012, the *Voluntary Guidelines on the Responsible Governance of Tenure of Land, Fisheries and Forests in the Context of National Food Security* were adopted. Canada failed to consult Indigenous peoples on the countless issues in this instrument that affect their rights (GCCEI 2012b: para. 117). The practice of obtaining state consensus was used to set low standards.

A key rationale for adopting "voluntary" guidelines is to encourage states and others to strive for higher human rights and environmental standards than they might be willing to agree to in a legally binding instrument. Yet the *Guidelines*, as drafted, appear to significantly lower international standards and unjustly favour states to the detriment of Indigenous peoples.

The *Guidelines* characterize land and resource tenure rights as rights outside of the "human rights" context. They subjugate Indigenous peoples and rights in a manner that may increase state domination and control: "All tenure rights are limited by the rights of others and by the measures taken by States necessary for public purposes" (*Guidelines*: para. 4.3). The new instrument seeks to undermine the legal concept of "free, prior and informed consent" (GCCEI 2012b: paras. 112–16).

In his 2012 report to the General Assembly, Special Rapporteur James Anaya urged the FAO and other international organizations to initiate substantive and procedural reforms. In particular, he concluded: "Operational policies or guidelines relating to indigenous peoples … should be reformed as necessary, or interpreted to ensure compliance with relevant international standards as set forth in the Declaration, applicable treaties and other sources" (General Assembly 2012a: para. 86).

Deficient Approaches to Environment, Development and Climate Change

In June 2012, the government adopted the omnibus Bill C-38, which included seventy different bills and did not allow time for careful scrutiny by members of Parliament. This was followed by the adoption of a second omnibus bill, Bill C-45, which comprised sixty different pieces of legislation. The parliamentary process was highly undemocratic, allowing for virtually no amendments. The integrity of Parliament was seriously impaired (Coyne 2012: A15). A significant portion of these bills had adverse implications for the environment and for addressing climate change.

It is unjust and deceptive for the federal government to adopt amendments to a host of environmental provisions or laws through two omnibus "budget" bills totalling about nine hundred pages. Many aspects of these omnibus bills have real and potential impacts on Indigenous peoples' rights and interests. Indigenous peoples across the country expressed their outrage and a social protest movement, Idle No More, emerged.

In 1999, Canada's highest court highlighted in Corbiere (para. 116) that "the best remedy is one that will encourage and allow Parliament to consult with and listen to the opinions of Aboriginal people affected by it." Regardless of what duty Parliament may have prior to passing legislation, the government has a duty to consult when contemplating measures that potentially affect Aboriginal or treaty rights. As indicated by the Alberta Court of Appeal: "the duty may still fall upon those assigned the task of developing the policy behind the legislation, or upon those who are charged with making recommendations concerning future policies and actions" (*Tsuu T'ina Nation* 2010: para. 55).

As illustrated by the Polaris Institute, there is a correlation between the issues raised with the federal government by some of the wealthiest oil and gas corporations and their lobbyists and the amendments adopted through the omnibus bills (Polaris Institute 2012: 6, Tables 5 and 21 (Appendix F)). In a follow-up letter to the editor of the *Globe and Mail*, the Executive Director of Polaris said: "a system which makes it possible for government officials to meet and communicate with oil industry officials 463 per cent more than with environmental groups, let alone First Nations, is hardly operating in the public interest" (Clarke 2012). Such a disparity in favour of the corporate sector serves to distort the priorities of government and its perceptions of public interest.

In a 2008 press conference, Canada's environment minister stated that the UN-DRIP "has nothing whatsoever to do with climate change" (Curry and Mittelstaedt 2008: A10). Yet rights in the UNDRIP that are likely to be affected by climate change include: self-determination, treaty rights, lands, territories and resources, subsistence, health, culture, environment, development, peace and security. For example, rising sea levels and severe flooding in Indigenous traditional territories could prevent or otherwise jeopardize the exercise of many of these rights.

In regard to environment and development issues, Indigenous peoples have repeatedly urged a human rights-based approach consistent with the UNDRIP. As affirmed by the Human Rights Council, "environmental damage can have negative implications ... for the effective enjoyment of human rights," and "environmental damage is felt most acutely by those segments of the population already in vulnerable situations" (2011b: Preamble).

In aggressively pursuing major resource development, the Canadian government has shown little regard for related environmental and climate change concerns. It has sought to discredit Indigenous peoples and environmental organizations opposing the Northern Gateway Pipeline proposed by Enbridge from Alberta to British Columbia, among other projects. Natural Resources Minister Joe Oliver has generally slammed "environmental and other radical groups" that are getting in the way of forestry, mining and energy projects (Babad 2012). The government is also selectively reviewing the charitable status of organizations "as a threat to encourage silence" on environment and resource development issues (Sajoo 2012: A11). Further, it has taken measures to influence environmental review processes and reduce federal oversight, so as to favour proposed resource development. As a result, the human right of Indigenous peoples to an effective remedy is being significantly reduced.

A stark example is found in Bill C-38. Among the diverse range of problems arising from Bill C-38 is that it reduces fisheries protection for fish. It empowers the government to approve projects even if they have been refused approval by the National Energy Board. At the same time, the government may significantly limit the time period for environmental assessments. Public participation in environmental assessment of projects is restricted and the number and types of projects subjected to environmental assessment are reduced.

In regard to the proposed Northern Gateway Pipeline, the federal government's overall approach to consultation on Indigenous peoples' rights has raised serious questions. It was illogical for the National Energy Board to examine the environmental effects on Indigenous peoples' rights, when the government had not first consulted on what rights were potentially affected. The Supreme Court has indicated, for example, that Aboriginal title differs significantly from other Aboriginal rights: "aboriginal title encompasses the right to exclusive use and occupation of the land held pursuant to that title for a variety of purposes, which need not be aspects of ... aboriginal practices, customs and traditions " (*Delgamuukw* 1997: para. 117). Yet such distinctions were not taken into account by either Northern Gateway or the Joint Review Panel that assessed the proposed project, since neither had such a mandate (Canada (National Energy Board) 2013: vol. 2, 47).

A similar flaw affected the Joint Review Panel's consideration of the "public interest," which was affirmed as being "local, regional, and national in scope," and inclusive of Indigenous peoples (Canada (National Energy Board) 2013: vol. 1, 11). Yet Aboriginal title was not explicitly considered in assessing the public interest. Oil sands expansion in Alberta is linked to the Northern Gateway Pipeline.

This raises climate change concerns relevant to present and future generations of Indigenous people.

Clearly there is a need for the government to adopt an effective rights-based approach in regard to development. Current policy approaches are not working. An internal Aboriginal Affairs' report indicates: "There is a tension between the rights-based agenda of Aboriginal groups and the non-rights based policy approaches" of the federal government (Lukacs 2014).

Unjust Actions on Free Trade

Canada is engaged in negotiating trade agreements with a large number of countries. In regard to the negotiations with the European Union (EU), Canada's trade minister indicated that provincial, territorial and municipal governments have been consulted: "these are the most transparent and open negotiations that Canada has ever undertaken … if you contact our stakeholders, you will find that they have been consulted on a regular basis on the issues that affect them" (Shane 2012: 18). Indigenous peoples, however, were not consulted.

A major concern with investor-state dispute processes in trade agreements is that they have "resulted in dozens of absurd corporate lawsuits against public health, environmental and conservation measures, and other matters" (Trew and Lui 2014). These are all measures that could impact Indigenous peoples. The European Union is currently consulting the public on whether such a process should be included in future trade agreements, but the Government of Canada has yet to do the same.

Serious questions have been raised by trade experts and Indigenous peoples about the Canada-China agreement, signed by the parties in September 2012 (Van Harten 2012). In regard to this trade agreement, the Hupacasath First Nation (HFN) filed for judicial review since there was no prior consultation with HFN and other Aboriginal peoples by the federal Crown. HFN has raised a number of concerns, including that it may be prevented from exercising its rights to conserve, manage and protect lands, resources and habitats in accordance with traditional Hupacasath laws, customs and practices.

The Federal Court of Canada ruled that the potential legal impacts of the trade agreement raised by HFN are "non-appreciable and speculative in nature" (*Hupacasath First Nation* 2013: para. 3). The Court added that ratification of the trade agreement by Canada without engaging in consultations with HFN "would not contravene the principle of the honour of the Crown or Canada's duty to consult HFN" (para. 3). This ruling is currently being appealed by HFN.

This ruling has been severely criticized. For example, a major concern is that Canada's "commitment to protect Chinese investors' interests in Canada is a step toward paving the way for unfettered resource development" (Tucker 2013: para. 38). This could in the future affect Indigenous peoples' constitutionally protected rights to lands and resources. In addition, modern First Nations' agreements with the Crown "invariably include provisions specifically requiring consultation prior to the adoption of an international agreement" (Tucker 2013: para. 41). Indigenous peoples would be denied the right to an effective legal remedy if courts do not recognize a failure to consult in the context of such international agreements.

In regard to their lands, territories and resources, Indigenous peoples are not only stakeholders but also rights holders. As one legal expert commented, "it is impossible to maintain the fiction that trade and human rights issues are separate questions and that the trade law community can continue to claim that they should be considered separately in separate international fora" (de Mestral 1998: 78). Human rights must remain paramount in any free trade agreements. "The primacy of human rights over trade liberalization is consistent with the trade regime on its own terms. The institutions that are the official guardians of trade law pose formidable barriers to the proper and full realization of this insight" (Howse and Mutua 2001: 24).

Yet, Indigenous peoples have not been consulted by federal and provincial governments on their human rights concerns with free trade agreements. Such a double standard is inconsistent with the federalism principle, which, according to the Canada's Constitution, includes federal and provincial governments and Aboriginal peoples. As the Supreme Court of Canada indicated in *Reference re Secession of Québec* (1998: para. 57), "federalism is a political and legal response to underlying social and political realities." These realities include Aboriginal peoples, as highlighted more recently by the entrenchment of s. 35(1) of the *Constitution Act, 1982*.

The Special Rapporteur on the right to food has indicated that the human rights obligations of World Trade Organization (wto) members and the commitments they make through trade agreements "remain uncoordinated" within the wto. Often, at the domestic level, "trade negotiators either are not aware of the human rights obligations of the Governments they represent, or they do not identify the implications for their position in trade negotiations" (Human Rights Council 2009b: para. 33).

Underfunding of Essential Services

S. 36 of the *Constitution Act, 1982* affirms that federal and provincial governments and legislatures are committed to promoting equal opportunities, reducing regional disparities, and providing essential public services of reasonable quality to all. There continue to be urgent needs facing First Nations, Inuit and Métis communities in the different regions of Canada, based on decades of human rights violations and government neglect.

The 2009 Report on Canada by the Special Rapporteur on adequate housing emphasizes: "Overcrowded and inadequate housing conditions, as well as difficulties accessing basic services, including water and sanitation, are major problems for Aboriginal peoples" (Human Rights Council 2009c: para. 72). For example, despite existing constitutional commitments and repeated warnings from Canada's Auditor General (Office of the Auditor General of Canada, 2011: 5), Canada continues to discriminate in providing essential services to First Nations people on reserves, by providing significantly lower per capita funding as compared to similar situations off-reserve.

This situation was exacerbated when the federal government was elected in 2006 and refused to implement the $5 billion Kelowna Accord, which was "to address the serious conditions that contribute to poverty among Aboriginal peoples" (Joffe 2010: 154). This Accord had been agreed to in November 2005 by national Indigenous leaders and all heads of government — federal, provincial and territorial.

Attawapiskat is a Cree community in northern Ontario, which gained international attention when it requested the Red Cross to make an emergency intervention in 2011 to address the community's housing crisis. When Special Rapporteur Anaya publicly expressed concern about the "dire" conditions in Attawapiskat and other First Nations communities, which are "allegedly akin to Third World conditions," the Canadian government characterized his statement as a "publicity stunt" (Mackrael 2011: A10).

In the face of strong public criticism by the Attawapiskat Council, the government imposed a third party manager (TPM) to take financial control of the First Nations community. In the Attawapiskat First Nation case (2012: paras. 90, 91), the Federal Court of Canada ruled that the government's decision to appoint a TPM "does not respond to the problem" and was "unreasonable" in all the circumstances.

Harming Indigenous Children

Canadian government policies have inflicted significant harm on Aboriginal children. The 2012 Report of the Committee on the Rights of the Child underlined the "serious and widespread discrimination in terms of access to basic services faced by children in vulnerable situations" (para. 32(b)). The Auditor General of Canada, Sheila Fraser, reiterated that the number of First Nations children in state care in 2008 "was close to eight times the proportion of children residing off reserves" (Office of the Auditor General of Canada 2011: 23). She added, "there has yet to be a notable change in the number of First Nations children in care." State care is an extreme measure that should only be used as a "last resort" (Committee on the Rights of the Child 2003: para. 17).

In 2007, the Aboriginal Affairs minister testified before a parliamentary committee that the proposed repeal of s. 67 of the *Canadian Human Rights Act* would enable First Nations citizens to file a complaint against the Canadian government for discriminatory actions against them. The minister confirmed that this could include "access to programs, access to services, the quality of services that they've accessed, in addition to other issues" (Canada 2007).

A complaint was filed in 2007 with the Canadian Human Rights Commission

(CHRC) for alleged discrimination by the government in regard to federal funding of child welfare services on First Nations reserves. In response, the government tied up the complaint for years with technical arguments denying that the CHRC has jurisdiction to hear the complaint. Such tactics continue, even though the prime minister publicly stated that his government "extended the full protection of the *Canadian Human Rights Act* to First Nations Canadians living on reserves" (Government of Canada 2012).

The co-complainants — First Nations Child and Family Caring Society (FNC-FCS) and the Assembly of First Nations — alleged that Ottawa was providing 22 percent less than the provinces for Aboriginal child welfare services. In response, the government argued that the Act does not allow any comparison to be made with the provinces. Upon judicial review, the Federal Court of Canada rejected this argument. It noted that the government itself makes such comparisons in its programming manual and funding policies on child welfare services (*First Nations Child and Family Caring Society of Canada* 2012: para. 374). The Court added: "International instruments such as the UNDRIP and the *Convention on the Rights of the Child* may also inform the contextual approach to statutory interpretation" (para. 353).

The Canadian government is invoking technical arguments *to deny use of any provincial comparator*, with a view to evading responsibility for providing less funding for child welfare services on reserves. Yet in the Atlantic provinces, the federal government is *using provincial comparators* so that lower income assistance payments would be made to those in poverty on reserves. When sued by First Nations, the government unsuccessfully argued that the First Nations must administer such payments according to the rates and standards of the provinces — even though there had been no prior meaningful consultation by the government. The Federal Court ruled that the First Nations were "entitled to procedural fairness" and the government's administrative decision "would greatly affect the interests of … the majority of social assistance recipients" (*Simon* 2013: para. 122). The government was also chastised by the Court: "The recipients of social assistance are the most vulnerable in society and yet a decision affecting a number of them is made without any true comprehension of its impact" (*Simon* 2013: para. 155). In regard to using the UNDRIP, the Court indicated that it "favours an interpretation that will embody its values" (para. 121).

It is difficult to comprehend why the government would adopt policies that further impoverish Indigenous peoples. Poverty has its greatest impact on Indigenous children. In *The Future We Want*, heads of state and government affirmed by consensus: "Eradicating poverty is the greatest global challenge facing the world today and an indispensable requirement for sustainable development" (Rio+20 2012: para. 2). Such development has economic, social and environmental aspects that are interrelated (para. 3).

Failure to Provide Information on Residential Schools

In May 2006 the Indian Residential Schools Settlement Agreement (IRSSA) was concluded and signed by Canada, Aboriginal organizations, religious organizations and others. According to the terms of the IRSSA, the Truth and Reconciliation Commission (TRC)'s mandate includes the compiling of an historical record of the Indian Residential Schools (IRS) system and its legacy. The mandate also includes preparation of a report that includes the history of the IRS system (*Fontaine* 2013, para. 59).

In October 2013 the Truth and Reconciliation Commission (TRC) made a request for direction to the Ontario Superior Court of Justice, in order to obtain information from Canada that was stored in Library and Archives Canada (LAC) (*Fontaine* 2013). The federal government responded by unsuccessfully challenging the legal standing of the TRC to make any such request to the Court.

Canada also claimed that its obligation to search its files and provide relevant documents to the TRC applies only to the active and semi-active files of the departments of the Government of Canada — and not where those files have been archived at LAC (*Fontaine* 2013: para. 63). The Court ruled that Canada's obligation to provide documents to the TRC extends to the documents archived at LAC (para. 83).

In another case, in January 2014, the applicants, who had attended St. Anne's residential school, were successful in obtaining files of the Ontario Provincial Police (OPP) released by Canada (*Fontaine* 2014). This information would be used to support their claims for compensation for abuse.

As described by the Court, St. Anne's was the site of "some of the most egregious incidents of abuse within the Indian Residential School system." For example, "an electric chair was used to shock students as young as six years old" and "the staff at St Anne's residential school would force ill students to eat their own vomit" (*Fontaine* 2014: para. 105).

In 2003, the Government of Canada requested possession of the OPP records for 156 actions that Canada was defending. The government argued that the records were "relevant and necessary" to the adjudication of the pending civil trials and that it would be "unfair" to require Canada to proceed to trial without production of the records (para.111). However, the applicants and the Assembly of First Nations did not know about this information until 2013.

The Court ruled that Canada had failed to comply with its disclosure obligations. Further, the court concluded it "does have the jurisdiction to re-open settled claims but that jurisdiction must be exercised on a case-by-case basis" (paras. 224, 225).

In regard to the IRSSA, the government should be complying in good faith with its terms. In taking adversarial positions, the federal government was attempting to deprive the TRC and residential school survivors of possibly millions of documents. In international law, the survivors and victims and their families have the right to the truth (*Rome Statute of the International Criminal Court* 1998: Principle 4). Canada has the duty to preserve memory (Principle 3), which includes "fulfilment of the State's duty to preserve archives and other evidence concerning violations of human rights ... and to facilitate knowledge of those violations."

In cases of massive *or* systematic human rights violations, the right to the truth has been cited in relation to protection of the family guaranteed in the *International Covenant on Civil and Political Rights* (Article 23(1)), the right of the child to preserve his or her identity in the *Convention on the Rights of the Child* (8(1)), and the right of the child not to be separated from his or her parents in the same Convention (9(1)).

Decolonization

There are diverse ways in which the Government of Canada is undermining the security and human rights of Indigenous peoples. Key issues include resource development; environment and climate change; Indigenous children; essential infrastructure; food security; rights to land and resources, including genetic resources; and free trade.

Instead of protection of their rights being ensured, the vulnerability of Indigenous nations and their citizens is increased. A common failure of the government is the lack of genuine consultation and cooperation with Indigenous peoples. Their right to give or withhold free, prior and informed consent is simply dismissed or ignored.

Since 2006 the Government of Canada has engaged in deliberate strategies to undermine the UNDRIP. Such persistent actions have consistently occurred at the executive and legislative levels and in litigation. International forums are exploited for similar purposes.

The government has violated core Canadian and international principles of justice, equality, non-discrimination and respect for human rights when Indigenous issues arise. Such conduct is the antithesis of good governance. It constitutes racial discrimination.

Ongoing government actions fail to uphold the honour of the Crown. They are incompatible with international and constitutional objectives of reconciliation with Indigenous peoples. As underlined in Haida Nation (para. 17) by the Supreme Court of Canada: "In all its dealings with Aboriginal peoples ... the Crown must act honourably. Nothing less is required."

In the face of widespread criticisms, the government resorts to its oft-stated mantra that progress is being made and large sums are being spent on Indigenous peoples. The comments of former Indian Affairs Minister Chuck Strahl (2007) are illustrative:

> This government has acted on many fronts to improve quality of life ...
> for all Aboriginal people ... his agenda ... is leading to tangible progress

in a range of areas including land claims, education, housing, child and family services, and safe drinking water.

Such replies gloss over critical shortcomings on each of these issues and cannot justify ongoing strategies that violate Indigenous peoples' human rights. These types of responses camouflage attempts to devalue the UNDRIP and oppose its implementation. Comments relating to government expenditures are not a substitute for respect, protection and fulfillment of human rights.

Incredibly, Prime Minister Stephen Harper has claimed: "We ... have no history of colonialism" (Ljunggren 2009; see also Comack, this volume). In contrast, Canada's highest court ruled in *R. v. Ipeelee* (2012: para. 60):

> To be clear, courts must take judicial notice of such matters as the *history of colonialism, displacement, and residential schools* and how that history continues to translate into lower educational attainment, lower incomes, higher unemployment, higher rates of substance abuse and suicide, and of course higher levels of incarceration for Aboriginal peoples. (Emphasis added)

Federal and provincial governments continue to invoke the colonial doctrine of discovery, in order to claim that the Crown retains "underlying title" to Indigenous peoples' lands and territories. Until the Supreme Court of Canada repudiates this racist doctrine, governments will likely continue to rely on it to perpetuate the land and resource dispossession of Indigenous peoples. What is urgently required in Canada is a comprehensive and collaborative process of decolonization, consistent with Indigenous peoples' sovereignty, jurisdiction and human rights (Permanent Forum on Indigenous Issues 2014: paras. 22, 34).

When addressing Indigenous peoples' human rights, the Canadian government believes it can act with impunity. This ongoing abuse of power is at the expense of democracy, accountability, transparency and respect for the rule of law. Until such diverse injustices against Indigenous peoples are redressed, Canada as a country remains diminished.

Within the federal government, there are growing concerns that the government's approaches are not working. It is reported that internal government documents reveal "the current government's policy direction is alienating First Nations and leading to increased tensions" (Barrera 2014). In particular, "there is 'tension' between the 'rights-based agenda of Aboriginal groups' and the 'non-rights based policy approaches grounded in improving socio-economic outcomes.'"

The resolve and determination of Indigenous peoples should not be underestimated. Indigenous voices continue to grow at international and domestic levels. These voices are contributing to new and progressive human rights standards and jurisprudence. In this ongoing struggle, the UNDRIP remains a beacon, catalyst and blueprint for achievement, well-being and renewed hope.

Note

1. See, for example, *International Covenant on Civil and Political Rights*: arts. 1 and 27; *International Covenant on Economic, Social and Cultural Rights*: arts. 1, 2, 6, 11, 12 and 15(1)(a); *International Convention on the Elimination of Racial Discrimination*: arts. 2(1), 2(2), and 5(d)(v) and (e); and UNDRIP: arts. 1–3, 24 and 31.

References

Aboriginal Affairs and Northern Development Canada. 2010. "Canada's Statement of Support on the United Nations *Declaration on the Rights of Indigenous Peoples.*" November 12. <aadnc-aandc.gc.ca/eng/1309374239861>.

Agreement between the Government of Canada and the Government of the People's Republic of China for the Promotion and Reciprocal Protection of Investments. 2012. Done at Vladivostok on 9 September ["Canada-China Agreement"].

Amnesty International. 2012. *Matching International Commitments with National Action: A Human Rights Agenda for Canada.* December. <http://www.amnesty.ca/news/news-releases/canada-time-to-match-international-commitments-with-national-action>.

Amnesty International (Canada). 2007. "Canada and the International Protection of Human Rights: An Erosion of Leadership? An Update to Amnesty International's Human Rights Agenda for Canada." December. <http://www.amnesty.ca/themes/resources/hr_agenda_update_2007.pdf>.

Babad, Michael. 2012. "Joe Oliver taints all with talk of environmentalists, radicals." *Globe and Mail*, 10 September. <http://www.theglobeandmail.com/report-on-business/top-business-stories/joe-oliver-taints-all-with-talk-of-environmentalists-radicals/article4085710/#dashboard/follows/>.

Baird, John. 2012. "Canadian values 'the envy of the world,' says Baird." *Embassy* August 27. <embassymag.ca/dailyupdate/view/306>.

Barrera, Jorge. 2014. "Aboriginal Affairs 'unable' to do job, faces 'high risk' of deteriorating relationship with FN: Documents." *APTN National News*, 4 March. <http://aptn.ca/news/2014/03/04/aboriginal-affairs-unable-job-faces-high-risk-deteriorating-relationship-fn-documents/>.

Bill C-38. 2012. *An Act to implement certain provisions of the budget tabled in Parliament on March 29, 2012 and other measures.* S.C. 2012, c. 19. Short title: "*Jobs, Growth and Long-term Prosperity Act.*"

Bill C-45. 2012. *A second Act to implement certain provisions of the budget tabled in Parliament on March 29, 2012 and other measures.*" S.C. 2012, c. 31. Short title: "*Jobs and Growth Act.*"

Canada. 2007. Standing Committee on Aboriginal Affairs and Northern Development, *Minutes of Proceedings and Evidence.* March 22. <www2.parl.gc.ca/HousePublications/Publication.aspx?DocId=2786776&Language=E&Mode=1&Parl=39&Ses=1>.

____. 2012. "Address by Minister Baird to United Nations General Assembly." New York, 1 October. <http://www.international.gc.ca/media/aff/speeches-discours/2012/10/01a.aspx?lang=eng&view=d>.

Canada (National Energy Board). 2013. *Report of the Joint Review Panel for the Enbridge Northern Gateway Project*, "Connections," vol. 1 and "Considerations," vol. 2. <http://gatewaypanel.review-examen.gc.ca/clf-nsi/dcmnt/rcmndtnsrprt/rcmndtnsrprt-eng.html>.

Canadian Charter of Rights and Freedoms. 1982. Part I of the *Constitution Act, 1982,* being Schedule B to the *Canada Act 1982* (U.K.), c. 11.

Canadian Human Rights Act. 1985. Revised Statutes of Canada, c. H-6.

Canadian Human Rights Commission. 2008. "Still a Matter of Rights." A Special Report of the Canadian Human Rights Commission on the Repeal of Section 67 of the Canadian Human Rights Act. <http://www.chrc-ccdp.ca/pdf/report_still_matter_of_rights_en.pdf>.

Charter of the United Nations. 1945. Canada Treaty Series 1945, No. 76. <http://www.un.org/en/documents/charter/>.

Clarke, Tony (Executive Director of the Polaris Institute). 2012. Letter to the editor. *Globe and Mail,* Dec. 10. <http://www.theglobeandmail.com/globe-debate/letters/dec-10-the-catch-22-of-the-genome-project-and-other-letters-to-the-editor/article6143038/>.

Committee on Economic, Social and Cultural Rights. 2009. General Comment No. 21, *Right of everyone to take part in cultural life (art. 15, para. 1(a), of the International Covenant on Economic, Social and Cultural Rights).* UN Doc. E/C.12/GC/21, 21 December. <http://tbinternet.ohchr.org/_layouts/treatybodyexternal/Download.aspx?symbolno=E%2fC.12%2fGC%2f21&Lang=en>.

Committee on the Elimination of Racial Discrimination. 2002. *Concluding observations of the Committee on the Elimination of Racial Discrimination: Canada.* U.N. Doc. CERD/C/61/CO/3, 23 August. <http://tbinternet.ohchr.org/_layouts/treatybodyexternal/Download.aspx?symbolno=A%2f57%2f18%28SUPP%29&Lang=en>.

____. 2006. *Concluding observations of the Committee on the Elimination of Racial Discrimination: Guyana.* U.N. Doc. CERD/C/GUY/CO/14, 4 April. <http://tbinternet.ohchr.org/_layouts/treatybodyexternal/Download.aspx?symbolno=CERD%2f-C%2fGUY%2fCO%2f14&Lang=en>.

____. 2012. "Consideration of reports, comments and information submitted by States parties under article 9 of the Convention (*continued*): *Nineteenth and twentieth periodic reports of Canada* (continued)." Summary record of 1242nd meeting on 23 February, UN Doc. CERD/C/SR.2142, 2 March. <http://tbinternet.ohchr.org/_layouts/treatybodyexternal/Download.aspx?symbolno=CERD%2fC%2fSR.2142&Lang=en>.

Committee on the Rights of the Child. 2003. "Day of General Discussion on the Rights of Indigenous Children: Recommendations." 34th Sess., 3 October. <http://www.ohchr.org/Documents/HRBodies/CRC/Discussions/Recommendations/Recommendations2003.pdf>.

____. 2012. *Concluding observations on the combined third and fourth periodic report of Canada, adopted by the Committee at its sixty-first session* (17 September–5 October), UN Doc. CRC/ C/CAN/CO/3-4, 6 December. <http://tbinternet.ohchr.org/_layouts/treatybodyexternal/Download.aspx?symbolno=CRC%2fC%2fCAN%2f3-4&Lang=en>.

Constitution Act, 1982. Being Schedule B to the *Canada Act 1982* (U.K.), 1982, c. 11.

Convention on Biological Diversity. 1993. Concluded at Rio de Janeiro, 5 June and entered into force 29 December.

Convention on the Rights of the Child. 1990. 20 November 1989, 1577 U.N.T.S. 3, entered into force 2 September.

Coyne, Andrew. 2012. "Illegitimate use of omnibus bills renders Parliament a lame duck." *[Montreal] Gazette,* May 1. <http://www.montrealgazette.com/news/Illegitimate+omnibus+bills+renders+Parliament+lame+duck/6544558/story.html>.

Curry, Bill, and Martin Mittelstaedt. 2008. "Ottawa's stand at [climate change] talks hurting native rights, chiefs say." *Globe and Mail*, 12 December. <http://www.theglobeandmail.com/servlet/story/RTGAM.20081212.wclimate12/BNStory/National/home>.

de Mestral, Armand L.C. 1998. "Reconciling Human Rights and International Trade Law." *Canadian International Lawyer* 3, 71.

Declaration and Programme of Action. 2001. Adopted by World Conference against Racism, Racial Discrimination, Xenophobia and Related Intolerance, Durban, South Africa, 8 September. <http://www.un.org/WCAR/durban.pdf>.

Declaration of the High-level Meeting of the General Assembly on the Rule of Law at the National and International Levels. 2012. GA Res. 67/1, 24 September (adopted without vote). <http://www.un.org/ga/search/view_doc.asp?symbol=A/RES/67/1>.

Economic and Social Council. 1962. *Report of the Commission on Human Rights*. U.N. Doc. E/3616/Rev.1, 18th session, 19 March–14 April. <http://daccess-dds-ny.un.org/doc/UNDOC/GEN/N62/136/24/PDF/N6213624.pdf?OpenElement>.

FAO (Food and Agriculture Organization). 2010. FAO *Policy on Indigenous and Tribal Peoples.* Rome: FAO. <http://www.fao.org/docrep/013/i1857e/i1857e00.htm>.

____. 2012. *Climate change and food security: A report by the High Level Panel of Experts on Food Security and Nutrition of the Committee on World Food Security*, Rome. <fao.org//fileadmin/user_upload/hlpe/hlpe_documents/HLPE_Reports/HLPE-Report-3-Food_security_and_climate_change-June_2012.pdf>.

First Ministers and National Aboriginal Leaders Strengthening Relationships and Closing the Gap. 2005. Kelowna, BC, November 24–25 <http://www.health.gov.sk.ca/aboriginal-first-ministers-meeting>.

GCCEI (Grand Council of the Crees [Eeyou Istchee]). 2011. "*Nagoya Protocol*: Comments on Canada's Possible Signature and Draft Domestic Policy." Joint submission with other Indigenous and human rights organizations to the Government of Canada, October. <http://quakerservice.ca/wp-content/uploads/2011/12/Nagoya-Protocol-GCCEI-Joint-Submission-on-Canadas-possible-signature-Oct-28-11.pdf>.

____. 2012a. "Undermining Indigenous Peoples' Rights and U.N. Declaration: Urgent Need for Procedural Reforms in International Organizations." Joint submission with other Indigenous and human rights organizations to U.N. Permanent Forum on Indigenous Issues, Eleventh sess., 12 June. <http://quakerservice.ca/wp-content/uploads/2012/06/IPs-Rts-and-UN-Decl-Need-for-Urgent-Reforms-in-Intl-Organizations.pdf>.

____. 2012b. "FAO Voluntary Guidelines on Governance of Tenure of Land, Fisheries and Forests in the Context of National Food Security: Discrimination and Subjugation of Indigenous Peoples and Rights." Joint submission with other Indigenous and human rights organizations to Food and Agriculture Organization (Committee on World Food Security. Rome, Italy, April. <quakerservice.ca/wp-content/uploads/2012/05/FAO-Natl-Food-Security-Guidelines-Governance-of-Indigenous-Tenure-Rights-GCCEI-Joint-Submission-Apr-12.pdf>.

____. 2012c. "Response to Canada's 19th and 20th Periodic Reports: Alternative Report on Canada's Actions on the *Nagoya Protocol*." Joint submission with other Indigenous and human rights organizations to Committee on the Elimination of Racial Discrimination, January. <www2.ohchr.org/english/bodies/cerd/docs/ngos/NGOs_Nagoya_Protocol_Canada_CERD80.pdf>.

General Assembly. 1970. *Programme of action for the full implementation of the Declaration on the Granting of Independence to Colonial Countries and Peoples.* Resolution 2621 (XXV), October 12. <http://www.un.org/en/ga/search/view_doc.asp?symbol=A/RES/2621%28XXV%29&Lang=E&Area=RESOLUTION>.

———. 2005. *Right to Food: Note by the Secretary-General.* U.N. Doc. A/60/350, 12 September (Interim report of the Special Rapporteur of the Commission on Human Rights on the right to food, Jean Ziegler). <http://daccess-dds-ny.un.org/doc/UNDOC/GEN/N05/486/96/PDF/N0548696.pdf?OpenElement>.

———. 2006. *Report of the United Nations High Commissioner for Human Rights.* 61 sess., Supp. No. 36, UN Doc. A/61/36, New York. <http://daccess-dds-ny.un.org/doc/UNDOC/GEN/N06/532/20/PDF/N0653220.pdf?OpenElement>.

———. 2010. *Situation of human rights and fundamental freedoms of indigenous people: Note by the Secretary-General.* Interim report of the Special Rapporteur on the situation of human rights and fundamental freedoms of indigenous people. U.N. Doc. A/65/264, 9 August. <http://daccess-dds-ny.un.org/doc/UNDOC/GEN/N10/479/13/PDF/N1047913.pdf?OpenElement>.

———. 2012a. *Rights of indigenous peoples: Note by the Secretary-General.* U.N. Doc. A/67/301, 13 August (report of the Special Rapporteur on the rights of indigenous peoples, James Anaya). <http://unsr.jamesanaya.org/docs/annual/2012-ga-annual-report-en.pdf>.

———. 2012b. *Evaluation of the progress made in the achievement of the goal and objectives of the Second International Decade of the World's Indigenous People: Report of the Secretary-General.* U.N. Doc. A/67/273, 8 August. <http://www.un.org/ga/search/view_doc.asp?symbol=A%2F67%2F273+&Submit=Search&Lang=E>.

Government of Canada. 2012. "Statement by the Prime Minister of Canada at the Crown-First Nations Gathering." Ottawa, Ontario, 24 January. <pm.gc.ca/eng/media.asp?category=3&featureId=6&pageId=26&id=4597>.

Howse, Robert, and Makau Mutua. 2001. "Protecting Human Rights in a Global Economy: Challenges for the World Trade Organization." Paper prepared for the International Centre for Human Rights and Democratic Development. <http://papers.ssrn.com/sol3/papers.cfm?abstract_id=1533544>.

Human Rights Council. 2009a. *Report of the Special Rapporteur on the situation of human rights and fundamental freedoms of indigenous people, James Anaya.* U.N. Doc. A/HRC/12/34, 15 July. <http://daccess-dds-ny.un.org/doc/UNDOC/GEN/G09/145/82/PDF/G0914582.pdf?OpenElement>.

———. 2009b. *Report of the Special Rapporteur on the right to food, Olivier De Schutter, Addendum: Mission to the World Trade Organization.* 25 June 2008. U.N. Doc. A/HRC/10/5/Add.2, 4 February. <http://daccess-dds-ny.un.org/doc/UNDOC/GEN/G09/106/39/PDF/G0910639.pdf?OpenElement>.

———. 2009c. *Report of the Special Rapporteur on adequate housing as a component of the right to an adequate standard of living, and on the right to non-discrimination in this context, Miloon Kothari: Addendum — Mission to Canada.* UN Doc. A/HRC/10/7/Add.3, 17 February. <http://daccess-dds-ny.un.org/doc/UNDOC/GEN/G09/115/02/PDF/G0911502.pdf?OpenElement>.

———. 2010. *Report of the Special Rapporteur on the situation of human rights and fundamental freedoms of indigenous people, James Anaya: Addendum: Cases examined by the Special Rapporteur (June 2009–July 2010).* U.N. Doc. A/HRC/15/37/Add.1, 15 September. <http://daccess-dds-ny.un.org/doc/UNDOC/GEN/G10/161/02/PDF/G1016102.pdf?OpenElement>.

_____. 2011a. *Final report of the study on indigenous peoples and the right to participate in decision-making.* U.N. Doc. A/HRC/18/42, 17 August, Annex (Expert Mechanism advice No. 2 (2011)). <www.ohchr.org/Documents/Issues/IPeoples/EMRIP/AEVfinalreportStudyIPRightParticipate.pdf>.

_____. 2011b. *Human rights and the environment.* U.N. Doc. A/HRC/RES/16/11, 24 March. <http://www.ohchr.org/EN/HRBodies/HRC/RegularSessions/Session16/Pages/ResDecStat.aspx>.

_____. 2011c. *Report of the independent expert in the field of cultural rights, Farida Shaheed.* U.N. Doc. A/HRC/17/38, 21 March. <http://daccess-dds-ny.un.org/doc/UNDOC/GEN/G11/122/04/PDF/G1112204.pdf?OpenElement>.

_____. 2011d. *Incompatibility between democracy and racism.* UN Doc. A/HRC/RES/18/15, 29 September. <http://daccess-dds-ny.un.org/doc/RESOLUTION/GEN/G11/166/89/PDF/G1116689.pdf?OpenElement>.

_____. 2012a. *Expert Mechanism on the Rights of Indigenous Peoples: Study on the role of languages and culture in the promotion and protection of the rights and identity of indigenous peoples.* U.N. Doc. A/HRC/21/53, 16 August, Annex – "Expert Mechanism advice No. 3 (2012): Indigenous peoples' languages and cultures." <http://www.ohchr.org/Documents/HRBodies/HRCouncil/RegularSession/Session21/A-HRC-21-53_en.pdf>.

_____. 2012b. *Report of the Special Rapporteur on the right to food, Olivier De Schutter, Addendum: Mission to Canada,* UN Doc. A/HRC/22/50/Add.1, 24 December. <http://www.ohchr.org/Documents/HRBodies/HRCouncil/RegularSession/Session22/AHRC2250Add.1_English.PDF>.

IFAD (International Fund for Agricultural Development), 2009. *Engagement with Indigenous Peoples: Policy.* Rome, November. <http://www.ifad.org/english/indigenous/documents/ip_policy_e.pdf>.

International Convention on the Elimination of All Forms of Racial Discrimination. 660 U.N.T.S. 195. Adopted by U.N. General Assembly on 21 December 1965 and entered into force on 4 January 1969.

International Covenant on Civil and Political Rights. G.A. Res 2200 (XXI), 21 U.N. GAOR, Supp. (No. 16) at 52, U.N. Doc. A/6316, Can. T.S. 1976 No. 47 (1966). Adopted by the U.N. General Assembly 16 December 1966 and entered into force 23 March 1976.

International Covenant on Economic, Social and Cultural Rights. G.A. Res. 2200 (XXI), 21 U.N. GAOR, Supp. (No. 16) at 49, U.N. Doc. A/6316 (1966); Can. T.S. 1976 No. 46. Adopted by U.N. General Assembly 16 December 1966 and entered into force 3 January 1976.

Joffe, Paul. 2012. "*U.N. Declaration on the Rights of Indigenous Peoples*: Not Merely 'Aspirational.'" 16 September. <quakerservice.ca/wp-content/uploads/2012/09/UN-Decl-Not-merely-aspirational-.pdf>.

_____. 2010. "*U.N. Declaration on the Rights of Indigenous Peoples*: Canadian Government Positions Incompatible with Genuine Reconciliation." *National Journal of Constitutional Law* 26, 121.

Ljunggren, David. 2009. "Every G20 nation wants to be Canada, Stephen Harper insists." *Calgary Herald,* 26 September. <https://groups.yahoo.com/neo/groups/NatNews/conversations/topics/49522>.

Lukacs, Martin. 2014. "Aboriginal rights a threat to Canada's resource agenda, documents reveal." *The Guardian,* UK, 4 March. <http://www.theguardian.com/environment/

true-north/2014/mar/04/aboriginal-rights-canada-resource-agenda>.

Mackrael, Kim. 2011. "U.N. official blasts 'dire' conditions in Attawapiskat." *Globe and Mail*, 20 December. <http://www.theglobeandmail.com/news/politics/un-official-blasts-dire-conditions-in-attawapiskat/article2278146/>.

Miller, Robert J. 2011. "The International Law of Colonialism: A Comparative Analysis." *Lewis & Clark L. Rev.* 15, 847.

Nagoya Protocol on Access to Genetic Resources and the Fair and Equitable Sharing of Benefits Arising from their Utilization to the Convention on Biological Diversity. 2010. Adopted by the Conference of the Parties, Nagoya, Japan, 29 October.

Newcomb, Steven T. 1993. "The Evidence of Christian Nationalism in Federal Indian Law: The Doctrine of Discovery, *Johnson v. McIntosh*, and Plenary Power." *N.Y.U. Rev. Law & Social Change* 20: 303.

Office of the Auditor General of Canada. 2011. *Status Report of the Auditor General of Canada to the House of Commons — 2011*, ch. 4 (Programs for First Nations on Reserves). <http://www.oag-bvg.gc.ca/internet/English/parl_oag_201106_04_e_35372.html>.

OHCHR (Office of the U.N. High Commissioner for Human Rights). 2010. "The Right to Water." Fact Sheet No. 35, August. <http://www.ohchr.org/EN/PublicationsResources/Pages/FactSheets.aspx>.

____. 2013. "Statement upon conclusion of the visit to Canada by the United Nations Special Rapporteur on the rights of indigenous peoples, James Anaya." 15 October. <http://www.ohchr.org/EN/NewsEvents/Pages/DisplayNews.aspx?NewsID=13868&LangID=E>.

Permanent Forum on Indigenous Issues. 2011. *Report on the tenth session (16 –27 May 2011)*. Economic and Social Council, Official Records, Supplement No. 23, United Nations, New York, E/2011/43-E/C.19/2011/14. <http://undesadspd.org/IndigenousPeoples/UNPFIISessions/Tenth.aspx>.

____. 2012. *Report on the eleventh session (7–18 May 2012)*. Economic and Social Council, Official Records, Supplement No. 23, United Nations, New York, E/2012/43-E/C.19/2012/13. <http://undesadspd.org/IndigenousPeoples/UNPFIISessions/Eleventh/Documents.aspx>.

____. 2014. *Study on the impacts of the Doctrine of Discovery on indigenous peoples, including mechanisms, processes and instruments of redress: Note by the secretariat*. UN Doc. E/C.19/2014/3 (20 February) [Study by Forum member Edward John]. <http://daccess-dds-ny.un.org/doc/UNDOC/GEN/N14/241/84/PDF/N1424184.pdf?OpenElement>.

Polaris Institute (Cayley-Daoust, Daniel and Richard Girard). 2012. "Big Oil's Oily Grasp: The making of Canada as a Petro-State and how oil money is corrupting Canadian politics." December. <http://www.polarisinstitute.org/files/BigOil%27sOilyGrasp_0.pdf>.

Rio+20 United Nations Commission on Sustainable Development. 2012. *The Future We Want*. Rio de Janeiro, Brazil, 20–22 June, UN Doc. A/CONF.216/L.1 (19 June). <http://sustainabledevelopment.un.org/futurewewant.html. Endorsed by General Assembly, UN Doc. A/RES/66/288>. (27 July 2012) (without vote).

Rome Statute of the International Criminal Court. 1998. U.N. Doc. A/Conf.183/9 (1998), adopted in Rome, 17 July. Entered into force July 1, 2002.

Sajoo, Eva. 2012. "Tories squash public dissent." *Winnipeg Free Press*, 14 November.

<http://www.winnipegfreepress.com/opinion/westview/tories-squash-public-dissent-179242121.html>.

Scoffield, Heather. 2012. "U.N. food envoy provokes Ottawa with findings on hunger and poor diet in Canada." *Winnipeg Free Press*, 16 May. <http://www.winnipegfreepress.com/arts-and-life/life/health/un-food-envoy-provokes-ottawa-with-findings-on-hunger-and-poor-diet-in-canada-151723675.html>.

Shane, Kristen. 2012. "Feds talking EU trade deal enforcement." *Embassy*, 31 October.

Strahl, Chuck. 2007. Letter from Minister of Indian Affairs, Chuck Strahl, to Assembly of First Nations National Chief, Phil Fontaine. 10 December (on file with author).

Trew, Stuart, and Emma Lui. 2014. "Canada should follow EU lead on investment rules." *Embassy*, 4 March. <http://www.embassynews.ca/opinion/2014/03/03/canada-should-follow-eu-lead-on-investment-rules/45210>.

Tucker, Kathryn. 2013. "Reconciling Aboriginal Rights with International Trade Agreements: Hupacasath First Nation v. Canada." *McGill International Journal of Sustainable Development Law and Policy* 9: 109.

United Nations Declaration on the Rights of Indigenous Peoples. 2007. GA Res. 61/295 (Annex), UN GAOR, 61st Sess., Supp. No. 49, Vol. III, U.N. Doc. A/61/49 (2008) 15.

Van Harten, Gus. 2012. "14 reasons why Canada-China investment deal needs more time, debate." *Vancouver Observer*, 17 October. <http://www.vancouverobserver.com/politics/commentary/14-reasons-why-canada-china-investment-deal-needs-more-time-debate>.

Vienna Declaration and Programme of Action. 1993. Adopted by World Conference on Human Rights, 25 June 1993. U.N. Doc. A/CONF.157/24 (Part I) at 20.

Voluntary Guidelines on the Responsible Governance of Tenure of Land, Fisheries and Forests in the Context of National Food Security. 2012. Food and Agriculture Organization. Endorsed by FAO Committee on World Food Security, 11 May. <http://www.fao.org/fileadmin/user_upload/nr/land_tenure/pdf/VG_Final_May_2012.pdf>.

Whittington, Les. 2012. "U.N. food envoy blasts inequality, poverty in Canada." *Toronto Star* 16 May. <http://www.thestar.com/news/canada/2012/05/16/un_food_envoy_blasts_inequality_poverty_in_canada.html>.

Williams, Jr., Robert A. 2012. *Savage Anxieties: The Invention of Western Civilization.* New York: Palgrave Macmillan.

World Intellectual Property Organization. 2014. <http://www.wipo.int/tk/en/genetic/>.

Legal Cases

Attawapiskat First Nation v. Canada (Minister of Aboriginal Affairs and Northern Development). 2012. Federal Court 948.

Corbiere v. Canada (Minister of Indian and Northern Affairs). 1999. 2 Supreme Court Reports 203.

Delgamuukw v. British Columbia. 1997. 3 Supreme Court Reports 1010.

Elsipogtog First Nation v. Canada (Attorney General). 2012 Federal Court 387; appeal dismissed 2012 Federal Court of Appeal 312.

First Nations Child and Family Caring Society et al. v. Canada (Attorney General). 2011. "Memorandum of Fact and Law of the Respondent, the Attorney General of Canada," Respondent's Record, vol. 5, Federal Court of Canada, Dockets T-578-11, T-630-11, T-638-11, 17 November 2011.

First Nations Child and Family Caring Society of Canada v. *Canada (Attorney General)*. 2012 Federal Court 445.

Fontaine v. Canada (Attorney General). 2014 ONSC 283 (Ontario Superior Court).

Fontaine v. *Canada*. 2013 ONSC 684 (Ontario Superior Court).

Guerin v. The Queen. 1984. 2 Supreme Court Reports 335.

Haida Nation v. *British Columbia (Minister of Forests)*. 2004. 3 Supreme Court Reports 511.

Hupacasath First Nation v. *Canada (Minister of Foreign Affairs)*. 2013 FC 900.

Mabo et al. v. *State of Queensland* [No. 2]. 1992. 175 Commonwealth Law Reports 1 (High Court of Australia).

R. v. *Ipeelee*. 2012 Supreme Court of Canada 13.

R. v. *Sappier; R.* v. *Gray*. 2006. 2 Supreme Court Reports 686.

R. v. *Sparrow*. 1990. 1 Supreme Court Reports 1075.

R. v. *Van der Peet*. 1996. 2 Supreme Court Reports 507.

Reference re Secession of Québec. [1998. 2 Supreme Court Reports 217.

Samson Indian Nation and Band v. *Canada*. 2006. 1 Canadian Native Law Reporter 100 (Federal Court Trial Division).

Simon v. *Attorney General of Canada*, 2013 Federal Court 1117.

Taku River Tlingit First Nation v. *British Columbia (Project Assessment Director)*. 2004. 3 Supreme Court Reports 550.

Tsilhqot'in Nation v. *British Columbia*, 2014. Supreme Court of Canada 44.

Tsilhqot'in Nation v. *British Columbia*. 2012. British Columbia Court of Appeal 285 [also cited as *William* v. *British Columbia*]. Appeal pending in Supreme Court of Canada.

Tsuu T'ina Nation v. *Alberta (Minister of Environment)*. 2010. Alberta Court of Appeal 137.

Index

Aboriginal (also see Indigenous), 2, 3, 5, 19, 47, 49, 52–54

Aboriginal Justice Inquiry of Manitoba, 72, 76 146

Aboriginal legal traditions, 197, 211

Aboriginal rights, 195–197

African Court on Human and Peoples Rights, 176, 177

American Indian Boarding Schools, 86–91
    Boarding School Healing Coalition, 94
    cultural suppression, 87
    death, 90–91
    forced labour, 90
    lack of medical care, 88
    malnutrition, 88
    physical abuse, 88–89
    sexual abuse, 89–90

American Indian Report, 89

Amnesty International, 21, 23–24
    Canada, 146

An Act to Amend the Indian Act (Bill C-31), 102, 107–9, 118, 152, 155–6
    Bill C-31 Woman, 110
    patrilineal descent, 109–110
    status categories, 108–109
    women, 108

An Act to Encourage the Gradual Civilization of Indian Tribes in the Province and to Amend the Laws Respecting Indians, 104

An Act to Promote Gender Equity in Indian Registration (Bill C-3), 100, 102, 104, 107, 111–115
    provisions, 111
    amendments, 112, 115
    effects, 111, 115–116
    exclusion, 112
    sex discrimination, 102–104, 111–112, 115, 118–120

Assembly of First Nations (AFN), 95

assimilation, 4, 27, 31, 36, 148

autonomy, 127, 135
    collective, 126
    individual, 127

Beijing Platform for Action, 130,

biodiversity, 222–225

Canadian Bill of Rights, 153, 154,

Canadian Charter of Rights and Freedoms, 157,

Canadian Human Rights Act, 154,

citizenship (citizens), 3, 6, 18, 36, 47, 56

civilization, 144, 151,

climate change, 223, 227–229

collective remedy, 92,

colonialism, 2, 6, 7, 13, 19, 20, 28, 60–61, 69, 130, 131–133, 221, 235
    resistance to colonialism, 68, 78
    Saskatchewan rebellion, 66

colonization, 144, 148, 150, 158,

consent, 217, 225–226, 234

constitution (Canadian), 3, 4, 18, 19, 25
    Constitution Act, 1867, 148, 154,
    Constitution Act, 1982
        section 35, 202–204
        section 91(24), 148

criminalization
    "get tough" on crime, 77–78
    over-incarceration, 71

cultural rights, 83,

decolonization, 3, 12, 13, 83, 84–86, 93, 96

deficit framing, 45, 50–52, 54, 56

Delgamuukw v. British Columbia, 182, 184

discrimination, 132, 137, 218–222, 225, 231–232

drug trade, 73, 74

duty to consult, 32, 36, 217, 221–223, 225–230, 232, 234
    consultation and accommodation, 182–183, 209
    Endorois, 176